BARACK OBAMA

MASTER OF

WASHINGTON DC

FREDERICK MONDERSON

SUMON PUBLISHERS

SuMon Publishers
PO Box 160347
Brooklyn, New York 11216

sumonpublishers.com@sumonpublishers.com
blackfolksbooks.com@blackfolksbooks.com
fredsegypt.com@fredsegypt.com blackegyptbooks.com@blackegyptbooks.com

Copyright Frederick Monderson/ SuMon Publishers, 2011 All Rights Reserved.

No part of this book may be reproduced, stored in a retrieval system, or transmitted by any means without the written permission of the author.

ISBN – 978-1-61023-013-1
LCCN - 2010918486

In the Tribute to Professor George Simmonds, "Unsung Hero," Dr. Fred Monderson sat at the feet of his heroes, Brother X, Michael Carter, Dr. Leonard Jeffries, El Hombre Brath, Dr. Lewis, Prof. George Simmonds, Dr. ben-Jochannan, Sister Camille Yarbrough, among others.

FOREWORD

The "Buzz" these days is to criticize President Barack Obama left and right, Republican and Democrat, black and white, regarding his position on every conceivable issue, foreign and domestic, black and white, men and women and even gay and straight. Its general knowledge the President has been a victim of

All the best,

unrelenting Republican criticism in an obstructionist bent ranging from his birthright to his right to exercise the functions of the office he was elected to. What is unendingly evident, the people to this day are still not fully aware of the difficulties confronting this country that Barack Obama has dedicated his Presidency to combat and the many accomplishments he has attained in his short tenure. To the extent they are aware; the critique has become political then *ad hominem*, with the expressly stated intent of undermining his presidency.

What is surprising these days is the litany of prominent blacks as John Conyers, Tavis Smiley and now Cornel West who have come out vehemently criticizing the

President. John Conyers' critique is surprising in as much as he has been in Congress nearly 40 years and without question has scars that show how he earned his stripes. Equally, privy to Congressional infighting and enacted legislation and their significance makes his critique of Mr. Obama even more surprising, though he has said he still wants to make him a better President.

THE WHITE HOUSE
WASHINGTON

June 25, 2009

Mr. Frederick Monderson

Brooklyn, New York 11216

Dear Frederick:

Thank you for your kind note. Your thoughtful words join a chorus of millions of Americans who are eager to lead our Nation towards a brighter tomorrow.

Each day, I am inspired by the encouraging messages of hope and determination I have received from people across the country. With the magnitude of challenges we face, we will only overcome them if our imagination is joined to common purpose.

The future we leave to our children and grandchildren will be determined by our willingness to shoulder each other's burdens, take great risks, and move forward as one people and one Nation. With your help, we will build on what we have already achieved and lay a foundation for real and lasting progress.

Sincerely,

Tavis Smiley's criticism may be more about ratings since he has not been able to "land the President" for a talk show or some expose of that nature. He too feels in criticizing he wants to correct and protect the president.

THE WHITE HOUSE

WASHINGTON

January 6, 2010

Dr. Frederick Monderson

Brooklyn, New York 11216

Dear Dr. Monderson:

We received the item you mailed to the White House, along with your request for President Obama to autograph this item.

Unfortunately, because of the high volume of requests and the demands on the President's time, we are unable to fulfill your request. We have enclosed your item, as well as a photograph bearing the President's signature that he would like you to have.

Thank you again for contacting us, and we appreciate your interest.

Sincerely,

F. Michael Kelleher
Special Assistant to the President and
Director of Presidential Correspondence

The criticism of high profile, particularly academic, individuals is another matter. There are those who, from inception, thought Obama was "not black enough." Today, they are accusing the President of not doing enough for black people! There is, therefore, something wrong with such intellectual who, at the "round-table discussions" would probably, as some have boasted to other blacks, 'Well, look at the size of my bank account' which seems to undermine the status accredited them as this "onion is being peeled back," exposing the true nature of such persons.

Granted everyone sees things differently and are entitled to their opinions since such is guaranteed by the First Amendment, but a different yardstick of measurement is expected from some people, particularly professed academics. For example, in the first essay of this current work entitled "The Obama Years" both Playthel Benjamin and Professor James Blake praised President Obama for successfully navigating the Washington minefield of Republican obstructionism, weathering the tornados of their social allies' nefarious assaults while still passing more and significant legislation than his counterparts in similar time in office. These professional individuals certainly recognize the minefield where Obama's office is situated, but they also perceive how his legislation, in its disguised forms, tremendously aids blacks as it does every other American. So, we ask; how could the same situation be viewed differently by two sets of academic minds, unless, perhaps, the mask of one is slipping because time, the great equalizer, ultimately exposes the true nature of those who profess what they are not, really. Such then is one symptom of the myriad of challengers President Obama has had to contend with, and if I may say so, he's doing a pretty damn good job of disarming their rhetoric.

President Obama represents new age leadership who wants to move America forward irrespective of race but believes people must be viewed from the "content of their character," good citizenship, and that all people should benefit from his actions and legislation. All this notwithstanding, what these critics refuse to acknowledge, President Barack Obama, though he comes from a mixed family has clearly professed his is a Blackman, African American. And, even more important, his ace in the hole is he is married to a Black woman whose heritage is that of a slave descendant. Obama loves his wife who is an intellectual powerhouse in her right. Now, he is not a philanderer and goes home to his wife every night and she would remind him of black issues. Equally too, he is a Blackman of incredible moral fortitude otherwise, with the "Hubble Telescope focused into his closet," his opponents would have sought political mileage against him. Nevertheless, Obama himself confesses if you're going to enter the political arena you must be prepared for hardball! Therefore, as leader of the American people he is prepared to follow the path he established through hard work and will not necessarily inform the opposition every step he intends to take to carry out his agenda.

BARACK OBAMA
MASTER OF WASHINGTON DC

TABLE OF CONTENTS

1. The Obama Years: Challenges of a Lifetime   7
2. Obama: Leadership Supreme   13
3. President Obama in Africa I   18
4. President Obama in Africa II   42
5. President Obama and Foreign Policy   54
6. Representative Peter King: Denounce the New York Post   72
7. Testing Barack   81
8. Defending Obama   87
9. Obama: The Eternal Optimist   100
10. Barack Obama: The First 30 Days   113
11. Anti-Racist Activism Alive

and Well	136
12. Stay Up, Barack	144
13. From the New Yorker to The New York Post	148
14. Why We Must Support Barack Obama	159
15. The Brilliance of Barack Obama	165
16. Obama: The First 100 Days	176
17. President Obama, 100 Days Again	188
18. Our Leader Goes Abroad	194
19. Michelle Obama: Boss Woman	198
20. The Confidence of Barack Obama	207
21. Barack Obama and Leadership	212
22. Stay On Track, Barack	217
23. Barack Obama: Man of The People	224
24. Barack Obama and the Black Agenda	233

BARACK OBAMA
MASTER OF WASHINGTON DC

25. Barack Obama and Arizona State University — 241
26. Barack Obama: The People's Champion — 246
27. Edward Kennedy, Obama's Ally — 256
28. Some Perspectives on Obama's Health Care Reform — 275
29. Further Considerations on Health Care Reform — 284
30. Leaderless Republicans — 294
31. Obama and "Gates-Gate" — 302
32. President Obama and the Republicans — 312
33. President Obama and Women — 325
34. The "Obama Doctrine" — 340
35. Obama: Proud to Be President — 357
36. Wither The Republicans — 363
37. The President Abroad — 370

38. The Buck Stops with Barack! — 378
39. Barack Obama: A Majority of One — 382
40. Barack Obama: Man for All Seasons — 390
41. Michelle Obama: Mother of the Year — 398
42. Barack Obama and the Supreme Court — 408
43. Barack Obama and the Voting Rights Act — 426
44. Barack Obama and the Power of Symbolism — 438
45. Obama Versus The Man of Steel — 445
46. Obama's Many Hats as President — 454
47. The Excitement of Barack Obama — 462
48. So Obamasque — 465
49. From Dred Scott to Barack Obama — 472

BARACK OBAMA
MASTER OF WASHINGTON DC

50. Barack Obama:
    Man With the Plan   488
51. Michelle Obama and
    The Gorillas   498
52. President Obama and the
    Power of Appointment   503
53. The Quintessential Obama   510
54. Barack Obama and the
    Powers of the Presidency   519
55. The Idiocy of Alan Keyes   530
56. Obama's Stimulus and
    Dance of Legislation   533
57. Obama, "Doin' Too Much"   537
58. Obama and Compromise   541
59. President Obama and
    Affirmative Action   544
60. President Obama and
    War Powers   548
61. Man of Steel or Rust   553
62. Fiasco on the Mall   557
63. Reflections on
    Barack Obama   561

64.	Shirley Sherrod: Superstar	567
65.	Barack Against the Rest	569
66.	The President's Cabinet and the Order of Succession	576
67.	The State of the American Union	578
68.	Rally Around Barack	580
69.	President Obama and Congress	586
70.	Obama as Education Reformer	591
71.	Barack Obama: The Great Visionary	595
72.	Obama: Uneasy Lies the Head	599
73.	Vote or Die! Well,	603
74.	Reflections on the New "Obama Age"	606
75.	Barack Obama Master of Washington DC Postscript	612

BARACK OBAMA
MASTER OF WASHINGTON DC

"Yes We Can" BARACK OBAMA Campaign slogan, 2008

1. THE OBAMA YEARS
Challenges of a Lifetime
By

Dr. Fred Monderson

In the tradition of presenting diverse views on the most pressing issues of the day, CEMOTAP presented "THE OBAMA YEARS: Challenges of a Lifetime," A Panel Discussion based on "Research and Facts" held at Bethesda Missionary Baptist Church, Jamaica Avenue, Queens, Saturday, April 23, 2011, 2: 00 pm.

With an Opening Prayer by Rev. Charles Norris, Jr., the audience singing "Lift Every Voice and Sing" and Welcome by Sister Betty Dobson, whose Co-Chair, Dr. James McIntosh introduced the Panel Facilitator Imhotep, Gary Byrd, who in turn presented the Panel Participants Prof. James Blake, Manhattan Community College; Milton Allimadi, Publisher *Black Star News*; Dr. Leonard Jeffries, scholar, historian CUNY (not able to attend owing to an engagement in Ghana); Attorney Joseph Mack, lawyer and activist; and Brother Playthel Benjamin, journalist and musician.

After a noteworthy Introduction of Praise for Bethesda Missionary Baptist Church celebrating 100 years of service to the Queens community, and CEMOTAP for its wonderful work on behalf of defending the integrity of the Black community in media, Gary Byrd informed "President Obama has been the most threatened Chief Executive of all times." Next he identified his Program on WLIB, 1190 AM, Sunday evening 7:00-12:00 pm and that there's an "Obama Watch" segment at 8:55 pm. Pointing out "conversation is important, critical" and offering CUDOS to CEMOTAP for sharing information, he called attention to past debates between Al Sharpton and Cornell West and a **Like It Is** NY, TV 7, episode featuring Councilman Charles Barron and newspaperman Les Payne, that "produced fire, heat and high intensity, among conscious Blacks," then he admonished the audience "Let's come out of this discussion empowered."

FREDERICK MONDERSON

Insisting he was concerned with politics and policy and not philosophy and religion, the first panelist Playthel Benjamin began his presentation by quoting "A Negro preacher must be a poet in order to survive" and chided Glen Ford and Cornell West and Michael Erik Dyson for the theatricality of their performances as it related to President Obama. Calling Cornell West "Prof. Longhair" and Michael Erik Dyson "Chilly D. Knowledge" he insisted "they indulged in wishful thinking." He further pointed out "These people's critique of Obama portends trouble for our people." Next he defined the exercise of Power as "the ability to do what you want;" "the ability to get other people to do what you want;" and "the ability to get most of what you want." This last is significantly accomplished through compromise!

Moderator Gary Byrd introduces the Panel members starting with Prof. James Blake, Dr. James McIntosh, Attorney Joseph Mack and Journalist Playthel Benjamin. Publisher Milton Allimadi later joined the group.

The policy choices Obama has made, he stated, are considered "real politik" in the environment in which the man functioned, despite the watching opposition hand behind him. In this he expressed unambiguous and unequivocal support for President Obama whom he called the most humane president in the history of the American Presidency. Obama is a political genius, he noted, and the most progressive Chief Executive to occupy the White House. He did point out there were consequences of the President taking over this office. Offering an opinion, he insisted further, "This will be a Neo-Periclean age if Democrats win back the House and President Obama is re-elected." He described the President as a pragmatic technocrat not an ideologue for which he argued "Black people benefit

BARACK OBAMA
MASTER OF WASHINGTON DC

more from anything Barack Obama does more than any other group." Then he supported this view by mentioning the multi-billion dollar award to Black Farmers; the Lilly Ledbetter Law for equal pay for women; rescue of the Auto Industry that provides jobs for significant numbers of black workers; and aid to Historical Black Colleges, among others.

Prof. James Blake said Barack Obama's occupancy of the White House is worth more than a million words, as he identified "white hopes" in the person of the present Republican presidential contenders. That the Republican Party unleashed brutal attacks on the President determined to see him fail was well agreed upon. This position is clearly credited to Mitch McConnell who set out and stated his goal is to make a failure of the President. To everything the President did and proposed the Republicans "just say No!" Obama has had to face "white haters" and "black distracters" full of lies and acting as forces of distraction. They were interested in "Getting that Nigger and his family out of the White House." History has shown a powerful strategy of divide and rule is to "Separate the leader from his people before you murder him!"

Prof. Blake has insisted in 22 months Barack Obama has amassed some 2200 legislative accomplishments, an unheard of total. To understand how such legislative acts benefited blacks you have to examine the language it's couched in he argued.

In the book *Slave Songs in the United States* Prof. James Blake pointed out, there were subliminal messages in such songs as "Go Down Moses" and "Swing Low Sweet Chariot" and in the language "Childhood Obesity, Low Income, Health Care Reform, Healthy Child Reconstruct Act and Pre-Existing Health Condition" these are designed for and clearly the greatest beneficiaries are Blacks! Mr. Obama bailed out the auto industry and this has provided jobs for Blacks! Obama leveled the playing field in Education. He increased funding for Black Colleges and enacted a Childhood Obesity Act. Low income housing assistance and Choice Neighborhoods means the Projects, and so on!

FREDERICK MONDERSON

Prof. James Blake shakes hands with Milton Allimadi, members of the Panel on 'The Obama Years.'

The *New York Times* of July 12, 2009 informed President Obama had increased food aid from $15 billion to $20 billion. And the President made provisions in the Global Poverty Act that poverty be reduced by half by the year 2015. Prof. Blake insisted, "This Panel Discussion should not be called the Obama Years but the Obama Months for in 28 months he did more than Bush did in 8 years."

Next Prof. Blake pointedly asked, "It is not what Obama has done for us, but what have you done for Obama?" We are in an age of "Divide and Conquer." He insisted the "race card" has been played in presidential politics. Stating the President faces enormous challenges, he then asked the powerful question as to how history will judge us all in this Lenten season, "Where were you when they crucified our Lord (President)?"

Next Gary Byrd identified the "Counterpoint of the program" when he introduced Attorney/activist Joseph Mack who laid great store upon President Obama not supporting the Defense of Marriage Act. His theme seemed to be regarding the question of "Full faith and credit." He also raised the question of "Killing of the first born in Egypt" "Bethlehem" and the "Sacrificial Lamb" paying particular attention to events in North Africa, and that the target was not specifically Gadhafi but his son and successor. This action was aimed at eviscerating the future leadership of that oil rich African country.

BARACK OBAMA
MASTER OF WASHINGTON DC

Mr. Mack confessed, initially he supported Barack Obama but recent events caused him to reassess that support particularly after the bombing of Africa, Libya. This caused Mack to reject the President whom he accused of having "no spine" for allowing the Republicans to bully him. However, both Playthel Benjamin and Prof. Blake disagreed vehemently and pointed to Republican opposition and the minefield President Obama has to function in. We cannot be unmindful of the many threats to his personal safety despite the great work of the Secret Service.

Joining the group, Milton Allimadi informed he was in Libya in January and seeing the number of high rise buildings going up in that country, particularly by Italian and German investment groups, asked the Libyans 'Could American Black contractors and investors be given a chance?' To this the Libyans agreed. Next he proposed setting up 'Libyan banks in Black communities such as Harlem to finance Black investment and development.' This too, the Libyans agreed to. There was much agreement that oil was not the single driving force in the rebellious action but also to sever future Libyan leadership because of what the Libyans have done for Africa in general.

Barack Obama's Washington, DC Photo 1. The Amtrak Rail that brings visitors to Washington, DC.

FREDERICK MONDERSON

Barack Obama's Washington, DC Photo 2. The Amtrak rail that take visitors away from Washington, DC.

Overall, Playthel indicated his support for Barack Obama has been unwavering because the President has 'faced the hounds' while passing significant legislation that benefited all Americans particularly Blacks. Prof. Blake equally agreed that the President had passed significant legislation that equally aided Blacks but this was done despite the hostile environment of Republican obstructionism and some Blacks who were either ignorant of the facts or had resolved to throw the President under the bus, were "men of little faith!" He felt history would judge those who chose not to understand the nature of contemporary American politics and that "Republicans play dirty pool." Attorney Mack confessed to losing faith in the President particularly because of his allowing the Republicans to get what they want but more especially because of events unfolding in Libya, as elements sought to "kill the first born." Some in attendance believed, the "first born" they were attempting to kill was Barack Obama.

To the question as to what Dr. King would say regarding Barack Obama, the answer was "Dr. King would commend the President, recognize he had opened the door and given the hostility of the environment under which he functioned, was pleased with his accomplishments."

Thanking Rev. Norris and providing a donation for the use of the facilities, Dr. McIntosh thanked all in attendance and adjourned until the next significant gathering of CEMOTAP.

BARACK OBAMA
MASTER OF WASHINGTON DC

"There's not a Black America and a White America, and a Latino America and an Asian America – there's the United States of America."

2. OBAMA: LEADERSHIP SUPREME
BY

DR. FRED MONDERSON

Sitting and listening to one of the newest musical tunes entitled "Obama's Greatest Hits," familiar names as Osama bin Laden, Donald Trump, Joe "the Plumber," John McCain, Hilary Clinton, Sarah Palin, and with aspirants to the Presidency lining up as the Republican Party ponders who will be their next "best man," other names as Mitt Romney, Michelle Bachman, Gov. Tim Pawlenty, Mike Huckabee, Newt Gingrich have emerged; its finally becoming apparent to some people despite Republican claims, President Barack Obama is an extraordinary individual who has demonstrated outstanding leadership from the inception he appeared on the radar of national recognition. More important, in this short period, he has dumfounded his critics who used every trick in a political playbook to derail the man and his plans to serve and rescue his nation. Yet, despite the perennial criticism of his every effort, his resilience has proved a sustainable trait of the greatest magnitude allowing him to leave the competition in the dust, seemingly confused, as he goes about the people's business while chalking up significant military, terror, diplomatic, economic and legislative results. Despite what is said, a great many people still love and respect Barack Obama!

In a recent exchange the President exclaimed he was too busy to engage with "Circus criers" and as it turned out at the time, he was exercising his thinking cap in executing one of the most amazing military feats imaginable; that is, in addition to the herculean task of rescuing his nation; he has remained committed to and been at work from day one as President. That Mr. Obama is a man of great intellect despite the likes of the "Donald Trumps" who questioned his academic background and therefore his intellectual and leadership functionality, was evident in his organization of a Presidential campaign that trumped some of the most seasoned contenders possessing "political machines" of great experience. In addition, to his natural intellect developed at Columbia and Harvard Universities and the hard knocks gained as a Community Organizer in the Chicago urban environment; in sum they have all seasoned the man to the vicissitudes of the political jungle experience. Not forgetting his wonderful family, one of his greatest assets is his penchant for surrounding himself with some of the most capable

FREDERICK MONDERSON

minds of the American political, economic and educational landscape that adds an awful dimension to his thinking ability and leadership skills. In fact, during the rigors of the Presidential Campaign, when Senator Obama was accused of being deficient in an area of expertise, viz., economics, financial and foreign policy, education, diplomacy, military action in times of challenge, he would "go to school" on the opposition by consulting his reservoir of "wise men" and would come out demonstrating new mastery of some area his challenger focused on. This strategy, therefore, early established Mr. Obama in the tradition of great African American thinkers as Martin Luther King, Jr., and Malcolm X.

Case in point! Like all other candidates for the office of the President Mr. Obama has had to submit proof of his natural birth citizenship which is a constitutional requirement. He proved he was born in Hawaii and thought this was sufficient to qualify him for the office. While he went on to win the Presidency, amidst the many accusations he was subjected to, men pursuing ulterior motives still questioned the authenticity of his birth and therefore his Presidency. This led to a movement called "Birthers" who insisted to nauseating limits; Mr. Obama illegally occupied the White House! What an insult to the American people who elected him President! Let us also add, the world watched as some in this country heaped mud on our leader and the "leader of the Western World." Even more, these "rebels" generated quite a following as some observers labeled their actions racist; because Mr. Obama was a Black man, considering the history of this nation, particularly in reference to the role the institution of slavery has played in developing its economic and social foundations as the nation transformed itself. Now despite the birth certificate shenanigans and revelations some still believe Mr. Obama was not born in the United States and that he is also a practicing Muslim. Yet, one sign at the "Rally on the Mall" read "I don't care if the President is a Muslim!"

BARACK OBAMA
MASTER OF WASHINGTON DC

Barack Obama's Washington, DC Photo 3. Columns in the decorated interior of the Union Station.

Still, Mr. Obama probably viewed this distraction as just that, as he set about addressing the challenges facing the nation, the job he was elected President to combat. Let us not forget, he applied that great intellect together with his team of great minds so that from the inception of his new Administration, he secured TARP Funds and Stimulus Dollars then set about rescuing Wall Street, the Auto Industry, engineering significant and far reaching legislation for equal pay for women, as well as health care reform; issued a challenge to the scientific community to experiment and develop new forms of clean energy whether solar, wind, or battery power, with focus on the environment and insisted they employ any strategy that would help to alleviate America's dependence on foreign sources of that precious commodity, oil. He created incentives to encourage an overhaul of the American Educational system while emphasizing the relevance of new strategies for teaching; the need for more competent teachers and techniques and insisted on the need for greater proficiency in math and science to make America more competitive in this modern changing and complex world. Aiding housing recovery, he consistently wrestled with unemployment that has significantly impacted American society despite enormous efforts made to address this problem. Again, we must return to the root of the problem; that is, the chasm of policy and practice he inherited from Republican mismanagement!

FREDERICK MONDERSON

During the campaign and at the start of the Obama Administration, the full impact of the overall state of the American economy was not fully realized and now more than two years into his term, unemployment persists, despite the avalanche of effort expended to address this issue. We should not forget the significant growth in outsourcing of American jobs during the Bush years is the foundation of unemployment woes. Let us also pay particular attention to the national debt that has been growing in recent years, particularly since significant portions are owed to foreign nations. We cannot forget either, the national debt was raised some 18 times under Bush but Republicans are holding the line against one time for Obama! Nevertheless, while his economic team fights feverishly to contain and reduce unemployment, some light is seen in the tunnel but it's still quite distant.

Notwithstanding, as the image of the President faced the challenges of "party politics," even individuals as Donald Trump picked up the mantra of the "Birthers" quest. Perhaps Mr. Obama held out on the final birth revelation to allow critics to show the *venom of their underbelly*. However, while some called their actions racist, others saw wisdom in his birth holdout indicating the "clown nature" of some of his detractors.

Vowing he would get Osama bin Laden during his election campaign, as President, Barack Obama pursued the head of Al Qaeda relentlessly as he prosecuted the war on terror and the mastermind's network. Call it disinformation if you like, but whenever in recent years the question of bin Laden's whereabouts was raised, the standard response given was "He's somewhere in the Pakistan mountainous badlands" meaning the trail had gone cold! Even if it did, by keeping certain details out of the press, the team assigned to "Get bin Laden" kept working on their assignment, updating the President on progress, narrowing their focus and finally locating his hideout.

The military task force chosen to carry out the plan to "get their man," practiced, some say, 100 times on how to successfully storm the terror mastermind's stronghold. As they approached "D-Day" the President's leadership skills took center stage as he pondered all the unimaginable risks involved in the ambitious plan. In view of past failed military forays, viz., Kennedy's "Bay of Pigs" failure in Cuba and Jimmy Carter's "Iran hostage rescue" collapse, even the fiasco of the "Somali Invasion," President Obama was faced with a tough Presidential decision as to time and manner to execute the plan to get Osama. Combining "old faithful" listening to his people skills, and mindful of his "If we have actionable intelligence about high-value terrorist targets we will act" speech, he made the gutsy decision which turned out to be a spectacular triumph for his image, trumping the likes of Donald Trump who questioned his leadership abilities. Not only did Mr. Obama show the world he was a strong leader by proving he was tough on terrorism, he signaled to domestic opponents "You can't use the soft on terror argument" in your 2012 Presidential campaign. Some say execution of the operation, rapid disposing of bin Laden and seizing his treasure trove of terrorist data was as good

BARACK OBAMA
MASTER OF WASHINGTON DC

as it gets, and that the Obama Administration performed brilliantly demonstrating Mr. Obama is truly an outstanding leader, decisive and courageous.

Barack Obama's Washington, DC Photo 4. Even more columns in Union Station.

As he demonstrates these many traits, the hard working Mr. Obama continues his unrelenting domestic efforts to address problems in the economy, unemployment, fiscal policy, educational initiatives, the various forms of new alternative energy sources, passing legislation that's designed to make people's lives better, his chances of being re-elected seem to be getting much better despite the litany of contenders lining up to challenge him for the Presidency. Without a doubt, however, Mr. Obama has demonstrated extraordinary leadership at a critical time in America's history as he seeks to create a brighter future for this nation.

FREDERICK MONDERSON

"Hold firmly, without wavering, to the faith we profess!"

3. PRESIDENT OBAMA IN AFRICA I
By

Dr. Fred Monderson

After successfully attending a Summit establishing a new chapter in American-Russian relations, then on to Italy for a G-8 Economic Conference where he and the first family had an audience with Pope Benedict, President Obama arrived in Ghana, West Africa for a one-day visit charged with more significance and electricity than that of all past Presidents combined who have visited Africa. To recall, as a Senator from Illinois, Barack Obama visited Kenya, his father's homeland which provided a tremendous welcome to this "son of a son." Elders dressed Obama in traditional African garb and this provided a firestorm in the 2008 Presidential Elections at home as opponents sought to paint him as Muslim among so many other things. However, this time as the first African-American President, rather than return to his "roots" in Kenya, President Obama chose Ghana because of its symbolism as a thriving and vibrant democracy as evident from a recent election and peaceful transfer of power to the opposition.

In a historic address to the Ghanaian Parliament, carried by CNN and equally broadcast across the African continent, Mr. Obama was pragmatic, stuck to his guns and delivered a "tough love" speech outlining America's new relationship with African nations. He emphasized the simple and unmistakable fact, "we must start with the simple premise that Africa's future is up to Africans," and recognizing Europe's imperial role on the continent insisted, "a colonial map that made little sense bred conflict and the West has often approached Africa as a patron, rather than a partner; but the West is not responsible for the destruction of the Zimbabwean economy over the last decade, or wars in which children are enlisted as combatants."

BARACK OBAMA
MASTER OF WASHINGTON DC

Barack Obama's Washington, DC Photo 5. Scene on the busy station floor with a sit-down restaurant, a vendor's wares and passersby.

Despite these facts, five hundred years after the discovery of the Americas and the subsequent efforts to conquer this hemisphere, the European Slave Trade in Africans, and the ramifications of plantation slavery of Africans with attendant psychological and physical emasculation of the victims of such barbarism; in this, we see the legacy of slavery still functioning institutionally in many guises as we crossed the bridge of the new century. This forces us to remember that (in this emerging great nation of America, the English colonials under Britain fought the French, in the *French and Indian Wars (1756-1763)* and fought the British in the *War of Independence (1776-1783)*. This new great nation then fought the British in the *War of 1812 (1812-1815)*. Then we fought the *Mexican War (in 1845)* and the Spanish in the *Spanish American War (1898-1900)*; the Germans and their allies in *World War I (1914-1918)* though we practically entered the conflict in 1917; again, the Germans, Italians and Japan in *World War II (1939-1945)* though we entered that conflict on December 7, 1941; the *Korean War (1950-1953)*; and against the Chinese, Russians and their allies in the anti-*Communist Cold War*. Again, particularly the Russians, who have atomic weapons, probably still aimed at us that can devastate this nation; yet, these people can all come to these shores, blend in with the population and with some effort begin moving up the social ladder towards realization of the American Dream. However, the ravages and devastation of slavery and its legacy still identify sons and daughters of Africa in America and make us victims of racism that was born out of this dehumanizing experience of the MAAFA or "great enslavement!"

Barack Obama's Washington, DC Photo 6. Elevated semi-circular colonnade in white marble, a hallmark of Washington's government architecture.

Therefore, we need never forget, as we ended the Twentieth Century and crossed the bridge to the Twenty-First Century; it was W.E.B. DuBois who said the question of the "color bar" would dominate those past hundred years. All people must move away from this odious conception and practice that is very much alive and well in the world in today's 21st Century! Showing as an aspect of long memory, Fordham in *Geography of African Affairs* (1965: 58-59) has recounted how Africans worldwide were viewed then in the most disdainful manner, and supplied an example that indicated, "As late as 1928 a distinguished Englishman" could write, "The Negroes of Tropical Africa specialized in their isolation and stagnation in utter savagery. They may even have been drifting away from the human standard back towards the brute when migratory impulses drew the Caucasian, the world's redeemer, to enter Tropical Africa ... mingle his blood with that of the pristine negroes and raise the mental status of these dark skinned, wooly haired, prognathous retrograded men ...." The speaker capitalized Caucasian but not Negroes!

BARACK OBAMA
MASTER OF WASHINGTON DC

Barack Obama's Washington, DC Photo 7. Colonnade with figures on the cornice on the façade of Union Station.

He continued (1965: 59) that: "Echoes of this attitude were still to be heard in the British House of Lords in 1961" when he quoted Lord Barbizon of Tara, on March 23, 1961, in *Hansard* Vol. 229, No. 57, Cols. 1277-9. It stated: "As I went to it [the United Nations] I really got the impression that there was a convention of nigger minstrels going on ... the Commonwealth is a piebald set-up, and a pie-bald set-up is a poor form of organization that will never last." Of course, contrary to such a mindset, that is not to say, some of our people have not progressed despite difficult odds, as they struggled with and without bootstraps.

However, as we celebrated another Martin Luther King birthday and head towards Black History Month in February, 2009, the voices of such commentators as Julian Bond, Kwame Mfume, Leonard Jeffries, Tony Martin, Sonny Carson and a whole host of others, all have pointed to the disparities and difficulties of high unemployment, police brutality, racial discrimination, poverty, lack of proper medical care, drug infestation, crime, poor education, etc., that still plague Black communities. This odious legacy remains viable principally because of the African heritage of Black people that seems anathema to many in this nation. But it must be remembered, Black people paid the ultimate sacrifice to build America, and we intend to earn our place at the table of this nation, under the philosophic and humanistic banner believing in the fatherhood of God and the brotherhood of man!

With that, all need to understand the forced removal of Africans, called the Atlantic Slave Trade, began soon after the Portuguese landed in West Africa in 1441. That year, a trickle of Africans was first taken to Lisbon, Portugal. Lloyd (1972: 51) has shown these early contacts by the Portuguese along the West African coast was beginning to clear the way for the later onslaught.

Barack Obama's Washington, DC Photo 8. Panoramic view of the entrance façade of Union Station with "Old Glory" flying half-mast against a blue sky background.

"In 1434 Portuguese ships passed Cape Bojador in Mauretania; by 1475 Fernando Po had been reached, and in 1483 Portuguese sailors visited the capital of Benin, probably the most highly organized coastal kingdom at this period. The Portuguese were impressed by it and established a trading port at Ughoton (Gwatto) in 1486, but their main attention was directed to the Gold Coast with its more valuable exports; the castle of San Jorge da Mina was erected at Elmina in 1482. Gold apart, the West African coast offered little to attract European trade until the discovery of the Americas provided a demand for slaves."

However, from 1485 onward we witness a number of significant events in Europe. First there was the unification of Spain and defeat of the Moors and the fall of Granada. Then in 1492 Columbus' expedition was underway. Decades thereafter, Africans began to be shipped to the Americas to cultivate plantations. By the end

BARACK OBAMA
MASTER OF WASHINGTON DC

of the century, plantation culture utilizing enforced African labor were producing sugar cane and derivative products; particularly in the British West Indies, e.g., Barbados and Trinidad; Slavery came after 1814 in Cape Town, South Africa; and after the Dutch in Guiana now Guyana, enslaved Africans who were harnessed to exploit this sweet product with its derivative industries.

Barack Obama's Washington, DC Photo 9. View of the stairs and columns from the Senate side of the front of the Capital Building, with visitors milling by.

FREDERICK MONDERSON

Barack Obama's Washington, DC Photo 10. From the luscious greenery, view of that magnificent building with its columned dome, symbol of democratic power.

Iliffe (1995: 127-128) recounts: "The Atlantic slave trade began in 1441 when a young Portuguese sea-captain Antam Goncalvez, kidnapped a man and woman on the Western Saharan coast to please his employer, Prince Henry the Navigator-successfully, for Goncalvez was knighted. Four years later the Portuguese built a fort on Arguin Island, off the Mauritanian coast, from which to purchase slaves and, more particularly, gold, which was especially scarce at this time. After failing in 1415 to capture the gold trade by occupying Ceuta on the Moroccan coast, Portuguese mariners groped down the West African coast towards the gold sources. Arguin was designed to lure gold caravans away from the journey to Morocco. Yet slaves were not merely by-products, for a lively market in African slaves had existed since the mid-fourteenth century in southern Europe, where labor was scarce after the Black Death and slavery had survived since Roman times in domestic service and pockets of intensive agriculture, especially the production of sugar, which Europeans had learned from Muslims during the Crusade. As sugar plantation spread westwards through the Mediterranean to Atlantic islands like Maderia and eventually to the Americas, they depended increasingly on slave labor. The Atlantic slave trade was largely a response to their demand."

BARACK OBAMA
MASTER OF WASHINGTON DC

Barack Obama's Washington, DC Photo 11. Another view of the Capital Building from behind the decoration so characteristic of Washington, DC.

Significantly, by 1505 or thereabouts, exploration of the "New World" had become ingrained. The result was systematic and widespread destruction of indigenous cultures, viz., the Incas, Mayas, Aztecs, etc., that were flourishing in this hemisphere. Commenting on the people who followed Columbus into North, Central and South America at the end of the Fifteenth Century, Davidson (1996: 202) wrote: "These others, who were Spanish soldiers and adventurers, ruined the [native] American peoples whom they found. Their intention was not trade, but loot; not peace, but war; not partnership, but enslavement. They fell upon these lands with greed and the fury of destruction. And the [native] American peoples, unlike the Africans, were unable to defend themselves. Being at an earlier stage of social and technical development than the Africans, these people were easy victims to Spanish violence. Along the coast of Guinea, the Portuguese and other Europeans had begun by trying their hand at violence. But they had given that up. The Africans they met were too strong for them. In the Americas it was different."

Even further, Davidson (1996: 203) continued: "There was terrible destruction of the 'Indians,' the name that was mistakenly given by these raiders to the native-born American people. A Spanish report of 1518, only twenty-six years after the first voyage of Columbus across the Atlantic, says that when the island of Cuba was discovered it was reckoned to contain more than a million 'Indians,' but today their number does not exceed 11,000. And judging from what has happened, there will be none of them left in three or four years' time, unless some remedy is applied."

That unfortunate state of affairs, forced Bishop Bartholomew De Las Casas to petition the papacy. He requested that Africans be brought into the Americas for labor purposes, to replace the rapidly disappearing indigenous population. Losing the battle to "save the Indians," he unleashed an even greater tragedy that lasted for centuries, and claimed many, many more lives. This stain on humanity's integrity was Europe's Slave Trade in Africans to America!

The Age of Exploration created new opportunities for discovery and transformation of the new lands, introduced by Columbus and the other explorers, for which they sought official sanction. The Papal division of the world in a Papal Bull in 1492 gave half to Portugal and the other half to Spain, Christian nations and ardent defenders of their religion and the papacy. Two years later in 1494, the demarcation was enshrined in the Treaty of Tordesillas, moving the boundary line 300-leagues to the west. The new official pronouncement gave most of the New World to Spain. That excluded the Portuguese foothold in Brazil that is today the largest country in South America. As such, this Papal beneficence prohibited the Spanish from involvement in the trade in enslaved persons from Africa. The Portuguese, however, did have a free hand there. Iliffe (1995: 130) continued that: "The first West African slaves went mainly to Portugal, then to Maderia, and then to Sao Tome. Direct shipments from Africa to the Americas began in 1532. As European and African diseases destroyed the Amerindian peoples, African slaves replaced them, because Africans alone were available in the required numbers, and then were cheaper than white indentured laborers, and they had the unique degree of immunity to both European and African diseases which came from living in the tropical periphery of the Old World."

By the late sixteenth century nearly 80 per cent of all exported West African slaves went to the Americas, especially to Brazil, where plantation sugar took root during the 1540s.

BARACK OBAMA
MASTER OF WASHINGTON DC

Barack Obama's Washington, DC Photo 12. Still another view of one of the most photographed sites in Washington, DC.

The Spanish *Haciento Treaty* was agreed to in 1713. Whosoever held it had permission to supply the Spanish possessions in America with enslaved persons from Africa. In fact, Moore and Dunbar (1968: 110) have written: "The British took a leading part in this trade from the middle of the seventeenth century, with the development of the plantation colonies. New impetus was given when at the Peace of Utrecht in 1713 [Britain] obtained the Asiento." This Spanish contract was to supply cargo to and from the Spanish "New World." For the African victims involved, this dreaded official instrument, yet, provoked many wars at sea among slaving European nations. Dreaded, in the sense that, the Spanish could not get slaves in Africa, so they had them brought to their "New World" plantation. For Africans, it provided death and hopelessness of Slave Trade and Slavery. Oliver and Fage (1970: 120) have argued the Spanish territory was very lucrative and: "The early Spanish colonies there had been supplied with African slaves, mainly through the Portuguese, from about 1510. But it was not until the competitive irruption into the West Indies of the Dutch, French and English in the seventeenth century, when there was a rapidly growing European demand for sugar - a crop making heavy demands on labor - which the transatlantic slave trade began to dominate European activities in West Africa. Compared with an estimate of some 275,000 Negro slaves landed overseas by 1600, the seventeenth-century figure is thought to be about 1,340,000; the figures of the eighteenth and

FREDERICK MONDERSON

nineteenth centuries seem to have been about 6,050,000 and 1,900,000 respectively. The new development ousted the Portuguese from the Gold Coast. For a short time the trans-Atlantic trade was almost a Dutch monopoly, but their success provoked English and French hostility, and by the eighteenth century it was the traders of these two nations who were the principal competitors in the international trade, thought the Portuguese continued with a private slave trade of their own, from Angola and San Thome to Brazil. In terms of the trade alone, victory went to Britain. By the end of the eighteenth century her ships were carrying nearly half the slaves taken to America." Let us not forget the operative word here is "landed" in the "New World."

And so it continued for centuries. But that is not to say, though we mentioned the Portuguese, English, French and Dutch, that these were the only nations involved. We must remember colonial America was also an active participant in Slave Trade development. This systematic and undeniable sustained holocaust provided an inexhaustible supply of free labor required by slave trading nations then transforming the American landscape. Those other nations involved included the Brandenbergers or Germans, the Danes, and Swedes. Still, though not involved in carrying Africans to the "New World," the Spanish, because of the needs of empire, helped maintain a system of slavery in America, for three centuries after Columbus; that encouraged the perpetuation of this ghastly degrading and deadly labor-supply phenomenon.

From the Atlantic Slave Trade's inception, it would appear that few of the traders worried or were concerned about carrying conditions aboard their ships. As a result, the terms "tight packers" and "loose packers" came to characterize how enslaved Africans were transported to the Americas.

As Malcolm X has said, "We did not land on Plymouth Rock, Plymouth Rock landed on us." Thus, the treatment in the "Middle Passage" and "Triangular Trade" promised nothing but death, hopeless melancholy and despair. Enslaved Africans were devastated or killed at inland capture; in forced march to the coast; in holding cells on the coast before shipment through the "Door of No Return." That is, after the coastal areas had been depopulated. Let us not forget those killed or died in the inhuman conditions on those "Coffins of death" who were then thrown overboard to be devoured by sharks that trailed such ships!

BARACK OBAMA
MASTER OF WASHINGTON DC

Barack Obama's Washington, DC Photo 13. Another view of Union Station's entrance with the flags flying half-mast.

Relative to mortality and in view of this situation, in 1788 and again in 1792, the House of Commons of the British Parliament conducted inquiries on the Slave Trade. They found that "persons transported from Africa to the West Indies are kidnapped, solely for the purpose of selling them to the traders." Alexander Falconbridge (1788: 13), a surgeon in the Slave Trade, had written there is: "great reason to believe that most of the Negroes shipped from the coast of Africa are kidnapped." Sold to European slavers, the enslaved Africans faced a difficult journey. It took some fifty-two days to cross the Atlantic from Africa to America. At times the voyage was longer. However, it was seldom shorter!

Significantly, a constant problem of the Slave Trade was overcrowding. The famous slave ship BROOKES, out of Liverpool, sailed to the West Coast of Africa in 1783. This 320-ton frigate was built without forecastle and pierced for 20 guns that enabled every square foot of the vessel to be used to store its human cargo. *Minutes of the Evidence on the Slave Trade to Parliament* (1789: 43) indicated calculations were made of the men's room, boys' room, women's room, the gun-room, cabin, half-deck and a number of platforms.

FREDERICK MONDERSON

Barack Obama's Washington, DC Photo 14. Another view of the Capital Building.

Barack Obama's Washington, DC Photo 15. Still another view of the Capital Building.

A. Stuart-Brown (1932: 48-49) described some carrying logistics of this famous vessel: "The slaves were lodged on the lower deck, the men in a room 46 feet by 25 feet 4 inches and 5 feet 8 inches high, the women in a smaller room 28 feet 6 inches by 23 feet 6 inches and the boy's room was 13 feet 9 inches by 25 feet."

BARACK OBAMA
MASTER OF WASHINGTON DC

In one instance, this slaving ship spent 10 months on the coast and collected 609 enslaved Africans. Those who boarded first experienced the horrors of "holding" before the "Middle Passage."

Dr. Thomas Trotter, the BROOKES' surgeon, according to *Evidence of Robert Stokes Esq., Before the Select Committee of the House of Lords in 1948*, reported seeing Africans all over the ship. In testimony to the Committee of Parliament, Stokes (1849: 5) describing his observations on the ship, stated the: "slaves in the passage were so crowded below, it is impossible to walk through them without treading on them." These conditions existed in the "pre-regulation period" when "tight packers" was the rule. "Tight packers" meant purchase and carry as many enslaved persons without concern about safety. Pack them in tight! In the *Frontispiece* of this same source, Charles Fox, an abolitionist had stated: "True humanity consists not in a squeamish ear; it consists not in staring or shrinking at tales such as these, but in a disposition of heart to relieve misery. True humanity appertains rather to the mind than to the nerves, and prompts men to use real and active endeavors to execute the measures which it suggests."

After regulation in 1789, BROOKES was restricted to carry only 454 enslaved Africans. The ship was still crowded with 450 aboard! One could only wonder how it managed to transport 609! After regulation, "loose packing" or carry fewer based on ship's tonnage, helped reduce the mortality rate aboard this and many other British slavers. While in this essay the British example is often used, the practice applies for colonial America and other slave-trading European nations, making Britain the "best of a bad lot." Some have disagreed and believe they were the worst during the 1700s-1800s. Fact is, British regulation was not a pre-requisite of other nations. Business operated on the conscience of the monetary unit whether pound, frank, mark, or dollar. The stark inhumanity of the trade victimized and physically dehumanized the African man, woman and child.

According to *An Historical Account of the Liverpool African Slave Trade* (1884: iii) there was an old saying in the City of Liverpool: "Get slaves honestly, if you can, and if you cannot get them honestly, get them!" Of course, a colleague of mine in the 20th Century, Stanley Simpson, reviewing this comment asked: "What is meant by the term 'honestly' in this context during the 1700s?" Does it mean pay first for the merchandise? Or, pay a good price for what you got? If so, what would be the true value of a human being? That is the question! In fact, it forces us to wonder 'what is the true value of an African man, woman or child?' When we apply this context to the present state of relations among our people, it does not matter if persons are killed by their own or by others, a human life should not be regarded as being without value. That is why the Theme of 1997 Black Solidarity Day was: "No (Black) one should die at the hands of another."

FREDERICK MONDERSON

In those times, in the principal British slave trading city of Liverpool and elsewhere, it was a popular belief, notes *Historical Account* .... (1884: 14) that: "Slavery was right; it was supported by the Bible, and strenuously advocated by the clergy of the time; as well as the politicians. They asserted it was divine right that the blacks were of an inferior race and were to be bought and sold by the white man; with his brand on them .... How many crimes have been committed in the name of the book?" Perhaps, however, it was not in the name of the Book but in the name of profits!

We are told further in the same source (1884: 16) of George Franklin Cook, tragedian, who was born April 17, 1756 and died September 26, 1812. While drunk at a performance in the Liverpool Theater, he is quoted as saying to his jeering critics: "I have not come here to be insulted by a set of wretches, of which every brick in your infernal town is cemented with an African's blood." We are also informed in *Edinburgh Review* (1908: 26) the "chief center of the African trade Liverpool, [was] remarkable in the commercial history of the United Kingdom." Even further, the same source, in *Edinburgh Review* (1908: 33) states: "Of all English communities, Liverpool derived the most wealth from the debasing trade." More, in the *Illustrated London News* (1957: 18) we are again reminded of descriptions of the city's investment in the Slave Trade as an "impressive array of commercial institutions, banking houses, insurance companies, trading associations and produce exchanges." In addition, *Illustrated London News* (1957: 18) informs further, "Liverpool merchants performed a variety of economic functions incorporating the means for financing and insuring the commodities they bought and sold, and controlling the ships which carried the commodities overseas." Even more, that the "Liverpool merchant body exerted a powerful influence over Parliament through the Liverpool Parliamentary Office." This was probably because the prosperity of the port was tied to the import of raw cotton, sugar, wheat, flour, rum, and tobacco, and to the export of cotton piece goods, woolens, salt, coal, iron products, chemicals, glass and soap. However, this profit motive notwithstanding, things have an uncanny way of working themselves out, for there were individuals whose conscience and high moral standards dictated that they resist and challenge this plague perpetuated by their countrymen. One such instance can be cited of James Fox, an abolitionist quoted as saying during the English Parliament's attempt to regulate the Slave Trade, that: "There can be no regulation of robbery and murder."

BARACK OBAMA
MASTER OF WASHINGTON DC

Barack Obama's Washington, DC Photo 16. Greenery in front of the Capital Building under a clear blue sky.

Barack Obama's Washington, DC Photo 17. Flowers, statue and the wonderful structure that so fascinates because of its political power and architectural magnificence.

FREDERICK MONDERSON

Barack Obama's Washington, DC Photo 18. More of the Capital Building.

We know the Atlantic Slave Trade began after Bishop De Las Casas sought papal approval to ship Africans to the Americas to save lives of Amerindians. Foxburn (1932: 56) has shown: "Las Casas, ... saw no harm in subjecting African Negroes to the treatment from which he sought earnestly to save the aborigines of the new world." However, some have argued that de Las Casas thought this the lesser of two evils. Perhaps he never thought it would escalate as it did. Yet, and arguably, the trade was continued under religious sanction through the belief that Africans were not Christians, not Europeans, had an "exotic culture" and easily definable by skin color. Therefore, official policy held it was okay to enslave them. Thereafter, in 1562-63, Sir John Hawkins, the first Englishman to trade in enslaved Africans, sailed to Africa in the slave ship *Solomon*. Two years later in 1564-65, he sailed in the slave ship *Jesus*, blazing a trail for his countrymen.

Harris (1972: 72-73) has written: "It was a combination of European attitudes about blacks and the demand for cheap labor that sired the Atlantic Slave Trade and New World black slavery." When the Portuguese arrived in Africa they began seizing Africans to take to Europe as 'curiosity pieces' which confirmed that a "new land had been reached." The early African victims were honored in Portugal, taught Portuguese, and used as informants and guides for future Portuguese voyages to Africa.

BARACK OBAMA
MASTER OF WASHINGTON DC

However, as the number of Africans increased in Lisbon they gradually were relegated to menial tasks, and by the middle of the fifteenth century, a lively trade in African (slave) labor developed. Thus, even before the Americas were settled by Europeans, Europe witnessed the development of black slavery, especially in Portugal, Spain, Italy, and Sicily. It has been estimated, for example, that between 1458 and 1460, from 700 to 800 slaves were exported annually from Africa to Europe, with an estimate of 35,000 for 1450-1500.

Barack Obama's Washington, DC Photo 19. Ever remindful statuary that attest to the struggle for freedom and to maintain the unity of the Union.

Some authorities have calculated that from 50,000 to 100,000 Africans were taken to Europe during the whole course of the trade. Whatever the numbers, the point to emphasize here is that a half century prior to their settlement in the Americas, many Europeans (especially the inhabitants of Spain and Portugal, the two countries that spearheaded American settlement) had become accustomed to the enslavement of the Africans.

Yet, and conversely, by the 18th century, a religious conviction motivated men of good will to lead the fight to outlaw the slave trade. In Britain, many important abolitionists were involved including Granville Sharpe, Thomas Clarkson, Charles Fox, Wilberforce, Macaulay, and the Reverend John Newton, a reformed slave

FREDERICK MONDERSON

dealer. Reverend Newton authored the hymn "How Sweet the Name of Jesus Sounds," after a religious conversion, while aboard a slave ship he operated off the coast of West Africa.

In 1849, evidence was presented by Robert Stokes before a *Committee of the House of Lords*, as previously stated. This body, following inquiries of six decades earlier, reflected on the high mortality rate of English seamen in the trade before regulation. Their results revealed the following percentage of mortality rates: 50, 20, 20, 30, 33, 25, 30, 50. This showed an average of 32 per cent death rate for seamen on board some English slavers. Well, if the slavers were experiencing such high rates of mortality, imagine what it was among their cargo!

John Latimer (1893: 474-75) in *The Annals of Bristol in the 18th Century* recounted the view regarding "one captain from the port of the slave trade who did not deserve long ago to be hanged."

Barack Obama's Washington, DC Photo 20. Barack Obama's Washington, DC Photo 20. Still another look at the foliage before the back entrance of the Capital Building with the Fountain in the foreground.

Slaving methods of procuring sailors were notorious. In the slaving business, these seamen were: "Dreadfully ill-treated .... drugged with liquor until impotent to offer resistance ... sailors ... encouraged to run into debt, and then offered the alternative of a slaving voyage or a goal ... never permitted to read the articles they

BARACK OBAMA
MASTER OF WASHINGTON DC

signed on entering a ship, and by the insertion in these documents of iniquitous clauses .... wages in the slave trade (30 s per month) though nominally higher, were actually higher in other trades."

Nonetheless, in his *Essay on the Impolicy of the Slave Trade*, Thomas Clarkson (1785: 35) mentioned the "difficulty of procuring seamen for the slave trade is well known at the ports where it is carried on." Again, Clarkson (1788: 57) notes "in the year 1786, 1125 seamen will be found upon the dead list in consequence of this execrable trade." That same year recalled Clarkson (1788: 60) among West India Seamen "1470 deserted or were discharged .... Only 610 seamen out of the whole number deserted or were discharged yet found their way out of the colonies; ... that 860 yet remain to be accounted for in the expenditure of the year 1786." These figures, reinforced the view that mortality rates were high aboard these frigates of death, and, once tricked, sailors seemed to want to get out of the business themselves. Still, and also important, not all sailors were shanghaied and money was being made by the investors, whose mantra was "Buy low, sell high!"

More importantly, however, was the high incidence of deaths among the Africans, victimized in this Atlantic Slave Trade's forced migration, being the subject of centuries of psychological and physical assaults. In 1788, Clarkson called for "Efficiency of Regulation of the Slave Trade" because of its effects on both victims in the trade, Africans and Europeans. He supplied particularly interesting data on the subject of mortality. In his evidence, sailors' testimony show: "we purchased 350 slaves and buried 61; in a second voyage, in the same ship, we purchased 350, and buried 200; and in ...we purchased 370 and buried 100 .... We purchased 700 slaves and lost 250 ... we purchased 300, out of which we buried 17 ... 350 were purchased, and 25 were lost as before .... about 500 were purchased, and 150 buried."

FREDERICK MONDERSON

Barack Obama's Washington, DC Photo 21. Moving right along, horse of the war chariot, the Fountain and the Lawn before the Grand Marble Terrace of the Capital Building.

Barack Obama's Washington, DC Photo 21a. Gathering of the "Millions More March" on the Mall before the Grand Marble Terrace in October, 2000.

BARACK OBAMA
MASTER OF WASHINGTON DC

Barack Obama's Washington, DC Photo 21b. Another view of the gathering of the "Millions More March" on the Mall before the Grand Marble Terrace in October, 2000.

Most deaths were due to overcrowding and the intolerable conditions of the voyage. Practically, the physical and psychological cruelties of slavers were significant factors Africans had to reckon with. Victimizers also became victims of conditions they created.

In the end, the African personality was denuded and broken from this experience. Or, as the Afrocentrists would say, the Africans were "detached, isolated, and de-centered." Arriving in the West Indies the African was again debased. There, a final merciless legislative act transformed him into chattel or property. For example, *Report of the Lords' Committee of Council* "... 1789, Part III, in Jamaica, slaves were considered as property as indicated Anno 1696 Act 38: XL .... That no slave shall be free by becoming Christian; and for payment of debts and legacies, all slaves shall be deemed and taken as all other goods and chattels are in the hands of executors or administrators; ... all children of slaves, born in the possession of tenant for life or years, shall remain or revert."

Again, in Jamaica, *Anno* 1719, Act 67: V "... no Negro, mulatto, or Indian slave shall hire themselves out to work, either ashore or on board any ship or vessel, boat, ferry, canoe ... every such slave so offending, shall be whipped at the

FREDERICK MONDERSON

discretion of any magistrate in the parish or precinct where such slave or slaves shall offer themselves for hire.

In Barbados, slaves were also considered as property, for according to Act No. 94 of April 29, 1668, the "Negro slaves of this island shall be real estate .... all Negro slaves, in all courts of judicature and other places within this island, shall be held, taken, and adjudged to be estate real ... and shall descend unto the heirs and widow of any person dying intestate."

Again, in Barbados, January 1672, Act No. 178 was considered "A Declarative Act making Negroes real estate in that: "... Negroes shall be deemed real estate and not chattels ... Negroes may be sued for and recovered by action personal ... Negroes continue chattel for the payment of debts." Even further, on August 8, 1688, Act No. 329 states: "here any Negro or other slave ... shall suffer death then shall such justices and freeholders, colonels and field officers who adjudged such Negro or other slave to suffer death, immediately after sentence thereof given inquire by the best means they are able of the value of such Negro or other slave, in which value they shall not exceed the sum of five and twenty pound sterling .... tempt or persuade any Negroes or other slaves to leave their masters and mistresses ... adjudged to pay the master of the said Negro or other slave five and twenty pounds."

Barack Obama's Washington, DC Photo 22. Some of the many columns in the Capital Dome and entranceway.

BARACK OBAMA
MASTER OF WASHINGTON DC

On November 28, 1705, Act No. 516 read: " ... for all Negroes and other slaves that shall be imported to this island and landed there, an importation or duty shall be paid, that the merchant or merchants ... pay into the treasurer of this island ... five shillings current money for each and every Negro or other slave imported, whether male or female, young or old ...."

Finally, a *Supplemental Act* was passed on February 7, 1715, No. 593 that read as follows: "Be it therefore enacted ... that no Negroes or other slaves whatsoever, which shall for the future be once imported into this island shall be exempted from paying the duty of five shillings a head, but such only which shall be within 48 hours exported in the same ship or vessel."

Therefore, the psycho-social ramifications of the centuries old experience seemed to, and still, so significantly plague the survivors of the greatest of all tragedies, that Prof. Donna Richards of Hunter College called *The Maafa* or "Great Enslavement;" which served as "the basis of the Western World's Economic Development on the Backs of African people!"

Barack Obama's Washington, DC Photo 23. Still another view of Union Station's entrance with the Post Office building at the end of the street.

FREDERICK MONDERSON

"Change will not come if we wait for some other person, or if we wait for some other time. We are the ones we've been waiting for. We are the change that we seek." BARACK OBAMA Speech during the 2008 Presidential campaign.

4. PRESIDENT OBAMA IN AFRICA II
BY
Dr. Fred Monderson

It is interesting how President Barack Obama visited Africa at different times to make two of his most significant addresses outside of the Continental United States. His Address in Egypt at Cairo University was designed to start a conversation, open a dialogue of mutual respect, mutual dignity "with the Muslim world." His speech at the Ghanaian Parliament in Accra was crafted to send a message to Africa and the world of America's intent to more closely engage the continent of his ancestral heritage. More particularly, to the African nations and their rulers, he insisted the will, interests and future of their people, their greatest resources, must be paramount if Africa is to emerge and play the significant role in world events that it is truly capable of.

Yes, Egypt is in North Africa, it has always been there. Importantly, of all African nations, Egypt benefits most from the potency of the geographical detritus impregnated in the life giving Nile River flowing from inner Africa, and the potentialities of cultural effluence that from time immemorial has enriched, energized and revitalized that nation and its people in all aspects of their existence. Ghana, in West Africa, is pivotal in the historical development of modern Africa for a number of reasons, and thus, was an ideal location for President Obama to make his historic address. The name Ghana piggybacks on the first of three medieval empires of Ghana, Mali and Songhai, which dominated Middle African history. This name was significant in influencing modern Ghana's march to independence in 1957 and the symbolism it represented in Kwame Nkrumah's vision of an independent and united continental economic, cultural and social African government, shedding the shackles of colonialism.

Also, Ghana became a principal transshipment point for enslaved Africans being forcefully embarked to New World plantation slavery. Elmira Castle, in Ghana, is one of many lining the West African coast where European marauders, in the age of "Naked Imperialism" used their enormous canon power to fight off Atlantic competitors and when turned around, terrorized the surrounding countryside in their insidious effort to marshal, accumulate, house, and ship Africans through the "Door of no return," to a life unknown, but of unspeakable horrors far away.

BARACK OBAMA
MASTER OF WASHINGTON DC

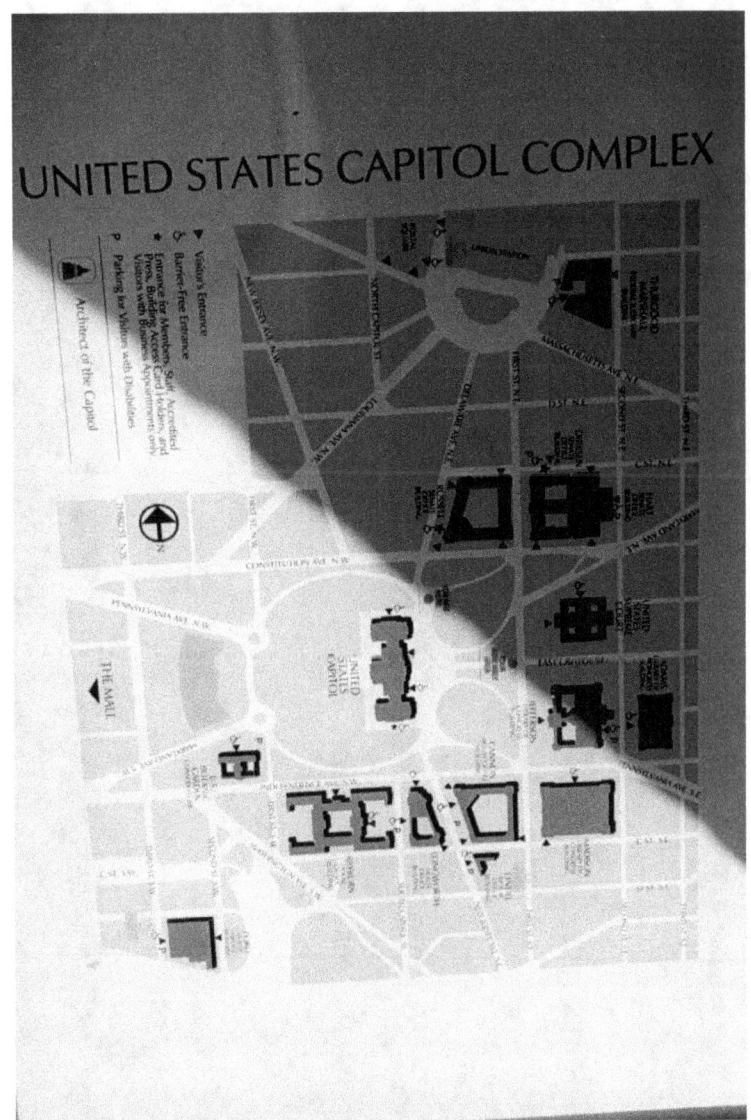

Barack Obama's Washington, DC Photo 24. Map of the Capital showing some of its most famous streets and important buildings.

FREDERICK MONDERSON

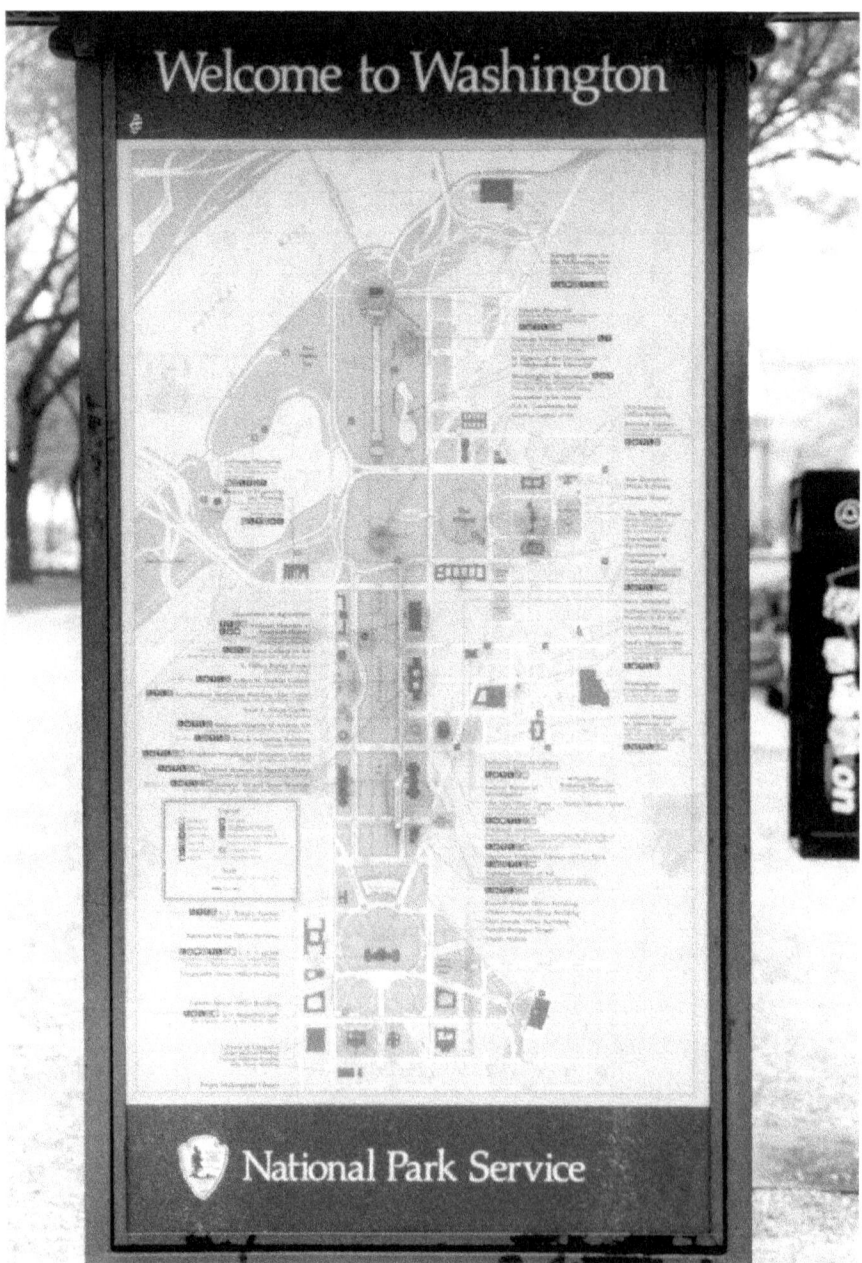

Barack Obama's Washington, DC Photo 24a. Welcome to Washington map of the Capital provided by the National Parks Service showing the more significant structures in the area.

BARACK OBAMA
MASTER OF WASHINGTON DC

Barack Obama's Washington, DC Photo 25. Columns of the Lincoln Memorial with its Doric Capitals.

It is also interesting that President Clinton visited Ghana in the last years of his tenure and was shown in a photograph looking through the "Door of No Return." The same may be said for President Obama. The important question, however, is whether the guides informed these two Presidents "an American activist named Sonny Abubadika Carson" reinterred his ancestor Samuel Carson, a US Navy Veteran of the War with Mexico (1845) here in Ghana, inaugurating the First Emancipation Day Festival, August 1, 1998, equally creating the "Door of Return." Now he is buried alongside a Jamaican slave named Crystal at Asin Manso, beside the river where the slaves took their last bath before being shipped through the same and infamous "Door of No Return." In a significant and historic move, Mr. Carson opened the "Door of Return" so African Americans can visit the site of pilgrimage and connect with their ancestral roots in Ghana. This can also be a first step as they search elsewhere on the continent. The guide's follow-up question to Mr. Obama then should have been, 'Sir, would you like to see the site of African American Pilgrimage at Asin Manso?'

America was essentially founded as a Christian nation and in that searing crucible, many un-Christian acts, such as the Slave Trade and Institution of Slavery were perpetuated against African people for centuries. In an age when people struggled with government to declare the Rights of Man and issue the Declaration of

FREDERICK MONDERSON

Independence, boasting of life, liberty and the pursuit of happiness, African people were denied much these universal principles were intended to achieve. Yet, in the religious contradiction in its founding principles, America struggled to evolve a level of tolerance so that through good works the American "melting pot" came to accept in its mix, Baptists, African Zionists, Moravians, Anglicans, Jehovah's Witnesses, Catholics, Jews, Muslims and atheists, all being allowed to practice their beliefs or non-beliefs, peacefully, in a society allowing religious tolerance.

However, upon his arrival in Cairo, Egypt, Mr. Obama, true to his campaign promises, wanted to dispel the myth that America was at war with Islam, Muslims. This is because of the recent history of events, particularly the attack on September 11, 2001, that led to the war on terrorism and subsequent developments that saw Americans fighting in Iraq and Afghanistan, and equally, seeming to ignore the fundamentals of the Arab-Israeli conflict which is fueled by the Palestinian-Israeli issue. So, therefore, in his initial greeting to the audience at the Cairo University and to Muslims worldwide tuned in to listen the young American President who promised fundamental change in American relations with Islam and the world; he therefore began with the greeting "Salaam-Wali-Kom" to which the response was "Wali-Kom-Salaam," not only from the live audience, but one could imagine hearing it through the TV sets and radios emanating from the worldwide listening audience. He had struck a positively sensitive nerve in this initial and fundamental show of respect. Thus, he could say, "I bring you peace from Muslims in my country" and, having Muslim forebears himself, he had broken the ice!

Seeking to defuse the time of tension, and being "proud to carry the good will of the American people," he reflected on the "historical conflict" rather than cooperation colonialism had generated between the Arab/Muslim world and the West, and particularly America. Thus, he wanted to create a new beginning in America's relations. Significantly, as a student of history he emphasized that Islam has always been a part of American history and that American Muslims have enriched American history. Then he went on to boast of "civilization's debt to Islam."

Here Mr. Obama spoke of a "partnership based on what Islam is, not what it isn't." He also sought to make it clear "America is not the crude stereotype of a self-interested empire" and that it's been shaped by events and people who contributed much to shape its creed, "Out of Many One."

Here again he emphasized, "Let there be no doubt, Islam is a part of America," and that "words alone cannot meet the needs of our people." Equally, with that astute historical perception, he stated clearly as a remindful warning to so many, at home and abroad, "Any world order that elevates one nation or group over another will inevitably fail." Here he particularly referenced and spoke against the issue of "violent extremism in all its forms" and that "America will relentlessly confront all extremism which poses a grave threat to our security." Reiterating the now known

BARACK OBAMA
MASTER OF WASHINGTON DC

fact, President Obama pointed out, "Al Qaeda killed over 3000 people on 9/11" and America in response "partnered with a coalition of 46 nations" to which "Afghanistan demonstrates Americas goals and our need for better relationship."

Next Mr. Obama dealt with the "Palestinian-Israeli issue" and emphasized his early dispatch of an envoy to the region, the recognition of a "two state' solution "and the need to end the construction of settlements," all while reiterating and reassuring "America's commitment to Israel" and the need to guarantee its "safe and inviolate borders;" but later he would insist "Israel must return to the 1967 borders" in order to encourage a lasting and good faith Middle East Peace.

Barack Obama's Washington, DC Photo 26. A better view of the back of the Lincoln Memorial with its wonderful colonnade consisting of ten in the back and equally ten in the front, with eight each on the two sides.

FREDERICK MONDERSON

Barack Obama's Washington, DC Photo 27. Another view of the side of the Lincoln Memorial with eights columns on each side. This makes for a total of 36 columns surrounding the Memorial, commemorating the 36 states in the Union when the President was shot.

By the time he ended, commentators agreed this was the "most powerful and most persuasive speech of any President to the Muslim world." They further pointed to Mr. Obama's "emphasis on soft power rather than hard power," and that this represented an "important shift in America's relations with the Muslim world." Commentators again believed, in this respect he had gained "enormous political capital around the world."

President Obama treated "any attempt to deny the Holocaust ever occurred as criminal behavior." He cited his great uncle, Charles Payne of the 89th Infantry Division, who was an eyewitness in liberating one of the death camps, Again, like Mr. Obama, "the New York activist Sonny Carson's uncle was a member of one of the first Black units to liberate one of the death camps." At a later date, after a visit to Russia, the President arrived in Ghana, West Africa, and addressed the Ghanaian Parliament in a message carried continent-wide. The essential message of his Address was that Africa's future is in Africa's hands. He expressed, "Africa does not need a strong man; it needs strong institutions;" and that Africa's "ruling elites have not thought of reinvesting in the well-being of the masses" of its people, its greatest asset.

BARACK OBAMA
MASTER OF WASHINGTON DC

Critics wondered why the President chose Ghana instead of Kenya, land of his paternal heritage. Clearly, as Secretary of State Hillary Clinton would later indicate, corruption is rife in Kenya and thus this would have been an unlikely venue for the President to have given such an important speech. However, the stated and most logical reason why Ghana was chosen is that it has a functioning democracy with easy transfer of power as evident recently following the last election. Notwithstanding this reality, the role of the military cannot be overlooked, some scholars have argued, for with "foreign interference" in overthrow of Prime Minister Kwame Nkrumah, Ghana's first elected leader and the names Adjai, Achaempong, and finally Jerry Rawlins, who, incidentally was in the audience, remained reminders of Ghana's troubling past and its image of "Neo-colonialist" activism.

President Obama, nevertheless, seemed to be building upon the little publicized initiatives in Africa begun by Presidents Clinton and Bush. In America's catch up in Africa, President Obama hoped to challenge major nations such as China who have been making investment inroads on the continent rich in natural resources. China, for its part, has a significant head start since the days of building the Tan-Zam railroad free of charge and having been an active supporter in the struggles against Apartheid in South Africa, Rhodesia and South-West Africa (Namibia.) Mr. Obama, on the other hand, because of his African American heritage, this appears helpful for his new initiatives of bringing Africa into the hub of global commerce. In addition, terrorist infiltration of the African continent and the East African ports as naval operational points for military action in the Middle East and Pacific, are issues that drive America's new interest in the long neglected Africa continent. However, he could not emphasize this new involvement without speaking out against corruption, nepotism, mismanagement and inefficiency in Africa as well as the disruptive nature of civil wars and lack of fundamental respect for the rights of Africa's citizens. It is a conundrum that Africa is a resource powerhouse, yet its people are economically impoverished and not well served.

FREDERICK MONDERSON

Barack Obama's Washington, DC Photo 28. Still another view of two sides - together for eighteen of the thirty-six Doric columns surrounding the Lincoln Memorial.

The practical and diplomatic side of his visit over, the President began an emotional tour of the slave dungeons with his wife, children and mother-in-law, as Anderson Cooper of CNN reported on July 18, 2009. The President thought this was a "powerful moment for myself, Michelle and the girls." As he toured the slave castle dungeons and looked through the "Door of No Return" he equated it with his trip with Eli Wiesel to Buchenwald, a Holocaust site, and felt "as if the walls could talk," creating a profound, shocking experience.

Acknowledging his wife Michelle is a descendant of slaves, Mr. Obama declared "people were willing to degrade others if they appeared different." Realizing a church was in the castle's yard, President Obama expressed, "Slave merchants may have loved their children and gone to that church above the dungeon."

Taken below to the "Door of No Return," he muttered, "Through this door the journey of the African-American began" and rightly stated "profound sorrow must have been felt as people were hauled off to the great unknown." Dr. DeGruy said, these African victims "experienced profound emotional feelings from sorrow to rage."

BARACK OBAMA
MASTER OF WASHINGTON DC

The CNN Program's Host, Anderson Cooper of AC 360, mentioned "12-40 million people were forced to make the Middle Passage." This is somewhat inconsistent with conservative traditional doctrinal beliefs that 12-15 million were actually transshipped. In fact, W.E.B. DuBois in his 1896 Harvard PHD Thesis *The African Slave Trade 1638-1888* gives a figure of "100 million souls lost to Africa."

These figures included dead and dying in the kidnappings and the march to the coast; on shore in the holding pens; and those thrown overboard in the trans-shipment. Let us not forget, March 9, 1732 when 132 slaves were thrown alive overboard in three sets and the ship's owners had the audacity to file for insurance coverage in London under a clause entitled "perils of the sea."

The dead and dying on shore was a significant factor in the equation. First of all, we were reminded by President Obama that the slave trade was "very, very big business controlled by royal families of Europe." Let us not also forget, New England merchants built ships and their seamen provided slaves for southern plantation owners. Also, New England merchants established a price of "140 gallons of rum for 1 male African; 120 gallons of rum for 1 female African; and 90 gallons of Rum for 1 pre-puberty female." We could also add the employment opportunities in boat building and ancillary trades as painters, barrel makers and makers of metal hoops that bind barrels, etc. Not to omit the metal fetters that bind the African captives en-route to be slaves on "New World" plantations and as punishment for rebelling against the slave system.

It is clear, profit motives required strict rules and punishments that were harsh and deadly; all designed to make examples of slaves; or as Terence Stampp in *The Peculiar Institution* indicated in a chapter entitled "To Make Them Stand in Fear!" All manner of owner actions were designed to instill fear and trepidation among the slave lot. Among the many tools of intimidation used by perpetrators of the system in addition to a wide range of restraining devices, in vicinity of the "Door of No Return" were female slave dungeons and punishment cells in the slave castles. In the female slave dungeons, 150 women were packed in a single room. This was really eerie. The punishment cell was a death sentence for those about to die. With no ventilation, lighting, or relief facilities, the room contained a "foot thick of feces." The dungeon's odor coupled with the odor of feces, two centuries later is debilitating, imagine the psychological and emotional impact in the "fresh state" as the enslaved endured, some praying for death or "escape" through the "Door of No Return." From these horrible beginnings stem the historical disadvantages and misadventures African people in the Americas were victims of, for a long period of time.

FREDERICK MONDERSON

Barack Obama's Washington, DC Photo 29. Front of the Lincoln Memorial.

Out of the dungeon's hole, in the courtyard, President Obama reflected on his wife Michelle's slave roots. He spoke of her great, great, grand-father and great, great grand-mother Jim and Louisa Robinson who started in sprawling South Carolina, about 1850. These people were victims of, according to President Obama, "a terrible labor regime that was oppressive and created deep wounds in our nation."

Essentially, from Ghana on the West African Coast, to Slave Street in Georgetown, South Carolina, the slave experience and its legacy of racial discrimination has imprinted with long lasting emasculating implications on the psychological and emotional well-being of slavery's institutional victims, African-Americans.

Yet, when all is said and done, President Barack Obama's trip to North and West Africa was a double pointed stroke of genius. In Egypt he was able to deliver a strong message designed to improve America's relationship with the Muslim world and in Ghana, he critiqued Africa's leadership, while outlining preconditions for American assistance and partnership were key elements of his strategy. At the same time, he shined the light on a dark chapter on Western and American slave history experience. While this article does not seek to examine the relations of foreign companies in ownership, extraction and price setting for Africa's natural resources and raw materials, suffice to say Europe, America and the West, some have argued, still continue to undermine Africa and other areas' economic structure. Also, let us not forget the role of corruption among African and other leadership that facilitates the resulting process of "under-development." Therefore, as a good faith broker, America needs to help level the playing field in Africa's relationships to create a reliable partnership that will be able to extend

BARACK OBAMA
MASTER OF WASHINGTON DC

dependable cooperation as world events become more complex and America seeks more "true friends."

Barack Obama's Washington, DC Photo 30. Photograph shows the fountain and Reflecting Pool with the Lincoln Memorial in the distance.

FREDERICK MONDERSON

"The best way to not feel hopeless is to get up and do something. Don't wait for good things to happen to you. If you go out and make some good things happen, you will fill the world with hope, you will fill yourself with hope." BARACK OBAMA

5. PRESIDENT OBAMA AND FOREIGN POLICY
By

Dr. Fred Monderson

President Obama inherited a foreign policy nightmare where he had to contend with two wars in Iraq and Afghanistan, a seemingly ubiquitous war on terror, marauding Somali pirates along a major shipping lane, the problem of Middle East Peace fueled by the Palestinian-Israeli conflict, Iran's reckless pursuit of nuclear capability for military advantage that would destabilize a volatile region, North Korea's nuclear brinksmanship, emergence of leftist regimes in Latin America stoked by Venezuelan strongman Hugo Chavez, while drug lords were rampaging through the region creating havoc and mayhem in Mexico, on America's south-western border.

In addition, America's image has been tarnished abroad owing to the arrogance of the Bush Administration even as the leader of the Western Alliance; however, under President Obama the nation has sought to mend fences with key players, court our strongest allies, while delicately balancing Eastern Europe's application for membership in NATO and the European Union and encouraging Russia's economic interest, while also keeping an eye on its military ambitions and constructively employing its position of power as leverage against recalcitrant foes seeking to rattle our nerves. Meanwhile, China, Japan, Korea and Indonesia pose special economic challenges as neighbors India and Pakistan, always a powder keg, are reminded they must channel their energies towards internal tranquility and economic development rather than external conflict that is counter-productive. Africa is a special case, for besides being the ancestral home of a significant portion of this nation's population, land of President Obama's paternal heritage, it is loaded with the greatest concentration of the globe's mineral resources, though its political leadership reeks of corruption and the business and social elite are disconnected from the broad masses of the population. Notwithstanding, and lacking a colonial heritage in Africa and in the past allied with "Africa's traditional

BARACK OBAMA
MASTER OF WASHINGTON DC

enemies," America is now making a significant push to secure its place in the African sun through "tough love" talk, economic cooperation, social/medical assistance and assessing new security considerations. Faced with such a full plate, President Obama chose the ablest foreign policy team comprising Secretary of State Hillary Clinton, Defense Secretary Robert Gates, Treasury Secretary Timothy G. Geithner, Commerce Secretary Gary F. Locke, Homeland Security Secretary Janet A. Napolitano, US Trade Representative Ambassador Ronald Kirk and United States Ambassador to the United Nations Susan Rice, all coordinated by White House Chief of Staff Rahm I. Emanuel destined with a mission to restore America's place of leadership on the world stage.

Barack Obama's Washington, DC Photo 31. People coming and going from and to the front entrance of the Lincoln Memorial.

FREDERICK MONDERSON

Barack Obama's Washington, DC Photo 32. Street view of the Dome of the Capital Building.

In this effort, the extraordinary team has helped win praise for President Obama by changing America's image abroad, helping to stabilize the global economic downturn and allowing him to be the "strongman" against potential foes. Yet, his suave, sincere and determined effort has enabled the nation to begin to be perceived, as former President Bill Clinton remarked, "By the power of our examples rather than the example of our power."

Notwithstanding, in order to understand where we are today, and the road ahead, its enlightening to look back at the history of significant foreign policy milestones, for out of these examples solutions to some of today's problems may be found.

From the beginning of the new nation, foreign policy and foreign relations have been challenging and troubling propositions for American Presidents. In the dynamic climate of 18th Century revolutionary Europe, once America declared independence, Britain's traditional enemy France rushed to recognize the young state, cementing a long-lasting relationship between the two nations. Despite this budding relationship, George Washington warned in his **Farewell Address** in 1789, "America should forego foreign alliances, be friendly to all, but maintain neutrality in its foreign policy dealings." Out of this admonition, for more than a century until **World War I**, America had to contend with and was involved in

BARACK OBAMA
MASTER OF WASHINGTON DC

fending off the British in the **War of 1812**, Andrew Jackson's incursions into Spanish Florida to chastise Seminoles who were aiding runaway slaves, and dynamics of the nation's unfolding **Manifest Destiny** expansion westward at the expense of the native Americans and Mexicans.

Barack Obama's Washington, DC Photo 33. Naval recruits on parade with an audience.

Barack Obama's Washington, DC Photo 34. Statue of Thomas Jefferson seems to be looking out from between the columns of his Memorial.

FREDERICK MONDERSON

Nonetheless, the first significant foreign policy challenge to the United States resulted in the nation having to issue the **Monroe Doctrine** in 1822. This was a show of force without the power to back it up. Apparently, as the Napoleonic Wars ended and a semblance of calm returned to Europe, colonialist nations, particularly Spain, wanted to undermine the newly independent Latin American states and re-establish their "New World" empires. Despite the bloody War of 1812 under President James Madison because the British were seizing or "impressing" American merchantmen at sea; a decade later Britain with its mighty navy backed America's plan in enforcing the **Monroe Doctrine**. Equally, this helped cement these two nations relationship and two centuries later they are the strongest of allies.

Barack Obama's Washington, DC Photo 35. What a beautiful contrast, green grass, fallen brown leaves, green trees and buses fronting a wonderful colonnade with blue sky in the background.

The War with Mexico was long in brewing as **Manifest Destiny** fueled westward expansion resulting in the seizure of Texas, New Mexico, and California and much more from our neighbors to the south and west. We cannot overlook the treatment of the Native Americans! Yet, besides these conflicts, however, the Monroe Doctrine reinforced the isolationism of America for the remainder of the 19th Century, only pushed by "Jingoism" and "Yellow Journalism" into war with Spain in 1898. However, during the Civil War (1860-1865), President Abraham

BARACK OBAMA
MASTER OF WASHINGTON DC

Lincoln was worried Britain and France would break the North's blockade of Southern ports for the badly needed cotton consumed by the ever expanding textile industries of those two nations.

Barack Obama's Washington, DC Photo 36. View of the Jefferson Memorial from across the bay.

Into the new 20th century, Teddy Roosevelt, whose Black soldiers among the Rough Riders "saved his bacon" in the "Charge up San Juan Hill," turned out to be the greatest imperialist President of the United States. He fermented the breakaway of Panama from Columbia, built the Canal under the Hay-Pauncefote Treaty and strengthened the **Monroe Doctrine** by issuing the **Corollary to the Monroe Doctrine** in 1903. This "walk softly and carry a big stick" strongman practiced "gunboat diplomacy" and was determined to secure Latin America as an exclusive preserve of the United States for economic investment and military security.

World War I was not much of a foreign policy question. The world was threatened, America was threatened, and so America fought the war. The Peace Treaty was another matter and President **Woodrow Wilson's 14-Points** for peace dominated the talks and some of its provisions came to significantly influence post-war developments.

FREDERICK MONDERSON

The cause of World War I, viz., colonialism and imperialism, industrialization and military build-up, notwithstanding, foreign policy up to this time was simply a set of cordial relations among nations. These can be described as a sort of "open-the-door-for-the-other-guy-get-along" relationship. That is, except when one nation sought to impose its will on another through the use of force. This happened in 1931, and it changed forever, the way nations related to each other, set precedents and reinforced the significance of "doctrines" as a tool of foreign policy.

Barack Obama's Washington, DC Photo 37. Serenity underlies the Supreme Court with its powerful function as one branch of the American political system.

A "doctrine" seems to imply the use of force to uphold a foreign policy position in response to a single or set of developments involving relations among nations. Equally, in the doctrine's evolution, it became increasingly clear that doctrines are not exclusively a President's preserve but they can be issued by others with the same force of enforcement. That is to say yet, in the following example, while the individual may have his name attached to the doctrine, he is actually acting on behalf of the President acting on behalf of the American nation.

BARACK OBAMA
MASTER OF WASHINGTON DC

Barack Obama's Washington, DC Photo 37a. Close up of a youngster saluting before the doors and column bases of the Supreme Court.

FREDERICK MONDERSON

Barack Obama's Washington, DC Photo 38. Part of the Viet Nam Veteran's Memorial showing three men, two whites and one black, patrolling the rice paddies of Viet Nam. Many consider the veterans of this conflict the most neglected of all such soldiers who have fought America's wars though some effort is now being made to address this neglect.

BARACK OBAMA
MASTER OF WASHINGTON DC

Barack Obama's Washington DC Photo 38a. Plaque of the Viet Nam Veterans Memorial showing the true symbols of the Wall, the men in the field and the flag.

In 1931, Japan invaded China and the US sent Secretary of State Stimson to Japan to deliver what became the "Stimson Doctrine." The "Stimson Doctrine" said essentially, "The United States will not recognize any nation that seizes land by force." This "Stimson Doctrine" did more for maintaining the physical territorial integrity of the State in the 20th Century than any other single document or policy. For example, colonialism created some 50 states in Africa, today 54, many through single-villages. Yet, after independence no nation has credibly challenged its own border. That is, with the exception of Sudan which split into north and south primarily due a civil war brought about for religious and economic reasons. Dating to treaty agreements in 1896, Venezuela has, since the 1960s, challenged the limits of Guyana's border. Yet, this has not gone forward. Vietnam's unification is a different matter. Even significant, when the Iraqi strongman Sadaam Hussein invaded Kuwait in 1991, as a friend, the United States was called on to repel the invader. President George Bush (No. 41) invoked the "Stimson Doctrine," assembled a coalition of nations and defeated the invader. While in the 1930s the "young Stimson Doctrine" did not halt Hitler's invasions, it probably motivated America to aid Britain in the "Lend Lease" program. Nevertheless, ever since, the "Stimson Doctrine" "has kept the peace" and proved to be one of the most profound American foreign policy positions.

FREDERICK MONDERSON

Barack Obama's Washington, DC Photo 39. Paying tribute at "The wall" of the Viet Nam Memorial.

BARACK OBAMA
MASTER OF WASHINGTON DC

Barack Obama's Washington, DC Photo 40. Another view of the Supreme Court from across the street. Notice the flag at half-mast and intricacies on the cornice.

As a result, doctrines have been important in characterizing the foreign policy positions of Presidents Truman, Eisenhower, Kennedy, Carter, Clinton, and Bush, which brings us to President Barack Obama in the 21st Century world.

With an excellent foreign policy team in place, President Obama has confronted the far-reaching challenges facing America and seems to be winning or at best keeping his challengers at bay. He has changed perceptions of America abroad; his outreach to the Muslim world has helped disarm militant preponderance; despite common belief, al Qaeda and the Taliban are on the run and their leaders are basking in the safety of their caves, fearful of drone attacks. Two members of President George Bush's "Axis of Evil" Iran and North Korea, with their economies seriously challenged and facing more serious economic sanctions for pursuing nuclear military potential, in view of Obama's foreign policy firmness, now seem to be seeking exit strategies so as to be reintegrated into the world community of nations. Nonetheless, in a kind of "double speak" Iran has offered to talk while testing several missiles lately and finally admitting to the existence of an undisclosed nuclear processing site, though Western intelligence has known about it for years. Drawing a line in the sand at the recent Pennsylvania G-20 Economic Summit, along with western nations courting Security Council members Russia and China, President Obama has "tightened the screws" on Iran calling for more tougher sanctions.

FREDERICK MONDERSON

Barack Obama's Washington, DC Photo 41. Statue and colonnade fronting the Treasury of the United States.

As leader of the "Western Alliance," President Obama has moved away from former President Bush's plan to install a missile defense shield in Eastern Europe. Perhaps this costly measure is technologically outdated and as such the strategy is to downplay the challenge to Russia while deploying more subtle yet effective measures to check Russian expansionist ideas. Meanwhile, Afghanistan has remained a "stone in the President's shoes." There are calls for more troops to counter the increasing Taliban insurgency and equally Americans want to get out of that mess. The President has insisted Afghanistan is crucial to combating the war on terror because any Taliban re-emergence will surely accommodate Al Qaeda and American troops will probably have to return. Afghanistan has indeed proved to be a foreign policy challenge for President Obama.

President Barack Obama is the first sitting president to preside as President of the United Nations Security Council and he used this platform to explain much of his foreign policy concerns, particularly on the Palestinian-Israeli conflict; United States role in the World; Iran Nuclear Program as well as Global Warming and its Environmental Impact. Calling for a "new era of engagement" with a new spirit of cooperation among member nations, in his address, regarding the Palestinian-Israeli conflict, he stated: "We continue to call on Palestinians to end incitement against Israel. And we continue to emphasize that America does not accept the legitimacy of continued Israeli settlements …. The United States does Israel no favors when we fail to couple an unwavering commitment to its security with an insistence that Israel respect the legitimate claims and rights of the Palestinians.

BARACK OBAMA
MASTER OF WASHINGTON DC

And nations within this body do the Palestinians no favors when they choose vitriolic attacks against Israel over constructive willingness to recognize Israel's legitimacy and its right to exist in peace and security."

On the United States' role in the world, he was firm in insisting: "Those who used to chastise America for acting alone in the world cannot now stand by and wait for America to solve the world's problems alone. Now is the time for all of us to take our share of responsibility for a global response to global challenges." These challenges he pointed out are extremists sowing terror, rogue nations seeking nuclear capability for military purposes, genocide, melting ice caps, persistent poverty and pandemic diseases.

As in his campaign position to talk to adversaries, on the Iran Nuclear program issue, President Obama told the United Nations, "This should be resolved diplomatically and I am on record as being committed to negotiate with Iran in a serious fashion to resolve this issue. However, if Iran does not respond during negotiations, serious additional sanctions remain a possibility."

On the issue of Global Warming he reiterated the significance of this threat, insisting: "Now is the time for all of us to take our share of responsibility for a global response to global challenges. If we continue down our current course, every member of this assembly will see irreversible changes within their borders."
On the economic front, strong economic and fiscal policies have not simply pulled America back from the brink, but also played a pivotal role in helping stem a global economic downturn. President Obama's trip to West Africa and Secretary of State Clinton's 11-nation tour of Africa was a 1-2 strategy to engage Africa in a new approach to benefit both America and Africa. However, while these efforts seem to be bearing fruit, the President has, despite tremendous effort, still not been able to break the stalemate in the Palestinian-Israeli conflict. Yet, the struggle continues to find a solution to this longstanding dilemma that is costing lives and property damage and sowing ill-will.

These then are some of the foreign policy challenges President Obama and his foreign policy team are struggling with in this new era of heightened challenges and immediate expectations. However, despite what may be said about foreign policy experience or inexperience, particularly in the Presidential Primary and National Campaign "young Obama" never took a back seat to involvement in issues beyond the nation's border. The following are some of the Foreign Policy initiatives as supplied by "Outside the Beltway" site where Alex Knap stated: "I think that it's perfectly fair to criticize Barack Obama's experience. I do not think it is fair, however, to outright lie about his experience. Obama has been quite active in the Senate and despite his short career there has actually accomplished quite a bit. Here's a sample of some rather significant pieces of legislation that Barack Obama had a major hand in. I don't necessarily agree with all of the policies below, but these were pretty significant and Obama played a major role."

Then he goes on to list "**The Lugar-Non-Proliferation Act**; **The Coburn-Obama Transparency Act**; **Relief of the Democratic Republic of Congo**" but Obama has also worked with others to remain involved in his short Senate career. "Outside the Beltway" site provides the following regarding Barack Obama's involvement in government.

- FactCheck: Campaign prevented committee meetings, not rules. (Sep 2008)
- Global Poverty Act: spend 0.7% of GDP on foreign aid. (Aug 2008)
- In Cold War, we won hearts & minds; now do same to world. (Jul 2008)
- Dangers of intertwined world can't be contained in borders. (Jul 2008)
- OpEd: Policy views based on experience in Kenya & Indonesia. (Jul 2008)
- Important to undo the damage of the last seven years. (Feb 2008)
- Never negotiate out of fear, and never fear to negotiate. (Jan 2008)
- President must abide by international human rights treaties. (Dec 2007)
- Obama Doctrine: ideology has overridden facts and reality. (Dec 2007)
- No Obama Doctrine; just democracy, security, liberty. (Oct 2007)
- $50B annually to strengthen weak states at risk of collapse. (Aug 2007)
- No "strategic ambiguity" on foreign policy issues. (Aug 2007)
- My critics engineered our biggest foreign policy disaster. (Aug 2007)
- Meet with enemy leaders; it's a disgrace that we have not. (Jul 2007)
- We cannot afford isolationism. (Mar 2007)
- Never has US had so much power & so little influence to lead. (Jul 2004)
- US policy should promote democracy and human rights. (Jul 2004)

Africa

BARACK OBAMA
MASTER OF WASHINGTON DC

- Dressed in Africa in traditional garb, not "Muslim attire." (Aug 2008)
- Majored in international affairs based on living abroad. (Jul 2008)
- Moral obligation to intervene in Darfur to avoid spillover. (Jul 2008)
- Wrote 2006 law stabilizing Congo with $52M. (Oct 2007)
- Increased aid to Republic of Congo. (Aug 2007)
- Visited largest slum in Africa, to publicize its plight. (Aug 2007)
- No-fly zone in Darfur; but pay attention more in Africa. (Jun 2007)
- U.S. funds for humanitarian aid to Darfur. (Mar 2007)
- Protested South African apartheid while at college. (Feb 2007)
- Focus on corruption to improve African development. (Oct 2006)
- Visited Africa in 2006; encouraged HIV testing & research. (Oct 2006)

Americas

- Meet with Cuban leaders only with agenda of US interests. (Feb 2008)
- Cuba: Loosen restrictions now; normalization later. (Feb 2008)
- Willing to meet with Fidel Castro, Kim Jung Il & Hugo Chavez. (Nov 2007)
- Invest in our relationship with Mexico. (Sep 2007)

Asia

- We must be tough with Pakistan & stop coddling Musharraf. (Sep 2008)
- Must be tough on Iran, but talk to them too. (Sep 2008)
- Learned privilege of being American by living in Indonesia. (Jul 2008)
- China is a competitor but not an enemy. (Dec 2007)
- U.S. needs to ameliorate trade relations with China. (Mar 2007)

Europe

FREDERICK MONDERSON

- We've been reactive for 8 years; be proactive with Russia. (Oct 2008)
- Recent Russian actions in Georgia are unacceptable. (Sep 2008)
- In Berlin: proud citizen of US; fellow citizen of the world. (Jul 2008)
- Cooperation among nations is not a choice; it's the only way. (Jul 2008)
- Chairs European subcommittee; could hold Afghanistan hearing. (Jul 2008)
- Engage Russia regarding nuclear proliferation. (Jul 2008)
- Strengthen NATO to face 21st-century threats. (Aug 2007)

Mideast

- Kissinger agrees with me on meeting with enemy leaders. (Sep 2008)
- FactCheck: Kissinger opposes presidential meetings with Iran. (Sep 2008)
- My record on Israel is same as McCain's. (Jul 2008)
- Appropriate for Israel to take out Syrian nuclear reactor. (Jul 2008)
- Jerusalem should be capital of Israel, pending final status. (Jul 2008)
- Jerusalem as joint Palestinian-Israeli capital is ok. (Jul 2008)
- Palestinian people suffer-but from not recognizing Israel. (Apr 2007)
- FactCheck: Palestinian suffering from stalled peace effort. (Apr 2007)
- Supports Israel's self-defense; but distrusted by Israelis. (Oct 2006)

Resolutions

- At college, protested for divestment from South Africa. (Aug 2007)
- Voted YES on cooperating with India as a nuclear power. (Oct 2008)
- Sponsored aid bill to avert humanitarian crisis in Congo. (Dec 2005)
- Implement Darfur Peace Agreement with UN peacekeeping force. (Feb 2008)

BARACK OBAMA
MASTER OF WASHINGTON DC

- Urge Venezuela to re-open dissident radio & TV stations. (May 2007)
- Let Ukraine & Georgia enter NATO. (Jan 2008)
- Condemn violence by Chinese government in Tibet. (Apr 2008)
- Sanction Mugabe until Zimbabwe transitions to democracy. (Apr 2008)
- To this can be added Afghan law tolerating marital rape is abhorrent. (Apr 2009)

Thus, whatever is said about Obama, to not have been involved in the anti-Apartheid struggle like so many young people in America and worldwide could have been a legitimate issue his critics could have used, but to no avail!

Barack Obama's Washington, DC Photo 41a. The beauty of Ionic (female) capitals on a raised colonnade on the side of a building.

FREDERICK MONDERSON

"We lose ourselves when we compromise the very ideals that we fight to defend. And we honor those ideals by upholding them not when it's easy, but when it is hard." BARACK OBAMA

6. REP. PETER KING: DENOUNCE THE NY POST! By

Dr. Fred Monderson

OBAMA LOVES HIS WIFE!

Representative Peter King:

At first I was terribly incensed, and feel his family too was shocked, over your insensitive comment that "there was nothing good about this guy," at this particular time of mourning the passing of Michael Jackson; but then I realized you had a role to play. After all, God created the devil to find work for idle hands and Judas had a role to play in the betrayal of Jesus, otherwise he could not have accomplished his mission. So, therefore it seems a King representing Queens had to make such scurrilous remarks about the "King of Popular culture" music at a time, across the globe, when nearly one billion people were in the joys of celebrating the passing of a man who touched their lives for decades or generations. You probably heard the story of the party pooper; if not, let me tell you about him. Apparently, some people were in a wonderfully happy party mood, getting down and having the most enjoyable time, really "letting their hair down." Then this fellow wanted to relieve himself, I think his name was Party Pooper. He let loose a terrific foul wind and just spoilt the good mood everyone was in and so the name stuck. While I hate to say this, your comments are somewhat akin to that fellow but the interesting thing was, this time the foul wind came from a representative of the national government, the House of Representative, and this was totally unexpected by not only Americans but sensitive people all over the world.

BARACK OBAMA
MASTER OF WASHINGTON DC

Barack Obama's Washington, DC Photo 42. The Civil War Memorial.

OBAMA LOVES HIS WIFE!

You certainly would not have made those insensitive comments about Michael Jackson to the *New York Amsterdam News* but you gave it to the *New York Post*, a newspaper whose objectivity is questionable from its actions over an extended period of time, demonstrating ramifications that antagonized many people. After all, the *Post's* insensitivity was again manifested a few months ago when they published the controversial "Ape Cartoon" with the police shooting alluding to President Obama. You may have heard of the commotion this created and when the people mobilized, I think, and pressed for closure, of what some called a "racist rag," yet others saw it as a glorious "birdcage dropping mat," full of it! Some protesters believe Rev. Al Sharpton made a mistake when people mobilized behind him, and that he should have pressed for closure of the *New York Post* newspaper that time!

Recently, evidence surfaced in London and elsewhere that the management and representatives of the newspaper empire to which *New York Post* belongs, are under investigation for inappropriately and criminally accessing personal information about celebrities for whatever reason. This you should probably have known before you gave your interview. Nevertheless, you went ahead with your

FREDERICK MONDERSON

attack on Mr. Jackson with those inappropriate comments given to that newspaper, the *Post*. Now, there's a line from an old song that reads, "Fools rush in where wise men fail to go," but I believe as a national government representative, you should at least be wise and circumspect in your comments, particularly to news agents such as the *New York Post*. Or, is there an ulterior motive in your behavior? Is it race or are you posturing for votes? Either way this was an inappropriate way to project either position.

When elections of late have been so close, for example, Franken and Coleman, if there are any of your constituencies who were celebrating, showing empathy and condolences towards Michael Jackson, then you may have alienated them, considering you may have an opponent who will certainly bring back your words in a haunting manner. Should I remind or inform you, the Democratic Party has you on its radar as a Republican whom they wish to target and to relieve you of your electoral position.

Anyway, much has been said about Michael Jackson and without a doubt there has been much speculation and innuendos but not many people have risen to Mr. Jackson's defense. For sure, Michael Jackson has been a figure subject to much press publicity but the *New York Post* seems to have a vendetta against him. If you recall, they seldom had anything positively constructive to say about Barack Obama during the Presidential campaign.

Let me give you an example of the *New York Post's* coverage of Mr. Jackson. I contrast this with a major coverage of the *New York Times*. In the *New York Times* article, "Jackson's Estate: Piles of Assets, Loads of Debt" by Tim Arango and Ben Sisario, June 27, 2009, Front page and p. 11. In addressing Michael Jackson, this article names the following number of times: Michael Jackson 1, Michael 4, Mr. Jackson 30, and Mr. Jackson's 19. Contrast this with an article by K. Li in the *Post* entitled "Mom wins grandkids as war for 'million$' looms" by Lachlan Cartwright in LA and David K. Li and Kate Sheehy in NY on Tuesday, June 30, 2009, p. 12, in which a comparatively shorter article lists "Jacko" eight times and Michael Jackson's once. Seems like the *New York Post* relishes in calling Michael Jackson "Jacko" and Mr. Li is a principal!

BARACK OBAMA
MASTER OF WASHINGTON DC

Barack Obama's Washington, DC Photo 43. The wonder of government architecture of the nation's capital with its magnificent colonnades.

FREDERICK MONDERSON

Barack Obama's Washington, DC Photo 44. The almost magical nature of the Capital Building as represented in this particular photo.

At the Apollo Theater Memorial to Michael Jackson on Tuesday, June 30, 2009, at 5: 26 pm, Rev Al Sharpton called for a moment of silence and told the audience: "He isn't Jacko, as some have called him in their attempts to denigrate him. We

BARACK OBAMA
MASTER OF WASHINGTON DC

are here to salute a legacy, to praise an icon. He's ours and we don't care what other people say. Without him there would be no Oprah, no Tiger, no Obama." This is where we stand! Let me remind you there was no violence in Michael's songs, it was about love, healing, about changing the world for the better. Also, he held the Guinness Book's Record for giving charity the most money of any artiste or entertainer. He gave to some 38 charities $300-500 million dollars and even left endowments for charities in his will. To show his love and potential healing powers, he entered a Jaccoussi with an AIDS victim to comfort him as an act of friendship. Such an act would certainly heal his mindset into acceptance of his condition. Perhaps it was Michael Jackson's business acumen that annoyed so many, yourself included, particularly his purchase of the Beatles Catalog and even his marriage to Elvis Presley's daughter, Lisa. Therefore, for you to say "there is nothing good about this guy" perhaps your glasses need to be cleaned or that you are grinding your axe.

FREDERICK MONDERSON

Barack Obama's Washington, DC Photo 45. The author and son share a wonderful moment on the steps of the Capital Building.

As you probably know, Michael Jackson was involved in much publicity regarding child molestation, accused once which was settled out of court and charged, tried and then found not guilty on a second set of charges. These experiences were certainly painful and costly to Mr. Jackson. However, Larry King on CNN interviewed Mr. Mesereau, the attorney who represented Michael Jackson in the

BARACK OBAMA
MASTER OF WASHINGTON DC

trial. Mr. Mesereau pointed out Michael was found not guilty on 14 charges, and that "he was not a child abuser." When a black man is found not guilty critics disagree with the verdict, viz., O.J. Simpson, Michael Jackson, etc. However, when a white is found not guilty, general agreement is that the system works!

A new book purportedly about personal issues of Michael's life and among some other things claimed, "Michael was not a child abuser!" Latoya Jackson on Piers Morgan, claiming her brother was murdered, indicated the autopsy revealed there was no drugs in Michael's system the night he died except the drugs administered to him then! If we look at some of the major accusations in history, many of those accused were truly innocent. Yet, papers like the *Post* constantly act as if with malice and continue to seem to make news by their insensitive behavior. In the first instance of a settlement over child abuse, it's now coming out that as Mr. Jackson's popularity was rising and the charge of child molestation was brought, it was the insurance company that pressured him to offer "go away money" to the accuser.

OBAMA LOVES HIS WIFE!

Again, President Obama was recently abroad, attending a summit in Russia and again in Italy for the G-8 Economic Conference, which as a Congressman you are probably aware. The *New York Post* published a front page picture of President Obama turning to look at the rear of a young Brazilian female. It turns out the paper to which you made your now famous comments about Michael Jackson had, as we now know, intentionally published a picture that has been turned out to be false! It seems this is in keeping with the public's belief this paper would do anything to gain attention. We know there is an old saying, "Birds of a feather flock together," and old folks often said, "Show me your friends and I will tell who you are." Thus, this interview puts you in poor company, Mr. King! Have you thought how Katherine Jackson or the Jackson family would feel about your remarks, being a national figure and all? Have you expressed thoughts on anyone "Hiking the Appalachian Trail" or "extending their hands under public bathroom partitions?"

Essentially, Representative Peter King, I call on you to "Denounce the *New York Post*" for its continued misrepresentation and attempts to demean African Americans and showing no sensitivity in its coverage. For certain, even if your views about Michael Jackson are written in stone, which is rather archaic in an age of news technology, for sure you can call up the *Post* on misrepresenting the President. After all, if someone in the far reaches of this nation saw the *Post* front page picture about the President looking at the young woman's behind and not know of the clarification other news media carried, then for sure they would think less of the President. How then can you sit in the House of Representative knowing your favorite newspaper, the *Post*, did this and not say anything. So, Rep. King, "Denounce the *New York Post*!" Let us not forget, Edmund Burke said, "The only thing necessary for evil to triumph is for good men to say nothing!" Are you a good man Representative Peter King?

OBAMA LOVES HIS WIFE.

Barack Obama's Washington, DC Photo 46. Always something going on, trailers placed in front of the government's business.

BARACK OBAMA
MASTER OF WASHINGTON DC

"If we think that we can secure our country by just talking tough without acting tough and smart, then we will misunderstand this moment and miss its opportunities. If we think that we can use the same partisan playbook where we just challenge our opponent's patriotism to win an election, then the American people will lose. The times are too serious for this kind of politics." BARACK OBAMA

7. TESTING BARACK
BY

Dr. Fred Monderson

Senator, now Vice-President Elect, Joseph Biden caused a stir when he remarked, during the presidential face-off between Senators John McCain and Barack Obama, "the world will soon test Senator Obama within six months of becoming President," on issues that would challenge his leadership ability. This assessment from an experienced lawmaker and expert in foreign relations easily became an important talking point among the media and Senator Obama's competitors, Senator McCain and Governor Sarah Palin.

Another of the wise Biden's pronouncements, during the early stages of the Democratic Presidential Primary, is whether Senator Barack Obama "is fit to lead." This too was seized upon by the other contestants and became a virtual plank of Senator Hillary Clinton; and ultimately picked up by McCain and Palin in the Presidential race, questioning his ability. Nonetheless, and victorious in the Democratic Primary, Obama chose Biden as his running mate. The hawks soon swooped down on Biden's remarks about Obama not being "fit to lead;" then they queried why Biden would now follow Obama.

From his veritable reservoir of foreign policy and international relations experience, Biden confessed Senator Obama had grown tremendously during the rigorous challenges of the Primary. He went "to school on the issues," and consulted with some of the "great minds" of American military, foreign policy and economic issues. These two pronouncements notwithstanding, Senator Obama's personal and intellectual growth and his enhanced social demeanor and leadership deportment found favor with the American electorate who swept him into power as the President-Elect of these United States. Barack's ethnicity aside, being the first African-American to head a major political party, the combination of his demonstrated attributes and mannerisms, caused the voters young and old, to feel confident, as President he could effectively lead and help solve some of the nation's pressing problems during these challenging times.

On eve of Senator Obama accepting the Democratic Nomination, a local New York newspaper carried a front-page article entitled "Oh My God, Dems Erect a Greek Temple for Obama." On the inside, an image depicted him in toga and laurel. Interesting and while not explored in that article, the colonnade of columns, a significant feature of the Greek temple, had its origin in Egypt, along the Nile River in Northeast Africa. Whereas, the Greeks in Egypt and Graeco-Roman intentions of the founding fathers of America in crafting the foundations of the young American nation, an analogy can be made on leadership style and success in ancient times and now. Without question several books show evidence of ancient Egypt in the architecture, science and thought processes of the foundation and practices of the American republic.

Barack Obama's Washington, DC Photo 47. The massive nature of the constructive technique employed in such buildings is indicative of the permanence of these structures as well as the permanence of the government that they service.

For the first we turn to Margaret Murray's *The Splendor that was Egypt* in her assessment of the Pharaoh Amasis handling of Egyptian-Graeco relations. In this she writes: "Amasis owed his throne to the Egyptians' hatred of foreigners; at the same time he was keenly aware of the importance of foreign trade and the necessity of keeping on good terms with his nearest neighbors, the Greeks. He

BARACK OBAMA
MASTER OF WASHINGTON DC

solved this difficult problem by giving the city of Naucratis to the Greeks as their own possession, with special trading facilities, so that Naucratis had a monopoly of all goods coming by sea from Mediterranean lands. This gratified the Greeks; at the same time he destroyed the other Greek settlements in Egypt and so gratified his own people by confining the foreigners to the one port. This is one of the few examples in history when two diametrically opposing parties have been completely satisfied with the same arrangement; Amasis must therefore be ranked as one of the greatest diplomatists in the history of the world."

For the second, President-Elect Barack Obama, as heir to the Graeco-Roman mantle of American political leadership, on eve of assuming this position, has enjoyed an enormously high presidential rating by his constituency. Though the nation is in the throes of an economic and foreign policy quagmire, its confidence in Barack Obama's ability to handle the pressing challenges gives him the wherewithal to forge his "bridge over the troubled waters." Here again, another analogy is certainly appropriate.

The problem we faced with the catastrophe of 9/11 is that all of America's defenses were pointed towards an external threat and hence the enemy appeared within. Equally, President Elect Obama never expected to be "tested" from within his own party, in his home city and state, for the seat he once held, by a scandal ridden Governor Blagojevich administration. On the other hand, the Mumbai and Middle East "Tests," while credible are not on Obama's "watch." Nevertheless, the superb leadership acumen he demonstrated in his choice of the dream cabinet members, coupled with his suavity, ability and intellectual finesse, has enabled his parallel or "shadow government" to stay abreast of, study, learn from and craft a method of solving some of these problems. All this while insisting "there's only one President at a time" which has given him time to learn how to assess and handle such issues. More importantly, his rapid grasp of the issues, ability to conceptualize readily and well, his cool demeanor and like a magic wand, is indicative of his approach to pressing domestic issues such as retooling the nation's technological expertise to be globally competitive.

The economy in recession needs significant infusion in an economic recovery stimulus to confront joblessness and the housing problems of foreclosures, enable housing starts with requisite need for purchases of appliances, carpets, furniture and other big money items, perhaps reinforced through bank loans. While some remark any stimulus package will impact the next generation, right thinking dictates if we don't act now, we won't get to the next generation! Equally, infrastructure repairs to roads, bridges, tunnels, ports, railways will provide important jobs to help jump start the domestic economy. Putting people back to work will provide some relief to states bearing the brunt of budget shortfalls due to lack of jobs, increased spending particularly for health care and dwindling unemployment benefits as well as uncertainty of retirement options.

FREDERICK MONDERSON

Barack Obama's Washington, DC Photo 48. Another building, this time with Ionic capitals. Notice these capitals seem as a female hairdo while the Doric ones, on the other hand, are plain and more masculine.

Barack Obama's Washington, DC Photo 49. Here's a more frontal view of the previous building with its columns sporting Ionic capitals.

The campaign pledges of tax cuts for the middle class; the need for a comprehensive tax review; universal health care or close to it; overhaul of the Security Exchange Commission with greater regulations on all forms of financial transactions and stiffer penalties for securities fraud; as well as a better grasp of

BARACK OBAMA
MASTER OF WASHINGTON DC

inherent Social Security ramifications are all challenges facing soon-to-be President Barack Obama. There is great expectation for immigration reform with a pathway to legalization, not at the head of the line, but within a regulated process involving paying a fine, proof of paying taxes, and evidence of good citizenship. To this we could add comprehensive border security to provide protection against unlawful intrusion of people and drugs. Energy independence through the development of wide diversity of energy resources, viz., wind, solar, clean coal, nuclear, natural gas, oil, etc., will create more jobs of a lasting duration, with ultimate impact on domestic spending and trade imbalance.

Barack Obama's Washington, DC Photo 50. Magnificent building with its semi-circle colonnade at a raised level.

A special approach to the nation's schools in the form of new and upgraded buildings, state of the art technology and science facilities, improvements in teaching techniques of math and sciences, and better pay for teachers; will all go a long way to make American education more competitive, when the new president accedes to *de facto* and *de jure* power on January $20^{th,}$ 2009.

FREDERICK MONDERSON

Barack Obama's Washington, DC Photo 51. The nature of the domestic architecture is equally eye-catching as its government counterpart.

An extraordinary leadership skill, undergirding his visionary outlook and concern for American domestic and foreign image, will craft the changes necessary to rescue this great nation from the perdition it did not deserve; perhaps the last and greatest hope for humanity amidst the challenges and circumstances of the times. Therefore, creating and enforcing policies of change at the head of his dream team administration, with "all his dogs barking," President Obama will have an opportunity to become as astute and exceptional a leader as Pharaoh Amasis. It's a pity "grandmother" did not live to see the beauty and magnificence of her handiwork come to fruition. Significantly, one profound characteristic of African cosmological belief is that the glorious dead remains within memory to guide and protect the ones they nurtured and loved. Perhaps "Grandmother Toots" is still protecting her handiwork in soon to be President Barack Hussein Obama, perhaps the best hope for a new day in America.

BARACK OBAMA
MASTER OF WASHINGTON DC

"Our predecessors understood that government could not, and should not, solve every problem. They understood that there are instances when the gains in security from government action are not worth the added constraints on our freedom. But they also understood that the danger of too much government is matched by the perils of too little; that without the leavening hand of wise policy, markets can crash, monopolies can stifle competition, the vulnerable can be exploited. And they knew that when any government measure, no matter how carefully crafted or beneficial, is subject to scorn; when any efforts to help people in need are attacked as un-American; when facts and reason are thrown overboard and only timidity passes for wisdom, and we can no longer even engage in a civil conversation with each other over the things that truly matter -- that at that point we don't merely lose our capacity to solve big challenges. We lose something essential about ourselves." BARACK OBAMA Speech to Congress September 9, 2009

8. DEFENDING OBAMA
By

Dr. Fred Monderson

Recently in Harlem, New York City, a well respected African-American media watchdog group held a well-attended forum on President-Elect, now President Barack Obama of the United States of America. As already known, Obama's election was a heralded and well-observed historic event, watched across the globe. Importantly, however, and because of the liberal nature of this group, presenters at the forum were wide-ranging in their commentaries. Young and old, experienced and novice presented far-reaching pro and con commentary on the newly elected and soon to be President Barack Obama. So much so, the principal Master of Ceremonies, in tandem with the audience often burst into chants, "Respect our heroes," whether it was the presenters themselves or the subject of their presentation.

Many in the audience sat there cheering and others were surprised at what they were hearing pro and con on Obama. Much confusion was in the air and this has to do with folks' assessment of their "leaders' pronouncements" whether these are "researchers" or "Soldiers in the struggle."

FREDERICK MONDERSON

The interesting thing is that all through the primary and presidential campaigns, Barack Obama was accused, as all are well aware, of "not being black enough," "being too black," being "Muslim," being "inexperienced in economics, government and foreign policy," "palling around with terrorists," "against the surge," "a socialist," "not a citizen," "not wearing the flag on his lapel," and who knows what, including threats of physical harm. So, any new criticism, no matter what, pales in significance because it now cannot threaten his election. That done, and so much more before Barack Obama ascended to the presidency after his oath of office.

Our people need to develop and fine-tune analytic skills that allow critical evaluation of "leaders" because "no matter how good intentioned" they can "get it wrong." In response, however, a more positive assessment of personalities and events providing a constructive view trumps the destructive mentality and mindset that threatens the significance of the moment. One of the criticisms of Barack Obama is that he refuses to use the name of Dr. Martin Luther King, in his speeches, referring to him as a "preacher from Georgia." This is not true as evidenced from his pronouncements on Dr. King's birthday, January 19, 2009.

Barack Obama's Washington, DC Photo 52. A regular view of people, vehicles and architecture with the prominence of colonnades everywhere, reminiscent of founding fathers' desire to create "an ancient Rome" in America.

BARACK OBAMA
MASTER OF WASHINGTON DC

Barack Obama's Washington, DC Photo 53. Clearly the designs of buildings are wide, unique but never tall.

Sure Barack Obama is a product of the Civil Rights Movement, and if for strategy reasons he did not, on the campaign trail, trumpet Dr. King's name, he certainly identified with and alluded to his life's work. After all, Dr. King was a giant tree in the forest of the Civil Rights Movement, but there were also other trees. If we accept the argument, he did not trumpet Dr. King's name, then he certainly did not also mention Dr. King's precursors and contemporaries, Rev. Shutllesworth, A. Philip Randolph, Stanley Levinson, Cleveland Robinson, John Lewis, and Wyatt Tee. Walker, Whitney Young, Fannie Lou Hamer, James Farmer, Hosea Williams, Baird Rustin, Andrew Young, Harry Belafonte, Walter Fauntroy, Clarence Jones, Rev. Joseph Lowery, etc. Let's not forget, Rev. Lowery was front and center and made his famous pronouncement!

To validly accept criticisms of Barack Obama, we need to examine the commentary of stalwarts of the Civil Rights Movement, people of prominence and just plain folks who were pleased, excited, and ecstatic about Obama's campaign and election success. Jesse Jackson said Barack Obama was "the best the Civil Rights Movement has to offer." John Lewis was dumfounded, having lived through it all and never thought this day would come. Oprah Winfrey thought the earth "moved." Martin Luther King III is certainly impressed with Barack Obama.

FREDERICK MONDERSON

Colin Powell gave him his blessings and said, call me anytime! We certainly have to agree with these visionaries.

Some were upset because Barack Obama indicated his heroes were Abraham Lincoln and Franklin D. Roosevelt. Well, Lincoln was from Illinois, Obama's home state; he was a great president and issued the Emancipation Proclamation, instrumental in ending slavery and ushering in the 13th, 14th, and 15th Amendments. He has a significant memorial in Washington, D.C., and this is where Dr. King gave his famous "I have a dream" speech. The use of the Lincoln Bible in his oath, a ritual of the position, is to inspire the man and the people at this convergence of crisis and opportunity, as the nation forges ahead. This is why Diane Feinstein proclaimed that Martin Luther King's "Dream echoed from the Lincoln Memorial finally reached the White House."

F.D.R. faced the tumultuous catastrophe of the depression and with his "New Deal Programs" helped transform the economy and moved America forward and this effort was aided by World War II. These were certainly men in government and tremendous moral suasion, of which to emulate. The problem with the critics is that these two heroes of Obama were white and not black! White men certainly can be emulated, as well as black men. It's not particularly the man you're emulating but essentially what he stands for. Are we to believe there are no blacks who are heroes to white people! Those civil rights persons quoted above for sure must have inspired all peoples. Whites voted for Shirley Chisholm, Jesse Jackson, Al Sharpton, Major Owens, Jitu Weusi, etc. What about the cooks and cleaners on the White House staff who have waited forever to serve a Black President. How about the untold numbers of enslaved blacks who built the White House, while their masters were compensated? These all are finally relieved! From the chief cook and bottle washer to the captain in the White House today are black! Now there are even black cops in the White House. Nelson Mandela is black and a hero worldwide. John Brown gave his life to end slavery!

BARACK OBAMA
MASTER OF WASHINGTON DC

Barack Obama's Washington, DC Photo 54. Close-up of the previous photo showing the magnificence of the Doric capital in this elevated colonnade.

One of the rights and responsibilities of a citizen, as many are aware; many were beaten and bruised to attain this cherished ideal; is the right to vote. Follow me on this. In the general election, there were two candidates, one black and one white. If anyone voted it had to be for the black guy or the white guy. Therefore, if you did not vote for the black guy, either you did not vote or you voted for the white guy. If any of the latter two, how valid is your criticism of the black guy.

Did you see the millions of people, young and old, black and white, who came to Washington to seen and support the vision of Barack Obama, and those were all waving the red, white and blue! These people were attracted to Obama because of his cool demeanor, his organizational ability, his studious approach to an issue, his consensus approach to problem solving and his coalition building strategies. These qualities attracted people and generated intense motivation, energy and a deep sense of hope and anticipation among them and made this a deeply moving experience. After all, he is a man of deep and enormous conviction, possessing tremendous skill and capability, and he even reached over to the other side.

Again, another criticism has to do with President Obama's pick for his cabinet, some claiming Erik Holder at Attorney General and Susan Rice at the United Nations are not enough black faces. Of course, they missed Valerie Jarrett, the

FREDERICK MONDERSON

Transition Team's Co-Chair; Lisa Jackson to head the Environmental Protection Agency; Mona Sutphen, Deputy Chief of Staff; Melody Barnes, Director of White House Domestic Policy Council; Desiree Rogers, White House Social Secretary; and Cassandra Butts, Transition Team's General Counsel, etc. Significantly, President Obama essentially gets one shot at this, that is, fix the economy, defend America and put the nation back on the road to solvency, security and satisfaction. Notwithstanding, speculation will still allow Obama to appoint blacks in a multitude of federal middle-management positions including Supreme Court and Circuit Courts, and ambassadorships. After all, he had Jimmy Carter and Bill Clinton as examples of men who appointed blacks in meaningful positions. Even George Bush who appointed Colin Powell, Condoleezza Rice, and Secretary Paige at Education is an example. The man Barack Obama is a great visionary, great intellect; there is so much he will and has to do.

Barack Obama's Washington, DC Photo 55. Even from a distance we have Doric columns peeping out from between the trees highlighting the National Theater.

BARACK OBAMA
MASTER OF WASHINGTON DC

Barack Obama's Washington, DC Photo 56. Domes are of different sizes and shapes but they still adorn and this one highlights this building with its Ionic colonnade of columns.

We must consider the energy this new president has generated at home and abroad. We need not mention his tumultuous welcome in Germany. Some say he would be voted President of Germany. This would shake Hitler to his soul, if he had such. The French President Sarkozy is now considering non-whites for his cabinet. Fidel Castro said Barack Obama is a "sincere," "honest" and "a good man." It's been said, the "Freedom of a people to choose its own leaders is the root of a free democracy." It's a pity this lesson was not taught Mayor Bloomberg and Council Speaker Quinn of New York City, when it came to choosing the name of a street in the Black Community in honor of Sonny "Abubadika" Carson. Just as Hofstadter had said about the American Revolution, "The revolution was in the minds and hearts of the people," Sonny Carson will forever remain a revered ancestor and a stalwart in the minds and hearts of the people of Brooklyn and across America.

Notice the student response in St. Vincent during the inauguration? This was happening all across the world! This was happening worldwide and CNN claimed they broadcast into 250 nations and territories! No man has ever commanded so world-wide an audience at any one happening. One could well imagine what was happening in Kenya, home of Barack's father. Have you seen the picture of the

FREDERICK MONDERSON

man standing on a bicycle in the street so he could get a better look, perhaps at a television monitor?

How often has anyone seen a black man and his family portrayed constructively on the front page of the *New York Times*? How many inaugural affairs have featured black entertainers in such prominence as this recent event? Mary J. Blige, Will-I-Am, Usher, Beyonce, J-Zee, Shakira, Kanye West, Stevie Wonder, Aretha Franklin, Denzel Washington, the young singers at the Ron Clark Academy, the Brooklyn Steppers, even the "9-year old reporter." Sure Ronald Reagan had Ray Charles up there singing "America the Beautiful," but for the most part blacks do not get prominence at these affairs.

Barack Obama's Washington, DC Photo 57. View of a busy street with its trees shadowing government buildings with their columns.

BARACK OBAMA
MASTER OF WASHINGTON DC

Barack Obama's Washington, DC Photo 58. How interesting that the Washington Monument seems to project a street light, from this angle.

All these notwithstanding, the American people elected Barack Obama President because of the need for a change in the way government works but also to help cure the ills plaguing the nation. This extraordinary man of talent and wisdom must present and work an economic recovery package that works, withdraw from Iraq, create a new Middle East Peace initiative, engage in early and aggressive diplomacy, and a whole lot more. He has to put people back to work, re-evaluate and make appropriate adjustments to the tax code, regulate Wall Street, deal with the deficit level and the foreign trade imbalance. He has to encourage granting of credit to small businesses, take a new look at "pork barrel spending," fix Social Security and Medicare, examine government waste and pentagon procurement practices, and develop energy independence through natural gas, coal, wind-power, solar, etc., while keeping the military strong and addressing the needs of veterans. His is a tall order and he has inspired a new generation to hope and look to the future.

FREDERICK MONDERSON

Barack Obama's Washington, DC Photo 59. Imagine two for the price of one. The Washington Monument and the Lincoln Memorial, all in the same picture.

In this, the new president cannot forget Black America. However, we must remember this man is married to a black woman and every night he goes home to Michele Obama and Sasha and Malia, their daughters. Michele is a known descendant of slaves and will never let her husband, who loves her very much, forget this. Who would ever believe there would be "Black love in the White House?" There are now blacks cops in the White House. Notice how history is revealing itself by reminding us, "The White House and the Capital Building were built on the backs of slaves." Don't forget that's a black man's statue that sits above the Capital dome! There may be much more to come out!

So in response to the criticisms leveled against Barack Obama, all we have to do is examine some of the things ordinary people said about this hero. One elder gentleman said "All I want is to see Barack Obama, as President, just climb the stairs, enter the White House, and close the doors."

BARACK OBAMA
MASTER OF WASHINGTON DC

Barack Obama's Washington, DC Photo 60. Washington's architecture is generally made of two kinds of stone, white marble and brown-red granite indicative of its majestic beauty and permanence, like the American system.

FREDERICK MONDERSON

Barack Obama's Washington, DC Photo 61. As the sun fades, the color of the buildings seem to play games with the eyes, still they project their beauty as in case of this structure with its Doric columned colonnade.

Barack Obama's Washington, DC Photo 62. While the columns add a wonderful décor to the buildings, the decorative features of the cornice add a distinct dimension that further enhances the beauty of these structures.

BARACK OBAMA
MASTER OF WASHINGTON DC

Barack Obama's Washington, DC Photo 63. Again, it's like an experience of building passing in parade rather than the visitor who strolls along in admiration.

While Reverend Warren in the Invocation remarked to the new President, "History is your story," there must be a "commitment to freedom and justice for all," and "Dr. King is shouting in heaven;" he also admonished Barack to "Share, serve, and seek common good for all." Nevertheless, he was trumped by Reverend Joseph Lowery, "Dean of the Civil Rights Movement," who perhaps put the event best when he called for love not hate, inclusion not exclusion, and tolerance not intolerance. But, his most telling pronouncement is that "now the black does not have to stay back, the brown can stick around, the yellow can be mellow, the red man, can get a head man, and white should do right!" Even more important was the reassurance the new president gave the nation that "The challenges will be met." "The time has come to set aside childish things" because "All deserve to pursue their full measure of happiness." And, finally, "The world has changed and we must change with it." It's a pity in Obama's White House quest, many refuse to accept this admonition!

FREDERICK MONDERSON

Barack Obama's Washington, DC Photo 64. Imagine this beautiful sight on a clear day in the afternoon when the sky is blue and from a distance, perhaps from across the Mall, as these buildings' beauty is further accentuated.

"We lose ourselves when we compromise the very ideals that we fight to defend. And we honor those ideals by upholding them not when it's easy, but when it is hard." BARACK OBAMA Noble Lecture, Dec. 10, 2009

9. Obama: The Eternal Optimist
By

Dr. Fred Monderson

The Dictionary defines an Optimist at one who believes in or has "an inclination to anticipate the best possible outcome of any action or event!" In retrospect, this is the attitude Obama took in the "Debt Ceiling" debacle!

Importantly, President Barack Obama, in confronting the many challenges facing his young administration from left, right and center, has described himself as an

BARACK OBAMA
MASTER OF WASHINGTON DC

"Eternal Optimist." How true, for with the challenges and hurdles he has had to overcome to reach the "mountain top," clearly that optimism has been a profound asset that served him well. And, if events of the past are a valid barometer, he will certainly meet the new challenges and fulfill his destiny in moving America into the contemporary modern age. Even more, perhaps that optimistic spirit can really infect and help transform America to make this nation live out the true nature of its creed, "we hold these truth to be self evident that all men are created equal," in terms of treatment and opportunity, as the Declaration of Independence and Constitution have long held. In these difficult times, optimism is certainly one powerful exhilir that is inexpensive but can work wonders for those with the faith in its potency.

A credible argument can be made that Barack inherited the optimistic outlook from his parents; for, looking at his father's picture with that cocked pipe in his mouth, portrays a man of confidence, courage, character and optimism. His mother, young, free-thinking, professional and imbued with that "Kansas upbringing," added so much to the "work in progress." Even more important, "Grandma's hands" in the upbringing added care and spice to the masterpiece baking in the oven. All these, notwithstanding, the young Barack had to find himself challenged by the vicissitudes of passage of the rite of youth. Nevertheless, emerging from that tunnel or turmoil of uncertainty and perhaps as realization of his youthful upbringing; Barack began to manifest himself, as the challenges and benefits of a sound education were themselves motivating factors in his decision to excel in an environment where benefits accrue to hard work in pursuit of excellence. And, though there may have been bouts of insecurity, and dismay, the inherent spark of optimist may have ignited a flame of possibilities in his desire for achievement and finally success.

FREDERICK MONDERSON

Barack Obama's Washington, DC Photo 65. Columns in review!

Barack Obama's Washington, DC Photo 66. An observed feature is that columns are sometimes many, sometimes few.

BARACK OBAMA
MASTER OF WASHINGTON DC

Barack Obama's Washington, DC Photo 67. So there we are, paralleling the Mall.

The new realization of potentialities coupled with possibilities and challenges leading to success propelled the young optimist to realize the sky could be the limit. Yet, rather than being sidetracked with the falsity of glitter and fluff, having accomplished academic success, young Obama set out to work in the fields of social inequities rather than be drawn to the aspirations of financial gain. An old adage of ancestral wisdom holds, "don't love money, let money love you." Who knows, a similar outlook may have motivated Barack Obama upon graduating from first Columbia University and then Harvard University, to head to Chicago for social work give-back rather than the great and tantalizing promise of Wall Street. Who would believe the journey of social service could be more beneficial than the quest of financial gain. Then again, in retrospect, maybe clairvoyance and destiny played a role that Obama did not end up on Wall Street and possibly down a crooked road! In Wall Street he may not have met "Mighty Michelle" Robinson.

So, Barack Obama put down roots in Chicago where he met Michele Robinson. He began a family and plied his intellectual and organizational skills and grew from first hand experiences in the trenches of trying to transform psycho-social and economic iniquities. That optimistic outlook coupled with a dogged determination to right social wrongs, perhaps lead him to, as Malcolm X admonished, "Look in the mirror for the change agent to correct the myriad problems" plaguing an urban community, as in Chicago. This realization led the young hero to the next political

FREDERICK MONDERSON

level. That is, legislative involvement to effectuate meaningful change, first as a State Senator and finally as a Federal Senator from the great state of Illinois. Thus, optimistic Barack Obama, buoyed by a stable family relationship with a beautiful and professionally accomplished wife Michele and two wonderful children Sasha and Malia, and with a wonderful extended family, had arrived at a pinnacle where meaningful social change could be effectuated.

Barack Obama's Washington, DC Photo 68. Even though the people are not there, the stillness of the night adds an ornate beauty to the architecture.

Notwithstanding, and from the zenith of being able to realize the American universe is badly flawed; like the weary and war-worn soldier struggling to return home and having to fight one last battle, Senator Barack Obama decided to seek the Presidency of the United States of America.

Barack, Who? Obama? Osama? Osama bin-Laden? Name confusion, yet this guy is a Muslim and he wants to be President of the United States! What is this world coming to?

BARACK OBAMA
MASTER OF WASHINGTON DC

Barack Obama's Washington, DC Photo 69. Everyone may not be working but some people still seem to be burning the midnight oil.

Barack Obama's Washington, DC Photo 70. The circular pattern in arrangement of building façades and entranceway adds a unique beauty to these creations.

FREDERICK MONDERSON

Barack Obama's Washington, DC Photo 71. The other side of the previous picture.

In all probability Barack Obama sat his wife Michele down and said: "Honey, I wish to run for the Presidency of the United States." She may have responded, knowing the optimistic capability and dogged determination of her husband, "I believe in you, but this will be an enormous challenge. Still, you're up to it. After all, your optimistic attitude will guide you." With that, Barack launched his Presidential campaign and, well, the rest is history. Now, having succeeded to the Office of the Presidency, he set about to quickly keep campaign promises but also worked to stem the bleeding economic arteries of the nation.

Success has been described as "when opportunity meets preparation" and having the power, the new president began setting things in motion. Yet, and despite partisan bickering in Washington, President Obama, within less than a month, had accomplished tremendous gains in his young administration. Perhaps no other president has accomplished as much in so short a time; but this may attest to the urgency of the times and America's love affair with the dynamic new leader bubbling with confidence, commitment, concern and a desire to rescue his nation, re-direct its focus and set it on a path possibly more glorious than ever before. Equally important, he wants the next generation to be as assured of the American dream as this generation is, and such is a prime concern of his. Moving rapidly, the president evaluated and overturned many important Executive Orders of his predecessor, George Bush, the 43rd president.

BARACK OBAMA
MASTER OF WASHINGTON DC

With a view to repairing America's image abroad, President Obama, in keeping with a campaign pledge, announced his intent to close the Guantanamo Detention Center in Cuba where combatants in the war on terror are held. While many have expressed the need for caution in this directive, the president has reassured the families of victims of terror, he is not being soft on terrorism but that justice for such individuals will be fair, swift and appropriate.

Barack Obama's Washington, DC Photo 72. The Jefferson Building in the Library of Congress. This building's exterior beauty is a pale comparison to its internal decoration and the reservoir of knowledge it holds.

FREDERICK MONDERSON

Barack Obama's Washington, DC Photo 73. Oh, what a wonderful stroll with the Capital Building at your back.

The new president has appointed a Middle East Envoy to tackle the mercurial Middle East peace process in order to end the suffering of so many and try to stabilize the region, helping to better the life of its residents. He has signaled his desire to hold discussions with Iran while holding the line on what America views as its undesirable behaviors. This includes Iran's support for Hamas and Hezbollah, meddling in Iraq that puts American lives in great danger, and most important its quest to achieve nuclear weapons with an evil intent. He sent Vice-President Joe Biden to Europe to reassure the NATO Alliance America is turning a new page in its foreign policy. His Secretary of State Clinton has sought to check "Axis of Evil" types to convince them America still means business and signal to Asia, America wants good and meaningful relations!

To pursue his visionary agenda, the president was quick to assemble an impressive economic, foreign policy and security team; so much so, even his detractors praised his choices as visionary. The optimistic Mr. Obama, however, believed only the most skillful individuals can help him accomplish the daunting economic and social challenges that lay ahead to set America on the right path.

BARACK OBAMA
MASTER OF WASHINGTON DC

Barack Obama's Washington, DC Photo 74. In bright of day, colonnades upon colonnades.

To cap it all off, President Obama was able to achieve the passage of his stimulus bill, the most significant Congressional financial allocation in history, within a month of his young administration. This was an unbelievable accomplishment despite significant elements of the legislative body voting against it. Of course, because he won the election by as significant a majority as he did, and with some difficulty, the bill passed. Naturally, and perhaps secretly Obama must have thought as Havelock Ellis (1859-1939), who in the *Dance of Life* (1923) wrote: "The place where optimist most flourishes is the lunatic asylum." Nevertheless, the legislative process of the bill did send a message to the President, yet he remained optimistic.

FREDERICK MONDERSON

Barack Obama's Washington, DC Photo 75. Again, columns may be few or many.

The negativity of Republican members of both houses of Congress, notwithstanding, the bill will focus on energy and the environment; science; the safety net; education; health; taxes; and infrastructure. The *New York Times* describes dynamics of the above as: "The Bill Smiles on Power Programs;" "Research and Development Aid Restored;" "For the Needy, a Variety of Help;" "Schools get Large Infusion of Money;" "More Money for Medicaid and the Jobless;" and "Cuts for Individuals and Business."

What is interesting in the process of achieving this significant part of the president's program to rescue and reposition the nation, he suffered a number of disappointments. The first of these had to do with his cabinet choices, for Governor Richardson's withdrawal as Secretary of the Commerce Department was derailed due to a conflict of interest, and much later Senator Judd Gregg for the same position, though the latter claims the reasons are different, his being ideological rather than questionably criminal. Senator Tom Daschle's withdrawal as Secretary of Health and Human Services was for tax problems; Nancy Killefer as Chief Performance Officer – also because of tax problems; and Timothy Geithner as Secretary of the Treasury, who yet was confirmed, even though he himself had tax problems, while Hilda Solis was also confirmed, though her husband also had tax problems. Despite all of these setbacks with potentially negative public relations image problems, even while the Stimulus Bill was being debated, President Obama kept his positive outlook and sought replacements, while still remaining focused.

BARACK OBAMA
MASTER OF WASHINGTON DC

The interesting thing is the American people, realizing the gravity of the nation's plight and that Barack Obama inherited the situation, yet remained cool as cucumber, so they continued to express unqualified support for the man. Perhaps they saw in Obama what Francois Marie Arouter Voltaire (1694-1778) believed in *Candide* that optimism is "a mania for maintaining all that is well when things are going badly." Equally, Sigmund Freud (1856-1939) in *Future of an Illusion* may have expressed a view that seems to typically describe President Obama: "The voice of the intellect is a soft one, but it does not rest until it has gained a hearing. Ultimately, after endless repeated rebuffs, it succeeds. This is one of the few points in which one may be optimistic about the future of mankind, but in itself it signifies not a little."

Finally, McLandburgh Wilson in the *Optimist and Pessimist* (1915) put it best in describing the Congress' challenge to the President: "The optimist sees the doughnut, but the pessimist sees the hole." Maybe now having crossed the legislative Rubicon of his Stimulus Package, the doughnut of his optimism will carry President Barack Obama successfully to his destiny; while the Republican Congress will find itself in a pessimistic hole when the next election rolls around in four years time.

Barack Obama's Washington, DC Photo 76. Close-quarter architectural competition?

FREDERICK MONDERSON

Barack Obama's Washington, DC Photo 77. Oh, well. There's that youngster lining up to take that memorable photo to later boast as he sits on the bench, "I remember when they were doing repair work to this building, but now I preside as Jurist."

BARACK OBAMA
MASTER OF WASHINGTON DC

"What the American people hope — what they deserve — is for all of us, Democrats and Republicans, to work through our differences; to overcome the numbing weight of our politics. For while the people who sent us here have different backgrounds, different stories, different beliefs, the anxieties they face are the same. The aspirations they hold are shared: a job that pays the bills; a chance to get ahead; most of all, the ability to give their children a better life."
BARACK OBAMA State of the Union Address January 27, 2010

10. BARACK OBAMA: THE FIRST 30 DAYS BY DR. FRED MONDERSON

For all new political administrations, the measure by which they are judged is how well they are doing and this is assessed by how much is accomplished in the first 100 days. Such a development is standard. However, when it came to President Barack Obama, what he has been able to achieve in the *First 30 Days* is remarkable to say the least. He certainly had a plan when he arrived in Washington after waging a successful campaign, but the assistance his Transition Team received from the Bush Administration certainly had something to do with his success. Even more, the team he put in place most assuredly helped in his achievement, but the dogged determination of the man, his working long hours crafting his plan and his desire to succeed with the intent to rescue his nation, all worked in his favor, producing the results it did. Additionally, while this is still somewhat sufficient to judge the effectiveness of his young administration, in some ways, it is not surprising in that the "black guy" is always expected to be more, and be more for most people. He has more to prove, not by his own doing, but naysayers expect more, even though many know the previous man messed things up and it may take even longer to fix. Still, the strategy is a measure of how well and how serious Obama has approached his responsibility and his intent to deliver results.

Elsewhere, I have mentioned an old tale of "Somewhere in the Islands." There a youngster visited his father at work in a bank, where the layout of the office was such that one could see rows and rows of desks of men in white shirts manning them all. Everywhere the boy looked he could see white men in white shirts, all, except his father, a black man in white shirt, sticking out like "fly in buttermilk."

FREDERICK MONDERSON

Later in that father and son interaction, the boy enquired as to why this is so. To which the father replied, "Son I did not get this job by having the same education as the other workers, I had to have more." That is, if the job required a BA Degree, one had to have a Masters; and if a Masters, then two or three Masters is a safe bet for the "black guy" to land the job. That is the nature of institutional discrimination, but we live with it, until it's time to prove one's self, and we deliver!

Barack Obama's Washington, DC Photo 78. Straight and curved sides are unique.

BARACK OBAMA
MASTER OF WASHINGTON DC

Barack Obama's Washington, DC Photo 79. View of the previous picture but notice the artistic piece in the foreground and the four columns to the right.

Barack Obama's Washington, DC Photo 80. The foreground trees seem to accentuate the beauty of the Capital Building.

FREDERICK MONDERSON

In this case of Barack Obama, the same applied and he delivered because he realized the gravity of the nation's situation he inherited. In this, he put together a remarkable Cabinet and an effective collection of advisers; appointed a Middle Eastern Envoy not only to work on the Peace Process but also to build better rapport with Muslim countries; he acquired the Second Part of President Bush's Bank Rescue Funds; announced his intention to close Guantanamo Bay Prison for terror detainees; announced a new emphasis on clean, renewable energy, to make America less dependent on Middle Eastern and other sources of oil, and to put this nation at the forefront of 21st Century industrial innovation; he intends a new cooperative effort with leading nations to combat climate change and global terrorism; he sought to reform and strengthen the American educational system for innovation and competitiveness; effectively passed the greatest "Stimulus Bill" in the history of the nation's economic relationship; he proposed a new high speed rail system; and he made his first official visit to a foreign nation, Canada, as President of the United States. Later he announced his new budget to effectively cut the nation's deficit in half by the end of his first administration. In this latter, insisting on honesty and transparency, he argued against fiscal deficits and runaway spending, while calling for sacrifices and hard decisions, and asked that the American people hold their Representatives accountable. In summary, therefore, his Recovery Plan, Stability Plan and Housing Plan are essentially designed to transform how things are done nationally to meet the new challenges facing the nation. How things have speedily changed!

All this was achieved in a remarkably short time period, despite lack of cooperation particularly from the Republican controlled House of Representatives after the 2010 elections and next to nothing Republican support in the Senate that has really been a tremendous hindrance. Nevertheless, the charismatic personality of the new President, the rush to bring into fruition creative ideas enunciated in his political platform, his ability to surround himself with the best particularly economic and foreign policy minds whose ideas easily encompass and seek answers to the gravity of the situation facing the nation, as well as his ability to seek consensus and reaching across the aisle, are all assets that have been well used to achieve the success he has accomplished so far.

Throughout his campaign, Senator Barack Obama hammered away at President George W. Bush, blaming him for the economic calamity in which the country found itself under his stewardship over the last 8 years. Considering that President Bush's predecessor President Bill Clinton had achieved a budget surplus having created several million jobs and set America on a terrific period of economic growth, Obama insisted the current situation created under Bush's watch, gives him a failing grade for stewardship. Now, critics are insisting its Obama's economic baby and he must deliver especially on jobs, but as a local New York

BARACK OBAMA
MASTER OF WASHINGTON DC

"philosopher" Kenrick Merez has opined, "Perhaps after Obama is removed job creation will boom."

Barack Obama's Washington, DC Photo 81. No the building is not sinking; it's just the photographer's hands that appears crooked.

Barack Obama's Washington, DC Photo 82. White marble as opposed to red granite.

FREDERICK MONDERSON

Barack Obama's Washington, DC Photo 83. The author and a wonderful family who had come to Washington for the Million Family March in 1995.

President Obama's Economic Team was headed by Paul Volker, former head of the Federal Reserve. It's interesting, particularly for the young people to understand the value of knowledge and experience, and why they must fortify themselves in this respect. After he stepped down from the Federal Reserve, Volker was "put out to pasture" and they brought in Greenspan and then Paulson and later Bernanke! When Barack needed an experienced economic hand, he turned to Volker, who, only willing to put his experience in service to the nation, answered the call. As has long been the case during the campaign, when Obama was accused of being inexperienced in a particular area, "he went to school," without being observed, and shored up his knowledge in a particular area, as he demonstrated such knowledge in the debates. This he did in *Economics* 101 and 201, probably with Volker's assistance. Talk about being trained by the best!

This new President chose his Security Team carefully, retaining Robert Gates at Defense, even though Gates belonged to the Bush Republican Administration, simply because Secretary Gates had experience in the important war on terror and had knowledge of all the global hot spots. Even thought the President may choose his replacement later on, this early knowledge and expcrience trumped ideology. This was clearly a brilliant move on the part of the young President as all eyes were on him! One thing is certain, even though it could come at a later time; this

BARACK OBAMA
MASTER OF WASHINGTON DC

was not the time for ideological reasons to change the head of the Security Team, giving the President breathing space to concentrate on other equally pressing matters. So far he has held the terror wolves at bay!

Mr. Obama put together a rather credible Cabinet of the best minds for the key areas that require the greatest input from his government, to accomplish the requirements to make his administration successful. He suffered some setbacks because, for personal reasons Governor Richardson and Senator Daschle were unfit for office and the Senator who turned back was more ideologically motivated than concerned with working for the common good.

Nevertheless, the President took it all in strides, and probably thought, "Though a few branches of my philosophic tree may be shaky and need some pruning, fundamentally the trunk of my game plan is sound and can achieve the sought after results." Similarly, were Cheikh Anta Diop's stated views of his thesis expressed in his book *African Origins of Civilization: Myth or Reality* regarding ancient Egypt being a black civilization!

The Middle East problem has been a thorn in the side of American Administrations for more than half a century and it appears there is no solution in sight. In the past, however, most administrations took up this issue, sometime later in their term, but this time President Obama speedily appointed his Middle East Envoy at the inception so he could hit the ground running. Clearly no one could accuse him of dragging his feet in seeking solutions to this problem. He knows the Middle East problem is intricately linked with the success of his administration's efforts and interest in the region, and globally.

FREDERICK MONDERSON

Barack Obama's Washington, DC Photo 84. This "Grove of Tranquility" seems even more beautiful with the white marble in background.

Barack Obama's Washington, DC Photo 85. So much is happening here, but, no, the lights in the rear are not a part of the author's headwear.

BARACK OBAMA
MASTER OF WASHINGTON DC

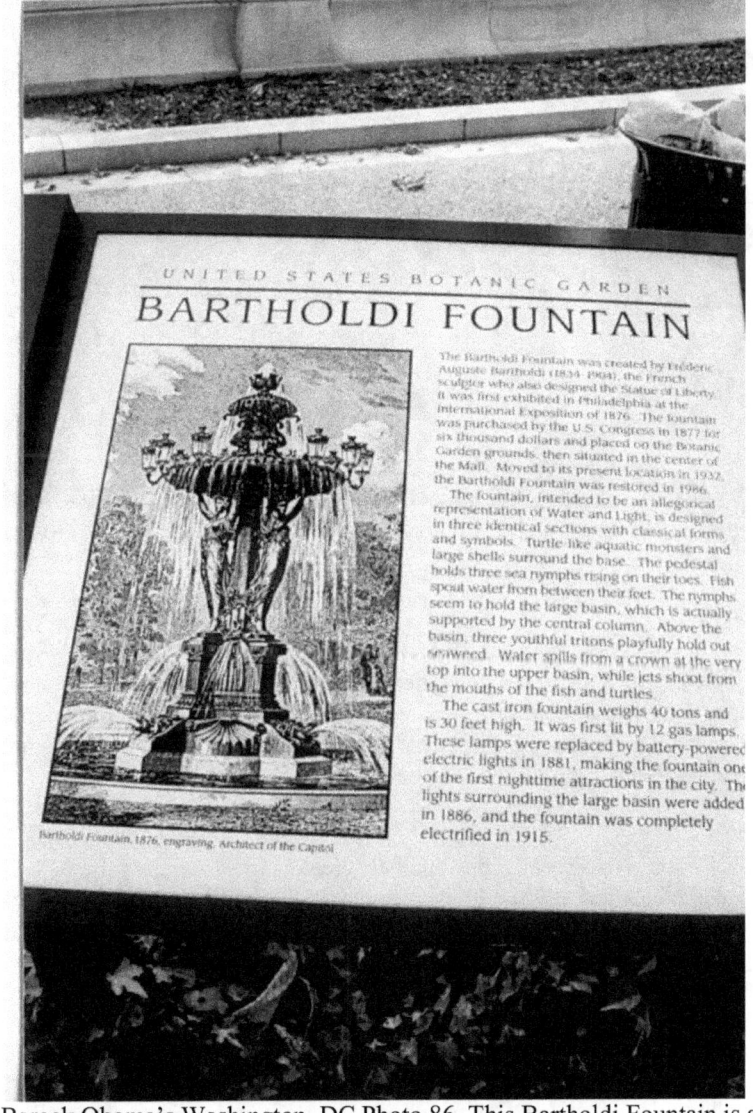

Barack Obama's Washington, DC Photo 86. This Bartholdi Fountain is a wonderful memorial representing Water and Light.

FREDERICK MONDERSON

Barack Obama's Washington, DC Photo 87. Sports on the lawn with a kiosk in rear.

President Obama never doubted the abilities of Senator Clinton and that's why he made her Secretary of State. That done, her first assignment to Asia was to signal to that region, the Obama Administration considered it important and to convince India, China, and Japan, the US considers them significant players in his global economic and diplomatic initiatives. She seems to have done an excellent job.

The Stimulus plan is essentially designed to create infrastructure jobs and aid development in education and the housing industry putting people back to work, investing in research and development to make inroads into the nation's hurting energy dependence. Clean energy, new energy initiatives, liquid gas, solar power, wind and even nuclear energy will relieve the American dependence on foreign sources of energy, create new jobs and make America a leader in this form of future energy resources technology. Attention to global warming, more concerned environmental stewardship and assistance to the world's poor and particularly aiding Bill Clinton's global AIDS outreach, and that of George Bush especially in Africa, are considered sound policy initiatives.

The President's trip to Canada was well received and as demonstrated, he listened

BARACK OBAMA
MASTER OF WASHINGTON DC

well to the concerns of this important neighbor and ally who has stood with America in its most challenging times, and will continue to be a key partner in American foreign policy and trade initiatives.

Barack Obama's Washington, DC Photo 88. Another view of the Kiosk on the lawn.

FREDERICK MONDERSON

Barack Obama's Washington, DC Photo 89. The Capital Building photo taken from the bus.

Barack Obama's Washington, DC Photo 90. An even better view of the Great Dome.

BARACK OBAMA
MASTER OF WASHINGTON DC

Barack Obama's Washington, DC Photo 91. Still another view of the Capital Building from street level.

Despite the gauntlet of criticisms from House of Representatives and even Senate Republicans, the President's ratings are very high because the public sees him as an honest broker, doing the best, assisted by an able team, trying to clean up the mess he inherited.

Naturally the President has his critics outside of government, including Rush Limbaugh, who seem to be emerging as the Republicans' leading ideologue in setting their agenda. Interesting however, in his most recent criticism of the President's supposed new helicopter, "The American economy is fundamentally sound" and "The Mac is Back" John McCain seems to have forgotten he did not even realize how bad things really were. Nevertheless, the President gently slapped him down in referring to the helicopter question statement by saying essentially, "I like my old toy, and I'm not getting a new one. After all, I have never had a helicopter before." All this goes to show, the President is on the right track after only 30 days, which says much for his confidence and determination to set things right in Washington and the nation. Thus, he seems well on his way to becoming a Master of Washington, DC! New York attorney Marc Aronson believes "Obama will go down in history as a great president. My whole family voted for him."

FREDERICK MONDERSON

Barack Obama's Washington, DC Photo 92. A side view of the Capital Building.

Barack Obama's Washington, DC Photo 93. Layers and layers of columns on the Capital Building, as a visitor stroll by.

BARACK OBAMA
MASTER OF WASHINGTON DC

Barack Obama's Washington, DC Photo 94. Another view of the previous photo showing close-up of the Senate entrance colonnade (right) and the House further to the left. Notice the stone of the near and far columns is different to the center columns.

Barack Obama's Washington, DC Photo 95. Oh no, the Capital Building is not about to capsize. It's just the nervous hand of the photographer that took this shot.

FREDERICK MONDERSON

Barack Obama's Washington, DC Photo 96. That's more like it as the Capital Building assumes its upright position.

BARACK OBAMA
MASTER OF WASHINGTON DC

Barack Obama's Washington, DC Photo 97. White marble columns on a building with blue sky and white clouds in the background.

FREDERICK MONDERSON

Barack Obama's Washington, DC Photo 98. "Slim" seems a "column" in his own right.

BARACK OBAMA
MASTER OF WASHINGTON DC

Barack Obama's Washington, DC Photo 99. Youngster stands before a figure considered "The contemplation of Justice."

FREDERICK MONDERSON

Barack Obama's Washington, DC Photo 100. Oh, to be young, free, and American, enjoying the joys of youth with the security of the Capital Building in the background.

BARACK OBAMA
MASTER OF WASHINGTON DC

Barack Obama's Washington, DC Photo 100a. Oh, to be young, happy and among many in the nation's capital walking the walk!

Barack Obama's Washington, DC Photo 100b. View of the Composite Columns in front of the House of Representatives' side of the Capital Building with "Old Glory" at full mast.

FREDERICK MONDERSON

Barack Obama's Washington, DC Photo 100c. Youngster before the Fountain that blocks out the view of the Capital Building.

Barack Obama's Washington, DC Photo 100d. A better view is afforded the front of the Capital Building from the Jefferson Building of the Library of Congress.

BARACK OBAMA
MASTER OF WASHINGTON DC

Barack Obama's Washington, DC 100e. Here's what the front of the Capital Building looks like from close-up on the Senate side.

FREDERICK MONDERSON

"We can't expect to solve our problems if all we do is tear each other down. You can disagree with a certain policy without demonizing the person who espouses it. You can question somebody's views and their judgment without questioning their motives or their patriotism. Throwing around phrases like "socialists" and "Soviet-style takeover" and "fascist" and "right-wing nut" -- that may grab headlines, but it also has the effect of comparing our government, our political opponents, to authoritarian, even murderous regimes. Now, we've seen this kind of politics in the past. It's been practiced by both fringes of the ideological spectrum, by the left and the right, since our nation's birth. But it's starting to creep into the center of our discourse. And the problem with it is not the hurt feelings or the bruised egos of the public officials who are criticized. Remember, they signed up for it. Michelle always reminds me of that. The problem is that this kind of vilification and over-the-top rhetoric closes the door to the possibility of compromise. It undermines democratic deliberation. It prevents learning -- since, after all, why should we listen to a "fascist," or a "socialist," or a "right-wing nut," or a left-wing nut"? It makes it nearly impossible for people who have legitimate but bridgeable differences to sit down at the same table and hash things out. It robs us of a rational and serious debate, the one we need to have about the very real and very big challenges facing this nation. It coarsens our culture, and at its worst, it can send signals to the most extreme elements of our society that perhaps violence is a justifiable response." BARACK OBAMA, *remarks at University of Michigan, May 1, 2010*

11. Anti-Racist Activism Alive and Well By

Dr. Fred Monderson

Thanks to the likes of newspapers that print racially insensitive and false information such as the *New York Post* has done and equally racist white supremacist groups and individuals who threaten and try to demean President Barack Obama, Civil Rights activism is alive and well! This was clearly demonstrated today when more than a thousand people turned out to protest at noon, Thursday, February 19, 2009, in front of the *New York Post* on Sixth Avenue at 48th Street in Manhattan. The message was clear, Barack Obama is President of the United States of America as well as of Black America, and the

BARACK OBAMA
MASTER OF WASHINGTON DC

likes of any who threaten or demean him in any way will face the organized wrath of the activist community, backed by people of goodwill, black and white, everywhere.

Barack Obama's Washington, DC Photo 101. The capital Building as cherry red!

As in days of old, activists of all ideological persuasions, races and ethnicities assembled in front of the *New York Post* to send a message. The "Chimp Political Cartoon" is racist, distasteful and has fired up opponents who will not take it anymore. So stated activists Al Sharpton, Councilman Charles Bar on, Reverend Herbert Daughtry, Hip Hop Minister Conrad Mohammed, Viola Plummer, Dr. James McIntosh, Queen Mother of the Middle Passage Dr. Blakely, Chief Bar Kim Parker, Erik Monderson, Michael Hooper, Members of the National Action Network and a whole host of others, including union members, and Eday Fox, Councilwomen Letitia James and Darlene Mealy, as well as 100 Men in Law Enforcement Who Care, and people from various activist movements and many whom this reporter could and did not identify. Throughout, the chant was "Shut Down the Racist Rag New York Post," "Shut it Down, Yes We Can," "Shut it Down, Yes We Will."

FREDERICK MONDERSON

Barack Obama's Washington, DC Photo 102.   Another view of the Capital Building.

The utter insult that generated this type of response had to do with the *New York Post's* Political Cartoon of Wednesday, February 18, 2009, that depicted two Policemen, one shooting a chimp dead and the other uttering the following: "They will have to get someone else to sign the next Stimulus Bill." This insensitive comment became a national issue as modern communication avenues, television, radio and other newspapers aired and highlighted its depiction and message across the country and in concert with the Internet, the issue became even more widespread.

BARACK OBAMA
MASTER OF WASHINGTON DC

Barack Obama's Washington, DC Photo 103. The Dome from a different angle.

FREDERICK MONDERSON

Barack Obama's Washington, DC Photo 104. "Equal Justice Under Law" is a powerful guarantee of fairness and protection in all types of legislation.

BARACK OBAMA
MASTER OF WASHINGTON DC

Barack Obama's Washington, DC Photo 105. Another of those magnificent buildings with the Doric colonnade arranged in an elevated spot.

One has to remember, after the election of Barack Obama to the Presidency of the United States, many shortsighted individuals began harping that now we have an African American as President there is a need for the end of Civil Rights activism, and they have also called for the end to Black History celebrations. Many who argued for the end to such activism wishfully envisioned President Obama's election meant a rapid transformation of America in a manner that there would be no need for such in a "Post Racial America." Those who have struggled to make these movements meaningful and effective have responded with a resounding NO! Neither group ever dreamed Barack Obama would become so much of a target! In fact, Civil Rights activists really believed they would have to keep the new president honest, not that they would have to come to his defense and they are prepared!

Now, regarding the *Post* item, a number of issues are appended from deconstructing the political cartoon that have raised the sensitivity with racial implications, and one has to wonder how the CNN lady analyst could not see racial overtones therein.

The *New York Post* waged a negative campaign against Barack Obama; for while in favor of his rival, John McCain, the paper had very little that was positive to say about the winner of the elections.

The whole notion of the police shooting of black men and women, viz., Amadou Diallo, Patrick Dorismond, Eleanor Bumpers and so many more, and the whole notion of open season on blacks, terrorism of the KKK and establishment and literary mechanisms of lynchings, are all stark reminders America must move beyond such odious behaviors; for after all, black soldiers at home and on the frontiers are protecting this nation and its citizens, and they are watching and taking notes!

On the previous page, the *Post* had a big write-up, capitalizing on the president signing the Stimulus Bill.

The next page, the *Post* and its cohorts are stoking the hornets' nest by graphically associating a police-shooting, a dead ape with 2 bullet holes in his chest, and the now famous line "They will have to find someone else to sign the next stimulus bill."

When the editor and cartoonist were called on to retract or denounce their handiwork they drew a line in the sand and affirmed, this is parody of the Stimulus Bill passed by Congress and we're standing by it. They claimed the Bill belonged to Nancy Pelosi and not the President and thus she and Congress is the subject of the parody. So, why is Nancy not signing the Bill on the previous page?

However, nowhere is Congress mentioned in the cartoon; the seeming darkening of the ape is ominous; mention of the Stimulus Bill and the image of the First African American President signing it on the previous page; historic associations of blacks with apes, chimps, and orangutans made many mad who decided to **call** the paper out.

This issue has national and worldwide implications of a historical nature and those who see otherwise are historically ignorant.

Remember the black man in McCain's audience who gained notoriety by telling his candidate "We must stop him (Obama)!" raised the question, strange as it may seem, is this one such attempt?

BARACK OBAMA
MASTER OF WASHINGTON DC

Clearly, Obama has a lot of support but this insult during Black History Month is even more hurtful, and thereby galvanized the activist movement.

The activists' message is clear, *The Post* has a long history of insulting Blacks and this cannot continue. There is another demonstration scheduled for Friday at 5:00 pm. They intend to encourage people who have subscriptions to *The Post* to cancel such; others not to buy *The Post*; and also they intend to broaden the action by picketing and boycotting those businesses who advertise in *The Post*. Again, thanks to the insensitivity of the newspaper they have mobilized activists of goodwill who will send an unmistaken message to all the likes of *The Post*: "Do not take Blacks for granted!" Even most important, "Stay off the President" for even though protocol dictate he not get down in the mud, many of his followers are only itching to take on all comers!

Barack Obama's Washington, DC Photo 106. What a magnificent view of the lawn, clump of bushes as the Capital Building hides behind and "Old Glory" flies proudly beneath a clear and blue sky.

FREDERICK MONDERSON

"In reaffirming the greatness of our nation we understand that greatness is never a given. It must be earned. Our journey has never been one of short-cuts or settling for less. It has not been the path for the faint-hearted, for those that prefer leisure over work, or seek only the pleasures of riches and fame. Rather, it has been the risk-takers, the doers, the makers of things -- some celebrated, but more often men and women obscure in their labor -- who have carried us up the long rugged path towards prosperity and freedom." BARACK OBAMA, Inaugural Address, Jan. 20. 2009

12.   STAY UP, BARACK!
By

Dr. Fred Monderson

The New York Channel 7, TV show, **LIKE IT IS** with Host Gil Noble began on Sunday March 15, 2009, with guests Milton Allimadi of *Black Star News* and Herb Boyd of the *Amsterdam News* who mentioned the past week's deaths of 5 prominent New Yorkers including the Schomberg's designer, Levina Pointer, Chuck Sutton and Bill Tatum, longtime Publisher of the *Amsterdam News*. As the discussion waged, an even more disturbing revelation was made regarding a "credible" reporter; I did not get his name; who in referring to President Barack Obama, regarding the policies he's trying to implement, said he was "crazy." The gall of this fella!

Nearly two months ago, the tabloid *New York Post*, before the "Chimp Cartoon;" after the President had criticized Wall Street technocrats who gave out large bonuses, at a time when they were experiencing tremendous financial setbacks; printed comments by a Wall Street trader, **Jose something** who in response said, "We work long hours, and deserve these bonuses, so FU-K OBAMA." However, while this disrespectful clown should be reminded he received a paycheck for his labors, the notion of the bonus is these difficult times is entirely another matter.   The disturbing part is this creep has the disgusting and unmitigated gall to curse the President and the *New York Post* had the shameful temerity to publish this insulting disrespect of the President of our country. This pattern of behavior was continued with the "Chimp Cartoon" and such actions are simply a "long train of abuses."

BARACK OBAMA
MASTER OF WASHINGTON DC

While this reporter has not followed this up, the local TV news media has shown clips of racist white supremacy organizations, through their internet web sites, calling for the death of President Obama! It's common knowledge, throughout the Presidential campaign, "men with guns" were found in Obama's vicinity; an elected Sheriff in Florida ranted and raved against 'Barack Hussein Obama;' Obama was accused of untold numbers of questionable but groundless conduct; and even Governor Sarah Palin, the Republican Vice-Presidential candidate was accused of fermenting a climate of anti-Obama hatred in her campaign stops, so much so, respectable Republicans as Colin Powell took a stand against this form of political fear-mongering. Nevertheless, Barack Obama persevered, not unmindful of those behaviors, for in a manner of speaking, such race-baiting were designed to take his eyes off the prize. This flawed and malicious strategy never achieved its intended purpose, but it has, however exposed the racist underbelly of this vile practice, motivated by racial hatred, perpetrated by people of questionable character and those who chose to be associated with them. The Republicans never upbraided her, and their empty non-cooperative attitude makes her and them non-credible candidates in 1212.

Despite this cultivated, threatening and malicious behavior on the part of these "losers," the President's ratings are at remarkable highs. This means a tremendously large percentage of the public has expressed faith and confidence in the President as he demonstrates creative leadership to a nation battered by the tremendously damaging storms of a global economic downturn. Its well known, Barack Obama inherited the problems confronting the nation, but he has gloriously risen to meet the challenge with not just words but creative ideas designed to sail this ship of state beyond the perilous waters of the economic meltdown and into the calm seas with new and better energy policies; national infrastructural refurbishment; forward looking scientific breakthroughs; creation of jobs and revamping of the housing market; providing incentives for banks to more creatively address consumer needs; creating a more manageable and effective national health care system; crafting of an immigration policy that considers all the factors; drawdown Iraqi and surge Afghanistan military forces; remain unrelenting in the war on terror; all while providing leadership to the Western Alliance; recognizing the role of Asia in today's globalization; and remembering equally the importance of Africa in the scheme of things.

FREDERICK MONDERSON

Barack Obama's Washington, DC Photo107. This great and stately structure appears so majestic against a clear and blue sky.

Barack Obama's Washington, DC Photo 108. The rear of the House side of the Capital Building with its stately lawn.

BARACK OBAMA
MASTER OF WASHINGTON DC

Barack Obama's Washington, DC Photo 109. View from across the Great Lawn, the government buildings with their brown stone and ubiquitous columns seem so connected.

All this notwithstanding, continuously and assiduously employed as he is, in that creative factory of credible solutions to multifaceted problems, sometimes called the Oval Office, the President can lose track of those of non-cooperative and questionable intent, because of his confidence in his structural security apparatus. Nevertheless, it's reassuring for him to know, there's a cheering section rooting for him as well as putting the miscreants on notice, "Behave, or else!"

The story was told of an incident in a past New York City Marathon, with upwards of 60,000 entrants, one fall Sunday afternoon. As this grueling challenge began to take its toll, a Kenyan runner took the lead coming off the George Washington Bridge, heading towards and through Harlem, New York City. As he rounded the bend into Harlem, the onlookers lining both sides of the route were flabbergasted and broke out in a tumultuous cheering uproar, ecstatic to see an African in the lead. As he confessed later, he was shocked and emboldened to see so many Black people out there cheering for him. They both fed each other! From there it was all down-hill to the finish line in Central Park.

That's why we say "Stay Up Barack!" "Work your magic!" "We've got your back!" When you come around, if they're still standing, we'll deal with them!

FREDERICK MONDERSON

Barack Obama's Washington, DC Photo 110. People just milling around on the Great Lawn as the government buildings show their majesty in the rear.

STAY UP, BARACK!

"The true test of the American ideal is whether we're able to recognize our failings and then rise together to meet the challenges of our time. Whether we allow ourselves to be shaped by events and history, or whether we act to shape them. Whether chance of birth or circumstance decides life's big winners and losers, or whether we build a community where, at the very least, everyone has a chance to work hard, get ahead, and reach their dreams." BARACK OBAMA, speech, Jun. 4, 2005

13. FROM THE NEW YORKER TO THE NEW YORK POST
By
Dr. Fred Monderson

On his nightly show, **Larry King Live** the host tackled the *New York Post* political cartoon issue that made such a big stink. In the discussion with guests

BARACK OBAMA
MASTER OF WASHINGTON DC

Floyd Abrams, lawyer (white) and Prof. Richard Thompson Ford (black) of Stanford University, the former thought the cartoon offensive and racist, while the latter argued about stifling honest debate; yet, he too, found the cartoon racist. Larry King, one the other hand, could not, at first, despite his enormous media experience, detect racism in the cartoon, nor its identification with President Obama. As the discussion waged, with emphasis on parody, the *New Yorker* magazine piece published earlier in the campaign, whose cover depicted both Barack and Michele, came into play. Again, and yet, despite Larry's lengthy time in the media, the many faces he has seen in his countless interviews, all he could conclude, high profile individuals like Obama should expect to be parodied, for that is the nature of their visibility as public figures.

Well, sorry to say, Larry was wrong on both counts. If we take, for instance, the *New Yorker* magazine cover Mr. King did not fully grasp the implication and ratifications of the *New Yorker* piece.

Barack Obama's Washington, DC Photo 111. More of the colonnade feature of these buildings running parallel to the Great Lawn.

FREDERICK MONDERSON

While the *New Yorker* cover was done during the presidential election campaign, it was part of a "broad brush mentality" that attempted to besmirch Obama's personality and character. To recall, Barack Obama was accused of being inexperienced in foreign policy dynamics; against the war and the surge; being a Muslim; "palling around with terrorists;" not remembering the name of the soldier whose bracelet he wore; of being a Chicago politician; being a socialist; and a whole lot more. However, in the depiction of Barack in Middle Eastern garb along with his wife, the magazine unintentionally blundered in unconsciously depicting Michele, not as an ordinary spouse, but as a rifle-packing wife. Pardon the pun, but you many have seen a sign showing a hand holding a pistol that read "Never mind the dog, beware of owner!" Well, unintentionally and unconsciously the magazine may have stumbled onto something in portraying the "true nature of Michele Obama." Importantly, the magazine misplaced its intent for in trying to paint Barack as Muslim, it showed Michele as revolutionary spouse watching her husband's back and not afraid to use force, if necessary.

This glimpse at a hitherto unknown side of the First Lady not only put others on notice, galvanized her army of supporters, but also helped by perception and practicality, to equip her for the *tour de force* role she has now stepped into, equally showing her intellectual abilities, bubbling personality, remarkable smile, as sincere spouse and if need be, bodyguard to her best friend. This is certainly one example where the intent of the depiction portrayed has even more far reaching implications.

BARACK OBAMA
MASTER OF WASHINGTON DC

Barack Obama's Washington, DC Photo 112. What a magnificent view, looking out from the Lincoln Memorial across the Reflecting Pool with the Washington Monument and the Capital Building both reflects in the pool as folks look on.

FREDERICK MONDERSON

Barack Obama's Washington, DC Photo 113. More of the "jointed buildings" paralleling the Great Lawn.

Equally too, the *New York Post* "chimp cartoon" manifested far beyond the supposed intent of a "harmless" parody of the Stimulus Bill. It should be understood, there are often undercurrents to practically every situation and hence molding opinion in the public sector demands an enormous amount of sensitivity towards the various ethnic components of the American demographic quilt.

A major problem depicted in *The Post* piece showing the police, an ape, police shooting an ape dead, and the Stimulus Bill; let's not forget the history of insensitivity of *The Post* negative portrayal of Black people and the first African American as President of these United States, takes this issue beyond harmless parody. The truth about Barack Obama, in the mind's eyes of African Americans, he is one of the brightest stars in the Black pantheon, and even though he has not yet reached deification status, this "Moses" perhaps does know he has an unconventional army out there watching his back.

What has incensed this army, truth be told, it is and has been under attack and having its brightest star so assaulted, is as they say, fighting words!

BARACK OBAMA
MASTER OF WASHINGTON DC

We can use history as an example for so much is contained therein. The Slave Trade that captured and transported Africans to America, then trapped them in the vicious institution of slavery, some have argued, reversed the process of evolution, since *Science* holds mankind evolved from the Primates in Africa. However, in that brutalizing experience, the crime of not only physical excoriation, intellectual deprivation, denial of the humanity of the African being, most far reaching was the psychological assault involved in equating him with the lower animals. Hence, in a society where race was first, participating in this hideous crime, even the "lowest white person" enhanced his humanity by further debasing that of the African and all this was sanctioned, *de jure* and *de facto*, by law and social practice. All this occurred in a land where the Declaration of Independence boasted, "All men are created equal." Yet, the enslaved African was not a man and all he could finally muster by force of law was three-fifths of a person.

Barack Obama's Washington, DC Photo 114. A policeman guards a gate to the Capital Building.

FREDERICK MONDERSON

Barack Obama's Washington, DC Photo 115. Through flowery greenery the apex of the Washington Monument stands in all its magnificence.

Barack Obama's Washington, DC Photo 116. From the street level, most of the Washington Monument reveals its message and elegance.

BARACK OBAMA
MASTER OF WASHINGTON DC

Barack Obama's Washington, DC Photo 117. Another view of the Washington Monument.

Barack Obama's Washington, DC Photo 118. Still another view of the Washington Monument.

FREDERICK MONDERSON

Coupled with the terrorism directed against black people in the 19th Century and much of the 20th Century, the "monkey angle" became a potent psychological attack that had to be resisted. From the KKK lynchings to Bull Connor's police attack dogs and forceful water hoses, racial profiling, police brutality, numerous cop shootings, assassination of black leaders and threats to the President despite the terrific job of the Secret Service, ongoing white racist web sites calling for Obama's death, for us to allow *The Post* piece to go unchallenged, not only opened the door, but removed it altogether. The message is clear, we will fight! Lest others forget Claude McKay's Poem "If we Must Die," ... pressed to the wall, we'll be dying, but fighting back!

The message is crystal clear, while Barack Obama is President of the United States, Commander-In-Chief of the military as well as the Secret Service, Michele Obama heads her own unofficial army, with her generals left and right; thus and equally, her role is not simply to protect Barack's back, but also enhance the black agenda and this must assume a most serious tone. Let us not ignore Michelle as the slave ancestors' spokeswoman!

The reality of the election of Barack Obama conveys a manifestation of numerous proportions for though 95 percent of blacks voted for him, 5 percent did not; and while 47 percent of whites voted for him, 53 percent did not. Yet he prevailed. So much so, the "talking heads" floated a profound concept contained in a two-pronged strategy, such as now we are in a "post-racial America" and that "there should be an end to Black History." How laughable!

When we found out Columbus did not discover America, no one said we should stop celebrating Columbus Day. After the election of the first Irish American President John Kennedy, no one got incensed "when the Irish are smiling." While black don't have 100 organizations, we have the *National Association for the Advancement of Colored People*, *Trans Africa* and Reverend Al Sharpton's *National Action Network*, and "untold numbers of non-card carrying members" to remind all, Black History will remain relevant until, "Justice rolls down like a mighty stream."

Another concept also lost in this whole situation has to do with Europeans' claim to have originated "everything." However, while *Science* teaches "man originated in Africa," rising from the apes, and is therefore, the Africans' ancestor, in some respects this concept, like so many was stolen from him.

BARACK OBAMA
MASTER OF WASHINGTON DC

Barack Obama's Washington, DC Photo 119. A typical news day with all the news trucks lined up with the Washington Monument in the background.

Barack Obama's Washington, DC Photo 120. Classic view, seems as if, from an old photograph, the Capital Building.

FREDERICK MONDERSON

Barack Obama's Washington, DC Photo 121. The Washington Monument on a late fall afternoon, as the sun begins to wane far in the distance.

Barack Obama's Washington, DC Photo 122. From ground level, the entrance to the Capital Building with guard on the lookout.

BARACK OBAMA
MASTER OF WASHINGTON DC

"Hope is what led a band of colonists to rise up against an empire; what led the greatest of generations to free a continent and heal a nation; what led young women and young men to sit at lunch counters and brave fire hoses and march through Selma and Montgomery for freedom's cause. Hope is what led me here today--with a father from Kenya, a mother from Kansas; and a story that could only happen in the United States of America. Hope is the bedrock of this nation; the belief that our destiny will not be written for us, but by us; by all those men and women who are not content to settle for the world as it is; who have courage to remake the world as it should be." BARACK OBAMA, speech, Jan. 3, 2008

14. WHY WE MUST SUPPORT BARACK OBAMA BY

DR. FRED MONDERSON

Capping a hectic week, last, according to Ben Fuller, an AP writer, after he had announced "the launch of a more detailed plan to help struggling home owners avoid foreclosures; a new credit plan to spur lending for people and businesses; an overhaul of the way the government hands out private contract to reduce waste and a summit on how to overhaul health care" President Obama told the nation, in these struggling times, we must "endure, find creative opportunity in these hard times and ultimately prosper from the challenge." If that is not leadership, I don't know what is!

We must continue to support President Barack Obama because where he sits at the top of the trail of power is really a lonely place. It is not unusual to be alone in a crowd. The weight of the Office of President is so burdensome to do a good job, one has to totally enmesh one's-self in the task and this can wear down mind and body. Former President Bill Clinton, on **Larry King Live** remarked that the President needs the support of his family and friends and supporters as a release from the technical demands of the office. This, then is why

FREDERICK MONDERSON

we must give Barack Obama our support to be reassuring we're out there for him. Let's not forget, when Bill Clinton faced his greatest challenge in the impeachment proceedings, the evidence notwithstanding, the Senate as the Court of the trial had to take notice that he enjoyed, among others, unwavering and unequivocal black support and this certainly helped mold the final verdict allowing him to continue in office; everything else, notwithstanding, neither him nor we have forgotten the power and influence of such unqualified support!

Some of us may have the belief Barack Obama has reached the mountaintop and this is an end. Quite the contrary, it's only a means to an end. In fact, it's only the beginning of the means to an end. While we cannot forget our votes put him in the White House, we must put wood in the fire to keep him burning and also keep his feet to the same fire to remind him, that we too have issues and priorities that need the weight and influence of his position to make them realities. In fact, without saying so, he wants the challenge of the Black Agenda to force him to act on its behalf.

Barack Obama's Washington, DC Photo 123. The Capital Building in the distance.

BARACK OBAMA
MASTER OF WASHINGTON DC

Barack Obama's Washington, DC Photo 124. The Capital Building entrance from in the shade.

Barack Obama's Washington, DC Photo 125. Another view of the Capital Building, from the shade.

FREDERICK MONDERSON

The story is told of the entrepreneur in the old west who was so successful; he had "his own train." In those days this was an enormous achievement for an individual. One day, while rolling down the tracks, one of his assistants said, "Boss, you should take it easy; after all you have your own train." The lucky man pulled over and turned around and said: "You see this train, it only runs when my feet are on the pedal. When I take my foot off the pedal, it stops." There is a message in that and this is why we must continue to support Barack Obama. He must know we still and will continue to "Got his back."

There is more to this than just that. Those of us who can, must receive his message, analyze and filter it to those who cannot easily access and interpret the message. We must explain to the broad masses of the people what the President is doing on their behalf. We must explain his plans and policies and the actions he has taken on their behalf. We must also explain the opposition stands in waiting as "fifth wheels," to sabotage the coach under the ideological guise of keeping him honest; not giving credence to the fact, he is trying to clean up the mess their party bequeathed him.

We must support President Barack Obama as he works feverishly towards the ideals of that mythical 100 days by which his administration will be subject to the most intense scrutiny. We must equally keep the support on so he can confidently work his economic, educational, housing, banking, scientific, energy, foreign policy, military, health care and immigration plans and policies as he cruises toward that 1000 days in office. By then, having "crossed the Rubicon" of administrative durability, he can begin to pay dividends.

Then, there's really the question of "why, seriously, should we support Barack Obama?"

The answer is crystal clear! Let's get past the idea he's African-American; that's unquestioned. Seriously, he is captain of a ship we're all sailing on; our children and grand-children, our history and their future is at stake. The ship must make port or we'll all drown out there. The demonstrated leadership he has exhibited since coming to office; in essence, he has acted Presidential and this is an important reason why we must support Barack Obama. In this, he has allayed the fears of many who now see the gravity of the nation's plight, equally the world economic downturn, and realize the president is seriously working on the problem. This is certainly a reason we must support him!

Even more important, the President has outlined an economic plan, a housing plan, an education plan, and he is still crafting his energy plan. This is future thinking,

BARACK OBAMA
MASTER OF WASHINGTON DC

and has the promise of national solvency and we must provide the "wind beneath his sails."

The economic plan was designed to clean up the mess on Wall Street, provide stability to the banks so they could begin to make loans to help create confidence on Main Street, by allowing people to start using credit as part of the many pronged effort to help jump start the economy. Job creation can benefit someone we all know. The housing plan will offer assistance to home owners and check foreclosures. What better way to help the nation and ourselves in turn by supporting the President's efforts by telling Congressional Representatives to get on board the ship of state. The Stimulus Bill is part of this mix to create infrastructure jobs as repairing roads, bridges, ports, tunnels; building and repairing schools, and equipping them with state of the art equipment and rewarding teachers with greater expectations and accountability; efforts to stem foreclosures and encourage new building; retooling and assisting mass transit for more efficient and improved services and assistance to states and municipalities to strengthen their police, fire and other security services. We can't afford to lose police, firemen and other security personnel. Teachers are also important!

Barack Obama's Washington, DC Photo 126. Flowers in bloom add to the décor fronting the Capital Building.

FREDERICK MONDERSON

Barack Obama's Washington, DC Photo 127. Elevated columns on the building's side.

Barack Obama's Washington, DC Photo 128. Another view from the lawn.

This is a tall order and President Barack Obama has handled it rather well. To oversee and execute this broad recovery effort he will naturally have to step on some toes and in process generate hard feelings and even create enemies. However, his two aces in the hole are "I have the support of the people." Need I say more, why we must support Barack Obama! Naturally, unwavering support will generate unwavering rewards. Therefore, these and a whole lot more reasons are why we must support President Barack Obama!

BARACK OBAMA
MASTER OF WASHINGTON DC

"In an interconnected world, the defeat of international terrorism – and most importantly, the prevention of these terrorist organizations from obtaining weapons of mass destruction -- will require the cooperation of many nations. We must always reserve the right to strike unilaterally at terrorists wherever they may exist. But we should know that our success in doing so is enhanced by engaging our allies so that we receive the crucial diplomatic, military, intelligence, and financial support that can lighten our load and add legitimacy to our actions. This means talking to our friends and, at times, even our enemies." BARACK OBAMA, speech, Nov. 20, 2006

15. THE BRILLIANCE OF BARACK OBAMA
By

Dr. Fred Monderson

The brilliance of Barack Obama can be ascertained from a number of perspectives including the dynamics of his campaign strategy, his choice of key individuals to positions in his administration and the positively constructive manner in which he tackled the myriad of problems facing the nation. However, if we focus on one example, Civil Rights enforcement, this can perhaps be the exception that proves the rule!

It's generally agreed; everyone, critics and supporters alike, applauded President Obama on the choice of his cabinet and advisers, from first to last. Naturally, he was chided for those selected and rejected for one reason or another. However, as St. Paul believed, "Every man to his own order," President Obama chose wisely in assigning individuals because of their capabilities to function in their respective jobs in his administration; as for example, Robert Gates as Secretary of Defense, because you don't replace commanders during a war, especially when they are versed in the strategy and tactics of the enemy.

FREDERICK MONDERSON

Secretary of State Hillary Clinton, following in the footsteps of the brilliant Condoleezza Rice, is a formidable and knowledgeable replacement who brings a wealth of experience of a multi-faceted nature to the post. Timothy Geithner as Secretary of the Treasury must certainly be among the top 5 bureaucratic administrators of the world with a grasp of not just the American, but also the global economic infrastructure dynamics. Even Eric Shinseki, a retired general officer to head the Department of Veterans Affairs is nothing short of brilliance, for who would understand the plight and concerns of veterans but a veteran himself. And so on down the line.

Barack Obama's Washington, DC Photo 129. More flowers to decorate the surroundings of the Capital Building.

BARACK OBAMA
MASTER OF WASHINGTON DC

Barack Obama's Washington, DC Photo 130. A scene from the battle to save the Union remains a reminder how costly democratic freedom truly is.

Barack Obama's Washington, DC Photo 131. The Water Fountain eloquently decorates the scenery fronting the green lawn before the Grand Marble Terrace of the Capital Building.

FREDERICK MONDERSON

Now, probably the most important of all his appointments, the one of Eric H. Holder as Attorney General, will go a long way in helping shape the historical view of his Presidency. It is not inconceivable his wife Michele has had a role in this particular selection, given her roots, as a descendant of former slaves.

What is more important, however, recent pronouncements of the Attorney General are a tremendous indication that he will not be constrained and do a terrific job in the areas of civil and human rights and their enforcement. Whereas, in the early days of his young administration, African American critics of Obama, perhaps out of ignorance, chided him for not appointing more African Americans in high visibility roles in his cabinet. They held this view, rather than recognizing the President chose the best people for those positions, he thought would more effectively manage the daunting problems, in their assigned areas, that he inherited. That is why, as some have argued, he chose Rahm Emanuel as the "Pit Bull" to guard the White House gates. Conversely, he chose Eric Holder to rectify the Civil Rights issue. Even further, Civil Rights application and enforcement, which has not gotten the attention it deserved, may now be rectified and administered to finally level the playing field.

The Attorney General, a general of law, is the top law enforcement officer in the country. Some have called him the people's lawyer since he represents the government comprising the people's representatives. In this role, the Attorney General prosecutes those who violate federal law and advises the President in legal matters, as well as representing the People in court. He heads the enormous bureaucracy of the Federal Bureau of Investigation; the Drug Enforcement Agency; the United States Marshals Services; Bureau of Alcohol, Tobacco, Firearms and Explosives; the Federal Criminal Division; Civil Rights Division; and the Bureau of Prisons. Equally, while he must ensure all facets of the law is effectively and efficiently administered, he will probably pay more attention to Civil Rights legislation and enforcement more so than a great many of his predecessors did. Even more significant, in wake of his so called "controversial pronouncements" and the *New York Post* "chimp cartoon," civil rights violators are now put on guard, "the new sheriff is quick on the draw."

To have an understanding of Civil Rights statues, one must have an equal understanding of the history of Civil Rights legislations to be able to gauge how and if the Attorney General is making any meaningful enforcement in its execution. Again, a glimmer of the brilliance of Barack Obama is reflected in his concern for Civil Rights since recent Attorney Generals did not seem to make this a priority and now, hopefully, with the President's blessing, Holder will.

BARACK OBAMA
MASTER OF WASHINGTON DC

Barack Obama's Washington, DC Photo 132. Postcard picture of the Capital Building.

Civil Rights legislation was first passed after the Civil War by the Radical Republican Congress who engineered the 13th Amendment that freed the slaves (1865); the 14th Amendment (1868), Section 1, accordingly read; "All persons born or naturalized in the United States, and subject to the jurisdiction thereof, are citizens of the United States and of the State wherein they reside. No State shall make or enforce any law which shall abridge the privileges or immunities of citizens of the United States; nor shall any State deprive any person of life, liberty, or property, without due process of law; nor deny to any person within its jurisdiction the equal protection of the laws." The 15th Amendment (1870), Section 1 states: "The rights of citizens of the United States to vote shall not be denied or abridged by the United States on account of race, color, or previous condition of servitude." Section 2 reads: "The Congress shall have power to enforce this article by appropriate legislation."

Now, while the Harlem Renaissance highlighted artistic and intellectual capabilities of blacks, the Depression years took a tremendous toll on black aspirations for economic gains, as it did for so many others, whether in fair

FREDERICK MONDERSON

housing, quality education, physical safety and other basic human rights expressions. Notwithstanding, when government did not do for black Americans, civic organizations took the lead. One of the first, the Congress of Industrial Organizations, now the AFL-CIO began hiring blacks along with whites during the Depression years. However, while this approach was still in its infancy, by the dawn of World War II, A. Philip Randolph threatened to march on Washington to demand industrial contractors engaged in the war effort, hire black workers. This forced the hand of Franklin D. Roosevelt who passed an **Executive Order** in 1941, and at war's end, in fact, in 1948, President Truman, his successor, integrated the armed forces.

However, getting there and after was a dusty road of black aspirations, and such, in the **1875 Civil Rights Act**, amidst the waning years of Reconstruction, Congress declared it a misdemeanor to deny to anyone: "The full and equal privileges of inns, public conveyances on land or water, theaters, and other places of public amusement; subject only to the conditions and limitations established by law, and applicable alike to citizens of every race and color."

With withdrawal of federal troops following the election of 1876 that signaled the end of Reconstruction, the Supreme Court rolled back most gains in Civil Rights up to that time. So much so, except for the 13th Amendment, the other Civil War Amendments were severely curtailed, especially during the year 1883, culminating in the "infamous" *Plessey V. Ferguson* decision of 1896 arguing for *separate but equal facilities.* As it has been said, you can lie with statistics, so too, the Court stringently interpreted Civil Rights legislation claiming they were political not social rights or federal not state obligations and so on. In this, it could be argued; Attorney Generals did not act in the interest of the people! Nevertheless, people of goodwill were working to erode the stingy and innocuous interpretation of the law.

Still, the tide was turning, for since the *Dred Scott* Supreme Court decision of 1857 and culmination of Jim Crow legislation in *Plessey v. Ferguson* 1896, a number of legal activities slowly began to erode the bastions of racial suppression that limited full black participation in the constitutional guarantees. Within this mix, we cannot overlook the roles of Frederick Douglass and W.E.B. DuBois and so many others in emergent Civil Rights struggles, even while Booker T. Washington argued for "Gradualism" and technical rather than civil and political rights. Notwithstanding, as an example of important legal and constitutional decisions having an impact on Civil Rights expressions, the following may be mentioned:

The **Civil Rights Act of 1875** gave equal rights to use of inns, theaters, public conveyances, and other facilities as well as including African Americans on

BARACK OBAMA
MASTER OF WASHINGTON DC

juries. As John Newman and John Schmalback in *United States History* (1998: 296) informs: "The law was poorly enforced, however, because by this time, moderate and conservative Republicans had become frustrated with trying to reform an unwilling South – and also were afraid of losing white votes in the North."

Carl Brent Swisher's *Historic Decisions of the Supreme Court* (1958: 92) mentioned black "disillusionment" of prevailing events and in 1883, "the Supreme Court held that the Fourteenth Amendment had not given Congress substantive power to protect civil rights but only to correct abuses by the states. By this decision Congress was relieved of its basic obligation for the protection of civil rights of Negroes. Again the Court showed itself more concerned with the federal balance of power than with substantive rights."

1915 – Repeal of the **Grandfather Clause**. The **Grandfather Clause** was part of the enormous and odious effort designed to deny blacks the right to vote including intimidation and terrorism by organized bands including the KKK, White League and Knights of the White Camelia; Literary Tests requiring blacks to read and interpret any section of the Constitution; Poll Taxes; Property Ownership; and "Jim Crow" segregation on railroads, in restaurants, beaches and schools, and the list goes on, were hallmarks of the times some have labeled "The Age of Terrorism." *The Klansman* by Thomas Dixon Paige and *Rising Tide of Color* by Lothrop Stoddard are excellent sources providing evidence of terrorism against blacks in the 19th and early 20th Centuries. We could also mention *100 Years of Lynchings*. The Democratic Party denied blacks membership and so many blacks did not vote. Where was the Attorney General, in those days of terror and intimidation? Who knows!

1915 – *Guinn v. United* States outlawed the White Primary as unconstitutional
1927 – *Nixon v. Herndon* – argued blacks could participate in Democratic Primaries
1932 – *Nixon v. Condon* – determined the White Primary was unconstitutional
1938 – *Missouri ex Relations Gaines v. Canada* – Creation of separate graduate schools for Negroes.
1944 – *Smith v. Albright* – outlaw *Garvey v. Townsend* (1935), ruling against the White Primary.
1950 – *Sweat v. Painter* – Supreme Court ordered the admission of a Negro to a white college.
1950 – *McLauren v. Oklahoma State Regents* – Ruled the University could not segregate McLauren, a Negro.

FREDERICK MONDERSON

1966 – *Harper v. Virginia State Board of Elections* – Outlawed Poll Taxes
1954 – *Brown v. Board of Education of Topeka, Kansas*, ruled that segregation for purposes of education was unconstitutional.

1957 - Civil Rights Act – Created the Civil Rights Division in the Justice Department designed to enforce all "federal Civil Rights laws which prohibit discrimination, or national origin in the areas of voting, education, employment, and housing in the use of public facilities and public accommodations, and in the administration of federally assisted programs." This also created the Commission on Civil Rights, as Bone (1977: 253) notes "as an independent agency to investigate complaints of civil rights violation, review of government programs and recommend remedial action to the President and Congress."

1960 – Civil Rights Act – again Bone (1977: 253) writes "increased the penalties against any effort to obstruct either voting or the application of court orders designed to remove impediments to voting." Finally, the Justice Department was given the power to appoint "Referees," to "register potential voters where a court had found a 'pattern or practice' of discrimination. Even more, a new law made it a crime to destroy any voting records for 22 months after an election so that full documentary evidence would be available if any complaints come up."

1964 – Civil Rights Act – Can be considered as landmark as the 1954 *Brown V. Board* Case. Passed by President Lynden B. Johnson, its major provisions, according to Bone (1977: 253) were in the areas of:

> Voting
> Public Accommodations
> Public Schools
> Private employment

1965 – Voting Rights Act – Provided that: "The Attorney General, with the concurrence of the Civil Service Commission may replace local registers by voting examiners where literacy and other tests are used and fewer than 50 percent of the voting-age individuals participated in the 1964 election."

"When evidence indicates that literacy tests are being used as a means of discrimination, the federal registrar may suspend them."

1976 – In *McDonald and Laird v. Santa Fe Transportation Company*, the court ruled "Whites as well as blacks were entitled to equal protection against discrimination under the 1870 and 1964 civil rights laws."

BARACK OBAMA
MASTER OF WASHINGTON DC

The state of Florida held the key in determining who became President in 2000. Clearly, while there was much confusion in the form of ballots used, many voters were disfranchised for one reason or another. This practice certainly continued in 2004 and given the numerous complaints raised in 2008, one could plainly see how Barack Obama, as a lawyer, would appoint Eric Holder, an experienced advocate to the Attorney General position to ensure that each vote gets counted.

Barack Obama's Washington, DC Photo 133. Imagine "You and the Mrs." strolling through such foliage in company of such a remarkable structure with its historic significance.

FREDERICK MONDERSON

Barack Obama's Washington, DC Photo 134. It's like the building's just there, in the middle of the street.

Barack Obama's Washington, DC Photo 135. Another uniquely classic building with its colonnades.

BARACK OBAMA
MASTER OF WASHINGTON DC

The brilliance of President Obama may be manifest further because he believed Abraham Lincoln may be turning over in his grave when he realizes how descendants of the Radical Republicans have become timid regarding Civil Rights expressions of black people in America. After all, it was the Republican Party's abandonment of guarding the hard won rights of blacks that caused them to switch party in the 1932 election to vote for Democrat Franklin Roosevelt. Perhaps this is why Barack Obama appointed Eric Holder as Attorney General, among other things, but importantly, so that he would vigilantly guard the enforcement of the cherished attainment of Civil Rights enjoyment. Therefore, this appointment can be added to the mountain of evidence extolling the brilliance of Barack Obama. As such, hold fast to cherished ideals for there is more to come!

Barack Obama's Washington, DC Photo 136. Beautiful greenery between the statue and this nucleus of American political power always reflects a stark contrast.

FREDERICK MONDERSON

"I think that one of the things that we all agree to is that the touchstone for economic policy is, does it allow the average American to find good employment and see their incomes rise; that we can't just look at things in the aggregate, we do want to grow the pie, but we want to make sure that prosperity is spread across the spectrum of regions and occupations and genders and races; and that economic policy should focus on growing the pie, but it also has to make sure that everybody has got opportunity in that system." BARACK OBAMA, New York Times, Apr. 28, 2009

16. OBAMA: THE FIRST 100 DAYS
By

Dr. Fred Monderson

Having conquered that mythical milestone of "The First 100 Days," Barack Obama can now boast to the world he has demonstrated the wherewithal of effective leadership to put his nation on the irreversible course of overcoming the present American and world economic slowdown, while setting a course that will see America soar to heights in economic revitalization; scientific endeavors of experimentation and progress; lessening American reliance on foreign sources of energy while cultivating initiatives in clean energy technology; educational reform; and advancement of foreign policy initiatives; and moral and military leadership that protects and guarantees the nation's democratic strength to similarly symbolize the American eagle and space program, as they soar into the heavens.

In Barack Obama, the old adage that "One man can become a majority" if his truths are firm and his ideals can withstand the vicissitudes of critical scrutiny and malicious intent, finds classical expression in his posture and administrative and legislative efforts and accomplishments thus far. So much accomplished, so much more to come from a man of tremendous brilliance and vision, one has to wonder how we can clone him to get more "bang for our buck!" Now that the mist of campaign rhetoric has cleared into the reality of hard and moral leadership, a transition team seemingly flawless in its efforts, clear sighted policy initiatives and implementation and visible results oriented expectations, the dawn of a new era brings clear skies and calm seas for this vigorous new captain to sail his ship of state into the bright future he envisioned and had the boldness to plan for and craft its manifestation.

BARACK OBAMA
MASTER OF WASHINGTON DC

Malcolm X held, "History is a good teacher!" Since previous presidents have a tendency to examine the actions of past administrations, it stands to reason this is the path the Obama Transition Team took as they prepared to assume power, a nd prepare for the "First 100 Days."

David Gergen's *Eyewitness to Power* (2000:128) provides an important synopsis of the significance of the "First Hundred Days," in that, he considers: "They are the most precious time in the life of a president to defin e who he is and what he is seeking to achieve through his leadership. In those fourteen weeks, more than any other time in his presidency, he sets the stage for his entire stewardship. Before he reaches the White House, both the public and the press have been able to judge him only as an aspiring politician. They judge him on his past. Once he takes the oath, they must take his measure afresh – what is he actually like as president? They judge him on what he will be like in their future. That assessme nt can only begin after he raises his right hand and formally assumes the mantle of leadership. The public's judgment forms in a matter of weeks and, once formed, soon calcifies. It's a matter of public psychology."

Barack Obama's Washington, DC Photo 137. Greenery to accentuate the white marble of the Capital Building.

FREDERICK MONDERSON

Barack Obama's Washington, DC Photo 138. Still another beautiful view.

From the inception, Barack Obama publicly indicated he admired Abraham Lincoln and Franklin D. Roosevelt. Its understandable Lincoln was from Illinois, same as he; and FDR faced a cataclysmic set of circumstances that questioned the survivability of the American nation. However, beyond his admiration, these two presidents have been, perhaps, the most studied because of how they responded to the emergency of their day. With Lincoln it was the Civil War that threatened to tear the nation apart but with Roosevelt, it was the threat to the economic lifeblood of the nation. This development of Roosevelt's age had worldwide repercussions. Therefore, the latter situation is similarly what President Obama inherited and has sought to correct. How he handles this important national economic calamity with its global ramifications is what the nation and ultimately the world will judge him by during those critical 100 days, and even after.

BARACK OBAMA
MASTER OF WASHINGTON DC

Barack Obama's Washington, DC Photo 139. Classic view of the Grand Marble Terrace.

Barack Obama's Washington, DC Photo 140. Still another view of a classic structure.

FREDERICK MONDERSON

Franklin Delano Roosevelt's "First Hundred Days" in 1933 is recounted by David M. Kennedy's *Free From Fear* (New York: Oxford University Press 1999: 131-132) where he describes the new president's response to the Depression he inherited and actions of "Bank Holiday" or closing an important bank that signaled a move against the banking industry. He states: "This drastic action in a key industrial state set off tremors throughout the country. Public apprehension about the crisis in the banking system and disillusionment with bankers were amplified at this moment by revelations emanating from the Senate Banking and Currency Committee hearing room, where committee counsel Ferdinand Pecora was daily extracting scandalous admissions of malfeasance, favoritism, tax avoidance and corruption from the Princes of Wall Street."

In one measure, Congress announced "publishing institutions receiving RFC loans, a policy that amounted to broadcasting an official roster of the shakiest, most endangered banks." Kennedy (2000: 140) continued: "The original Hundred Days forged Roosevelt's principal weapons in the battle against the Depression and shaped much of the New Deal's historical reputation. They have a modified generation of effort to appraise their precise economic and social impact and, perhaps even more vexatious, their collective ideological identity. Like the man who presided over them the First Hundred Days, and beyond them, the New Deal itself, has puzzled historians neatly encompassing definitions of this politically creative era." The principal reason is Roosevelt unleashed a great number of bills, programs and administrations, viz., bank bill, farm bill, agricultural bill, beer bill, budget bill; Federal Emergency Relief Administration (FERA), Agricultural Amendment Act (AAA), Civilian Conservation Corps (CCC), National Industrial Recovery Act (NIRA), and Public Works Administration (PWA), among a whole host of others; and this approach is what scholars and presidents have studied since as characterizing the First 100 Days response.

Gergen, in comparing some of the Presidents (2000: 167) wrote: "Roosevelt had become 'Doctor New Deal,' as he called himself, helping a sick patient recover. Eisenhower slipped away from reporters and flew off to the Korean War front during his transition, becoming a president in search of peace. While Nixon spoke in his inaugural address as a man who wanted to 'Bring us together' at home, he showed quickly that his attentions were elsewhere as he flew off to Europe. People soon realized that he would mostly be a foreign policy president. At the end of a Hundred Days, Americans were less sure what Kennedy was all about, though they liked and admired him, and even less certain about Carter, who left them scratching their heads. Clearly, Reagan had to put his own stamp on his presidency."

BARACK OBAMA
MASTER OF WASHINGTON DC

Equally too, "it was obvious that the First Hundred Days were also a time of great peril, when presidents made some of their biggest mistakes. Kennedy had his Bay of Pigs in the First Hundred Days; Ford had his pardon of Nixon; Carter had a small disaster over a proposal to cut water projects and a bigger one with announcement of his energy plan."

Harry S. Truman succeeded Roosevelt and he assumed the Presidency April 12th, 1945 while becoming embroiled in events of the war's end and transition from war footing to integrating returning veterans into civilian life. While not within the First 100 Days period, but later that year he became associated with the 21 points. Gary W. Reichard in *Politics as Usual: The Age of Truman and Eisenhower* (Illinois: Harlan Davidson, 1988: 3) points out: "Among the twenty-one points he urged were Social Security extension, housing legislation, national health insurance, an increased minimum wage, further regional development programs modeled on the Tennessee Valley Authority (TVA), a full employment bill, and continuation of wartime wage and price controls."

Dwight Eisenhower brought his military experience as Allied Commander in World War II to the political arena, and his success in the 1952 elections came during the Korean War. The price of peace caused him to be in conflict with Congress as to allocation of funding. However, as Eisenhower would later report, his appointment of Earl Warren as Chief Justice of the Supreme Court was "the worst damn thing" he did. This is because Earl Warren presided over the historic *Brown v. Board of Education* decision in 1954, which he as a Republican wasn't really in favor of.

John Kennedy was a unique president, intelligent, young, Catholic and very good at delegating responsibilities to his aides. He met infrequently with his cabinet though the inner circle met with him frequently. He listened to his brother Bobby Kennedy, the Attorney General, most often of all his advisers. Perhaps his biggest blunders were the "Bay of Pigs" invasion, the later steel crisis in 1962 and his forceful integration of James Meredith into the University of Mississippi.

FREDERICK MONDERSON

Lyndon B. Johnson (1963) succeeded to the presidency with the murder of President Kennedy and he gets credit for creating a smooth transition during that time when the nation was in mourning. He created a culture of continuity rather than change. In his first public broadcast he emphasized the "legacy to continue" and this was successful in more ways than one. He successfully pushed much of the legislation Kennedy had proposed, very much within the "legacy to continue."

In the case of President Richard Nixon (1969), the American nation was experiencing a number of issues in terms of economic, political, diplomatic and cultural challenges to its power; yet, Nixon chose to focus more on foreign policy. In *Nixon in the World: American Foreign Relations, 1969-1977,* Edited by Fredrik Logevall and Andrew Preston (2008: 4), they describe the president as thus: "Shy and awkward in person but deftly sure-footed on the world stage, Nixon was a hawkish, staunchly anti-communist politician whose signature adventure was the frequency with which he negotiated with communists." They say further, within these parameters, he was faced with, "The reshaping of U.S. foreign policy, from its traditional roles of liberal interventionism and conservative isolationism into a policy of active but conservative engagement," which was "very much a journey of 'Nixon in the world.'" Therefore, the philosophic outlook which Nixon brought to the office placed him in a precarious position given: "The erosion of American power, the simultaneous ascent of rivals, the truculence of normally loyal allies, and the outbreak of severe international crises made the 1960s and 1970s perhaps the most challenging era for the makers of U.S. foreign policy. Inheriting a disastrous and unpopular war in Southeast Asia, facing myriad crises elsewhere, challenged by a resurgent Soviet Union and a recalcitrant People's Republic of China, burdened with mounting economic difficulties, and finding little help from traditional allies in Europe, Japan, and Canada, it was Nixon who found himself in the eye of this geopolitical hurricane." As such, then, Fredrik Logevall and Andrew Preston (2008: 27) wrote: "Nixon's foreign policy was complex: flexible yet inconsistent, realistic but also ideological, strong as well as weak. Everything was linked to everything else, from nuclear weapons to European communism, from relations with China to domestic politics, and from Vietnam War to Latin America and the Middle East."

David Gergen in *Eyewitness to Power: The Essence of Leadership* (New York: Simon and Schuster, 2000: 125) noted that Gerald Ford inherited "the worst inflation in the country's peacetime history, the highest interest rates in a century, the consequent severe slump in housing, sinking and utterly demoralized securities markets, a stagnant economy with large-scale unemployment in prospect and a worsening international trade and payment position." However, in his comparison with Roosevelt he says of the two presidents, first of Roosevelt: "He showed how essential it is to success that an elected leader demonstrates a mastery of his job in

BARACK OBAMA
MASTER OF WASHINGTON DC

his early weeks in office, especially during the first hundred days. As we see repeatedly, those weeks are more important than any other. While he need not be FDR, he must take great care to build the trust and confidence of the public, and Ford fell down on that one. It is equally essential, especially in a large organization, that someone take charge of the troops. If the leader does not have the temperament to crack the whip, he must empower someone else who will – and fast. Once words spreads that a leader and his team do not have a firm grip, a belief takes hold that he is not up to the job, and it then becomes devilishly difficult to reverse that narrative. On those fronts, too, Ford had trouble, largely because he had been thrust into the presidency without benefit of preparation."

Jimmy Carter took office in January, 1977. Regarding his presidency, Gergen explained "Ever since the New Deal, White House advisers have generally assumed that an incoming president should emulate FDR, overwhelming Congress and spellbinding the country with a flurry of legislative proposals during the First Hundred Days. But as we have now learned from a series of presidents, the importance of the First Hundred Days is not in how many legislative achievements or how much razzle-dazzle a new White House can produce. Jimmy Carter would send forth a blizzard of legislative proposals and new regulations, but neither the press nor the public could make sense of his priorities. The effort backfired. By contrast, as we shall see, Ronald Reagan had a limited, more focused agenda that, combined with other factors, built a much stronger presidency."

William Jefferson Clinton's presidency is today viewed as successful because he brought great economic prosperity to the nation. Perhaps Reagan's economic policies finally began to work, but Clinton built on these and so was able to add several million jobs. However, in the critical First 100 Days he failed miserably because, according to Gergen, Clinton: "failed to create a team that could govern" and he "failed to use the transition to make elaborate plans for his first weeks in office and to mobilize congressional support behind him. He was handicapped in part because his campaign, while politically appealing, did not lay out clear, precise ideas for his presidency." Even more, "he simply would not prepare himself physically for the ordeal ahead." He wasn't sleeping well and he did not condition himself to the many physical and emotional challenges he would encounter. Nevertheless, in time he was able to make the proper adjustments and economically speaking, his presidency was a success.

FREDERICK MONDERSON

George Walker Bush's big challenge came on September 11, 2001, months after his 'First 100 Days' but he was able to transition into that critical period with the assistance of his father who had been President and also CIA head as well as having a lot of connection and pull. He had a "go it alone philosophy," was a "risk taker" and was famous for his one-liners, "bring em' on" and Osama "wanted dead or alive." He ignored the polls and wanted to privatize Social Security and he had some difficulty with Congress and was an avid tax cut proponent. Nevertheless, the terrorist attack changed much and together with the Iraq war, helped define the presidency contributing to his overall negative rating at the end of his second term. He left an enormous budget deficit for his successor Barack Obama!

Barack Hussein Obama assumed the United States Presidency on January 20, 2009 and set to work immediately to address the fast deteriorating domestic economic meltdown in the country, with its impact on the global economy.

It seems to reason, Barack Obama studied and emulated FDR's and other presidents' emergency remedial and long-range reform measures, as well as the idea of infusing enormous sums into the economy. In the case of the present crisis as in so much of his march to the presidency, Obama has shown he recognizes and focuses on what is important. The first significant move, in that critical "honeymoon period" was getting Congress to release the remainder of President Bush's bank bailout TARP funds, then Obama was able to get his Stimulus Bill passed by his Democratic majority in Congress. He appointed a Middle Eastern Envoy to work the Palestinian-Israeli Conflict, dispatched Secretary of State Hillary Clinton to Asia to inform China, India, Japan and Indonesia, America considers them important players in the global economy and political stage. He announced intentions to close Guantanamo Bay prison, he negated many of Bush's Executive Orders, and unleashed a great many plans to address homeowner foreclosures, toxic assets in banks to enable their re-issuance of credit, problems in the automobile industry, emissions, health care, education, jobs creation in infrastructure repairs and even spoke out against exorbitant bonuses by big investment firms. Next, he visited Canada, then Europe to attend the G-20 Economic Summit, NATO Conference and Commemoration and made an address to the Turkish Parliament. Throughout these efforts President Barack Obama demonstrated extraordinary poise, a cool demeanor, a tremendous grasp of the issues and an excellent *modus operandi* of explaining his actions to the American people who love straight talk and old-fashioned values.

Next the President attended the Summit of Latin American nations where he handled the question of sanctions against Cuba, relations with Venezuela and the combined nations' response to climate change, narcotics flowing to North America, energy and trade. Even more important, regarding the staffing of his

BARACK OBAMA
MASTER OF WASHINGTON DC

administration, while it suffered a few bumps in the road, it took off and successfully unfolded, that is the more than 2000 positions in the White House. However, there's more to that and as Gergen explains: "As Thomas Mann and Norman Ornstein have pointed out, 'The task of staffing a new administration is staggering: more than 6,000 presidential appointments, including roughly 600 Senate-confirmed cabinet and subcabinet members .... If appointments are not made well before the inauguration, they can be delayed for months into the presidency, creating uncertainly in agencies and gaps in policymaking." This is what President Obama had to contend with and from the looks of things his team did a splendid job, even though he is still filling some positions.

Throughout all this, whether his actions at home or his demonstrated abilities abroad, Barack Obama has certainly changed America's image of itself and how others viewed it abroad. Clearly his actions over these First 100 Days are indicative President Obama is a true patriot with the best intentions and the best interests of America at heart. This is seen in every action he takes and that is why his percentage of approval is so high in the eyes of the people.

Hazel Trice Edney's "First 100 Days: Civil Rights Leaders give Obama an 'A'" in *Daily Challenge* (April 21, 2009: 2) which gives the following as Obama accomplishments in registering their grade.

His immediate confrontation with the nation's failing economy amidst which he now sees "glimmers of hope;"

The reversal of a string of anti-union executive orders issued by the Bush Administration;

The establishment of a Middle Class Working Families Task Force;

His stated views on the closing of the controversial Guantanamo Bay lockup for alleged terrorists, though this is still to be done;

His tour of Europe with First Lady Michelle Obama, which raised good will for America abroad during the G-20 economic conference;

His trip to Mexico with hopes of stopping violent drug cartels and preventing them from entering the U.S;

FREDERICK MONDERSON

His reaching out to Cuba for the renewed relationship, supported by the Congressional Black Caucus;

A new commitment to pour millions of dollars into the prevention and awareness of HIV/AIDS in America.

The grade given on the economy by many people is *Incomplete* because it's a work in progress and so far the results are mixed.

Essentially then, and taking an objective view, President Obama had inherited a number of problems that have created a debilitating effect on the American psyche, economics, foreign policy, global perception. Applying a wonderfully constructed managerial team and style, he set about treating the ailment at home and revamping America's image abroad. The litany of bills and programs he introduced has had a terrific effect on the perception people now have of him. They realize he inherited these problems and is doing his best to solve them.

Thus, the first 100 days of President Barack Obama is unlike any faced by other presidents because the times and circumstances were different, but not altogether dissimilar. To understand this statement, we recognize all comparisons of this nature refer to the Franklin D. Roosevelt Administration during the Great Depression as a yardstick. However, while President Obama's first months in office are probably as grand a scale as that of FDR; the latter probably did not face many of the issues Obama has had to. FDR's challenge was primarily economic, while Barack Obama's is much more multi-faceted, viz., FDR had cheap energy, not so with President Obama; the threat of Nazi extremism had begun in far away Europe, while modern terrorists attacked America and remain a threat; FDR did not face World War II until much later, while Obama inherited two wars; in foreign policy, FDR dealt mainly with Empires, Obama with nations; FDR's "global challenge" did not exist while Obama's is real; FDR probably did not have to deal with radical elements at home, while Obama is threatened by radical white racists and their cohorts; and so on. Therefore, for future comparison of Presidential strategies during the First 100 Days, President Barack H. Obama will become the new yardstick for the multi-faceted manner in which he attacked the multitudinous economic and other woes he inherited.

All this notwithstanding, among the many issues this first African American President faced was the composition of his Cabinet which reflected a diversity of

BARACK OBAMA
MASTER OF WASHINGTON DC

the American cultural demography; and included many women in very high profile positions in his administration, probably more so than any other president and most important there were black women visibly in positions of power. He visited 12 states to promote his plans and policies. Naturally the most pressing problem he faced was economic and he attacked it like a whirlwind, by deploying a great many strategies including securing the remainder of President Bush's TARP money, passing a Stimulus Bill, passing the Lilly Ledbetter Bill giving women equal work for equal pay, all while surrounding himself with some of the greatest minds America could muster in economics, energy, science, and so on. He passed some 14 bills that tackled jobs, infrastructure repairs, housing foreclosures, the automobile industry woes, banks issuance of credit and critique of Wall Street bonus. Turning to Foreign Policy, he appointed a Middle Eastern Envoy to jump start peace talks in that region, appointed and deployed Hilary Clinton to work her magic first in Asia and then elsewhere, stated his position on nuclear non-proliferation, made overtures to Iran and declared the United States is not at war with Islam. He declared his intention to drawdown in Iraq. Then he went abroad to Canada, Europe, Mexico and then Trinidad and Tobago. In all, he made foreign visits to 9 countries where he met 27 heads of state; he demonstrated tremendous grasp of the issues; displayed a remarkable intellectual acumen as he laid out his vision of the future for America and the world in news conferences, town hall meetings and parliamentary addresses.

Some have held, the grade President Obama received for his 100 days in office, focusing on the economy, is based on a person's politics. For example, Rudy Giuliani, former Mayor of New York City and Republican Presidential Candidate in 2008, while admitting to the genius of Barack Obama, equally held, the President is taking the nation, "way, way, in the wrong direction." Such a vote reflects the negativity and non-cooperation of Republicans in general. However, this is not the direction most people believe the country is presently heading and the confidence they expressed in Barack Obama, is based in the rising confidence the nation now has in the President, certainly in his First 100 Days, which provides hope for the future.

FREDERICK MONDERSON

Barack Obama's Washington, DC Photo 140a. Another view, from the side, of the Bank of America building affiliated with PNC Bank.

The Atlanta Georgia native "philosopher" Walter Brown believes after what has been done to him, "The Lord Almighty is on Barack Obama's side!"

"I think that one of the things that we all agree to is that the touchstone for economic policy is, does it allow the average American to find good employment and see their incomes rise; that we can't just look at things in the aggregate, we do want to grow the pie, but we want to make sure that prosperity is spread across the spectrum of regions and occupations and genders and races; and that economic policy should focus on growing the pie, but it also has to make sure that everybody has got opportunity in that system." BARACK OBAMA, New York Times, Apr. 28, 2009

17.　　PRESIDENT OBAMA, 100 DAYS, AGAIN
By
Dr. Fred Monderson

President Barack Obama has reached the second significant artificial milestone in his young administration, the second 100-day mark; and, much unlike the first 100-days, his forward progress, while just as great, has not been as universally

BARACK OBAMA
MASTER OF WASHINGTON DC

supported and accepted. He has, however, vigorously waged unrelenting strategies making strides in both domestic and foreign relations policies and practices; but, as some say, his honeymoon with the media seems over and thus, he keeps getting lots of "knuckle sandwiches," while the progress he is making is generally unnoticed and unheralded.

Despite criticisms by Republican lawmakers who offer no cohesive constructive plan on the domestic front, the $785 billion American Recovery and Reinvestment Act or Stimulus Bill was not designed to be disbursed over a six month, but a two-year period. As such, the Obama Administration has doled out some stimulus funds that have helped retain jobs of police officers, firemen and has funded some "shovel ready" road construction projects. Vice-President Joe Biden has always been accused of speaking out of turn; yet, with his insider knowledge, he was able, at a public meeting, to declare the "stimulus a success."

At the milestone, CNN graded the President's handling of the economy among several areas of his involvement, and he got the best grade of all categories on this. There is no question President Obama instituted confidence in the American people. The respected adviser to presidents and CNN Commentator David Gergen gave the President a grade of B+ on the category saying: "The economy was going over a cliff. He stopped it and brought us back." Donna Brazile, Presidential Campaign Manager and CNN Commentator thought the President's strategy represented the "Rescue, Recovery and Reinvest" approach, and now the reinvestment part will soon unfold. Others were not as kind.

This notwithstanding, and contrary to some skeptics, the President set the bar high and set about working to rectify the situation because he realized the gravity of the situation facing America. Yet, in commentary, many would say he still underestimated the problem and that the $785 billion stimulus was too small, talks circulated such as that of the "financial guru" Warren Buffett of the need for a second stimulus. Nevertheless, the President challenged Wall Street to clean up its act; Federal Reserve Chairman Ben Bernanke submitted more rigorous and stringent economic policies; and Treasury Secretary Timothy Geithner and the Council of Economic Advisers tacked issues in housing foreclosures, the banking industry's use of TARP's funds and issuance of credit to consumers and small businesses to unclog spending and encourage investments.

While the President challenged Wall Street and bankers over the size of their bonuses, he also took on the car industry, forcing General Motors and Chrysler

FREDERICK MONDERSON

into bankruptcy from which GM rapidly emerged to solvency. The "cash for clunkers" program advocated during the Presidential Campaign inserted some $3 billion of government credit to trade in old for new vehicles has proved a successful venture. For the initial $3 billion consumers may have spent some $20-$25 billion indicating a rise in commitment to credit spending and confidence in the nation's financial future.

While some 10 percent of stimulus money has already been spent and significant amounts projected for the fall, it stands to reason plans have mapped out areas of the most intense focus for upcoming spending, perhaps in school construction and upgrade; refurbishing of roads, ports, tunnels and waterways; research and development in clean energy initiatives; and repairs to transportation structures including creation of a high speed rail development project as the President publicly outlined.

With the upgrade of schools, emphasis has been placed on modernizing science and math labs with state of the art technology; hiring, retraining and upgrading pay scales of teachers to improve teaching techniques, strategies and results. Without a doubt President Obama's economic techniques have stabilized the housing foreclosure market, contributing to the rise in new construction work and job loss seems to have stabilized with unemployment insurance picking up the slack, these efforts fueling the uptick of home purchases with concomitant rise in home values.

Iraq and Afghanistan are undoubtedly important issues in the President's foreign policy undertakings. Having withdrawn American troops from principal cities and now they are reduced to supporting Iraqi troops, with the spike in recent bombings as the government has moved to restore a sense of normalcy, the US President awaits word from his ground commanders as to phased withdrawal from Iraq over the next two years. The surge of American troops in Afghanistan has rescued a volatile situation, stemmed a pending retreat of that government in wake of an escalating Taliban resurgence halted in face of US Marines' advance enabling normalcy to permit national elections. Again, awaiting word from ground commanders, the President mulls further increases in combat troops to Afghanistan.

BARACK OBAMA
MASTER OF WASHINGTON DC

Barack Obama's Washington, DC Photo 141. Seems like sixteen sets of two columns.

Barack Obama's Washington DC Photo 142. Notice how these Doric columns are paired as if on review.

FREDERICK MONDERSON

Barack Obama's Washington, DC Photo 143. A break from the norm, regular people on foot on the street with a dome in the background.

President Obama's foreign policy initiatives go beyond Iraq and Afghanistan, to include unrelenting pursuit of Al Qaeda in various theaters of operation including cooperation with Pakistan. He has made significant appearances and speeches in Canada, Mexico, Trinidad, England, France, Germany, Turkey, Egypt and Ghana, outlining America's military, nuclear, economic and scientific policy positions and goals. He has been ably assisted by Secretary of State Hillary Clinton in Asia, Africa and Europe; Ambassador Holbrooke in Iraq and Afghanistan and Senator Mitchell in the Middle East. While Mr. Obama focused on Latin America, NATO and the Western Alliance, he improved America's image and restored confidence in its global leadership. Major players as China, Japan and Russia have become effective partners in the global economic rescue and are working against extremists and nuclear proliferation.

The President's one-two strategy in Turkey and Cairo has created much goodwill between America and the Muslim world, while defending the right to relentlessly pursue extremists as Al Qaeda who threaten Americans but also encourage amicable relations among nations of various continents, cultures and religions. Continuing to focus attention on the Arab-Israeli conflict fed by the Palestinian-Israeli problem, as he has done from day one, the President has won kudos for his sincere efforts to find a solution to the Middle East unrest fueled by military threats, extremist behaviors and the debilitating consequences of poverty in a

BARACK OBAMA
MASTER OF WASHINGTON DC

region where people only want to live normal lives with a view to providing a better future for their children.

One of the most disingenuous charges leveled against President Obama is that he is "doing too much," too fast, too soon. Such claimants are blinded by their obstructionist behaviors designed to create a climate of fear, intimidation and, as some have dedicated their efforts to bring about resultant failure of the Obama Administration. Unfortunately, as Edmund Burke has pointed out, "Little minds and empire go ill together." The reason the President is attempting so much is because the problems are so many. The well-known African American scholar Dr. Joy De Gruy is quoted as saying "He in the frame cannot see the picture." This appropriately applies to Republicans who, wallowing in the mess they created, and refusing to take a step back, cannot, as the cliché goes, "see the forest for the trees" or the mess they created. Thus, blinded, they are unable to understand why President Obama must clean up the mess before its odor stinks up the whole damn place.

Barack Obama's Washington, DC Photo 144. People in motion in vicinity of the Castle.

FREDERICK MONDERSON

"We should be more modest in our belief that we can impose democracy on a country through military force. In the past, it has been movements for freedom from within tyrannical regimes that have led to flourishing democracies; movements that continue today. This doesn't mean abandoning our values and ideals; wherever we can, it's in our interest to help foster democracy through the diplomatic and economic resources at our disposal. But even as we provide such help, we should be clear that the institutions of democracy – free markets, a free press, a strong civil society – cannot be built overnight, and they cannot be built at the end of a barrel of a gun. And so we must realize that the freedoms FDR once spoke of – especially freedom from want and freedom from fear – do not just come from deposing a tyrant and handing out ballots; they are only realized once the personal and material security of a people is ensured as well." BARACK OBAMA, speech, Nov. 20, 2006

18. OUR LEADER GOES ABROAD
By

Dr. Fred Monderson

Our leader, President Barack Obama has made his first official visit across the big pond to represent the United States of America in Europe. While he previously visited Canada, this was just next door, to a staunch U.S. ally, and the current global economic downturn had been nowhere near its current proportions. In addition, there President Obama, how nice it sounds, sat across from a single head of state, with customary friendlies waving all the bells and whistles. Conversely, now our guy heads to the G-20 Economic Summit in London comprising the world's most powerful economies, along a road strewn with professional demonstrators, entrenched, prepared and his arrival is anticipated. In this milieu, where attending members represent the richest nations of the world whose constituencies are hurting and the entire globe is aflame in the meltdown, President Barack Obama will walk the gauntlet of great expectations and try to convince many people he can fix the US and global economy. This is indeed a tall order.

To recall, less than a year ago, amidst the Presidential Campaign, Senator Obama was vigorously struggling to weather the storm generated by his opponents on both sides of the aisle, Democratic and Republican. He was accused of being "inexperienced" in everything but particularly foreign policy. As a result, Senator

BARACK OBAMA
MASTER OF WASHINGTON DC

Obama went into his "school bag," announced his intent to travel, visited Iraq and Afghanistan and then on to Europe. There he received "rock star" treatment, particularly in Germany and Britain where he is now attending the G-20 Summit. Without a doubt, his "going to school" to shore up his weakness and coming out stronger, was much to the chagrin of his opponents. This strategy as demonstrated in subsequent contests proved to be successful, and, well, the rest is history.

Barack Obama successfully won the Presidency by waging a superb campaign that involved consensus building, unrelentingly staying on message, deploying his surrogates and effectively and efficiently mobilizing an enormous internet database to get out the vote and later to support his policies. Meanwhile, his economic team was quietly laying the groundwork of his economic vision to stem the hemorrhage in the nation's economy, housing, energy dependence; then bandage and treat the malady through financial infusion and finally be able to face the future with well-thought-out policies designed to stimulate infrastructure refurbishment, stem foreclosures and generate construction developments in the housing market, creatively engineer new energy initiatives, build and equip schools with new technologies to encourage teaching strategies to significantly improve American education and science, thus setting the nation on a path to a strong future our offsprings will inherit and be proud of.

Barack Obama's Washington, DC Photo 145. Ionic capitals adorn this colonnaded building. Notice how the Ionic capital seems as if a feminine hairstyle while the Doric is more robust or manly.

FREDERICK MONDERSON

Amazingly, President Obama, riding an extremely high wave of popularity, was able to command from Congress, within a relatively short period, an enormous financial largesse consisting of the second part of President Bush's "Wall Street Bailout Funds" and the passage of a whopping Stimulus Bill. All of this he did, after he had put together a fabulous team of economic, security, and foreign policy people in positions and with professionals to head the various departments of his new administration. In addition, the President appointed a Middle Eastern Envoy to tackle the festering Israeli-Palestine-Middle East question, announced his intention to close Guantanamo Bay Prison housing captured terror suspects, and dispatched Secretary of State Hillary Clinton to visit China, India, Japan and Indonesia. He spoke out against waste, greed and corruption on Wall Street as well as being critical of the bonus mess on that financial well-spring and sought to rescue the auto industry. Meanwhile he signaled his intention to confront rising health care costs and announced his housing plan to rescue that troublesome industry. Even further, he announced a plan to rid banks of toxic assets and stimulate their issuance of credit. All the while, his ratings have remained high, more so than many popular modern presidents.

Barack Obama's Washington, DC Photo 146. There's nothing more majestic than to see columns stretching across the broad front of a building.

With these many accomplishments to his credit, President Barack Obama has stepped out onto the world stage, the lion's den, where friendly, neutral and opposing heads of state await his arrival, comprising an entourage of 500 persons including their own cooks and 200 Secret Service personnel. However, this time

BARACK OBAMA
MASTER OF WASHINGTON DC

there are tremendous differences, as the President heads across the Atlantic Ocean, to when he traveled previously. Then he was an "inexperienced" Senator from Illinois; now he is a creative, concerned, and hard-working new American President, head of state, and leader of the "Western Alliance," who can now boast of the many initiatives he has taken to rescue his nation. Whereas on the first trip he headed to Iraq and Afghanistan, then on to Western Europe; now he heads to the United Kingdom for the G-20 Economic Summit and will spend Wednesday and Thursday there listening intently to the various world leaders' positions on the world's economic ills. Then it's on to France for a NATO meeting on Friday. On Saturday in Germany he will celebrate the 60th Anniversary of the founding of the North Atlantic Treaty Organization, and then attend a summit of European Union leaders in Prague, the Czechoslovakia Republic. Monday he will fly to Ankara, Turkey to make another tremendously importing speech to the Muslim world and confer with students in a round table there.

This trip is still more symbolic and substantive than his first in that the President and his wife Michelle will sit down with Her Majesty, Queen Elizabeth, for tea and a state dinner. However, within the G-20 configuration the President will meet with 3 principal groups to get their leaders on board to support his Stimulus Plan. These are the reliable allies of Britain, Canada, Japan and Australia. Then he will contend with Chinese power games regarding the dollar and the Russian challenge in oil and energy. France, Germany, India, Spain and Brazil have rejected his stimulus option calling for tighter regulation of banks and financial firms.

Nevertheless, the greatest asset President Obama will be traveling with, that he did not have previously, is his wife Michelle, empowered as First Lady of the United States. Oh, the power and majesty of a beautiful, intelligent, creative, fashionable and powerfully empowered black woman; first among equals among the great women of the world, with a twist. After all, France's President Sarkozy's wife is a supermodel. The German Chancellor is a woman, Angela Merkel and the Chinese Premier Hu Jintao's wife could boast my husband's constituency is the largest in the world. Notwithstanding, Obama will be able to unleash his beautifully sparkling and fashionable "Fly in the Buttermilk" wife, who can hold her own with the best of them and at the state dinner in London, Queen Elizabeth will have to think, "I thought I was the most powerful woman in the room." Then when Queen Elizabeth reaches over to compliment Michele Obama on her beautiful outfit, in that customarily majestic royal demeanor, our First Lady will respond, "Why thank you, Your Majesty, do come visit us some time, we're re-doing the White House." And, while the Queen's butter melts, she'll simply say, "I'll be there!"

FREDERICK MONDERSON

"The best judge of whether or not a country is going to develop is how it treats its women. If it's educating its girls, if women have equal rights, that country is going to move forward. But if women are oppressed and abused and illiterate, then they're going to fall behind." BARACK OBAMA, Ladies' Home Journal, Sep. 2008

19. MICHELLE OBAMA: BOSS WOMAN
By
Dr. Fred Monderson

Michelle is the boss' woman, I mean wife; but in her own right, she's a "boss woman!" Intelligent, professional, beautiful, caring, concerned, fashionable, she married Barack Obama and they have two children, daughters; and has obviously demonstrated the fact she's a loving mother, also daughter, sister and wife and partner. She held her own as an attorney, before and during their marriage, and burst on to the national political scene after her husband declared his candidacy for the Presidency of the United States. While some believe she may have made a misstep in the beginning of the campaign, the "hero-haters" waded into her with the most critical commentary imaginable trying to besmirch her personality and character. But, when the then Senator Obama looked deep into the TV camera and said pointedly, "If you're listening, stay off my wife," they got the message! Then this surrogate political wife of the now President, took to the campaign trail to represent and sell Barack Obama, and in the process the people got a good look at the woman who would end up as the first African-American First Lady of the United States, in 2009.

When Barack Obama won the Presidency and was sworn in as President, Michelle stood there proudly with him, the symbol of the quintessential and successful black woman, mother with her daughters, and the loving wife. From then on she emerged as a partner with a professional outlook that took a driver's seat in praising and selling her husband, President Barack Obama.

Now, if we backtrack and follow her from that night of the President's acceptance speech in Chicago, after being declared the winner; the beauty of the accompanying First Lady began to enhance the image of Barack as she stood

BARACK OBAMA
MASTER OF WASHINGTON DC

there majestically in that red and black dress, as wife, mother, and beautiful partner. Then the people began to identify with her as an individual whose attributes and characteristics can be emulated! Possessing poise, articulate and well dressed, Michelle had come into her own! Even more, fully equipped, she came fully equipped! From there, through the Transition Period, her first visit to the White House, the domain she would now preside over, her reception and wonderful identification with the equally beautiful and outgoing First Lady, Laura Bush, signaled the baton, in that role, was being passed to capable hands.

Throughout that period up to Inauguration Day, Michelle Obama carried herself as a class act. On that historic day she rose above the stratosphere to bask and share in the success and historic moment and the tremendous challenges that lay ahead. There she stood in that yellowish ensemble by Cuban-American Isabel Toledo consisting of dress with matching overcoat and leather gloves, and holding the Lincoln Bible as Barack raised his right hand to take the Oath of Office. No one made the connection, but perhaps Chief Justice Roberts fumbled with the Oath because he was blinded in the corners of his eye by the brilliance of the stunning black woman standing in front of him. Some have tried, particularly English writers, to compare her to Jackie Kennedy who wore similar colors on equally momentous occasions and possessed the same graceful characteristics. Each in their own Solar System, Michelle is the star of her own Galaxy!

Throughout that day, during the swearing in ceremony in front of that tumultuous crowd, in the first official visit to the White House as First Lady, along the path of the Presidential Parade, Michelle dazzled in the bright Washington sun. Later that evening, Michelle stepped out on the arm of her man wearing that fabulous gown, Amy Diluna of the New York *Daily News* of January 21, p. 2, described as "a white, beaded, one-shoulder confection from Manhattan designer Jason Wu, embroidered with fluttering appliqués." There the new President stood in white tie and tails, and held his fabulous wife in gentle embrace, as the beautiful couple danced at the Inaugural Ball to the sounds of Beyonce's rendition of Etta James's "At Last, My Love has come around." How beautiful the first couple looked as they indulged in the aura of that historic occasion. The moment lingers! Then the Obamas danced through the night, attending in all, ten Balls held in different locations throughout the capital, and Michelle was no ways tired!

FREDERICK MONDERSON

Barack Obama's Washington, DC Photo 147. Many-sided building with columns.

Barack Obama's Washington, DC Photo 148. Notice unlike most with this large number of columns, these capitals are of the ionic form as opposed to the Doric type.

BARACK OBAMA
MASTER OF WASHINGTON DC

Barack Obama's Washington, DC Photo 149. Washington Police are always on duty!

Once day one was over, the new political fashionista set about her own agenda of welcoming people to the White House, starting a community garden, being a wonderful Host for **Black History Month**, allowing normal people to get a view of her new mansion, being a source of support for military families, and the demeanor of this fantastical looking beautiful woman began to make us all proud! The next thing she did that was remarkable, as perhaps no other First Lady did, was to visit each Department of her husband's Cabinet, to familiarize herself with and praise the personnel for their service, remind them of expectations and helped sell her husband's agenda efforts to tackle problems facing the nation; equally reminding all that his success depends on their continued support. Granted Firs t Ladies are given significant responsibilities of social work, but this seems the first time a First Lady has taken such a hands on approach in direct contact with all of these agencies or departments. With this much accomplished and even more set in motion, Michelle Obama next stepped onto the world stage spotlight.

FREDERICK MONDERSON

On President Obama's first trip overseas to attend the G-20 Economic Summit in London, England, with projected visits to France, Germany, Czechoslovakia, and Turkey much was riding on this meeting. Naturally, his ace in the hole as always is his beautiful wife, Michelle who accompanied him. The trip across the Atlantic aboard Air Force One, with an entourage of some 500 persons including more than 200 security personnel, cooks and the media, was certainly an opportunity for both to prepare for the public scrutiny when they arrived at the first leg of their journey at Heathrow Airport.

Some believed, from this part of the journey, while the President was concerned with diplomatic matters, he also had to be concerned, in the eyes of the people, the "Mighty Michelle," did not upstage him. After all, he was engaged with economic and political matters and she through fashion appears to have exuded a shining example of a creatively cultured and intelligent international fashion icon. We are told she wore a Thakoun ivory grey grain-trimmed coat aboard Air Force One. Then she changed and stepped off the plane in London wearing a modern chartreuse dress by Jason Wu, the Taiwan born fashion designer, with a black belt and a Michael Korduster coat. For their visit to Number 10 Downing Street to meet the British Prime Minister Gordon Brown and his wife Sarah, she wore a mint green lacquered skirt and a beaded cardigan by J. Crew.

This "Black Star's" versatility showed even more as she attended a tea reception with Queen Elizabeth at Buckingham Palace, where they were obviously briefed on royal protocols. The tabloids splashed all over the picture of the Queen, Prince Philip, Barack Obama and Michelle Obama. There the Queen was seen looking "pretty in pink," while Michelle wore a black and white ensemble with a bow at the dress' waistline and accompanying white pearls that seemingly contrasted. This allowed the Queen's colors to appear more dominant. These two important women blended so well, they embraced willingly and a controversy ensued regarding protocol for touching the Queen. Some commentators pointed out, the Queen was so taken with Michelle, she initiated the embrace and felt comfortable doing so. She was even heard telling the First Lady, "We must keep in touch!" Such an invitation is given only to someone whose presence creates an air of comfort for this longest reigning monarch who has met 10 United States Presidents.

As Michelle would tell young students at an all-girls school in London, my story is a remarkable one. Imagine a young black girl, a descendant of slaves, from the West Side of Chicago, growing up and becoming First Lady of the United States, coming to London, visiting Queen Elizabeth, the "Soul of the British nation," embracing with her and being told, "Let's stay in touch. Come back and see me!" Only a "Boss Woman" can carry on like this!

BARACK OBAMA
MASTER OF WASHINGTON DC

Barack Obama's Washington, DC Photo 150. What a beautiful work of art.

FREDERICK MONDERSON

Barack Obama's Washington, DC Photo 151. What beautiful architectural contrast.

BARACK OBAMA
MASTER OF WASHINGTON DC

Barack Obama's Washington, DC Photo 152. Colonnades can come in various sizes.

FREDERICK MONDERSON

Jane Ridley, writing in the New York *Daily News* "Brits go bloomin' wild over First Lady," quotes the English fashion writer and broadcaster Caryn Franklin who wrote "Michele is a statuesque woman with great style who knows how to dazzle." She continued, "Her clothes aren't always expensive, but they epitomize class. She always dresses very appropriately, very cleverly. She looks friendly and accessible." Even more, the commentator explained. "She is a successful mother of two and though she doesn't have the perfect body or face, she's fantastically attractive. Michele has proved that it is possible to look incredible and be a powerful operator."

Later while the President was attending to official business at the G-20 Summit Michelle attended a dinner for the wives of the visiting heads of state at 10 Downing Street. There she stood next to the Harry Potter author J.K. Rowling, British Olympic gold Medalist Kelly Holmes, and Naomi Campbell sat nearby. Within the company of these powerful women of the world, Michelle Obama was comfortably at home, "one of the girls!" She continued to give a razzle dazzling performance everywhere she has gone. Even more, Michelle is a powerful promoter of women's rights. She is truly interested in empowering women, at home and abroad.

The wherewithal Michelle Obama has displayed in London will be carried on to France, Germany and Czechoslovakia and will no doubt be continued, when she returns home, putting to shame American critics the likes of Juan Williams. Imagine a black American commentator could be so disrespectfully critical of Michele and conversely a white Englishman, Richard Quest of London describes Michelle as a "lively bundle of energy that people are identifying with. She has such freshness and receives rock star treatment."

So impressive in London, she received a rating of 72 there compared to that of her husband who got a 69 and the reception in France was just as breathtaking. Some believe Michelle had a higher people rating in France than her husband, the French President Sarkozy and his wife. This international praise and recognition probably makes the likes of Juan Williams squirm under their rocks!

Notwithstanding, all this and more we have seen in such short time with much more to come. Clearly, "Mighty Michelle" is a wonderful breath of fresh air, who carries well the banner of her responsibility as First Lady, but is also friend and protector of her husband, President Barack Obama.

BARACK OBAMA
MASTER OF WASHINGTON DC

"I have studied the Constitution as a student; I have taught it as a teacher; I have been bound by it as a lawyer and legislator. I took an oath to preserve, protect and defend the Constitution as Commander-in-Chief, and as a citizen, I know that we must never – ever – turn our back on its enduring principles for expedience sake. I make this claim not simply as a matter of idealism. We uphold our most cherished values not only because doing so is right, but because it strengthens our country and keeps us safe. Time and again, our values have been our best national security asset – in war and peace; in times of ease and in eras of upheaval. Fidelity to our values is the reason why the United States of America grew from a small string of colonies under the writ of an empire to the strongest nation in the world. It is the reason why enemy soldiers have surrendered to us in battle, knowing they'd receive better treatment from America's armed forces than from their own government. It is the reason why America has benefited from strong alliances that amplified our power, and drawn a sharp and moral contrast with our adversaries. It is the reason why we've been able to overpower the iron fist of fascism, outlast the iron curtain of communism, and enlist free nations and free people everywhere in common cause and common effort. From Europe to the Pacific, we have been a nation that has shut down torture chambers and replaced tyranny with the rule of law. That is who we are. And where terrorists offer only the injustice of disorder and destruction, America must demonstrate that our values and institutions are more resilient than a hateful ideology." BARACK OBAMA, speech, May 21, 2009

20. THE CONFIDENCE OF BARACK OBAMA
By
Dr. Fred Monderson

From the time he appeared on the nation's scene, in the Primary and Presidential campaigns, his approach to the economic problems facing the nation, his visit to Canada and now his first Economic Summit in Europe, NATO, etc., Mr. Obama has demonstrated a confidence in his posture and problem solving methodology that is the hallmark of leadership which inspires; and importantly, he looks to the

FREDERICK MONDERSON

future in a positive manner, while putting in place policies, despite the bleak outlook, that will prove fruitful in the long run.

The ideal leader, whether in tranquil or challenging times, must demonstrate and project a positive and confident attitude, while executing constructive policy decisions to address any perilous situation so as to convince and encourage the nation as it looks forward to constructive changes in the times and their circumstances. Clearly, a confident attitude by the leader goes a long way in reassuring his followers there is light at the end of the tunnel, because this view is reflected in the attitude and mannerism coming from the top or front.

That positive outlook, as similarly construed by John Milton (1608-1674) believed, "Confidence imparts a wondrous inspiration to its possessor. It bears him on in security, either to meet no danger, or to find matter of glorious trial." Dr. Davies, perhaps more reflecting on Biblical stories, sees in confidence a divinely begotten attribute, for he states "Let one but have his confidence, and then he will not put on the strong armor of Saul, nor be afraid of the flashing sword of Goliath; he needs only the sling and stone.' However, as Francois Due de La Rochefoucauld (1613-1680) gave a utilitarian argument in the statement, "Confidence always gives pleasure to the man in whom it is placed," conversely Dr. Robert South (1634-1713) explained "Society is built on trust, and trust upon confidence of one another's integrity." This then is the relationship Barack Obama has endeavored to build with his constituency, the American people.

In retrospect, the then Senator Barack Obama must have possessed a tremendous amount of confidence to first contemplate a run for President; launch a campaign against unimaginable odds and relentlessly and confidently wage a positive one even when things seemed very bleak; yet, he preserved, extolling his supporters to keep the faith, their feet to the metal, and lo and behold, Mr. Obama went from win to win and on to final victory, becoming the 44th and first African American President of the United States.

Throughout the Presidential Campaign, Mr. Obama hammered away at how the then President George Bush mismanaged the economy. In retrospect, he was right; but, when Senator John McCain, parroting George Bush said, "The American economy is fundamentally sound," Obama saw an opening and rammed it like a "Mack Truck." However, when Obama assumed the Presidency after January 20, and became familiar with all the "inside information," the correct assessment of the American economy painted a dire picture. Now, inheriting this gloomy legacy, the confidence of Barack Obama, which had been growing in the unfolding last two years, coupled with the benefits of surrounding himself with some of the best American minds, his strong suit grew tremendously and was projected in his efforts to communicate with the American people.

BARACK OBAMA
MASTER OF WASHINGTON DC

As we look closely, we see confidence reflected in his town hall meetings, press conferences, the address to Congress, wooing Representatives and Senators and campaign style meetings with the people whenever he could get away from Washington to make these open air, hand shaking contacts, that so characterized his campaign. This is even more so when he is beside or with his beautiful wife Michelle. Nevertheless, despite the somber state of the American economy, as he went about his Presidential duties, despite the non-cooperation of his particularly Republican adversaries, the President strove to project confidence so his people can also be confident in their dealing and expectations. Similarly, Ann Eleanor Roosevelt believed: "You gain strength, courage and confidence by every experience in which you really stop to look fear in the face. You are able to say to yourself, 'I lived through this horror. I can take the next thing that comes along.'... You must do the thing you think you cannot do!" Equally, James B. Simpson's *Contemporary Quotations* (1964: 34) mentions Jack Bell of the Associated Press who described Robert A. Taft's manner in handling political crises, as "with all the confidence of a man dialing his own telephone number."

Barack Obama's Washington, DC Photo 153. Ronald Reagan Building and International Trade with its paired Doric capitals.

FREDERICK MONDERSON

Barack Obama's Washington, DC Photo 154. These buildings seem to fit so neatly together.

Barack Obama's Washington, DC Photo 155. Here we have the third type of capital, composite.

As Mr. Obama unfolded the various strategies he envisioned would be required to deal with the conundrum facing the United States domestically and in foreign policy, he certainly demonstrated confidence in how he communicated his ideas. His emergency economic strategy involved seeking from Congress the second half of George Bush's Wall Street bailout funds. His $800 billion stimulus package, bank and auto industry bailouts, attempts to provide mortgage relief and stem

BARACK OBAMA
MASTER OF WASHINGTON DC

foreclosures, encourage banks to issue credit, plan to reform education, to buy up toxic assets held by banks and infusing enormous capital funds into the banking system, are all confidence building strategies designed to endear him to the American people. Such honesty in reporting to the people, when we look at the high rating the young Obama administration enjoys with the nation is akin to Learned Hands' (1872-1961) speech to the Board of Regents, University of the State of New York on October 24, 1952 which stated "The mutual confidence on which all also depends can be maintained only by an open mind and a brave reliance on free discussions."

In the two instances when Mr. Obama traveled abroad to represent the United States, whether in Canada or in Europe at the G-20 Economic Summit, at NATO Conferences and Anniversary, in Town Hall Meetings or Press Conferences, with the Queen of England, the British Prime Minister and contacts with the British, French, German and Turkish people, the President demonstrated tremendous confidence in his realism and pragmatic approaches in social outlook, command of his delivery and of the issues as well as foreign policy expectations. This is the realistic behavior he has demonstrated consistently in his cool, calculated and confident mannerism we have come to expect from Barack Obama, President of the United States.

Barack Obama's Washington, DC Photo 155a. What a view, knowing there's a "cool pool" at your back!

FREDERICK MONDERSON

"I always believe that ultimately, if people are paying attention, then we get good government and good leadership. And when we get lazy, as a democracy and civically start taking shortcuts, then it results in bad government and politics."
BARACK OBAMA, MSNBC interview, Sep. 25, 2006

21. BARACK OBAMA AND LEADERSHIP
By

Dr. Fred Monderson

Leaders are not born, they are made, based on the circumstances in which they find themselves and the desire to rise to the occasion to fill a void, correct a disparity, or similarly as a ship without a captain finds itself in troubled waters, the individual who stands up or out and assumes control is the quintessential leader! In this, the Lilliputians over whom he towers, whether they fell short of the position, being faint of heart or lacked the wherewithal to assume the mantle of leadership, they often assume a critical posture fueled by envy and short-sightedness that puts them diametrically opposed to the good individual who has gone the distance. Pendleton Horring in *Presidential Leadership* (New York: Farrar and Rinehart, Inc., 1940: 1) in describing 'The political basis of presidential power' wrote: "The president is a figure symbolic of national purpose: he is also a human being. The kind of man he shows himself to be is intimately related to the power and meaning he gives his office. Hence there are few common characteristics of all presidents. Perhaps the chief constant is that the president must prove successful as a politician before he can attain this highest elective office. Whether he proves to be a statesman depends more upon the historians than upon the voters. The people elect the president, but they are not organized to support him in office; it is to Congress that he must constantly turn for the fulfillment of his objectives." Again he tells: "If our president is to be effective, he must be a politician as well as a statesman. He must consider the political expedience of contemplated actions as well as their consistency with his concept of the public interest." Therefore, the dynamics of this script appropriately applies daily to Barack Obama, the circumstances and the supporting cast of players in the unfolding reality in Washington, DC. It is real!

BARACK OBAMA
MASTER OF WASHINGTON DC

Then again, in the Washington dance, the President's power is opposed by Congress as outlined in the Constitution. Therefore, "The choice of a responsible chief executive by the general electoral process is the unique appeals to the voters at large for his election, yet once in office he is dependent upon Congress for the realization of his program."

Upon his election on November 4, Obama became the leader of America, the Western Alliance, the Democratic Party, and being African-American, and *Ipso Facto*, the leader of Black America. All this, notwithstanding, despite his enormous efforts to provide credible leadership the new President and his administration have come under a barrage of criticism particularly from Republicans in Congress and some within his party as well as print and electronic media analysts and reporters. Within this vein, perhaps fueled by jealousy and envy, given the nation's economic situation, the fact President Obama's young administration is heir to these problems, is making a good faith effort to stem the nation's economic hemorrhaging, bind its wounds, administer healing strategies and look to the future confidently. The confederation of seemingly anti-Obama forces seem more interested in pursuing what appears "anti-American" sentiments, for we have heard of critical support, but their posture is more critical than supportive, or rather more destructive. Hence, one has to conjecture up all forms of rationale for not cooperating at a time when all good men should come together to aid their nation in distress under the leadership of President Barack Obama.

Perhaps a historic perspective can throw some on light aspects of this leadership question. Whether black or white, the anti-African-American hero has had tremendous success in their campaigns against every black leader who has emerged in this country with a mission to correct or change some disparity whether it is social, political or economic. Nevertheless, history has and will shows these advocates of destructively negative actions and criticisms have been and will be spitting in the wind for the ideals the black heroes stood up for, died for, or advocated were in the best interest of the ideals of America.

FREDERICK MONDERSON

Barack Obama's Washington, DC Photo 156. Quite a different style of cornice, still the third type of capital, Corinthian or composite.

In the various cases of Denmark Vesey, Gabriel Prosser, David Walker, Nat Turner and even John Brown, who challenged the debilitating and emasculating effects of the institution of slavery, the anti-black hero was certainly not kind, demanding the head of these heroes. The anti-black hero again had unkind words

BARACK OBAMA
MASTER OF WASHINGTON DC

and deeds for Henry Highland Garnett, Frederick Douglass, Booker T. Washington, and Marcus Garvey when all came in for the same treatment from both black and white critics, all the while untold thousands were lynched to satisfy the appetite for terror that so characterized terrorist activities against blacks in the 19th Century and black victimization experiences in much of the 20th Century. W.E.B. DuBois, Paul Robeson, Elijah Mohammed, Malcolm X, Martin Luther King, Jr., Stokely Carmichael (Kwame Ture), Randall Robinson, Dr. ben-Jochannan, Sonny Carson, Charles Baron, each came in for resounding criticisms in light of their advocacy to move America along the path of good and effective government that respects and defends all the rights of all its citizens while providing the wherewithal to help maximize their humane, intellectual, economic and social potential.

Barack Obama's Washington, DC Photo 157. Notice these capitals are Doric, the masculine type.

Barack Obama has said the climate of Washington, DC., the hub of the nation's political power and influence, together with print and especially electronic media, have described him as being a genius one day and the equivalent of a don't know what's going on the next.

Naturally, the Constitution, in seeking to define Executive or Presidential Leadership provided checks to create a balance. Pendleton Horring in *Presidential Leadership* (New York: Farrar and Rinehart, Inc., 1940: 4) wrote: "In theory the

FREDERICK MONDERSON

president was to be selected from among the class of wise and responsible men carrying the burden of public affairs. Although the weaknesses of the scheme became only too quickly apparent, the plan itself must not be dismissed as fantastic. It provided for an executive whose authority was to rest upon the confidence and support of that group which was most concerned with the conduct of government. The president's power would thus have a definite basis – nonpartisan, but nevertheless politically significant."

"The president was to act as a moderator between the two houses of Congress; he was to stand above all factional differences; he was to arbitrate between men of conflicting views. Washington endeavored to fulfill this conception of the chief magistrate's function, and only in the light of bitter experiences was the ideal modified. In the political theories of John Adams: 'The emphasis is constantly placed upon the executive magistrate being the third power needed for the balance between the two assemblies, with function as mediator, arbitrator, arbiter, umpire, to mediate, intervene, interpose, and decide between the senate and the people, between the few and the many, in the two chambers, and between two parties ... impartial, made so because its interest for ultimate self-preservation, is to side with the weaker of the other two, whichever it may be at the time being. '"

Barack Obama's Washington, DC Photo 158. Palace or fortress, take your pick!

BARACK OBAMA
MASTER OF WASHINGTON DC

"Today's 24/7 echo-chamber amplifies the most inflammatory sound bites louder and faster than ever before. And it's also, however, given us unprecedented choice. Whereas most Americans used to get their news from the same three networks over dinner, or a few influential papers on Sunday morning, we now have the option to get our information from any number of blogs or websites or cable news shows. And this can have both a good and bad development for democracy. For if we choose only to expose ourselves to opinions and viewpoints that are in line with our own, studies suggest that we become more polarized, more set in our ways. That will only reinforce and even deepen the political divides in this country. But if we choose to actively seek out information that challenges our assumptions and our beliefs, perhaps we can begin to understand where the people who disagree with us are coming from .... The practice of listening to opposing views is essential for effective citizenship. It is essential for our democracy." BARACK OBAMA, remarks at University of Michigan, May 1, 2010

22. STAY ON TRACK, BARACK
By

Dr. Fred Monderson

First it was a "struggle" to arrive at the steps of the White House to assume the Presidency, only to fully realize the new job faced even more daunting challenges and conditions than at first thought. As the old adage hold, "Fortune favors the Prepared Mind," and during the campaign Senator Barack Obama had been working his contingency plans to "hit the ground running," upon assuming the Presidency, because he was confident of his ability to succeed. Upon arrival at his destination the new President found he had his job cut out for him. Nevertheless, President Barack Obama went to work in deploying his very astute mind working in tandem with the geniuses he surrounded himself with, all focusing their expertise to addressing the responsibilities he now inherited.

As Barack Obama set about to address problems in the economy, viz., jobs, credit, home foreclosures, health care, taxes, infrastructure repairs, etc., he was sadly

FREDERICK MONDERSON

criticized; he and his principal players were derided; nor did he receive any support or assistance from Republicans in the House of Representatives despite reaching out to them in a bi-partisan manner. Nevertheless, and undaunted, the young President set about putting in place policies and practices he envisioned would address the myriad of economic problems facing the nation.

Naturally, in this as in any problematic situation, money is an important asset and while the President had thought out a number of plans and policies ready to go, he also made a grab for available funds to help support his vision. First he sought Congressional approval for the second and unused portion of President George Bush's TARP, the Wall Street, rescue funds, in order to reinforce his domestic economic agenda. Next, in appointing Timothy Geithner as Secretary of the Treasury, despite the problems and obstacles associated with this choice, Barack Obama unveiled his more than $800 billion Stimulus Plan.

Withering great political resistance and getting no support from Republicans in the House of Representatives and only 3 Republicans supporting the measure in the Senate; still, with a solid Democratic majority, Congress passed a $780 billion Stimulus Bill. Now with his financial largess secured, President Obama and his team set about unfolding a whole slew of "Plans," in his approach to the various problems besetting America. Interesting, he took and devised a strategy for any number of issues he had to contend with, yet he remained silent about the critics who were attacking his efforts, only to remind them, he had won the election! On their part, the Republicans insisted there were not sufficient tax cuts in the Stimulus Package and this is needed for job creation. However, the President was quick to point out, under George Bush's eight-year tenure, the massive tax cuts he offered did not create that many jobs, and in fact, that President's policies or lack thereof are responsible for the quagmire we find ourselves in today. Fighting a rear-guard battle, Republicans stonewalled in Congress and launched advertising campaigns against the President's efforts. Concurrently, their "allies," right wing cohorts and many "white racist supremacist groups," began spreading false reports about Obama's intentions and integrity, still the Republican machinery failed, or chose not, to speak out about the negative publicity generated towards the President of the United States, perhaps it was because he is a black man, or "not their man." This type of behavior by their members and the various threats by white supremacist groups were unique in the history of the American Presidency.

Nevertheless, the Obama "construction repair crew," despite those bumps in the road, kept plying their skills to rescue the nation. Through it all, while painting the true picture of the many woes, the President kept working and praying, in face of the negative reports of joblessness, foreclosures, lack of credit, industrial turmoil, growing trade and domestic deficit, energy dependence, etc., hoping things would turn around soon. As all this unfolded, the cool demeanor Barack Obama had

BARACK OBAMA
MASTER OF WASHINGTON DC

exhibited along the path he traveled to the Presidency emerged as his strong suit and it benefitted him immensely. People could see, despite the gloom, the President maintained a positive attitude.

Barack Obama's Washington, DC Photo 159. With the "new normal" barriers have become an architectural feature.

FREDERICK MONDERSON

Barack Obama's Washington, DC Photo 160. Not only different styles of capitals on columns but also different systems of numbering in the colonnades.

While his "sown seeds to heal the American malady" were at work, President, Barack traveled overseas on two occasions. First he traveled to Canada and second to Europe for the G-20 Economic Summit, to France, Germany and Prague on NATO business and then to Turkey in an outreach to the Muslim world. That far out, while not expected but logically feasible, the President made a surprise trip to Iraq. There he gave out medals, pressed flesh with the troops and gave them a pep talk outlining the realities of their situation and the future prospects.

An interesting photo was published in one of the local tabloids showing a group of soldiers, standing and paying attention to the President's address. Having been there, the look of these two black soldiers among their buddies carried a powerful message, for those who could read such things. The mystique of these black Iraqi soldiers' expressions tell the tale of aspirations of black soldiers who were in the first and all subsequent wars the United States has fought. Even further, these black soldiers' expressions were ones of stern over-joy, to know the Commander-in-Chief was one of them, an African American. For eons soldiers naturally thought this day would never come!

BARACK OBAMA
MASTER OF WASHINGTON DC

Coming home, the President encountered a great deal of destructive commentary as to how unsuccessful his trip abroad really was. They commented that Barack Obama was not able to get this concession and that concession from this nation and that nation. Some even questioned his sincerity and loyalty. All this negativity, despite the tumultuous welcome the Obamas received and their impressive showing at social occasions, press conferences, town hall meeting or even more formal occasions in London, France, Germany, and Prague in Europe, even addressing the Turkish Parliament. Some constructive commentators, reflecting on the relative youthfulness of the Obama administration, in its first major trip abroad to meet the great leaders of the world and the important contacts he made; the verbal concessions he received from major world players and invitations to visit China and Russia to dialogue later this year; in these contacts were evident the important seeds, again like the farmer, he sowed, that could be exploited later on.

After his return home, President Obama again began focusing on the domestic agenda, whether in dealing with the auto industry mess, foreclosures and education. He unfolded new efforts to address and relieve toxic assets in the banking industry, as well as efforts to tackle energy dependence and jobs. This is what the people saw, the President hard at work on their behalf, and so his popularity remained high. The record of joblessness had kept rising month after month and the President, perhaps, began to question whether and when his plans would bear fruit, signaling some positive sign. After Secretary Geithner rolled out his economic plan, Wall Street rebounded and it has for weeks. The American people now seem convinced the Recession has bottomed out due to the Stimulus Dollars circulating to stabilize the economy and the constructive approach the President has instituted; this even though there will continue to be job losses for the rest of the year. Still, the Obama administration has laid the foundation for recovery in the economy with a view to particularly strengthening the education, energy and health care sectors. He has encouraged development of new and innovative energy approaches to make the nation less vulnerable to overseas sources of energy but also to transform the American scientific infrastructure. In addition, the President has begun to focus more on health care and immigration as significant milestones his administration seeks to achieve early in his first term.

Notwithstanding, when all is said and done, like the farmer planting his seeds with the expectation of a bumper crop, Barack Obama has been unfolding various plans to deal with the many issues in various sectors of the economy, that is slowly beginning to bear fruit. So much so, the President recently confessed there seems to be "glimmers of hope" in the turnaround. To view this success constructively one has to understand the American economy is not unlike a battleship or aircraft carrier, and as such, these massive instruments of power are unable to turn rapidly but gradually. Therefore, while the country may continue to see job losses these will be on a lesser scale than previous months as the techniques set in place to solidify the economy begin to take hold. That is why the American people have expressed such optimism in the efforts the President has taken thus far in his administration. As such then, all we can say is **Stay on Track, Barack!**

Barack Obama's Washington, DC Photo 161. In late afternoon, the sun sometimes plays on the plants and buildings.

BARACK OBAMA
MASTER OF WASHINGTON DC

Barack Obama's Washington, DC Photo 162. What a beautiful arrangement, this time with two columns fronting the entrance.

Barack Obama's Washington, DC Photo 163. Look carefully, you can see the differences between the two principal types of columns.

FREDERICK MONDERSON

"For we know that our patchwork heritage is a strength, not a weakness. We are a nation of Christians and Muslims, Jews and Hindus, and non-believers. We are shaped by every language and culture, drawn from every end of this Earth; and because we have tasted the bitter swill of civil war and segregation, and emerged from that dark chapter stronger and more united, we cannot help but believe that the old hatreds shall someday pass; that the lines of tribe shall soon dissolve; that as the world grows smaller, our common humanity shall reveal itself; and that America must play its role in ushering in a new era of peace." BARACK OBAMA, Inaugural Address, Jan. 20. 2009

23. BARACK OBAMA: MAN OF THE PEOPLE
By

Dr. Fred Monderson

Every once in a great while, civilization is blest with a great leader, and whatever the time, continent or country, some event dictates the emergence of the great man (or woman) whose courage, intelligence, ability to galvanize people of all persuasions, and the force of his personality is then called upon to make his mark. Despite the circumstances, the application of the distinguishing characteristics that define him, the love, respect and support of the people help to propel him over the impending circumstances whether they are imperial, military, medical, religious, civil, economic or political. Globally and from time immemorial, these "once in a lifetime" individuals have appeared, viz., Narmer, Imhotep, Zoser, Thutmose III, Hatshepsut, Amenhotep III, Rameses, Taharka, Cleopatra, Confucius, Buddha, Jesus, Julius Caesar, Charlemagne, Gibral Tarik, Prophet Mohammed, Mansa Musa, Sundiata Keita, Robert Bruce, Lord Nelson, Napoleon, Mohammed Ali, Shaka, Samori Toure, Moshesh, Menelik, Queen Nzinga, Queen Victoria, Queen Yaa Asantewaa, Granville Sharpe, Wilberforce, Winston Churchill, Mahatma Gandhi, Kwame Nkrumah, Nelson Mandela, and a whole lot more.

On the American historical scene, George Washington, Thomas Jefferson, James Monroe, Andrew Jackson, Charles Wilberforce, William Lloyd Garrison, John Brown, Charles Sumner, Abraham Lincoln, Ulysses S. Grant, Teddy Roosevelt, President Woodrow Wilson, Franklin D. Roosevelt, Dwight Eisenhower, John

BARACK OBAMA
MASTER OF WASHINGTON DC

Kennedy, and Ronald Reagan have all rose to the challenges of their time. In the African-American experience, Estanvanico, Crispus Attucks, Toussaint L'Ouverture, Dessalines, Christophe, David Walker, Nat Turner, Samuel Carson, Frederick Douglass, Harriet Tubman, Booker T. Washington, W.E.B. DuBois, Marcus Garvey, Malcolm X, Martin Luther King, Jr., Randall Robinson, Harry Belafonte, Jesse Jackson, Rev. Lowery, and even Al Sharpton and Larry King, primarily because he has sat across from so many famous people; and now we can add the exceptionally outstanding Barack Obama. All these historical figures achieved some form of distinction acting on behalf of the people or their nation. In case of the latter individual, it's his time at bat! Of course, over time, as events and circumstances change, the situations themselves changed. Yet still, these individuals made their mark in rising to some occasion and advanced the cause of the pressing issue of their time.

Just as circumstances, social and domestic, demanded the rise and functionality of a Martin Luther King, Jr., so too events warranted the emergence and utility of a Barack Obama, as the American nation faced its most serious challenge in the 21st Century. Interesting that the grave racial, social, civic, human rights reality of the Post World War II America that demanded a Dr. King, probably no other historic person existed in an age when his nation was threatened to its core, like Abraham Lincoln with the Civil War and a divided America; Winston Churchill and the Battle for Britain is a foreign example; and now that America faces its gravest challenge brought about by an economic collapse of extraordinary proportions, may be equally as grave as any time since the Great Depression of the 1930s.

The pros and cons of the current situation in comparison with the Great Depression, indicates America has grown much more demographically, in gross national product, in areas of trade, infrastructure development, scientific and technological advancement and more global economic and other forms of integration; but we have more tools at our disposal to treat the malady than that earlier experience.

Not discounting the significance of the individuals previously mentioned and the circumstances of their era, if we focus on three individuals, the general import of their situation will suffice to convey the significance of the ideas being underscored here.

In Churchill's day, the threat was of an external, imperialistic aggressive nature that threatened the interests and fabric of the British Empire and its way of life.

FREDERICK MONDERSON

Whereas, William Shakespeare's old adage holds, "Some men were born great; some men achieved greatness; and some men had greatness thrown upon them." Clearly "Churchill was born great" and when the situation demanded it, he rose to the occasion in leading Britain during World War II. When the people were reeling under the yoke of Nazism and its military onslaught, Churchill demonstrated his greatness as a statesman by galvanizing the people and championing his nation to lead it to victory.

Dr. Martin Luther King, Jr., "achieved greatness" reluctantly because the fundamentals of the social process and functionality of America regarding the black experience had suffered tremendously. In this age of television, it was affecting the emotional fabric of American society with tremendous ramifications for its image at home and abroad. This, particularly since the global nation-state dynamics was changing with competing ideological spheres of interest and more and more African nations were becoming independent in the post-World War II era and they were beginning to exert ever-increasing influence on the world stage.

If truth be told, perhaps Dr. King would have loved to remain a simple preacher in Atlanta rather than be drawn into the vortex of the Civil Rights struggle. True to his belief, "It's not where you stand in times of comfort and convenience, but where you stand in times of challenge and controversy." However, once involved, he demonstrated those quintessential elements of leadership, intellectual wherewithal, literary genius, superb oratory acumen, the strength of moral authority, a determined and non-violent yet consistent disposition, that endeared him to the people, near and far.

BARACK OBAMA
MASTER OF WASHINGTON DC

Barack Obama's Washington, DC Photo 165. Composite capitals in the Capital.

FREDERICK MONDERSON

Barack Obama's Washington, DC Photo 166. Sheer genius in decoration.

Challenged by the vicissitudes of racist ideology embedded in the American social order and process psyche, this "David slew the Goliath" of intransigent racial oppression, bigotry, institutional racism undergirded by a history of hatred and "white on black violence" that has characterized much of the history of America society. Who knows the full extent of torment he suffered at the hands of "card-carrying" and "free-lancing" perpetrators of racial violence. As they say, 'while some gave some, he gave all!' Yet still, while he "dreamed" in laying the foundations for social change in America, the process of its crystallization has now began to take shape, though there are miles yet to travel. Still, Martin Luther King demonstrated greatness as a non-violent proponent of creative direct social action, but like many before and after him, the American society had refused to recognize and honor him. However, it was this intransigence that galvanized support among broad masses of people, of high and low persuasions, forcing the powers that be; challenged, and finally forced to recognize this great soul, making his birthday a national holiday.

So much has happened since; even businesses have gotten into the act of "honoring Dr. King," that annually in early January we even hear of "Martin Luther King Sale." Of course Dr. King was not about sales, but the betterment of the black condition in America and that of the poor as well, all victims of sub-

BARACK OBAMA
MASTER OF WASHINGTON DC

standard education, poor housing, joblessness, poor medical treatment and all the things that prevent great segments of the American society from experiencing the true meaning of the American dream and even contributing their creative genius to the American think tank.

Barack Obama represents the third of the examples of individuals called upon to serve on the "altar of greatness." In his case he has had "greatness thrust upon him." That is, notwithstanding, the preparation he had to make in being ready for the arduous task he undertook on way to that heavenly realization of power and leadership. However, while Churchill's adversary was of an external nature and Dr. King's of a segment of the society disaffected and affecting, infecting part of the body-politic; Barack Obama's challenge, on the other hand, is that the whole American system is threatened by the economic meltdown, housing foreclosures and shortages in new construction, joblessness, crumbling infrastructure, that needs critical and urgent attention. As an example, everyone knows he inherited the economic mess now consuming his full attention, and the Stimulus Bill he recently signed was an initial remedy to combat the pressing circumstances. Yet, the opposition, Republicans, have used the argument that he is burdening future generations with a substantial debt and this is their reason for opposing him. If that argument had held, the untold number of times the debt ceiling was raised, we would have perennially had no deficits. Perhaps these critics are blinded in not realizing there would not be any future generation, if today's problems are not tackled sternly and solved with far reaching implications. Ronald Reagan "built up to build down" and this is what caused the collapse of the Russian Empire!

Equally, what we have learned from the path out of the Great Depression, we now have in our power, mechanisms to chart and adjust the response to the great economic challenges facing us. Given this ability, Barack Obama has chosen to think big, and like the calculus applied to the depression malady, he intends to infuse sufficiently significant funds and strategies to address the great economic issues and find a path out of the quagmire. In putting the nations back on the road to solvency, mechanisms will ultimately address the deficit and restore solvency to the nation. After all, it was Edmund Burke in wake of the reaction after the French Revolution who said, "Little minds and empire go ill together." Thus, not to be constrained by little minds, Barack has chosen to think and frame the big picture and in process face the future confidently with great expectations.

While Barack Obama is African-American he is not just an African-American hero; he is an American hero. He is an American people's champion, a man of all the people; any way, some, or most of the people anyway. As such, he chooses to

FREDERICK MONDERSON

not give credence to those in the minority who think otherwise or may even think evil of him and his efforts. This is the reason why his ratings have remained high because the people see a genuine leader working hard to alleviate their situation. In Barack we see a great mind with a heart as large as continental USA!

Nevertheless, why is Barack Obama such a well liked man of the people? Beyond the obvious that he is African-American, he is a loving family man with a beautiful wife, Michelle, and two lovely young daughters, to whom he is devoted. This is an ideal all people choose to see in their heroes. Barack Obama is very intelligent and quick witted, hardworking, incisive, studious and decisive, determined, a visionary, a great orator, capable of consensus building, does not bear grudges, likes to surround himself with the brightest minds in some of the more significant fields of social utility and above all else he is honest. He encourages debate and welcomes new ideas that will contribute to the common good. He tells people what really is rather than what may sound palatable to them. As a leader he is tall, not that this is important, though he possesses a beautiful smile and a wonderful personality, listens well and in more ways than one, he is a people person.

These are the traits that endear him to the people, so much so, even those who did not like him at first, have come around realizing he is an honest and sincere individual who is working hard on their behalf. These then are the credentials that not only make Barack Obama a man of the people, but are the ingredients that will help him fulfill his destiny and truly become one of the great statesmen of the 21st Century.

Therefore, as he struggles in putting together the right formula to tackle the myriad problems inherited with the Presidency, the people have a true sense of a sincere and hard working leader and show their support for President Obama in those significant percentage numbers. They seem to see the genuineness of the young leader as he serves the interest of the nation in the most heartfelt manner. This is the same confident approach and attentiveness to detail in tackling the task ahead, he has demonstrated in the clutch days of his campaign, and what sets him apart as a leader. It is one of the reasons why the people love Mr. Obama, a Man of the People!

BARACK OBAMA
MASTER OF WASHINGTON DC

Barack Obama's Washington, DC Photo 167. How about that, square pillars instead of columns fronting this building.

FREDERICK MONDERSON

Barack Obama's Washington, DC Photo 168. Here's another unique style of column built into an arch.

Barack Obama's Washington, DC Photo 169. Again, the Doric type encasing windows.

BARACK OBAMA
MASTER OF WASHINGTON DC

"It's important to realize that I was actually black before the election." BARACK OBAMA, Late Night With David Letterman, Sep. 21, 2009

"Race is still a powerful force in this country. Any African American candidate, or any Latino candidate, or Asian candidate or woman candidate confronts a higher threshold in establishing himself to the voters ... Are some voters not going to vote for me because I'm African American? Those are the same voters who probably wouldn't vote for me because of my politics." BARACK OBAMA, Los Angeles Times, Dec. 11, 2006

24. BARACK OBAMA AND THE BLACK AGENDA
By
Dr. Fred Monderson

The great Civil Rights activist A. Philip Randolph told of his invitation in 1941 to speak at the White House, during the years of the Franklin D. Roosevelt Administration. As he delivered one of his outstanding addresses on the conditions, aspirations and obstacles facing the black man in America, and what were some of the prescriptions to remedy the situation he proposed, the President listened intently to his every word, then said essentially, "I recognize your very eloquent presentation about the plight of your people and your request to address them." Next Mr. Roosevelt handed out cigars to everyone in the room, waited a while and again said, "Now, go and make me do it!" Perhaps this admonition further emboldened that tireless Civil Rights Campaigner as he held the torch, later initiated the 1963 March on Washington, and handed the baton to Dr. Martin Luther King, Jr., then leading the firestorm protest movement sweeping the nation to address black grievances and forever change the face of America at home and abroad.

FREDERICK MONDERSON

Now that African Americans have made leaps and bounds in electing Barack Obama as President, and in as much as there is one significant difference now as opposed to Roosevelt's time, it is that blacks now have a sympathetic ally and his wife in the White House. Nevertheless, it certainly is time to press the Black Agenda; because I suppose, the President expects, wants us to, "Now, go and make me do it!" In that needed monumental mobilization effort, however, we must clearly define the multi-faceted Black Agenda, and to use Obama's analogy, "Aim high, so if you fall short, then there will certainly still be much that is achievable."

As such then, it would be helpful to identify 10 most important issues in the Black Agenda, in one man's opinion; and that, if corrected, can have a significant impact in moving Dr. King's "Dream" along the path of realization and our people getting to the "Promised Land."

While the following are not arranged in any order of most importance, they are all very important to the overall concept and concerns of the Black Agenda. There are also other intangibles that are just as important and extend the list even further and these will be amplified later.

First, **Education** will always be an important asset to any people or nation. In olden days of slavery, in this country, one of the hallmarks of the success of that institution was to keep the enslaved African uneducated and ignorant. The idea that "reading is fundamental" equally applies to the literary person being able to "locate" him or herself, and as Dr. Leonard James of New York City Technology would say, "decode their environment" to interact successfully in the world. This is why slave masters and the then legal system made it illegal for enslaved persons to learn to read. Going a long way to address this malady, after the Civil War, the founding of Black Colleges was a significant step moving the Freedmen towards improving their self worth and securing the benefits of intellect and justice. Yet, from that time to now, education for blacks has been classified as of a "substandard nature" in terms of instruction, facilities and materials provided and resulting low expectations. Lest we forget the significance of *Brown v. Board of Education of Topeka, Kansas*, 1954! For much of the 20th Century, the reinforcement of social stereotypes and racial discrimination rightly characterized the condition of blacks as little better that when in slavery. However, with a sound education and the identification with Africa as African Americans, certainly changed much of the self-hatred brought about by the dismal education afforded by a reluctant social system. That is why today black people look to Barack Obama, after helping elect him President, to seriously consider this aspect of the Black Agenda; for after all, not simply a black issue, a sound education is "key" to the nation's social, scientific, technological and industrial future. Hence, the tremendous need and responsive support from Head Start through academic and/or

BARACK OBAMA
MASTER OF WASHINGTON DC

vocational educational opportunities and consideration; assistance to particularly disadvantaged schools in high-poverty areas as well as consideration for special education and disabled students, not to forget higher education, will all help build integrity and self worth in black youth upon whom the future will depend.

Jobs are important assets for individuals to maintain their self worth, be socially conscious, raise families and plan for the future. As the nation's unemployment rates rises, that of black males and black youth have always been higher than the national average. When I queried New York City Councilmember Albert Vann about this phenomenon, he maintained "Black unemployment, for both adults and youth, is nearly fifty percent." Thus, blacks need jobs to maintain their dignity, provide for and raise their families and be able to indulge in all the benefits and opportunities offered by the general society, whether purchasing a home, a car or any other big money item to help their families pursue happiness.

Health Care is important and expensive and the many maladies that afflict the human body and mind demands the less fortunate still have access to the best medical care and expertise the American medical system can provide. This is a principal concern for African Americans, victims of some of the most serious medical maladies facing the nation including diabetes, AIDS, heart attacks, obesity, cancer, and a whole lot more. We could also add diseases of the mind, for the history of degradation, debilitation and social neglect has contributed to generations of victims.

For the longest time blacks have faced the humiliating economic experience of **Red Lining** and **Denial of the Issuance of Credit** on the part of banks, especially as it relates to purchase of "big money items." The government must survey and hold accountable banks that practice redlining and denial of credit to any constituency, especially if such institutions receive bailout funds or other forms of assistance.

Racial Profiling or doing anything "while being black!" **Racial Discrimination**, whether institutional or social; and **Police Brutality**, are all odious criminal behaviors masked under sanction of law enforcement authority coupled with traditional practice. These behaviors scar the conscience and body politic of the nation, and government must make a good faith effort to guarantee all its citizens the right to not be subject to this reprehensible behavior.

FREDERICK MONDERSON

Prisons pose a serious threat to the psychological, emotional and physical well-being of individuals, their families and the future, particularly of African Americans. Without a doubt, many blacks, young and old, commit stupid criminal acts that land them in jail! Many are framed! Oftentimes, judges are harsh in treatment of these individuals who receive sentences not comparable to whites who commit similar crimes. In the prison industrial complex, where black manhood is physically and psychologically emasculated on a daily basis, an even more sinister victimization is perpetuated under sanction and cover of legal authority. That is the denial of the right to vote, **disfranchisement**, after these ex-offenders have served their sentences and paid their debt to society. This phenomenon is spreading across many states in the Union particularly the South and perhaps the President can seriously seek to address this veiled injustice that robs citizens of that cherished ideal that so many have struggled to attain.

Voting irregularities, Statehood for the District of Columbia, and the efforts needed to **Repeal the Voting Rights Act** or make permanent this law guaranteeing blacks the right to vote, which must be renewed every 25 years, should become front burner issues of the Obama administration. And, as both Roosevelt and Obama would encourage the people to develop a "Go and make me do it" attitude, blacks must come to realize President Obama and government cannot do everything for them and they must step up to the plate to enhance their own well being. Parents must play a more active role in raising their children and helping them to develop a constructive futuristic social perspective based on hard work, good citizenship, a sound education and a true sense of their role and that of their ancestors in the pageantry of history.

Intangibles added to the list, perhaps just as important, include spending wisely the over 900 billion dollars earning and spending power Black America accumulates annually. This is a powerful weapon for targeted spending, economic boycotts, investing wisely in black businesses and infrastructure development, community enhancement and home and business ownership.

For the young at heart of the 1970s, the movie **The Liberation of L.B. Jones** explained the traditional black businesses were undertaking; liquor store ownership; and the street numbers. Subsequently, all the states expropriated the numbers business. The liquor stores have been taken over by other ethnic groups, though blacks drink even more alcohol, which is a significant contributor to alarming rates of diabetes in the black community nationwide. The undertaking business is holding steadily in black hands but this too is under threat to fall into that "foreign domain."

BARACK OBAMA
MASTER OF WASHINGTON DC

Barack Obama's Washington, DC Photo 170.   What a beautiful site to greet the visitor.

FREDERICK MONDERSON

Barack Obama's Washington, DC Photo 171. What a view! What a View.

Blacks used to own "Mom and Pots Stores" but these are rapidly closing or have closed. Grocery stores, fruit and vegetable stands, nail salons, variety stores, hand laundries, Laundromats, furniture stores, and newspaper stands are all slipping away. Blacks with money are not investing in the black community in those critical local businesses such as Laundromats, grocery stores, laundry, nail salons,

BARACK OBAMA
MASTER OF WASHINGTON DC

liquor stores, hardware stores, etc. We make the most, shop, but not wisely, and not among black businesses. Compared to other ethnic groups, the "Black dollar" does not circulate sufficient in the black community or through black hands. Equally, black businesses also have to act more responsibly in regards the service they provide.

I'll be remiss in not mentioning a trip to Maryland, "Crab Capital," and stopping for some seafood, and was surprised to see a line of about 25 black patrons, all saying "They make the best seafood here!" The proprietor was alien to the Black Community and so were all the employees, but only blacks were the customers in a community disproportionately black. Thus, in many of the above mentioned intangibles, President Barack Obama cannot have any particular influence, we must do it ourselves.

Barack Obama's Washington, DC Photo 172. More Blair House garden view.

The President, however, through the Federal Communications Corporation, can overhaul the way that agency's attitude relates towards black radio, regarding "black set asides," *advertising in black businesses and classification of "minority" wherein blacks get lost in the vast diversity of this group*. That buying power

FREDERICK MONDERSON

blacks possess must target businesses where they shop to insist these hire black workers and advertise in black newspapers, on black radio, and also advocate that blacks shop and buy from black businesses. However, let's not forget, these items do not exhaust the vast myriad of issues that comprise the Black Agenda that in itself is a work in progress.

Barack Obama's Washington, DC Photo 173. Here we stand before the Gates to the Treasury!

Therefore, despite Barack Obama's extraordinary efforts to heal America, improve its image abroad and move the nation forward; the non-cooperation of Republicans and the numerous false claims against the President's character and intentions, all determine Obama is not out of the woods yet. When we consider racist and false claims against the President on the Internet and elsewhere; such claims that he intends to abrogate the Second Amendment right to bear arms and preachers of hate telling others to stock up on armaments; gun purchases since Inauguration have risen a thousand percent; Republican non-cooperation with the President and failure to denounce falsity and hatred; then there must be a black groundswell of support for the leader, otherwise we could lose a great deal.

We need a tremendous gathering in show of support for the President, the likes of the "Million Man March" on the Great Lawn in Washington, DC in 1995. Not only will this beat back the "wolves at the door," we will not only further embolden the President, but the Black Agenda will certainly be highlighted and get the necessary attention it deserves as we "make him do it!"

BARACK OBAMA
MASTER OF WASHINGTON DC

"Discrimination cannot stand -- not on account of color or gender; how you worship or who you love. Prejudice has no place in the United States of America."
BARACK OBAMA, speech, Jul. 17, 2009

25. BARACK OBAMA AND ARIZONA STATE UNIVERSITY
By

Dr. Fred Monderson

Arizona State University has fumbled the ball being in the contradictory position of inviting the President of the United States to speak at its Commencement Ceremony and denying him an Honorary Degree which has been conferred on Presidents and non-Presidents alike. The rationale for this behavior is that "President Obama has not achieved much" this early in his administration. However, in assessing achievements there should not be any static criteria conditions as to how long one has been "toiling in the field" but rather how fruitful has been the "toil," as opposed to how much time spent toiling. After all, with hundreds of academic institutions in this country one has to wonder "Who's doing the honor, the institution or the individual, who happens to be the President of the United States." Therefore, it's a toss-up as to who actually bestows the honor and who benefits from the occasion.

What would normally happen is that President Obama would fly onto the university grounds, give his commencement address, and then fly out back to Washington, DC, to continue his many functions. As such, it stands to reason the enormous graduating class would benefit tremendously being motivated in anticipation of the address given by the President of the United States. Perhaps many more parents, family members and friends of the graduates may decide to attend because it's the President of the United States who is giving the Commencement Address. The university's image may be further enhanced having "snarled the President" to give this important address; and thus they would be the envy of academic institutions being able to boast of having the President at its facility.

FREDERICK MONDERSON

However, a number of factors can be considered in assessing the university's position, which quite naturally is purely speculative on part of this writer.

First, Arizona is the state presidential candidate Senator John McCain represents. It stands to reason this "McCain country" supported his campaign effort because for his many years in government his stature may have benefitted the institution. Since McCain "carried Arizona" in the presidential election because he was a "favorite son," one could legitimately question should the university honor McCain's opponent "so soon." Nevertheless, one of the drawbacks to being President, Mr. Obama would appear ungraceful if he were to decline the offer to give a Commencement Address to a prestigious academic institution, no matter how "busy" he was.

From another perspective, if we examine Barack Obama's *Resume* the public can make a judgment as to whether he "has achieved enough" so far in his career.

First, Barack Obama was the child of a Kenyan father and a mother from Kansas. His father died early and for a great while he was the child of a single parent; ultimately being raised by his grandparents. Despite these shortcomings, Mr. Obama attended and graduated from the prestigious Columbia University in New York. He also graduated from Harvard University Law School, becoming President of the Harvard University Law Review. From this school most graduates head to Wall Street for that's "Where the money is!" Whether following intuition, social conscience or realization that opportunities for a black graduate on Wall Street are not as prosperous as white graduates, Barack Obama headed to Chicago "to work among the people" as a Community Organizer. When we consider the power of correct choice and the results of such actions, two aphorisms come to mind. The one "working for the public good" ends up in the White House, while the one choosing the "mighty dollar" ends up in the quagmire of the "Wall Street mess." Equally, in one of his speeches, the "Ballot or Bullet," Malcolm X offered; the white electorate is so divided between Republicans and Democrats; the black vote becomes crucially important and can determine who goes to the White House and who goes to the dog house. Of course, today independents are also important!

With the experience of serving in the trenches addressing social inequity, Barack Obama chose to venture into public service, seeking to become a State Senator in Illinois. In 2004, given the opportunity to address the Democratic National Convention, Barack Obama proved outstanding, gaining important recognition from a national audience. Thereafter, he aspired to the office and was again successful as a federal Senator from the great state of Illinois.

BARACK OBAMA
MASTER OF WASHINGTON DC

As the nation sank into its domestic economic malaise due to wars in Iraq and Afghanistan, revealed CIA behavior, Abu Ghraib Prison's unconventional activities and claims of torture at Guantanamo Bay Prison confining suspects from the war on terror, Senator Barack Obama chose to be a candidate for the presidency of the United States of America.

Everyone is familiar with the uphill task Barack Obama faced but his brilliant thinking built consensus, created effective campaign organizations throughout the land, raised enormous sums on the Internet and elsewhere as well as significantly amassed a tremendous database of supporters that finally upset the "early projected winner" of the Democratic Primary. Becoming the first African American nominated for the Presidency by a major political party, Obama utilized organization, motivation, an enormous desire to succeed, unrelentingly keeping his "eyes on the prize," having a tremendous work ethic, he benefitted from a reservoir of prayers, and despite all the negativity directed by the team of Arizona's "favorite son," Senator Barack Obama succeed becoming President-Elect Barack Obama.

With the prize secured and appeals for cooperation from the outgoing Bush Administration, President-Elect Obama set his transition team in motion. His circle of "wise men" next began putting finishing touches on the plans he would unveil to combat the myriad problems facing the nation; that is now incidentally beginning to pay fruit. Next, President Obama traveled abroad to represent America and despite what has been said of how much the new American President did not achieve, not much has been said about what he lost, because he did not lose anything. In fact, along with his wife, the new first couple wowed the world at official meetings, press conferences, town hall meetings, social gatherings, fashion encounters, parliamentary addresses, pep talks to troops, in the eyes of many; the man is a winner and successfully demonstrated such behavior for the longest.

All this should have been known to the Arizona Honors Awards Committee and it raises the question about their intentions. Similarly, Notre Dame University equally wants service without "payment." Still, Obama goes about his work! What President Obama should now do is accept the speaking engagement from Howard University who would be only too happy to confer the Honorary Doctorate Degree, and have them other guys "Wait until Next Year!"

FREDERICK MONDERSON

Barack Obama's Washington, DC Photo 174. Beauty and strength with great significance in this massive piece of architecture.

Barack Obama's Washington, DC Photo 175. Enticing architecture that charms the visitor.

BARACK OBAMA
MASTER OF WASHINGTON DC

Barack Obama's Washington, DC Photo 176.   Landscape is as important as architecture.

Barack Obama's Washington DC Photo 176a. Youngster stands beside flowered walkway with the Capital Building in rear.

FREDERICK MONDERSON

"I don't believe that the American people want us to focus on our job security. They want us to focus on their job security. I don't think they want more gridlock. I don't think they want more partisanship. I don't think they want more obstruction. They didn't send us to Washington to fight each other in some sort of political steel-cage match to see who comes out alive. That's not what they want. They sent us to Washington to work together, to get things done, and to solve the problems that they're grappling with every single day." BARACK OBAMA, remarks to GOP House Issues Conference, Jan. 29, 2010

26. Barack Obama: The People's Champion
By

Dr. Fred Monderson

When a people have chosen their champion and send him forth to do battle, they're obligated to keep track of the unfolding of his fate. In fact, the people must track the progress, rise and fall and particularly pay attention to sidereal commentary, regarding his character, ideas, values, associations and demeanor, whether positive or negative. What is most important, however, the people's champion, having been charged, being knowledgeable about his mission and purpose, obviously recognizes the pitfalls; but understanding the significance of his mission, and what he represents to those under whose banner he fights, never lets such distractions dissuade him from his appointed tasks. What's obvious and foremost, Barack Obama, the people's champion, is African American and capable! Significantly, and perhaps Sir Walter Scott's (1771-1832) description of the likes of Senator Barack Obama in *Marmion* is apropos here, for the author's offering speaks of: "His square-turn'd joints, and strength of limb, show'd him no carpe knight so trim, But in close fight a champion grim, in camps a leader sage."

In such a quest, as so many have accepted this characterization, and sent him forth under their banner, they must consistently pay attention to those planting the minefield along the path their champion must traverse. As such, then, the anti-personnel barbs strewn in Senator Barack Obama's path to the White House, range

BARACK OBAMA
MASTER OF WASHINGTON DC

from attempts to link him with Osama Bin Laden, the Al Qaeda leader, to being a black man. The latter we know, all the others are spurious.

Barack Obama's Washington, DC Photo 177. Inside the Smithsonian Institution building, people can find all kinds of thing to do.

Looking at this phenomenon, Barack Obama, the first black man chosen to represent a major political party in America, has been accused of "not being black enough," then "being too black!" Next, he was accused of being too liberal, a Muslim, a "Wrightist," unpatriotic and not-wearing the American flag pin on his lapel. As if that's not enough, he was accused of being anti-American, "palling around with terrorists," and while he first voted in the Senate against the war in Iraq, he was then accused of wanting to lose that same war in Iraq. Equally, he was accused of being inexperienced in foreign policy. Even more, Barack Obama was accused of not remembering the name of an American soldier in Iraq whose bracelet he was wearing on his wrist.

FREDERICK MONDERSON

Along the way, the Republican challenger's camp sought to acquire Barack Obama's birth certificate to use whatever personal information they can to their advantage. As some have expressed, "Everyday there is a new attack on Obama." He was also accused of being a Marxist, socialist, implying communist tendencies. Late in the campaign, Senator Obama was accused of being a "distributor" for wanting to "distribute the wealth" as he told "Joe the Plumber," regarding the strategy of his tax plan. He and his wife Michelle were parodied as Arabs on the cover of the *New Yorker* magazine and Senator McCain had to correct a woman at one of his campaign stops, that Senator Obama is "not an Arab. He is a citizen, a decent man with a family, and we just have disagreements over positions," as all politicians do. The blond-headed woman said he was an "inadequate black man!" How do you say that about a Columbia University graduate, as well as a Harvard University Law graduate and President of the Harvard Law Review. Senator Obama was a Community Organizer, an Illinois State Senator and a federal Senator from Illinois whose 2004 Democratic National Convention Keynote Address impressed so many, signaling the birth of a new star on the American political horizon. In addition, he has a very pretty and intelligent wife with two lovely children and he has not been unfaithful!

I guess, to these, as in *Paradise Regained*, John Milton (1608-1674) would say: "Calling shapes and beckoning shadows dire, And airy tongues that syllable men's names, On sands, and shores, and desert wildernesses. These thoughts may startle well, but not astound, The virtuous mind, that ever walks attended, By a strong siding champion, Conscience."

And even further, "The childhood shows the man, As morning shows the day. Be famous then By wisdom; as thy empire must extend, So let extend thy mind o'er the world."

Last but not least, amidst the echoing of calypsonian Gypsy's famous song, "Captain this ship is sinking," the McCain/Palin team harped on a six-month old Los Angeles *Times* article about a 2003 meeting at which Obama attended and a Palestinian activist was also there. The LA *Times* refused to release a tape of the gathering on the principle of non-disclosure to its original owner. The CNN *Truth Squad* dismissed the contents as irrelevant. Still, when the McCain camp was asked why bring up this six-month old article; their only response was "Because Senator Obama is one week away from being President." Nevertheless, when at first, during a Palin rally, as she worked the crown into frenzy, and someone shouted "kill him;" the Governor never said "Hold it!" that's not what we're about! Thereabouts, the Secret Service and FBI reported "men with guns" near Obama's location. Days ago, Skinheads were arrested for planning to spread carnage at a black school, then "kill Obama." Let's not forget Ashley's hoax

BARACK OBAMA
MASTER OF WASHINGTON DC

about "The black man" who carved a 'B' on her cheek! All of these were softly dismissed as, Dell, Da, Da, Da!

Barack Obama's Washington, DC Photo 178. Yes, people can find all kinds of thing to do and experience in the Smithsonian Museum as this African American family seems to be enjoying.

Interesting, when former Secretary of State Colin Powell, a Republican, endorsed Senator Barack Obama, a Democrat, he described him as being a "transformational figure," who will bring about "generational change." Regarding Senator Obama being associated with terrorists, among the many attacks leveled against him, Secretary Powell thought such charges "a terrible stretch of demagoguery." Conversely, the Anchorage *Daily News* in Alaska, Governor Sarah Palin's hometown newspaper, in endorsing Senator Obama, said he "brings far more promise to the office. In a time of grave economic crisis, he displays thoughtful analysis, enlists wise counsel and operates with a cool, steady hand." In addition, the newspaper said, Senator Obama had "judgment and intelligence to shape a solution, as well as the leadership to rally the country behind it." This is what the Republican camp could not countenance and sought to demean and derail. But as

FREDERICK MONDERSON

history will show, the will of the people will always triumph. In addition, when we contemplate the many attack accusations leveled on the integrity of Barack Obama by the Republican Party, and by his opponents Senator John McCain and running-mate, Sarah Palin, clearly they have colored the complexity of this race to be President of the United States.

However and yet, in a note on reality, an analogy is a useful tool that throws light on causal connections between ideas and experiences. Everyone is familiar with the Biblical story of Noah and the flood when he made his selections for the voyage of the ark. Now, in America, while there's no Noah as Captain, still we could, however, conjure up a case similar in substance to Noah's actions. In parody, as Noah chooses the occupants of America's ark, he is sure to include Christians, Jews, Catholics, Muslims, agnostics, atheists, gays, lesbians, handicaps, criminals, mafia, etc. However, just before this Captain would close the hatch, someone would probably shout, "Don't leave those two racists, and the two Klansmen, as well as James Crow, Jr., Esq., next to them, for they are part of America's past, present and future." Thus, these insidious racists get a free ride.

Again, when Governor Sarah Palin, in her past incendiary rancor stoked the fire of elements eager to show their racist underbelly, what these simpleminded miscreants were incapable of recognizing is that these times are different to African Americans' ancestors' times. The African, enslaved, freed, exposed to unspeakable horrors during and after slavery; endured to persevere to provide the wherewithal for progeny. What these descendants have proved, they too love this country and will not countenance others "putting sand in their rice" or thwarting the destiny of their champion. We have indeed learned a lot along the way!

Even the latest flap uttered by Senator Biden, Obama's running mate, that: "It will not be six months before the world tests Barack Obama like it did John Kennedy," has elicited a response from Senator John McCain who said: "We don't want a President who invites testing from the world at a time when our economy is in crisis and Americans are already fighting in two wars." Having waged a vicious and unrelentingly negative campaign, metaphorically speaking, McCain's side finally threw in the kitchen sink to which Obama side-stepped and this missed. Then McCain rolled out "Joe the Plumber," and announced at Alfred E. Smith's Dinner: "I have fired my entire staff and replaced them with 'Joe the Plumber.'" No wonder he lost the election! This "instant celebrity" soon began doing the media rounds, stumping with Sarah Palin, and prognosticated about Obama's position on Israel on McCain's behalf! Imagine! To speak about foreign policy, what are Joe's qualifications!! His credentials! More important, it turns out Joe is not even a licensed plumber, which means McCain will hire 'Unprofessional' help. Additionally, however, while Senator McCain hoped to make hay of Senator

BARACK OBAMA
MASTER OF WASHINGTON DC

Obama, stating that as President he would be tested, is another symptom of Senator's McCain's inadequate assessment of the state of things. That line of argument presupposes the world will not test McCain as President. Does Senator McCain, admitting we're at war on two fronts, believe he will not be challenged by Al Qaeda and all the other "bad boys" who will "stand down" because McCain is President? Will these same troublemakers not test Sarah Palin, if she were to succeed President John McCain?

Barack Obama's Washington, DC Photo 179. This town seems to be constantly building as evidence from the square beams being erected here.

Finally, the problem with Sarah Palin's analysis of Senator Biden's statement is not only to show how shallow her thinking is, but also to depict her one-sidedness. We have credited Senator Biden with being a foreign policy expert with tons of years in the Senate. In this, experience has taught him America's enemies will challenge the next President, whoever he or she is. We talk about two wars in Iraq and Afghanistan as well as the threats from "rogue states," but maliciously presume they will test Obama, but they won't pose a threat if John McCain is

FREDERICK MONDERSON

President. Therefore, unquestionably, if Governor Palin succeeds President McCain these same enemies will challenge her, being a woman and inexperienced as well. Much more important is how the people's champion, Barack Obama, has been challenged, maligned, as attempts were made to sidetrack his campaign from the time of the Democratic Primary and then through the contest between the Republican and Democratic Presidential Candidates.

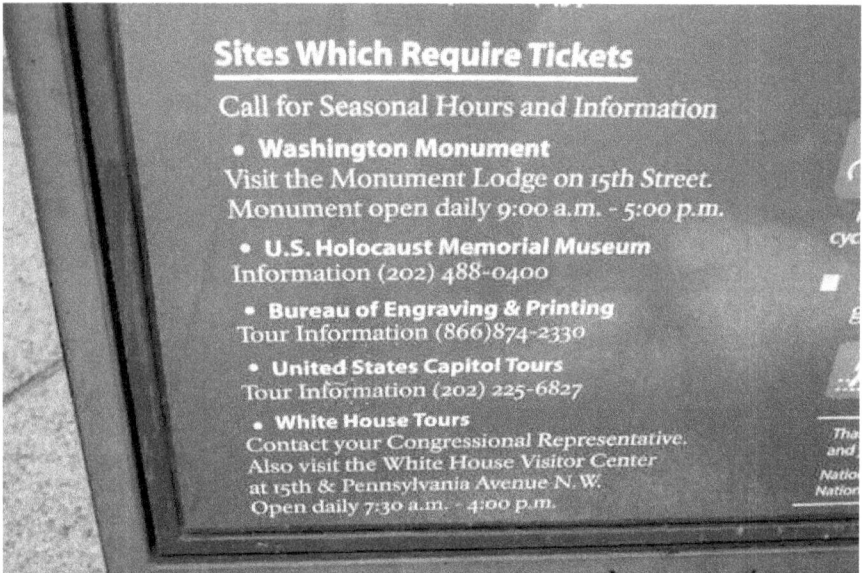

Barack Obama's Washington, DC Photo 180. Sites which require tickets and their times of being open with phone numbers to call.

All these, notwithstanding, Senator Barack Obama will persevere in his quest to be the first black leader of America and will again win respect for this nation abroad, as he has made blacks and whites across this country, proud.

BARACK OBAMA
MASTER OF WASHINGTON DC

Barack Obama's Washington, DC Photo 180a. What a remarkable view, across the tree-lined with the Capital Building's magnificent standing prominently under a blue sky with lazy clouds.

Barack Obama's Washington, DC Photo 180b. How conveniently this building seems to project the apex of the Washington Monument!

Perhaps Milton puts it appropriately: "All is best, though we oft doubt, What th' unsearchable dispose, Of highest wisdom brings about, And ever best found in the closet. Oft he seems to hide his face, But unexpectedly returns, and to his faithful champion hath in place, Bore witness gloriously; whence Gaza mourns, And all that band them to resist, His uncontrollable intent, His servants he with new acquist, Of true experience from this great event, With peace and consolation hath dismiss'd, And calm of mind all passion spent."

FREDERICK MONDERSON

Barack Obama's Washington DC 180c. Our young hero seems impressed with the purple flowers with the colonnaded building in the rear.

Unquestionably, so many would like to say, "Hold on Grandmother, stay up! You should see your handiwork brought to fruition, then be honored and smell your roses before you go! Deserving as you are! As history will be made and be thankful for your efforts along the way." Even more important and what America needs to realize, there's no turning back now! Without a doubt, if those young, uniformed students CNN has interviewed who demonstrated their analytic abilities and articulate expressions, is any indication, in time, many more black presidents, senators, congressmen, governors, principals, doctors, teachers, lawyers, judges, etc., will take their rightful places in making Dr. King's dream the reality so long in coming. And, all their efforts will make America an even better place, perhaps the last hope for the world!

BARACK OBAMA
MASTER OF WASHINGTON DC

Barack Obama's Washington DC 180d. Our young hero seems ready for the defense with pool and Capital Building in the rear.

FREDERICK MONDERSON

"The outpouring of love, gratitude and fond memories to which we've all borne witness is a testament to the way this singular figure in American history touched so many lives. His ideas and ideals are stamped on scores of laws and reflected in millions of lives -- in seniors who know new dignity; in families that know new opportunity; in children who know education's promise; and in all who can pursue their dream in an America that is more equal and more just, including myself.

The Kennedy name is synonymous with the Democratic Party, and at times Ted was the target of partisan campaign attacks. But in the United States Senate, I can think of no one who engendered greater respect or affection from members of both sides of the aisle.

OBAMA: His seriousness of purpose was perpetually matched by humility, warmth and good cheer. His compassion – [He] passionately battled others and did so peerlessly on the Senate floor for the causes that he held dear and yet still maintained warm friendships across party lines. And that's one reason he became not only one of the greatest senators of our time, but one of the most accomplished Americans ever to serve our democracy."

"The absence of hope can rot a society from within." BARACK OBAMA, Nobel Lecture, Dec. 10, 2009

27. EDWARD KENNEDY, OBAMA'S ALLY
By
Dr. Fred Monderson

Watching Rick Sanchez on CNN, August 26, 2009, the day after Senator Edward Moore Kennedy died, the ticker carried a Tweeter's comment, "Why should I mourn Ted Kennedy when I should be mourning children dying in Africa?" What a thing to say!

It's been said, "In difficult times," and we may add in excruciating and painfully sorrowful circumstances, "wise men say nothing!" This is certainly a somewhat controversial thing to say! Equally, it's also been said, in discussion, if you cannot add anything constructive to the dialogue, you should keep your damn mouth shut!

Let us get pass the Tweeter's right to free speech, if he's an American citizen. However, the comment by the above Tweeter is a perfectly good example why

BARACK OBAMA
MASTER OF WASHINGTON DC

young people should learn to think for themselves. Having learned to think for themselves, they would not accept statements even from "leaders" without analyzing the content, implications and whether there was a historical basis for the idea uttered, and to what extent such an idea is historically correct. Equally too, what are the consequences of that idea is also brought into question. Granted the Tweeter is entitled to his or her own views, beliefs and even biases, but it certainly deserves commentary. Still, expressing such thoughts on the Internet means its part of the public record that can influence others. After all, there is no attached caveat that said this is my idea and it's restricted with the intent not to influence others. Of course, he or she could and should have mourned African children, he did not have to mourn Ted Kennedy; but, putting the two together brought attention to him or her, and expressing this in public opens it to comment.

Barack Obama's Washington, DC Photo 180e. The magnificent Jefferson Building of the Library of Congress called a "Temple of Learning," the home of America's reservoir of knowledge.

Conversely, while this individual declined to pay tribute to the great oratorical legislator, legend, millions worldwide did! Thousands lined the route of his passing motorcade, 45,000-50,000 or so filed pass his coffin in the JFK Memorial Library in Boston and millions watched on television. Extending the statement further, one can also inquire whether the Tweeter would truly mourn African children or whether he or she has made any contribution, however miniscule, to the welfare or betterment of those African children's lives or the lives of people in

FREDERICK MONDERSON

general, black or white, wherever! Has that Tweeter donated to the cause of drought in Somalia or helped alleviate the carnage in Darfur?

There is a caustic, acerbic tone in the Tweeter's statement made at a sorrowful time that calls into question whether this person really cares about people, for such concerns would not lend itself to such a seemingly subjective and cold-hearted expression. Again, this is why young people should be encouraged to develop those critical faculties or skills that can teach them to evaluate and appreciate the good works of people particularly if its within the philosophic construct of the fatherhood of god and the brotherhood of man.

Ted Kennedy spent his life bettering the lot of humanity, evidenced in the 300 or more bills he personally authored and 1000 that bear his name. Thus, nearly anyone may have benefited from his enormous legislative work, perhaps even our "ungrateful" Twitter. Inasmuch as Edward Kennedy has been described due to his lengthy years as a U.S. Senator, through turbulent times, as "a great champion of human rights and dignity in America," a "folk hero of the left" who "cast votes on most of the crucial issues of the last half century;" he may have voted on issues that affected the parents of some of those same children in Africa. He is pictured with Nelson Mandela and with Kofi Annan, Ghanaian and United Nations Secretary General. Let us not forget the words of the Civil Rights icon, John Lewis, in referring to the presence of Ted Kennedy in the Senate during the tumultuous and challenging days of the 1960s and 1970s. He said, "It gave us great strength to know we had someone who cared. He never gave up, He never gave in, He never gave out." This "child of privilege who fought for the less fortunate" who, as Ted Sorensen, Presidential Adviser identified as "a national figure subject to words of scorn and hate," was also villainized for he took on the likes of Strom Thurman and Jesse Helms, even Ku Klux Klan Democrat Byrd, and spoke out against the Bull Connors and George Wallaces, among others, as the Civil Rights battles unfolded. In that era and climate, with two brothers already assassinated, he must have been fearful the same fate may befall him. Yet, "Kennedy championed so many causes popular or not," such a man must be honored, no matter what your philosophic or ideological persuasion happens to be.

BARACK OBAMA
MASTER OF WASHINGTON DC

Barack Obama's Washington, DC Photo 181. The *Blashfield Mural* or "Wheel of Knowledge" shows America leaning on ancient Egypt, the state in Northeast Africa, along the Nile River, as the foundation of all learning.

FREDERICK MONDERSON

Barack Obama's Washington DC Photo 181a. The *Edwin Blashfield Mural* or "Knowledge Wheel" comprises 12-seated figures to represent major nations who have either created or benefitted from the world of learning. However, while America has benefitted greatly we must look to the apogee of the wheel for the nation that started it all, Egypt the Nile River in Northeast Africa. These nations, Anthony Browder's *Egypt on the Potomac* (2004; 66) lists: "*Egypt*, typifying Written Records; *Judea*, Religion; *Greece*, Philosophy; *Rome*, Administration; *Islam*, Physics; *The Middle Ages*, Modern Languages; *Italy*, the Fine Arts; *Germany*, the Art of Printing; *Spain*, Discovery; *England*, Literature; *France*, Emancipation, and *America*, Science."

BARACK OBAMA
MASTER OF WASHINGTON DC

Barack Obama's Washington, DC Photo 182. Marbled entrance to the Library of Congress in the Jefferson Building.

Barack Obama's Washington, DC Photo 183. Picturesque detail of the muses of knowledge and information about the founding of the Library of Congress in 1800, serving as the nation's oldest federal cultural institution.

FREDERICK MONDERSON

In Claude McKay's poem, "If We Must Die," he reasons, "the monsters we defy will honor us though dead" for our demonstrated bravery in resisting their savagery. Thus, if "monsters" can honor their victims, we can certainly honor a "singular figure in American history who touched so many lives." During the Civil Rights Era, he was one of few legislators who unequivocally and vocally spoke on the protesters' behalf challenging all forms of brutalities and oppression, repression. Again, our Tweeter's vision seems devoid of historical consciousness, at a time, let's say, 1954-1974, that allows us to learn, for as Malcolm X has said, "History is a good teacher."

America changed dramatically in the two decades following the 1954 *Brown v. Board of Education* decision that ruled "separate but equal" educational and social conditions in this country are unconstitutional. Again, this was a time when as Malcolm X has so eloquently pointed out, the 1955 Bandung Conference helped change the world as the African continent intensified its struggle for decolonization and independence causing 40-odd African countries to become members of the United Nations and this unfolding impact influenced men and movements in this country.

Six years after *Brown*, 1960, John F. Kennedy, a Massachusetts resident of Irish heritage and Catholic religion succeeded to the Presidency of the United States. This was a monumental accomplishment concurrent with the Civil Rights Movement's emerging advocacy within the changing dynamics of the times, the visionary nature and liberal philosophic ideology of the Kennedy Administration that came to realize, given its history, America must either change or the internal combustion percolating would wreck irreparable damage to its social and psychological infrastructure. To combat this social, economic and political malady, President Kennedy drafted the fundamentals of what his successor Lyndon B. Johnson would dub the "Great Society" program. Equally, they intervened with federal troops to help speed up desegregation and integration, while aiding efforts of the movement led by Dr. Martin Luther King, Jr. Following Senator Edward Kennedy's death, Larry King asked Ted Sorenson, JFK adviser and speech writer, "Why should John F. Kennedy be considered great, given his short presidency?" The response was three important things. (1) After nearly 250 years of African American enslavement and discrimination, John Kennedy was the first President to take a stand to improve their condition; (2) He was the first to encourage Americans to explore the heavens; (3) with cool, calm and collective he weathered the 13 days of October, 1962, in the Cuban Missile Crisis.

As these events unfolded, the 1960s came to be described as the decade of assassination. First, President John F. Kennedy, then Medgar Evers, three little girls in a Birmingham church, and so many others including Chaney, Scherwin and Goodman, then Malcolm X, Dr. King and Robert Kennedy.

BARACK OBAMA
MASTER OF WASHINGTON DC

Edward Moore Kennedy succeeded his brother John F. Kennedy as Senator from Massachusetts in 1962, while the other brother Robert Kennedy was Attorney General. Two brothers killed in a 5-year period devastated the Kennedy family. Yet, from the battles of the 1960s to today, he has admirably carried the torch lighting the path of change and earning himself the title roaring "Lion of the Senate." This ascent, however, did not come easy as the fear of assassination lurked daily and one who stood up in the halls of power to advocate against social and civil iniquities, he was exposed to the whims of the unjust. Yet, Senator Ted Kennedy persevered as a man on a mission championing the cause of the voiceless fighting for economic and social justice. Vice-President Joe Biden, in the Senate some 36 years, described Kennedy as "an incredible man, with a lack of vitriol, lack of pettiness. He forced others to act big. People did not want to act small in front of him."

Barack Obama's Washington, DC Photo 184. Ceiling designed in the most intricately delicate manner highlighting the names of great literary heroes and in this case Browning and Longfellow are shown.

FREDERICK MONDERSON

Barack Obama's Washington, DC Photo 185. Browning is the individual pictured in the first part of the above photo.

Barack Obama's Washington, DC Photo 186. Longfellow is the individual pictured as the second part of the previous photo.

BARACK OBAMA
MASTER OF WASHINGTON DC

Barack Obama's Washington, DC Photo 187. Imagine the time it took to create such delicate work attests to the significance of the institution it covers.

Following the August 1963 Martin Luther King led March on Washington, the November 1963 assassination of President Kennedy his successor President Johnson tried to implement the "Great Society" program bringing into being the **1964 Civil Rights Act**, the **1965 Voting Rights Act**, etc. In the ensuing legislative battles, Senator Ted Kennedy steadfastly participated as if to see his brothers' dreams come through; emerging as a significant player helping to eventually usher this urgent legislation through the Congress, where, as David Gergen has said, he became "a voice of freedom for justice, a champion of lost causes." His liberal ideology was thus shaped by solidifying the merits of the Kennedy legacy laid in the shattered lives of his two brothers, killed by hate. Still, despite his dogged legislative determination, he was a man of peace, love.

FREDERICK MONDERSON

Barack Obama's Washington, DC Photo 188. "The poets who on earth have made us heirs of truth and pure delight by heavenly lays.

Again, this damn Twitter, wrong for the right reasons, for when Malcolm X spoke of the revolution without (outside) influencing the revolution within, he meant the African decolonization revolution having an impact on the Civil Rights Movement. However, while Malcolm did not apply this concept to purely domestic workings of the Civil Rights Movement, that revolution would have failed if it did not have significant assistance from within the halls of Congress. Here is a uniquely profound experience, playing out within the halls of power, a people struggling for their dignity under media and global scrutiny and we have a man, legislator of great humility, compassionate, fired by the ideas and ideals of seeing his brothers and friends assassinated, their work unfinished in the unfolding milieu, determined to see related constructive legislation a reality. This combination gave rise to the transformative coming of age of Senator Ted Kennedy, where he would become feared and loved at the same time.

BARACK OBAMA
MASTER OF WASHINGTON DC

Barack Obama's Washington, DC Photo 189. Imagine the majesty of thought and the magnificence of execution of the timelessness created as representative of this august institution.

FREDERICK MONDERSON

Barack Obama's Washington, DC Photo 190. Cultural motifs, ethos and creativity are the hallmark of a great people.

Barack Obama's Washington, DC Photo 191. Often imitated, sometimes duplicated but never can match the origination, the thoughts and actions that went into perfecting this ceiling is without question genius in its creativity.

BARACK OBAMA
MASTER OF WASHINGTON DC

Barack Obama's Washington, DC Photo 192. There seems no end to the wonder that so accentuates this ceiling in the Library of Congress.

FREDERICK MONDERSON

Barack Obama's Washington, DC Photo 193. Patterned tiled floor, marbled railing and columns and painted ceiling make this place a sight to behold and an unforgettable experience.

Barack Obama's Washington, DC Photo 194. The quote reads: "Beholding the bright countenance of truth in the quiet and still air of delightful studies."

BARACK OBAMA
MASTER OF WASHINGTON DC

Barack Obama's Washington, DC Photo 195. "The true university of these days is a collection of books."

Barack Obama's Washington, DC Photo 196. "Nature is the art of God."

FREDERICK MONDERSON

Barack Obama's Washington, DC 197. Composite capitals on marble columns, painted ceilings and a breathtaking view make this a remarkable experience that all people, particularly school children should have the opportunity to see.

BARACK OBAMA
MASTER OF WASHINGTON DC

Barack Obama's Washington, DC Photo 198. Part of the unforgettable experience on a trip to the Jefferson Building of the Library of Congress.

Barack Obama's Washington, DC Photo 199.

FREDERICK MONDERSON

Health Care Reform's biggest champion was Edward Kennedy and his passing was a terrible blow to Obama and his efforts to reform the system. Conversely, the Senator's passing galvanized and further motivated Barack and a Democratic Senate trying to honor their passing colleague's efforts and bring to fruition Ted Kennedy's greatest aspiration. However, as destiny would have it, the President lost a strong ally, yet his motivation bore fruit in passage of the Health Care Reform Act in 2010.

Barack Obama's Washington, DC Photo 200.

BARACK OBAMA
MASTER OF WASHINGTON DC

"The fact is, we are closer to achieving (health care) reform than we've ever been. We have the American Nurses Association, we have the American Medical Association on board, because America's doctors and nurses know how badly we need reform.... But look, because we're getting close, the fight is getting fierce. And the history is clear: Every time we're in sight of reform, the special interests start fighting back with everything they've got. They use their influence. They run their ads. And let's face it, they get people scared. And understandably -- I understand why people are nervous. Health care is a big deal. In fact, whenever America has set about solving our toughest problems, there have always been those who've sought to preserve the status quo by scaring the American people. That's what happened when FDR tried to pass Social Security -- they said that was socialist. They did -- verbatim. That's what they said. They said that everybody was going to have to wear dog tags and that this was a plot for the government to keep track of everybody. When JFK and then Lyndon Johnson tried to pass Medicare, they said this was a government takeover of health care; they were going to get between you and your doctor -- the same argument that's being made today." BARACK OBAMA, town hall meeting, Aug. 15, 2009

28. SOME PERSPECTIVES ON OBAMA'S HEALTH CARE REFORM
By

Dr. Fred Monderson

President Obama has undertaken the biggest project of his administration, the attempt to reform the nation's health care system. This has been a central theme of his campaign and will shape his Presidency. It is generally acknowledged, health care in America is a system in crisis with escalating costs that keeps rising. In addition, evidence points to the fact nearly 47 million Americans do not have health insurance coverage and something like 14,000 people lose their health insurance every day.

In this case, for example, with the figures continuing their upward spiral, by the end of his first term, a great many people will be added to the rolls, if the health care system is not mended or reformed. Thus, unable to deliver Health Care Reform, the President will have difficulty in being re-elected. If no reform of the system of providing medical assistance in this country, yet he is re-elected, upon which he becomes a "lame duck," the "goal post" will be moved much further back, thus making this a very difficult proposition. Then, as the President has warned, "If we do nothing, I can almost guarantee your cost will double in ten years." It is as he indicated, "When the Republicans were in power, in addition to the enormous tax cut they passed, benefitting the most-wealthy Americans, "They passed a Prescription Drug Plan and did not pay for it." As a result, "We dug ourselves a deep hole and now we have problems." Even further, in his town hall appeals to the American people, he has reiterated time and time again, "This is not about politics; it is about people's lives."

As such then, he is quick to point out, the "present system of care works for the insurance companies but not in the interest of the American people." Citing some centers as the "Mayo Clinic" in Cleveland, Ohio, and that "several others around the county have costs 20-30 percent lower, but higher quality of health care than the national average." That is why he insists, "Let us incentivize the hospitals, pay bonuses for solving problems the first time." Thus, his attempts to reform the health care system is simply to "improve quality and lower costs."

President Obama is being challenged "tooth and nail" by fellow "Blue Dog Democrats" and Republicans because of the significance of this piece of legislation. If the President succeeds with Health Care Reform, an issue he campaigned on, he would be unstoppable for other meaningful legislation, on the road to being a great president, re-election practically assured. If he fails in this venture, its jubilation for the opposition, he could very well be a one-term "lame duck" and re-election is therefore in jeopardy. As a result, all stops are pulled out! He makes concessions, compromises, says no to some and sells his own plan by taking it to the people in terms of town hall meetings, press conferences, advertising on TV and other media and also being aided by other entities as unions and even the pharmaceutical industry in trying to inform the public.

From the time of the Eisenhower Administration, through those of several presidents, the nation waited in anxious anticipation and disappointed rejection as the health care issue went down to defeat, time and time again. The last time Health Care Reform was an issue, it was in 1993-1994, during the Clinton Administration. Familiarity with the Republican dislike for Bill and Hillary explains why Health Care Reform was so detested and its failure to gain traction.

It could be pointed out opposition to Health Care Reform is fueled by the magnitude of the program undertaken by the government and the enormous costs over the long run. Thus, out of fear, Health Care Reform has remained in a "let alone stagnation" while, however, the costs have kept rising in an inefficient system. Therefore, when Barack Obama came along and decided to reform the system, those in satiated slumber allowing health care costs to rise became troubled by this awakening and rose in opposition raising spending and deficit concerns.

BARACK OBAMA
MASTER OF WASHINGTON DC

Barack Obama's Washington, DC Photo 201.

Barack Obama's Washington, DC Photo 202.

FREDERICK MONDERSON

What is troubling is language used by Republicans opposed to President Obama on this important issue. With the Stimulus Bill, 100 percent of House Republicans and all but 3 Republican Senators said no to the bill. This time the "Party of No" has gone further. For example, South Carolina Senator James De Mint shot from the lip: "If we can stop Obama on this it will be his Waterloo!" On the ABC TV program, *This Week* he again mouth off: "I like the President, but he is out of control." He "gives false promises." He "uses bogus numbers." "We must break him." Billy Crystal of *The Weekly Standard* offered "Go for the kill!" Others say: "We have got to stop him!" Such talk as "Republicans want to wound the President on Health Care Reform" has circulated.

Yet still, Congress continues to debate the issue; with both sides seeking compromises to arrive at a consensus package. Meanwhile, President Obama took to the road to sell his program and clarify much of its content for the American people most affected and caught in the middle between him and the various factions of Congress.

The President has insisted Health Care Reform is very central to rebuild the American economy. Its intent is stabilization of the financial system. The following relates to some of the more important aspects of Health Care Reform as preached by President Obama in his many town hall meetings and press conferences.

1. There will be no government takeover of health care. If you like your doctor, you get to keep your doctor. If you like your health care plans, you keep your health care plans.

2. If you have Health Insurance, the reforms will help you. The present system works for the Insurance Companies but not for the patients. We mean to fix this!

3. Health Care Reform will stop Insurance Companies from denying you insurance because of a prior ailment in your medical history. This will no longer be allowed.

4. With reforms, Insurance Companies will be held to a cap on how much they can charge per year. There will be no drop or watered down insurance. Simply put, reforms will bring security and stability to whatever insurance you now have.

5. We are only changing what does not work. There will not be any changes to Medicare benefits. Reforms will eliminate waste. We spend a lot of money that does little for your health. We are working to close the Donut Hole in patient billing. Have no fear about single payer option. Medicare and VA Hospital Care are both single payer options and they work very well.

BARACK OBAMA
MASTER OF WASHINGTON DC

6.   In his tele-town hall meeting with AARP, President Obama cautioned about much mis-information and myths in Health Care Reform. AARP, insisting it has not endorsed any bill making the rounds in Congress was told: "All Americans should have affordable health care. This is a historic opportunity to bring reform. We have waited some 60 years for Health Care Reform."

7.   When asked why the rush for passage of Health Care Reform, the President responded: "The rush is because families write me asking for help. If you do not set deadlines in this town, nothing gets done." "Doctors, nurses, hospitals, pharmaceutical industries, AARP, all say get it done!"

8.   This nation spends some $6,000.00 more per patient than any other industrialized nation and we are no healthier. The biggest driving cost in our budget is in Medicare and Medicaid. If we eliminate waste we can pay for 2/3 of the bill. The wealthy will pay the remaining 1/3 cost, much coming from taxing the Cadillac Plan insurance now valued from $25,000-$40,000.

9.   If you lose your job, move or change your job, you will still have Health Insurance. The reform plan would be very similar to the health plan for federal employees. As such, Americans cannot wait any longer for Health Care Reform.

10.   This Reform of Health Care is debated and supported for and against Barack Obama and those in support of Health Care Reform; stake holders; the Soft Drink Industry; Unions such as AFSME; Autism Speaks; Americans for Prosperity Foundation; Americans for United Change; Harry and Louise, 2009; all have their say as to the meaning of Health Care Reform and its effects on Americans and the American economy.

FREDERICK MONDERSON

Barack Obama's Washington, DC Photo 203. The magnificence of the colonnaded upper floor of the Jefferson Building.

Barack Obama's Washington, DC Photo 204.

BARACK OBAMA
MASTER OF WASHINGTON DC

Barack Obama's Washington, DC Photo 205.

As the Media continued its interest in Health Care Reform, Sunday Morning Talk Shows had much to say on the President's Health Care Reform Proposal. On ABC's *This Week*, July 26, 2009, George Will opined: "The Republican theory is if they get no Republicans they will lose some Democrats." This seems consistent with an idea put forward by David P. Calleo in *The American Political System* (London: The Bodley Head, 1968: 82-83) where he developed the idea: "Many of the legislative battles in Congress are, in reality, contests between two opposing coalitions: The Liberal 'Presidential' Democrats and Republicans on one side and the Conservative 'Congressional' Democrats and Republicans on the other. The former coalition generally represents the big cities, the minority groups and other interests who look to Washington and the President for positive policies in their favor. The other, representing rural areas, small towns, and particular regional interests, tends to oppose strong Presidential initiatives, regardless of nominal party affiliation" The "Blue Dog Democrats" fits this bill and unintentionally they ally with Republicans who oppose the President. As such, concessions, to the tune of $100 Billion given to the "Blue Dogs" for their support of the proposal has inflamed other liberal House Democrats who now see the Health Care Bill as being watered down.

Again, on *This Week*, in the Panel, Paul Krugman said: "If Democrats do not pass this they will be seen as losers" and that "if you get universality you will get cost control through the political process." Donna Brazile explained "The Public Option is what those who rally around the President want."

Senator Orin Hatch says: "The Public Option Plan will compete and give people a choice."

The significance of all this is that Health Care costs is draining the American financial system and President Obama means to fix it through Reform. The consensus is that he needs the help of all Americans to pass this legislation to help all Americans.

Barack Obama's Washington, DC Photo 206.

BARACK OBAMA
MASTER OF WASHINGTON DC

Barack Obama's Washington, DC Photo 207.

Barack Obama's Washington, DC Photo 208.

FREDERICK MONDERSON

29. FURTHER CONSIDERATIONS ON HEALTH CARE REFORM
By

Dr. Fred Monderson

Confronted by seemingly organized resistance fueling mistrust created by misinformation and myths, President Barack Obama has been making the rounds selling his Health Care Reform Plan and underscoring his obligations to the American people to get this done. Yet, despite his efforts to generate bipartisan support for health care reform, and the lack of bipartisan support, midway through the August recess, the President is moving to craft and pass a bill regardless.

Classic confrontations sometimes pit single individuals against tremendous forces of tradition, the might of military power or the boisterous rancor of orchestrated infiltrators armed with misinformation designed to hijack legitimate protests to sow confusion and racial hatred in attempting to stem progress. In many respects, semblances of the three scenarios can be found in the unfolding Health Care Debate. However, its generally believed one man can become a majority if he holds to ideals of his ground, his truths are immutable, then he can be successful. In all such encounters it's the power of the word rather than force of ideas that sometimes brings victory.

In 1806, in aftermath of the French Revolution, the backlash and results of the Napoleonic conquests, Napoleon approached the gates of Rome with a mighty force. Rather than entering the Holy City he encamped outside to which the Pope sent one of his bishops as an emissary. The bishop told Napoleon "The Holy Father would prefer you not enter the Holy City." Napoleon's response was, "I have 200,000 men under arms. How many guns does the Holy Father have?" The bishop retorted, "The Holy Father has the tradition of moral suasion." Napoleon and his army turned from Rome.

In 1944, in the waning years of World War II, the Germans launched a last minute blitzkrieg to stem the allied advance in France. The 101st Airborne Division of the American Army stood before the advancing German army in what became known as the Siege of Bastogne. With their overwhelming force the Germans approached the American line outlining their strength and promising the Americans would be treated fairly if they surrendered. The commanding American general responded with a single word, NUTS! He was rescued and the German advance collapsed!

BARACK OBAMA
MASTER OF WASHINGTON DC

Barack Obama's Washington, DC Photo 209.

FREDERICK MONDERSON

Barack Obama's Washington, DC Photo 210.

The rancorous behavior that characterized the early days of the health care debate was fueled by individuals with orchestrated instructions pedaling misinformation that resulted in disruptions we have come to associate with "August Town Hall" meetings around health care. Such revelations, however, can be viewed as the early beginnings of a baseball game with the results still in doubt. Notwithstanding, when the Republicans lose and the Democrats win, which they will, the victory can probably be credited to Massachusetts Representative Barney Frank for forcefully standing his ground. Representative Frank turned back a young woman with the comments "I don't know what planet you're from!" With that statement and his follow up, Congressman Frank may have singlehandedly turned back the pack led by a young woman who was truly surprised by the knowledge, calm and confidence he expressed. Clearly then, this movement, despite early successful disruptions, now seems unorganized, disjointed and fueled by misconceptions and misinformation expressing a perceived hatred for President Obama. Therefore, the dramatic images and behaviors some have argued, seems orchestrated or manufactured by people who did not vote for Mr. Obama and are funded by special interest groups, in alliance with the Republicans. As such, the issues they generally raise, viz., immigration, tort reform, government spending that's adding to the deficit, government spending on abortion, big government and environmental laws, are really about the President's policies not specifically about Health Care Reform. It's really about President Obama!Nevertheless, as Peter Hart has pointed out regarding President Obama and the people, "There is an intimacy in the relationship that is kind and personal about how the people relate to the President. They call him Barack. People want the President to succeed on this and so many other issues."

BARACK OBAMA
MASTER OF WASHINGTON DC

Barack Obama's Washington, DC Photo 211.

1. President Obama has rightly pointed out health care costs comprise 16 percent of the American economy and rising.

2. The American Health Care system is broken and unless it is fundamentally restructured, within a decade, costs will double, bankrupting the system. Today we spend $7200 per patient compared to an average of $3600 by most other industrialized nations. Even though we have the best medicine, our health care ranks lower than most nations. As Dr. Andrew Weil has pointed out, "We have to change the content of health care. We have nothing to show for what we spend on health care."

3. The President campaigned on Health Care Reform and essentially his position is thus, as indicated in a town hall meeting on August 8, 2009.

"We have a wonderful government run Medicare program. Bipartisanship is a wonderful thing. People write me expressing outrage, yet, they say keep your hands off my Medicare."

"The majority of Americans will still be getting their health care from private insurance. All we want is to set up a menu of options (an exchange) same as

FREDERICK MONDERSON

Congress has that will give the buyer greater leverage. Health Care costs will just keep skyrocketing until it is fixed."

"Somehow the House of Representatives voted for the 'Death Panel' on grandma because they thought it was too costly. I am not in favor of Death Panels."

"People's concern is that if we reform the Health Care system it will mean rationing. This is a legitimate concern. Systems such as Medicare are inefficient. It contains $177 billion give away over 10 years. This is subsidizing the Insurance Companies. Right now insurance companies are rationing care. The underlying fear will get better if reforms are made in health care."

"Right now, 9 out of 10 times the Generic drug works just as well. Why not get the Generic. If it turns out the Generic drug does not work as well, then you should get the Brand name. I want to speed up generics on the market. Right now, Insurance Companies are fighting to keep their patents on the market longer."

"We are not cutting Medicare. AARP will not endorse a bill that cuts Medicare, but making it more efficient by cutting out subsidies. This will result in savings for you. The biggest ones are on prescription drugs. Seniors are way over-paying. This is the "Donut Hole" because Medicare agreed not to negotiate drug prices."

"In the Single Payer and Public Option. – I am not promoting a Single Payer Plan. I am promoting a single plan that everyone has health insurance and if you don't have insurance, then you can go to an exchange, and having a public option in that menu, you will have competition."

"Competition is good. UPS and FED-EX are competing and doing just fine, while the Post Office continues to have problems.

"It is important to have a Public Option on the table.

"Mental Health is under-valued. I am a serious believer of Mental Health parity."

"There is much misinformation about how we do pay for this without raising taxes on the middle class. I said I will not sign a bill that adds to the national debt. This is in contrast to the Prescription Drug Bill passed by the previous administration and not paid for."

"Nearly $100 billion per year saving measures we will implement will pay for 2/3 of this. My ideas should not burden people who make $250,000 or less. Let's roll back the Bush Tax Cuts. We are still exploring ways to pay for Health Care."

"With 46 million people uninsured, with passage of Health Care Reform, we must focus on where we will get the doctors and nurses to cover these millions of extra people."

BARACK OBAMA
MASTER OF WASHINGTON DC

"The feds have an excellent employee plan. The Congressman's health care plan is no better than that of the janitor who cleans his office. In that large pool they have greater leverage."

"If you like your Health Insurance, you can keep your Health Insurance. If you like your doctor, you can keep your doctor. If you have Health Insurance you like, you do not have to use the Public Option Plan."

"There are legitimate concerns about the cost of the program. There are legitimate concerns about the Public Option. Right now the status quo is not working for you. Pre-existing conditions need to be covered. If we can set up a system that gives you Health Insurance at reduced cost and improved quality, that's what we are working for. Patients do not have free choice today. Single Payer Systems gives freedom of choice."

Yet, despite the President's clear cut outlining of his position, opponents of his measures, by and large, Republicans, have continued to sow misinformation to generate misconceptions. On the other hand, because of the importance of the matter, people want open and honest debate and answers to their pointed questions. Owing to false information particularly by Health Care Reform opponents, the nation is divided on Health Care. Now, let's look at some of the myths that have infuriated people causing genuine debate to be hijacked putting Health Care Reform in jeopardy.

1. READ THE BILL - Because the bill is large, the legislators were thought not to have read it. In the case of the young woman confronting Massachusetts Representative Barney Frank on her issue, she told him to "read the bill." Thereupon, he took out his copy, turned to the respective page, showed the falsity of her position and debunked that myth.

2. HEALTH CARE TO BE RATIONED - Politico Fact's President Bill Adair stated the plan will create a Health Choices Commissioner. For being ridiculously false, he gave it a "Pants on Fire" for extreme falsity.

3. ALL NON-CITIZENS - Legal or not, will be provided health care. Actually, if you're an undocumented alien you will get emergency care, but for general health care, you will have to pay your way. This too got a "Pants on Fire."

4. REGARDING QUALITY CARE – Health Care will be rationed. This too is determined to be false.

5. YOU WILL KEEP YOUR HEALTH CARE PLAN WITH PRIVATE INSURERS – This is not a sure thing, so it's given a half truth. Things may change in the future.

FREDERICK MONDERSON

6. THE PUBLIC OPTION WILL PROVIDE INCENTIVES – This will be dependent on changes in the market place.

7. THE GOVERNMENT WILL COME BETWEEN YOU AND YOUR DOCTOR – President Obama said, "Only you and your doctor should be in charge of your health care discussions. I don't think government doctors should be in charge of your health care. I don't want health insurance doctors in charge of your health care either."

8. DEATH PANEL FOR SENIORS – There is no such thing. Senator Specter pointed to a vicious, malicious, untrue rumor that a 74-year old will be written off because he has cancer. Politico Fact gave "Death Panel" a "Pants on Fire." "It is not what the President or any panel has proposed."

9. MUSCULAR DEGENERATION – You have to lose your sight in one eye before you can get optional care. CNN's Truth Squad gave this a false!

Barack Obama's Washington, DC Photo 212.

BARACK OBAMA
MASTER OF WASHINGTON DC

Barack Obama's Washington, DC Photo 213.

FREDERICK MONDERSON

Barack Obama's Washington, DC Photo 214.

Therefore, everyone agrees, the Health Care System is broken; it is inefficient, costly and does not serve as a safety net. While some have argued, "Preventive care does not save the government money," Dr. Michael Roizin, insisting health care reform must go forward, describes overall health as "a sink overflowing with

BARACK OBAMA
MASTER OF WASHINGTON DC

chronic diseases." To take back your health, you must, "Turn off the chronic disease faucet." This attitude therefore emphasizes wellness behaviors and practices.

Dr. Deepak Chopra insisted 80-90 percent of illnesses are preventable by exercise, diet and stress management. Dr. Sanjay Gupta pointed to $1.2 trillion over a 10-year period in 3 key areas of massive waste. Obesity costs $ 200 billion; smoking $1.91 billion; Clinical mistakes cost $92 billion and Defensive Medicine $210 billion. Operational costs and insurance paper number some $210 billion. These factors account for more than half of health care costs. Thus, analysts are insisting hospitals should be more creative and they should use generic medication.

Dr. Andrew Weil insists physicians should be trained to use "low tech" techniques and insist on intervention strategies.

Therefore, health care practice and reform are major issues in American economics and politics and that is why it has generated such intense pro and con response. President Obama came into office vowing to bring reform with a Public Option as a primary feature. He has tried to cultivate bipartisan support but to no avail, forcing some to wonder if he will waver on the Public Option. This has forced some Democrats in Congress to insist if there is no Public Option the bill won't pass, which means the President is prepared to "go it alone" without Republican support, to get a health care reform bill. Stay tuned!

Barack Obama's Washington, DC Photo 215.

FREDERICK MONDERSON

"What I've tried to do since I started running for President and since I was sworn in as President, is to communicate the notion that America is a critical actor and leader on the world stage, and that we shouldn't be embarrassed about that, but that we exercise our leadership best when we are listening; when we recognize that the world is a complicated place and that we are going to have to act in partnership with other countries; when we lead by example; when we show some element of humility and recognize that we may not always have the best answer, but we can always encourage the best answer and support the best answer."
BARACK OBAMA, press conference, April 2, 2009.

30. LEADERLESS REPUBLICANS
By

Dr. Fred Monderson

The quintessential leader is one who takes charge of a situation and demonstrates leadership behavior that in most cases results in a favorable outcome. Leadership theory holds leaders never sit on fences; they make decisions, good or bad. In business, leaders are expected to take chances, make judgments based on sound analyses and if anywhere from 60-65 or even 70 percent of their decisions are considered successful then they are hailed as wise decision makers.

The great Supreme Court jurists, chosen from whatever ideological spectrums, evolve into the ones who allow interpretation of the Constitution to be viewed not as a single rose boxed in a container with limitations of the past hindering its bloom, but actually becoming a wonderful bouquet, watered and exposed to the invigorating power of sunlight which then blooms magnificently to truly and legally nourish the great legal expectations of the American people.

Two of the most magnificent views in the nation's capitol are; first, the view from the Lincoln Memorial with "Old Abe" casting his glance beyond the Reflecting Pool, past the Washington Memorial and on to the dealings unfolding in the Capitol Building. Second, in a crisscross, is that of Thomas Jefferson looking past the Washington Monument, keeping an eye on happenings in the White House across the way. As a result, leadership transmitted from the White House to Congress along this axis must therefore consider the significance of these three great leaders whose influence looms great in the tradition of the best interest of the nation, and thus, only the best ideas should be cultivated and unleashed there from.

Barack Obama's election to the Presidency is more than the significance of being the first African American; the man chosen to revitalize America's economic and social structure at home and its foreign policy image abroad; his is the ideological

BARACK OBAMA
MASTER OF WASHINGTON DC

purity not of the right but the privilege to lead the nation. As such, Obama, the man, as race horses with blinders, only sees what's ahead, as history will see, in his view, what is best in the interest of the American nation. Equally, how to correct problems of a decaying past and cultivate new and revitalizing ideas that will restore America's scientific, educational and ideological leadership to a world waiting anxiously for this rebirth. This therefore, brings us to the nation's economic recovery, its new image abroad and the need to reform its Health Care System which, through fraud, mismanagement and inefficiency is significantly clogging the nation's economic lifeline.

In her "coming out" Sarah Palin blasted President Obama's Health Care Reform plan with its "death panel" on euthanasia as a system that is "downright evil." This position, not inconsistently negative is taken by more than 90 percent of Republican leadership on practically every issue President Obama has put forward from day one of his administration. We're all familiar with total House of Representative Republicans' rejection of the Stimulus Bill, and all but three in the Senate followed suit; the powerful "nine" Republican Senators who voted for Supreme Court Justice Sonia Sotomayor; and Republican members of the "gang of six;" who may know something their colleagues don't, and perhaps are subconsciously sending a message in their vote. Nevertheless, both Republicans and some Democrats, seeming near total rejection of President Obama's solutions to problems created by a Republican Administration over the last decade, raises questions of the whole notion of patriotism over party politics. For, after all, as the nation began to spiral downward in the domestic and global economic quagmire, one has to believe the interests of the nation has to come before all others, no matter what. However, Republican negativity seemed more motivated against the man, Barack Obama, than against his policies in the interest of the nation.

Republican *ad hominem* arguments against then Senator Barack Obama's campaign for the Presidency manifested in accusing him of being a non-citizen, Muslim, inexperienced, questioning his patriotism and without blatantly proclaiming such, they found problems with the audacity of an African American wanting to lead the nation. After all, from the earliest times, a la Crispus Attucks, African Americans have been dying to protect it.

FREDERICK MONDERSON

Barack Obama's Washington, DC Photo 216.

Barack Obama's Washington, DC Photo 217.

Notwithstanding, President Obama's love of America, his confidence, commitment and tremendously potent analytic ability, has put together a dynamic team of economic and scientific specialists, who, despite Republican non-

BARACK OBAMA
MASTER OF WASHINGTON DC

cooperation and invective, obstructionist behavior, ultimately steered the country towards the "light at the end of the tunnel," refusing to "turn back to the failed policies of the past." These days, President Obama, after examining the newest economic figures, has insisted "the worst may be behind us" and that, "we're heading in the right direction," inasmuch as we have a "steep mountain to climb" because "we started in a deep valley."

Now, as the plans he put in place have begun to take hold, and as he had campaigned on the issue of Health Care Reform, President Obama issued guidelines that Congress should present a bill for his signature before the August Recess. This insistence on Congressional legislative freedom set off an enormous negative campaign to stop the President's Health Care Reform agenda on the pretext it is too expensive and not in the best interest of the American people. All such ruckus now unfolding across the country, has forced observers at home and abroad to view the meaning, purpose and significance of this form of reaction and question whether such behavior is truly characteristic of American democracy. Some say yes, some say no! Some say constructive criticism is welcome, destructive obstructionist behavior is not welcome. This is evident, since the news media is replete with instances of people disrupting town hall meetings held by their elected representatives home for the August Recess and bent on explaining the dynamics of the Health Care Reform issue. Some have argued, this negative reaction is traceable to Republican begun behavior well before Congress recessed.

In this light, Republican Chairman Michael Steele was one of the first to fire a salvo against the President claiming he's taking on "too much, too fast, too soon." When we consider American citizens have waited more than sixty years for Health Care Reform, such a contention is out of place. In fact, when President Obama was asked "Why the rush?" he gave two reasons for the urgency. (1) "Because people write me asking for help," (2) "If you don't set deadlines in this town, nothing gets done." Also, "too much" means much has been ignored and thus the need.

Old folks have always said "Show me your company and I'll tell who you are." Importantly, they have also said, "Be careful of how you choose your friends" and "don't join gangs because you will be held responsible for the gang's behavior." And, finally, "be careful with whom you associate for this will show where your character and mind is." Significantly, in the aftermath of the French Revolution by 1791-1792, as the movement began to consume itself, the English theorist Edmund Burke wrote a treatise, "Some Considerations on the French Revolutions in France." A classic line from that classic work is: "The only thing necessary for evil to triumph is for good men (people) to say nothing."

This brings us to the question of Republican leadership; whether there is Republican leadership; and whether they are "good men." If so, why are they allowing "evil to triumph" by not denouncing malicious invective against the

FREDERICK MONDERSON

President and his policies. First of all, the "tail is wagging" Michael Steele's dog. His "cart is before the horse." His weak statement "we're not sending anyone to disrupt town hall meetings" forces us to realize "an enemy's enemy is a friend." Any behavior that is against Obama's policies is consistent with that of the Republican "Party of No!" that Steele leads, which holds similar views.

When the poor widow felt tired after traversing the land all day in search of sustenance and finally knelt down to pray near a bakery, two boys working there saw her kneeling and say, "Let's use some bread to stone that woman on her knees." As they started to hit her, she exclaimed, "Lord, I don't care how you send it, just keep it coming!" The question is, "Are Republicans listening to Michael Steele?"

Republican Senator Jim DeMint of South Carolina shot the first salvo on Health Care Reform obstructionism by saying "If we can stop Obama on this, it will be his Waterloo." Later he opined, the "President is out of control." DeMint claims the President "uses bogus numbers" and "gives false promises." Therefore, "we must break him." Billy Crystal of the *Weekly Standard* ordered "Go for the Kill!" Commentators have said, "Republicans want to wound the President on Health Care Reform." After such vile rhetoric, when world leaders gather for that memorable photograph, how proud would Americans be that their President is among the world's best? How about those men and women, particularly African Americans fighting on the front lines in Iraq and Afghanistan under the banner of the Commander-In-Chief, how do they feel? How do Veterans feel about this sully and vile behavior towards the President?

One thing for sure, Republican hostility towards President Obama and Health Care Reform has served as marching orders for people who disrupted town hall meetings. The disrupters use Republican slogans as "Just Say No!" Evoking "Joe the Plumber," whom Obama had to "flush with plunger" and all, they call him "Socialist" and his policies "Socialism." Images portray the President with Hitler's moustache and Nazi Swastikas and cries of "Nazism" abound. Members of Congress are also hung in effigy. That is not to say all people at town hall meeting are thugs and disrupters. There are intelligent people who want intelligent answers to legitimate questions about Health Care Reform but most are being drowned out in the disruptions. Fact is, whoever does the dirty work is irrelevant. As long as it gets done. When Henry IV exasperated: "Will no one rid me of this meddlesome priest" and two knights took off and murdered Sir Thomas Moore on the steps of the Whitenburg Cathedral, he did not send them, but the aim was accomplished!

In all this negativity, neither John McCain, John Boehner, Mitch McConnell, nor Representative Peter King of New York - Republican "leaders" have not come forward to denounce the hatred directed against the President and his policies. Let's not forget the 53 percent who voted against President Obama, they're the ones waiting in the wings. Without a doubt there are many people who hate President Obama because of his race. A new book, *In the President's Secret*

BARACK OBAMA
MASTER OF WASHINGTON DC

Service by Ron Kessler revealed 3,000 death threats against President Bush per year and 12,000 against President Obama!

Barack Obama's Washington, DC Photo 218.

Fact is, there's much misinformation given to many people by Health Care Insurance Companies, the Corporate Lobby, the Conservative Movement, Republican leaders, websites and "authorities" such as Sarah Palin who uses "death panel" rhetoric to misinform people that President Obama is pushing euthanasia, cuts to Medicare and Medicaid, government takeover of Health Care. In reality, the President has said, premiums have doubled in the last 10 years and will again double in the next. Health insurance is taking a bigger bite of the American dollar, as the cost of Medicare and Medicaid keep rising. This may break the federal budget. This nation spends $6000 more than most nations for health care with less result. Hence the need to fix the system before it truly gets out of control.

FREDERICK MONDERSON

Barack Obama's Washington, DC Photo 219.

Barack Obama's Washington, DC Photo 220.

BARACK OBAMA
MASTER OF WASHINGTON DC

Barack Obama's Washington, DC Photo 221.

Some commentators as David Sirota have pointed out, regarding the Health Care Reform plan, "This is really about how we pay for Health Care and not really about Health Care." Also, as Jim Greer says, "It's about financing and services."

Meanwhile, Barack Obama keeps pedaling, striding into the revitalizing possibilities of the new dawn and day coming into vogue because of his vision for America, buttressed by the work of his teams of "creative minds" dedicated to the goal of a new reality in this nation. Too bad, the Republicans will stand on the sidelines leaderless, as the marching bands go by and historians will trumpet, "He, the king (President) is clothed in a wonderful garment" as America finally evolves the true meaning of its creed!

FREDERICK MONDERSON

"Hostility and hatred are not match for justice; they offer no pathways to peace."
BARACK OBAMA, Speech, Feb. 27, 2009.

31. OBAMA AND "GATES-GATE"
By
Dr. Fred Monderson

"Gates gate" is bigger than Prof. Henry "Skip" Louis Gates! It is bigger than Sgt. James Crowley and it is bigger than President Barack Obama, who, during a national news conference was asked a question pertaining to the matter of Prof. Gates' arrest for disorderly conduct after an officer responded to a report of breaking and entering into his own residence. On Sunday, July 26, 2009, on *This Week*, ABC News commentator George Will offered "Some questions are not the President's responsibility" and that "we discuss race too much." Donna Brazile retorted, "For too long in our history we have not wanted to discuss this issue." Essentially though, the President did not speak uttering his now famous "The Cambridge Police acted stupidly by arresting a man in his own home." While these comments seemed inflammatory and inappropriate, other comments in his response have credibility. However, within 24 hours, because of national outrage, particularly from cops nationwide, the President entered the White House Press Briefing Room where Press Secretary Robert Gibbs presided and President Obama "walked back" his comments. He said he spoke to both gentlemen and invited them both to the White House for a beer.

This situation, however, needs a closer look, for in de-constructing both men, therein lies the problem.

Both Officer Crowley and Prof. Gates have exemplary records in law enforcement and in academia. However, the event that set this off and brought them together is, as indicated, police responding to a neighbor's report of seeing two black men with back packs breaking into the residence in question, that turns out to be Prof. Gates'.

The report itself has two parts. First there are black men whose behavior exposes all black men to ridicule and questionable responses in social relations, academia,

BARACK OBAMA
MASTER OF WASHINGTON DC

etc. Second, ingrained in the American psyche is the negative connotation regarding the "black man" and even more, "two black men." Let us keep in mind, the police are responding to "two black men" with "backpacks" breaking into the residence in an affluent neighborhood where, "black men" in all likelihood, were not supposed to be.

Evidently, Prof. Gates may have lived there for some time and, unless this was a new person in the neighborhood, she would have known "blacks lived there." We cannot fault the neighbor for her good neighborliness in reporting her perception of a "crime in progress." She could have realized for some time there was no activity at the house and did not know he was back. Nevertheless, there is a particular psychologically imbedded mindset in law enforcement when responding to a report regarding "black men." Now the neighbor is very upset claiming in her report she did not say "black men" or even mention "backpack."

Now, let us take Officer Crowley, a distinguished officer with an exemplary record in an upscale neighborhood with a black mayor, in a state with a black governor, in a country with a newly elected black President. He is responding to a report of two black men and the Cambridge police send out one of their best.

Sgt. Crowley was chosen by a black commissioner to teach a class on Racial Profiling at the Police Academy in Cambridge. Why? Because Racial Profiling occurs in Cambridge as it occurs throughout the country. All Sgt. Crowley's props notwithstanding, he was unable to diffuse the situation. He responded to breaking and entering and came away with a disorderly conduct charge. First and foremost, there was no crime and the charges were dropped. Anyone black or white would have been annoyed, if as "a man's home is his castle," and these events transpired there.

Now, Henry Louis "Skip" Gates!

FREDERICK MONDERSON

Barack Obama's Washington, DC Photo 222.

BARACK OBAMA
MASTER OF WASHINGTON DC

Barack Obama's Washington, DC Photo 223.

FREDERICK MONDERSON

Barack Obama's Washington, DC Photo 224.

Sometime around 1990 the *New York Times Magazine* featured Henry Louis Gates on its cover with his wife and kids, dubbing him, "The New Star in Black Studies." Quite frankly, this did not set well with many in the black community, particularly those who object to interracial marriages. However, there were others in the academic community of Black Studies who were toiling longer in the vineyards and did not get this or any kind of recognition from establishment media. Blacks do not like their leaders "chosen" and so while he was recognized as a black scholar, he was still an anomaly. In some forums and discussions participants would simply say, "Let's Skip Gates!"

However, and much to his credit, Prof. Gates trumped his critics by fulfilling the quintessential requirement for academic recognition; he published and published, prolifically. He worked in tandem with PBS and he launched the Genealogy

BARACK OBAMA
MASTER OF WASHINGTON DC

Project. "Skip Gates Goes to Africa" was a singular achievement. Single-handedly he filmed and exposed great portions of Africa to a wider audience in cooperation with PBS. Apparently, he had visited Africa previously and caused some consternation by bringing his "white wife" and this turned off some Africans. This time he came alone but a particular camera shot showed him as "lonely man" as he trekked across Africa.

Prof. Gates "discovered," then exposed to the world, a tremendous body of Medieval African history of literature, philosophy and law. This important body of knowledge is being translated, cataloged and readied for publication. On that Africa trip, however, he did antagonize Africans and African Americans.

Most Biblical scholars are familiar with the story of the encounter between King Solomon and the Queen of Sheba. Never mind the racial connotation over whether the queen said "I am black and comely" or "I am black but comely!" Or that Solomon pursued her because her empire was more extensive than his! It's agreed the encounter produced an offspring Menelik I, when the Queen returned to Ethiopia. Apparently, the Jewish "Ark of the Covenant" also disappeared about this time and became "lost to history;" or no one knew where it was for two millennia. That is, except the people who have it. These are the Ethiopians!

British investigators, just prior to Prof. Gates Africa trip had traced the location of the Ark to a place in Ethiopia, where the investigator was stopped at the gate to the building housing the Ark. This was shown on TV. Next we see Prof. Gates at the same gate. Some have argued, since the Ethiopian guardians refused to disclose the Ark to a white man, maybe they would show it to a black man. Some have also argued this was to be the high point of Prof. Gates' trip.

We therefore see Prof. Gates at the gate demanding to see the ark. The keeper's assistant who came out to greet him told Prof. Gates, "It's irrelevant what you think. We have the Ark of Covenant and we're not going to show it to anyone." However, he did explain to the previous investigator some aspects about the dynamics and power of the Ark; who is the chosen guardian, and what are the dangers of unintended exposure. Nevertheless, "Skip" returned home, aired his documentary, revealed discovery of the cache of knowledge and resumed his academic pursuits of teaching and publishing.

Like all successful people criticized, some have argued, Prof. Gates, residing in the "big house on the hill" "is of us but not with us!" Who knows, maybe with age he mellowed; maybe circumstances made him realize we're all in the same boat! That is why when faced with the situation he realized the "chickens have, in fact, come home to roost." Who knows if he overreacted? Who knows if he was overwhelmed by the situation? Maybe he really realized he was a black man in America and thus was annoyed he was being challenged in his own home!

FREDERICK MONDERSON

Officer Crowley, not wearing his name tag, later announced he was concerned about Prof. Gates' safety because he was responding to two men. He was not sure Prof. Gates may have been aware of the possibility of two men in the house who could threaten his safety. None of this was explained to the Professor when he was asked to come outside. Thus, Gates, challenged, forced to identify himself and asked to come outside by a white officer, finally realized he was no different from other blacks who were racially profiled. When asked to identify himself he stated, "I'm Professor Gates owner of this house" and Officer Crowley responded, we are told, "I'm the King of Siam."

As someone who teaches Racial Profiling classes to other officers, Crowley did not fare well in the practice run. The big man in Officer James Crowley should realize while he was not guilty of same, should now intensify a call for a national debate on Racial Profiling. He would be a terrific "Poster Boy" for Racial Profiling!

President Obama's initial measured statement, while point No. 2 was focused on, point No. 3 was generally ignored by the media. His point No. 1, being a friend of Prof. Gates was downplayed. Commentators speculated what would have happened if it was Dr. Henry Kissinger who was arrested by a black sergeant and President Bush had told the press the "Prof. Kissinger is my friend." However, having "walked his comments back" and invited both parties to the White House for a beer, President Obama should now make them chronicle and speak out, teach, about Racial Profiling that has had such a terrible impact on police/community relations.

We must not forget it's a small number of policemen who create the problem that stains good police officers like Sgt. James Crowley. Recently, an officer shown on TV stopping a white motorist was recorded ranting: "I will shoot you in the head and sleep soundly tonight." How pathetic! However, the painful history of Racial Profiling in its shameful aspects, date back to the Black Codes of the *Ante Bellum* South, relating to runaway slaves. Yet, despite the great social and racial progress made in America today, the emotional and psychological stain of Racial Profiling still increases the chances that a black or Hispanic would be arrested 10 times more than a white. In 10 years, prison populations increased fivefold and blacks are now 70 percent of prison, while only 10 percent of the general, population. Let us not forget, President Obama has been accused of moving America towards a police state, but, when he supposedly "checked the police" he was challenged. It lets us all know, Presidents, Professors, Police and the Public, how softly we have to tread in our relationships with one another. Marc Morial of the *National Urban League* advised that the President should embrace a strong national policy in the End Racial Profiling Act. He could then convene with Sgt. Crowley and Prof. Gates, a national forum with Civil Rights groups, Police Associations, Chiefs of Police and Community Activist groups. Such a significant focus can help rid the nation of the cancer of Racial Profiling and as we hope to make America a better

BARACK OBAMA
MASTER OF WASHINGTON DC

place, this may be a good start. Maybe the coming together of Sgt. James Crowley and Prof. Henry Louis Gates, despite the hoopla, is for the betterment of all.

Barack Obama's Washington, DC Photo 225.

FREDERICK MONDERSON

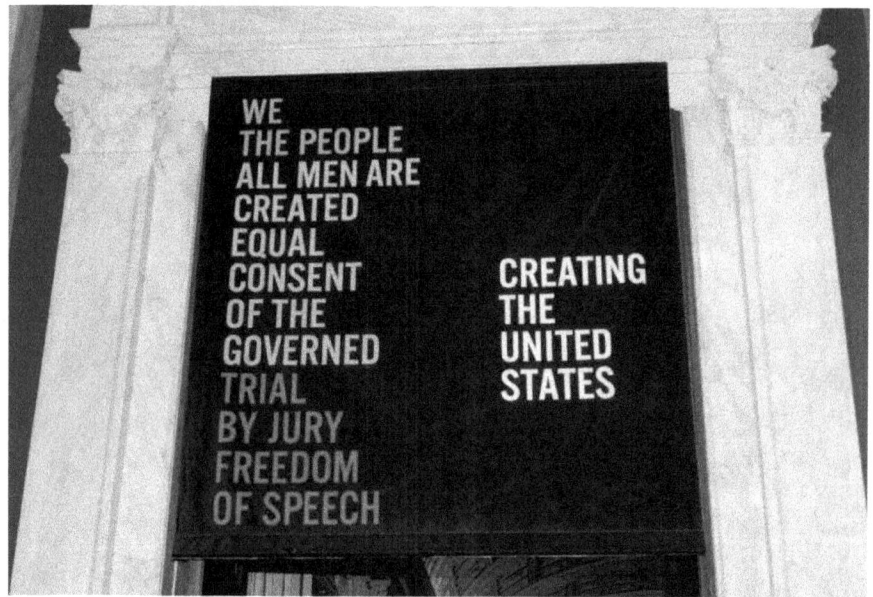

Barack Obama's Washington, DC Photo 226. The pillars upon which the American system rests.

BARACK OBAMA
MASTER OF WASHINGTON DC

Barack Obama's Washington, DC Photo 227.

FREDERICK MONDERSON

"If those Republicans come at me with the same fear-mongering and swift-boating that they usually do, then I will take them head on. Because I believe the American people are tired of fear and tired of distractions and tired of diversions. We can make this election not about fear, but about the future. And that won't just be a Democratic victory; that will be an American victory." BARACK OBAMA, speech Nov. 10, 2007

32. PRESIDENT OBAMA AND THE REPUBLICANS
By

Dr. Fred Monderson

Decades later, in the Smithsonian Institute, a youngster asks his granddad, "Grandfather, why are those statues labeled 'The Gang of Four?'" The grandfather responded, "Well son, back when I was your age, these four individuals, Senator John McCain, Governor Sarah Palin, Senator Mitchell McConnell and Representative Speaker John Boehner were Republican representatives whose political party was nicknamed the "Party of No!" They took on Senator Barack Obama, who became the 44th President of the United states. He beat them so bad, metaphorically speaking; it took them nearly forever to recover! However, while they served their country well; yet, they could never defeat the master strategist and tactician Barack Obama. When their statues were placed here, they were called "The Gang of Four!" "Tell me more grandfather!"

"You see son, it all began when the then Senator Barack Obama of Illinois decided to run for the Presidency of the United States. First he had to win the Democratic Nomination against Senator Hillary Clinton, which he did. That's when the Republicans began their strategies against Barack Obama that have all proved challenging but ineffective.

The Republican strategy in the Presidential Election was, first and foremost, to discredit Barack Obama in the eyes of the American people. He had run a tough campaign for the Democratic Nomination against Senator Hillary Clinton, wife of the former President Bill Clinton. Senator John McCain, a Viet Nam war hero, was seasoned, but one of the oldest candidates seeking the Presidency. Seeking to capture women who had voted for Hillary Clinton and disaffected because she was not chosen as Obama's Vice-President running mate, Senator McCain chose Alaska Governor Sarah Palin, a national political neophyte. The conservative right wing of the Republican Party loved her instantly because she was a woman,

BARACK OBAMA
MASTER OF WASHINGTON DC

young, almost Obama's age, articulate and spoke "Conservative speak!" Tremendous crowds turned out to glimpse the one potential Republican woman Vice-President, almost a heartbeat away from the Presidency.

Like a shiny new Lincoln penny she glittered, energized their base, gave McCain's numbers a tremendous bump in the polls; some believed she even overshadowed him. But, like that new penny, once in circulation, it began to get tarnished.

Senator McCain's "mis-speak" that the American economy was "fundamentally sound" when in fact two terms of Republican leadership under President George Bush and Republican control of Congress for most of the decade resulting in tremendous tax cuts for the wealthy, a prescription drug plan not paid for, and a turnaround in the economy resulting in catastrophic failures, tremendous Wall Street losses, enormous job losses, mounting housing foreclosures, loss of bank credit, consumer spending in decline, all added with Sarah Palin being perceived as inexperienced in key areas of government, foreign policy and equally important, much of her rhetoric was in fact guardedly scripted, raised many questions about Republican strategy and vision. Finally, the women's movement intellectual assessment of Governor Palin, determined she was a "lightweight" who, in fact, had too much baggage. As this aspect of the Republican strategy unraveled, equally devastating secondary strategies from their playbook exposed their "soft underbelly."

Surrogates such as "Joe the Plumber," in a campaign stop encounter with Senator Obama, accused the candidate of pursuing "Socialist policies." This relatively unknown individual instantly achieved celebrity status for a line the Republicans felt would be effective and then exploited. The name, "Joe the Plumber" was mentioned twenty-odd times in the Presidential Debate between Obama and McCain. Riding the wave, there was talk of Joe acquiring a singing contract and McCain promised to fire his whole campaign staff only taking "Joe the Plummer" to Washington. Like so many Republican moves, Joe too began to unravel. Turns out he was not a registered plumber and his income level would not be affected under Obama's $250,000 no-tax plan. However, he got his 15 minutes of fame but faded as the Republicans also did.

Whether intentional or unintentional, allies of the Republicans began to question Barack Obama's birthright, accusing him of being a socialist, attacking his blackness, that he was a Muslim, inexperienced in foreign policy, and that his wife Michelle was not a loyal American, implying she should not be First Lady, if her husband won. Obama took on his wife's critics first. Firmly, he stated to all comers: "If you're listening, lay off my wife!"

FREDERICK MONDERSON

Senator Barack Obama and his team had crafted a campaign strategy that was remarkable by modern standards. The energetic young Senator articulated towards, studied, targeted and motivated untold numbers of young people of all races.

Barack Obama's Washington, DC Photo 227a. The Library of Congress holds 5 million books on 500 miles of shelves.

Wanting to remain engaged, finding Palin shallow, the Republican message seemingly bankrupt, and Barack Obama stumping and striding, women flocked to his campaign as volunteers and voters. Independents were hedging their bets, but ultimately came aboard. Senator Barack Obama raised tremendous sums of money and continued to do so, particularly using the internet. Later he revealed he had amassed a 6-million Internet database of supporters.

BARACK OBAMA
MASTER OF WASHINGTON DC

Barack Obama's Washington, DC 228. The great American eagle in marble!

FREDERICK MONDERSON

Barack Obama's Washington, DC Photo 229.

Next, candidate Obama began deploying his big democratic guns, Bill Clinton, Al Gore, Hillary Clinton, Bill Richardson, Ted Kennedy, and high ranking, present and former members of the party he was now leading; including African-Americans, women, Latinos, Asians, gays and lesbians, young and old, physically challenged, all wanting to be part of history electing the first African-American as President of the United States. He stayed on message; his mantra was "Yes we can!" He called on supporters to spread the word and register voters, hold parties to clarify his message, he "went to school" to shore up weaknesses in his knowledge base in economic realities of banking, business, real estate, global trade and in foreign policy involving the Middle East, nuclear proliferation, environmental issues and energy independence. As the Republicans ebbed, Obama flowed. "Everybody was working" to pass the torch to a new generation of leadership. From his studied observations, Senator Ted Kennedy praised Senator Obama for "high principles, and bold expectations."

As the Republicans discombobulated and deconstructed, an energized Obama revitalized his teams, kept up the pressure bent on winning the election. The Republicans are good at utilizing unsolicited allies who could be disowned even though all parties have the same goal – Zero in on Obama! Stop him! Break him! Discredit him! As the election neared, Republican messaging, whether by phone or flyer indicated Republicans would vote on Tuesday, November 4th, Democrats

BARACK OBAMA
MASTER OF WASHINGTON DC

would vote on Wednesday, November 5th, 2008. People were told, "If you have a parking ticket and try to vote you would be arrested!" All manner of disingenuous disfranchisement strategies were directed against potential Democratic voters, especially blacks.

Threats and racial slurs were directed against Barack Obama. Objectively speaking, the Republicans could and did deny ownership, but would not denounce such insidious efforts to derail the Obama express. This is why Barack Obama won the election to become the 44th President of the United States of America and his victory ignited new interest in American issues unprecedented in world affairs.

There were probably some people, somewhere on the globe who believed the Inauguration would not happen. Many probably held their breaths until it did happen and then the world was treated to the fantabulous display of an American Presidential Inauguration, particularly one with the significance of number 44. Then it was time to get to work.

Senator Ted Kennedy, a man who never compromised his principles, yet recognized the historic renewal for the nation. He often echoed, "The work begins anew, hope rises, the dream lives on."

Owing to a carefully crafted plan of attack, during the transition period, President Obama hit the ground running by having his key cabinet heads, State, Defense, Treasury, Justice, Interior, Homeland Security confirmed relatively easily. The other department heads were approved by the Senate in a more pedestrian manner. Those chosen to head departments who had baggage withdrew their nominations.

Thanking President Bush for facilitating a flawless transition, President Obama encouraged Congress to grant him the remaining portions of the Bush bank rescue, TARP funds. Then he proposed an $800 billion Stimulus Bill entitled the American Recovery and Reinvestment Act, designed to, as Democratic Strategist Donna Brazile put it, initiate a strategy of "Rescue, Recovery and Reinvest" in the American economy. This is when the Republicans, seething from their 57% to 43% loss in the national elections, losing seats in both houses of Congress, put their foot down. No Republicans in the House of Representatives voted for the Stimulus Bill and only 3 Republican Senators crossed party lines to vote with the President's party to pass the measure designed to bind the wounds and treat the hemorrhaging US economy that equally and significantly impacted the global economic system.

FREDERICK MONDERSON

Barack Obama's Washington, DC Photo 230. A wonderful Coat of Arms.

Barack Obama's Washington, DC Photo 231. Marble angels, with and without wings, or, winged figure genius with stars in the background.

BARACK OBAMA
MASTER OF WASHINGTON DC

Barack Obama's Washington, DC Photo 232. Patterns that make a beautiful quilt.

While the Republicans engaged in obstructionist behavior, President Obama's assessment of the calamitous state of America's financial and economic systems, with good advice, intervened in the financial markets, banking system, automobile industry, housing market, paying attention to trends in jobless numbers, issuing and extending unemployment insurance assistance and health insurance. Dogged attention to detail, consistently working to address problems across the society's domestic spectrum and unafraid to make courageous decisions, the President's efforts at bipartisan rule received tepid support from the Republicans and predominantly "No to this and No to that!" So much so, the Republicans now earned the new title "The Party of No!" Criticizing the President, not showing any support, nor offering any viable alternatives to his proposals, they seemed to be fading in the distance of obscurity.

In the run up to the election, upon analysis of the current broken Health Care system and the fact Americans have waited more than half a century for reform; the fact Health Care consumes one sixth of the national economy, is fraught with waste and inefficiency; and that nearly 50 million people lack Health Insurance, candidate Barack Obama make the important plank of fixing Health Care a significant theme of his camping strategy. With the first 100-days milestone passed, the President received tremendous praise for the significant steps taken to address the myriad problems facing the nation despite Republican non-cooperation and obstructionist behavior other than just saying "No!" Despite his efforts at

FREDERICK MONDERSON

bipartisanship, Republicans would not get aboard the Obama Express, accusing him of not seeking true bipartisanship. The question is how many Republicans wanted bipartisanship, at what price, since they lost the election and were generally considered responsible for the economic and resulting domestic and foreign policy problems in the first place.

Bipartisanship is a two way street. If the President extended a hand, Republicans should have made every effort to grab it. In another context, Secretary of State Hillary Clinton in an interview question responded: "If President Obama walked on water, Bolton [former US ambassador to the UN] would say he could not swim!" Imagine! In eulogy at his passing, Senator Ted Kennedy was praised for never compromising his principles, though he "worked to bring consensus and bipartisanship." Too bad Republican Representatives could not emulate this "Lion of the Senate."

In the second 100-days, the President moved to reform Health Care and as Vincent Price said in the Michael Jackson song "Thriller," the "Hounds of hell" emerged. The "red in necks" began to show. The Insurance Industry and Conservative groups such as the Tea Party Express, Trust CommonSense.com, Americans for Prosperity, 60-Plus Association, Rick Scott's Conservatives for Public Rights, Freedom Works, all of whom can be considered "non card-carrying" members of the party or allies, created the mayhem of "Shutdown your Congressman," "Embarrass your elected representative," "Don't let an intelligent conversation develop," shouts of "Read the Bill," disrupt town hall meetings, record disruptions and post on U-Tube, so that people with legitimate concerns are "caught off guard," as people such as Talk Show Host Rush Limbaugh and Internet Chat throw gasoline on the fire of public discontent. Yet, Michael Steele could still shamefacedly affirm "We're not inciting anyone to go out and do anything."

Democrats at the town hall meetings were caught off-guard by negativity begun by South Carolina Senator Jim DeMint whose "Waterloo" and "Stop Obama" statements set in motion divisive actions even death threats to elected officials. However, individuals as Carrie Budoff Brown of Politico.com advised politicians to "prepare for these confrontations." Well-respected Presidential adviser and CNN commentator David Gergen, who had seen much, exasperated: "This has become very offensive." He asked, "Where's the Republican leadership?" Recognizing Republicans benefit from such ruckus, he said, "It's up to the leadership to quell this." Then he recognized such behavior had "roots in the campaign. The roots are in people who are upset with the election of Barack Obama. This has roots in anger seen over the last year." He further insisted, "Can we face the real challenges? Leadership on both sides needs to step up!" Democrats have stepped up. Republicans need to control the genii they let out of the bottle!

BARACK OBAMA
MASTER OF WASHINGTON DC

Barack Obama's Washington, DC Photo 233. Here the emphasis is on the "School Marm" who is the transmitter of the word of knowledge.

Many people believe Michael Steele's choice as Republican Party leader was a direct result of Barack Obama's election. The negative things being said to and about Representative David Scott and President Obama that relate to such as "Nigga," one has to wonder, does this characterization also apply to Michael Steele, who is also black? The question is how does he feel as the chickens come home?

Barack Obama's Washington, DC Photo 234. Pattern from the marble floor showing the four cardinal points of the compass, twelve squares with decorative patterns and twelve circles with the signs of the zodiac.

BARACK OBAMA
MASTER OF WASHINGTON DC

Barack Obama's Washington, DC Photo 235. Patterned tiled floor, marble stairs ascending to columns supporting a decorated ceiling.

Former Democratic National Committee chairman Howard Dean spoke of "lots of orchestrations, lots of organizations and reputable companies that are underwriting this" protest movement. He said further, "This is a handful of angry people who are overwhelming everyone."

Recently in the President's Joint Address to Congress, while making a point about illegal aliens not being covered in the new Health Care Reform bill, Congressman Wilson from South Carolina shouted "You lie" in the House Chamber. This is unprecedentedly blatant mark of disrespect in the Congress and directed towards the President was shameful. Senator John McCain, right after, said this was inappropriate and he should apologize. Wilson did and wanted to speak to the President who had one of his assistants accept the apology.

FREDERICK MONDERSON

There is something about South Carolina, first Senator DeMint and then Congressman Wilson and when we add some of the rancor from the "Tea Party Express" leader Williams invoking Charleston Heston's "from my dead cold hands" rant, this is a part of the serious Obama Derangement malady. Add to this Chris Brock "the black protester with guns" from Arizona who attended the Health Care Reform protest rally near the President, seemingly influenced by his pastor Anderson, the man who is "praying for the death of Obama;" we have had to say whoa! Imagine this Christian, I mean charlatan "Man of the Cloth" praying that President Obama may "have a brain tumor and die as did Senator Ted Kennedy." In the payback, Jesus will probably say to this fraud "Get thee hence from me Satan!" Meanwhile, the world was watching and wondering what was going on in America and why was there so much hate. There were new books out showing these people hate the President because of his race, pure and simple. Again, they were either "Card Carrying" or "Non Card Carrying" members or half-allies of the Republican Party. Again, one must wonder how Michael Steele must feel about all this.

All the while, President Obama had recognized the world was changing. He used his imagination to seize the opportunity to tackle the big issues to effectuate badly needed change with a constructive vision of a future with American leadership restored. Having employed effective leadership he rescued the American economy from the abyss, restored consumer confidence through calm wisdom and bold action that began to show results. He set the nation on a path to energy independence through clean energy initiatives and revamped educational structures, strategies and techniques. After his second term in office, he exited the Presidency and world stage with America at its pinnacle as a beacon of hope, a symbol to emulate and leading "by the power of its example, rather than an example of its power." All this America was able to accomplish under President Barack Obama's effective leadership with very little Republican support. No wonder, decades later, that party is still in tatters after the "thumpin'" administered by the First African-American President.

"So you see son, America was very lucky to have had Barack Obama as its 44th President."
"I'm glad you lived through that experience grandfather."

BARACK OBAMA
MASTER OF WASHINGTON DC

"Let us reach for the world that ought to be – that spark of the divine that still stirs within each of our souls." BARACK OBAMA, Noble Lecture, Dec. 10, 2009.

33. PRESIDENT OBAMA AND WOMEN
By

Dr. Fred Monderson

When the *New York Post* printed a misleading photo, on its cover, of President Barack Obama looking at the rear of a Brazilian model, that newspaper, some have called a "rag," "birdcage catcher," miscalculated over the reaction it would receive and what is the true relationship this brilliant leader has had with women. Such a relationship is evident from the number of women in his cabinet and particularly in this health care reform age, Linda Douglas of the White House Office on Health Care Reform and Kathleen Sebelius, Secretary of Health and Human Services, have been the President's most articulate and staunchest defenders of this policy position. When we add the female cabinet members at State, Homeland Security and the United Nations one gets some idea of the depth of his support for the abilities and capabilities of females, but even more important his recognition of the potential capabilities of this sex and his efforts to encourage their participation in the key aspects of his administration. We get an even better understanding of the man as a leader, intellect and human being. However, all of this is rooted in Mr. Obama's ancestral and familial history. As a result, any attempt such as the *Post's* to paint or besmirch President Barack Obama is false, bound to fail and a fundamental miscalculation of who the man really is.

Let us begin with his family and the female members who have influenced his evolution and sense of focus and humaneness. Mr. Obama was raised by his mother and grandmother. In his Autobiographies and graphic clips photographs of his mother holding "Baby Barack" and him sitting on the bench between grandmother and grandfather have gotten much press coverage. His mother would wake him at 4: 30 in the morning to do his homework before she went to work and when he complained she remarked, "This is no fun for me either, Buster." With her passing "Grandma Toots" took over; her influence was emphasized and with her passing on the eve of his triumph, he was visibly shaken. The sadness he

FREDERICK MONDERSON

experienced was due because (1) he lost the last maternal link; (2) he lost "Grandma Toots;" (3) she did not live long enough to see his greatest triumph, something she too worked long and hard to see accomplished. He does have a sibling and this allows him to remain connected to these two important women.

In a way, I see myself as a shade of Barack Obama, not by being able to accomplish what he had done, but simply being raised by grandma. In the military, she was my beneficiary and received gifts and cards from every port of call I visited. On mothers' day, I was challenged to show love to grandmother, mother, a wife, two daughters, two sisters, two aunts, and two nieces. I was terribly shocked when I lost grandma and then my mother!

I do believe in the health care reform debate, the likes of Sarah Palin and those she has influenced to run with the idea of "Obama pulling the plug on grandma" have so miscalculated, because it underestimates and undervalues his relationship with "grandma," and having given wings to such falsity, it will fly back in their faces like spitting in the wind.

Barack Obama's Washington, DC Photo 236. Early Printers marks from Britain and the United States, akin to a trademark or copyright as the written word began to spread.

BARACK OBAMA
MASTER OF WASHINGTON DC

Barack Obama's Washington, DC Photo 237. Marble sculpture showing the innocence of youth.

Upon graduation from college, Mr. Obama traveled to Chicago where he met the beautiful Michelle Robinson who "captured" him and has remained the wind behind his sails, giving him two beautiful daughters and a darling mother-in-law who all now inhabit the White House. The wonderful family of this man surrounded by these 4 beautiful females has sent a powerful message across America and the world of a functional black family, cohesive, loving, articulate, that can be emulated and proudly identified with. This shows his love and respect for females!

This modern age has seen women play significant roles in many arenas, whether in the general workforce, electorate, as corporate executives, business owners, students, heads of households, and in education, law and medical professions. Thus, futuristic thinkers, as Barack Obama has and will always prove successful by incorporating women power in their administrations and strategies.

As such, upon winning the Presidency, Mr. Obama decided to showcase women and their intellectual capabilities by including several in his government. Of the 15 cabinet departments in President Obama's Administration, 4 are headed by women, with Hillary Rodham Clinton at State; Hilda L. Solis at Labor; Kathleen

FREDERICK MONDERSON

Sebelius at Health and Human Services; and Janet A. Napolitano at Homeland Security. In positions of cabinet rank: Christina Romer is Chairperson of the Council of Economic Advisers; Lisa P. Jackson is Administrator of the Environmental Protection Agency; and Susan Rice is United States Ambassador to the United Nations. The White House Staff is replete with female members.

Barack Obama's Washington, DC Photo 238. The gold leaf Lamp of Enlightenment" or "Torch of Learning atop the copper-domed roof at the Thomas Jefferson Library dedicated to the Roman Goddess of wisdom Minerva and guarded by her uncle, Neptune god of the sea.

In the challenging days of the campaign after his win over Hillary Clinton for the Democratic nomination, many believed disaffected women would flock to Sarah Palin and the Republicans, despite this being a principal reason for McCain's choice. However, women realized Palin was "shallow" and Barack Obama

BARACK OBAMA
MASTER OF WASHINGTON DC

showed greater promise for the future of America. Therefore, women provided the margin of support that brought the Democratic victory and election of Mr. Obama as President. That is why so many women comprised his initial cabinet team. In fact, compared with other Presidents, he fared exceptionally well.

Bonnie Erber, in an online entry entitled "Barack Obama's Cabinet Appointments: More Women Needed," December 19, 2008, pointed out: "At the start of his first term President Bush nominated four women to his cabinet; Bill Clinton had five women in his cabinet at the start of his Presidency, and George H.W. Bush and Ronal Reagan each had two, according to research conducted by New York University's Wagner School of Public Service in partnership with the Washington Post." Hence, with 7 women in the above enumerated policy positions and even more in his White House Staff, President Barack Obama tops all previous Presidents for employing women in high level positions.

The road to this accomplishment has been long and challenging from the 19th century era of reform to the activism of the Women's Liberation Movement laying the modern foundations for equal rights. Plano and Greenberg (1989: 103-104) describes the Women's Liberation Movement as military, seeking to equalize society's views and treatment of both men and women. They write: "The main goal of the movement is to change society and its culture so that the 'dominant-inferior relationship of men to women' can be changed. Particular objectives for the more radical elements of the movement include the 'power-structured system of patriarchy' by which the father dominates family life, and wiping out 'sexism,' the conscious and unconscious male chauvinist attitudes that treat women as sex objects. Most liberationists, however, are concerned with less philosophical and

FREDERICK MONDERSON

Barack Obama's Washington, DC Photo 239. Marble bust of Thomas Jefferson, President from 1800-1808 and during whose tenure the Library was first started.

more immediate problems, such as ending job and pay discrimination, securing abortion reform, setting up tax-supported child-care centers, and securing equal treatment under national, state, and municipal laws."

BARACK OBAMA
MASTER OF WASHINGTON DC

Barack Obama's Washington, DC Photo 240. A hallowed corridor with decorated ceiling leading to even more goodies.

FREDERICK MONDERSON

Barack Obama's Washington, DC Photo 241. A reflective look back on the play of light on the columns and decorated ceiling.

They further emphasize the significance of the movement's objectives for the ballot. "The assumption of the feminists in those days was that the achievement of other basic rights and a dignified position in society would follow the securing of suffrage. The contemporary movement, which began in the early 1960s and gained momentum over the next decade, recognizes that this assumption has proved false, and that political, economic, and social discrimination against women still permeates American society. Women's Lib has taken on some of the characteristics of a radical mass movement, with protests, marches, invasions of male sanctuaries, condemnation of female sex symbols, and direct and indirect political involvement. Some scholars relate Women's Lib to the general problems of anomie and alienation growing out of the increasing urbanization and depersonalization of modern life. Since women constitute a majority of Americans of voting age, major political consequences could result from the movement's growing base of support. During the 1970s and early 1980s, most women's Lib activities were aimed at securing ratification of the proposed Equal Rights Amendment (ERA), led by the National Organization for Women (NOW), but the campaign failed. In 1984 Women's Lib hailed Walter Mondale's choice of Gerald Ferraro as vice-presidential candidate. In the 1980s, increasing numbers of women and minority group members became active in politics. Women, for example, in 1988 comprised 15.5 percent of the nation's elected state legislators, up from 4 percent in 1969." Today that number has increased, so too the diversity of elected women across the full spectrum of American ethnic composition.

BARACK OBAMA
MASTER OF WASHINGTON DC

Though much needs to be done, much has been accomplished in the recognition and promotion of women's capabilities. Still, the struggles for equal rights have continued along its tortuous path. In this respect, Plano and Greenberg (1989: 273-274) states: "Traditionally in American law, women have not enjoyed the same rights as men, and this has manifested itself in many areas of American life, including property rights, education, and employment opportunities. State laws vary widely, although many are protective of women rather than directly discriminatory. Women's suffrage led to a gradual narrowing of legal differences, but with increasing intensity since the 1960s, an extensive body of new laws and administrative regulations, as well as court decisions, has provided protection against sex discrimination. In March 1972, Congress proposed to the states a constitutional amendment that provided that "equality of rights under the law shall not be denied or abridged by the United States or any state on account of sex." The seven-year time limit for ratification expired in March 1979 and Congress, in an unprecedented move, extended the deadline to June 1982. Still, the proposal failed to receive the thirty-eight state legislative approvals necessary for ratification."

Like the significant milestones of the **Civil Rights Act of 1964** and the **Voting Rights Act of 1965**, Plano and Greenberg (1989: 274) explain the movement's significance in the following statement: "The concept of equal rights has had a dramatic impact upon American life, equal to, if not greater than, the impact of changing race relations. Many constitutional authorities believe that changes already brought about in behalf of women's rights as well as liberal application of equal protection of the law concepts diminish the need for an equal right amendment. Others note that an amendment will give rise to a host of constitutional problems relating to the traditional roles of men and women. The equal right movement achieved two major victories in the 1960s – the passage of the Equal Pay Act of 1963, which requires equal pay for men and women doing similar work, and the Civil Rights Act of 1964, which forbids discrimination against pregnant women in hiring and other personal policies. An end to sex discrimination in education was ordered by Congress in 1972 and the Equal Credit Opportunity Act was adopted in 1974. A 1978 enactment prohibits discrimination against pregnant women in any area of employment. Pension rights of widowed homemakers and of working mothers who temporarily leave jobs to raise families, were put under protection in 1984. In 1986, the Supreme Court declared sexual harassment to be unlawful sexual discrimination under the Civil Rights Act of 1964." Yet, despite all these gains, legal and societal, women still lagged. As such, in an effort to equalize American society and to reward women for their efforts in his election, one of the first bills President Obama signed upon coming into office was the **Lilly Ledbetter Fair Pay Act** designed to ensure basic protections against pay discrimination against women and other workers.

FREDERICK MONDERSON

Equally, a number of provisions in the American Recovery and Reinvestment Act (Stimulus Bill) were designed to assist women: "To help working mothers and fathers obtain quality child care, the Act includes an additional $2 billion for the Child Care and Development Block Grant, $1 billion for Head Start, and $1.1 billion for Early Head Start."

"The act also boosts family incomes by expanding Child Tax Credit to cover an additional 18 million children in working families and creating a new Make Work Pay Tax Credit."

"The Act also includes unemployment insurance reforms that will particularly benefit women, such as incentives for states to cover part-time workers and those who recently re-enters the workforce."

In addition, we are informed, President Obama signed an Executives Order establishing a "White House Council on Women and Girls to provide a coordinated federal response to the challenges confronted by women and girls and to ensure that all Cabinet and Cabinet-level agencies consider how their policies and programs impact women and families."

Barack Obama's Washington, DC Photo 242. Close-up of marble figures atop the Thomas Jefferson marble bust.

BARACK OBAMA
MASTER OF WASHINGTON DC

Barack Obama's Washington, DC Photo 243. On a visit to the Library, youngster stands beside bust of President George Washington.

FREDERICK MONDERSON

Barack Obama's Washington, DC Photo 244. Bronze close-up of George Washington.

Assessing the progress and impact women are making and having under President Obama, we can look at two influential women in the Obama Administration who recently conducted interviews on CNN, the Cable News Network. John King interviewed Ambassador Susan Rice on Sunday, August 9, 2009. Here are excerpts of her comments on various topics:

IRAN – "There are show trials going on against the post-election demonstrations. The Iranian government disrespects its people. There has been some torture. Reports of torture are a great concern. The regime in Iran is very unconcerned about the rights of its citizens."

"We must press Iran for a swift and safe return of all Americans."

"This was not a regime that was a golden child and suddenly turned evil."

"We are deeply concerned about the elections in Iran. The United States will push for new sanctions. We will do a stock taking in September. We are committed to preventing Iran from acquiring nuclear weapons."

NORTH KOREA – "This is a unique opportunity for a private citizen on a humanitarian mission to help release 2 American citizens. This was a private humanitarian mission. We have not negotiated with terrorists. We do not negotiate with terrorists. We want to see complete and verifiable denuclearization of the Korean Peninsula. Again, this was not a negotiation, this was a humanitarian mission."

BARACK OBAMA
MASTER OF WASHINGTON DC

President Obama said: WE ARE READY TO LEAD ONCE MORE! – "Things are a lot different now. We are renewing our leadership; restoring our stand on the global financial crisis. There is a changed approach in Iraq. We will be out by 2011. There is a completely new approach in Afghanistan and Pakistan. We are determined to disrupt, dismantle and displace Al Qaeda. We are renewing our relations with the Muslim world. We will initiate "new approaches to energy, climate change, China and Russia."

AFGHANISTAN – There are 62,000 US troops and 34,513 of other nations in the coalition. We are committed to strengthening the government and training its police. To be successful, we have to focus on 3 aspects of the problem. (1) We must focus on the military side; (2) we have to strengthen the Afghan government's ability to deliver for its people; (3) we must fight corruption.

"We expect the election to go forward on August 20. Afghanistan is extremely important. We need to defeat Al Qaeda. Make sure Pakistan is a level playing field. We'll probably spend another decade in Afghanistan. This strategy is important to disrupt and destroy Al Qaeda in Afghanistan and Pakistan. We're going to measure our progress every step of the way."

Fareed Zakaria of CNN's **Global Public Square** interviewed Secretary of State Hillary Clinton on August 9, 2009.

NORTH KOREA – "I have this policy; I never talk about what I talk to my husband about. North Korea can have a positive relationship with us. We pose no threat to North Korea. They rejected our approach and began to build up."

"The message came from the families, naming him (Bill Clinton) specifically. This was a private humanitarian mission. We were not rewarding hostage taking."

"It is not rewarding hostage taking. It had nothing to do with our policies."

"If President Obama walked on water, Bolton would say he could not swim."

"We have a world view that says America should lead by example. As Bill Clinton noted in a speech: "America should lead by the power of our example and not the example of our power."

"Both White Houses bring enormous intelligence to bear on domestic and foreign policy."

"The time in which Bill served is so much different that the time of President Obama."

FREDERICK MONDERSON

"Is power moving from the Secretary of State to the White House? The National Security Council. No. I am not exactly a shrinking violet."

Barack Obama's Washington, DC Photo 245. The path to effective government began with the state of Anarchy.

Barack Obama's Washington, DC Photo 246. Corrupt Legislation.

BARACK OBAMA
MASTER OF WASHINGTON DC

Barack Obama's Washington, DC Photo 247. Good Administration.

"The White House has to coordinate. It cannot execute. The NSC cannot execute policy. The State Department can execute policy."

IRAN – "The Iranian leadership is afraid of its people." "We did not move too soon (In regards the election). It was a hard judgment call. We were empowering protesters without getting involved."

As things unfolded and opposition mounted against President Obama particularly because of Health Care Reform, Mr. Obama remained calm. He refused to see the tremendous vitriol as race instigated, still continuing to persevere in carrying forth his responsibilities as the nation's leader. Dr. ben-Jochannan, the renowned Egyptologist, historian, etc., in one of his lectures spoke about African opposition to conquerors. As the men continued to fight, and fought and fought, they could not stem the tide of the continued onslaught. "Then we sent in the women!"

Mr. Obama deployed his most potent weapon, his wife, Michele Obama. Mrs. Obama was quick to galvanize women support, impressing upon them Health Care Reform is a woman's issue. The First Lady pointed out, women were the mothers who had to visit the hospitals with sick children, they themselves had to be treated, their families were caught in the mix and their elder parents were just as vulnerable. Working her magic, she seemed to turn back the "lunatics who had escaped from the asylum" and were provoking undeserved press coverage. While this was unfolding, President Obama next unfolded his most potent weapon. He showed how the women in his most immediate family, his mother-in-law, his wife and his two daughters were direct descendants of slaves. He made his critics realize this part of American history will not be forgotten then reminded them, as President, "I am the reality of power!"

FREDERICK MONDERSON

"I refuse to be lectured on national security by people who are responsible for the most disastrous set of foreign policy decisions in the recent history of the United States. The other side likes to use 9/11 as a political bludgeon. Well, let's talk about 9/11. The people who were responsible for murdering 3,000 Americans on 9/11 have not been brought to justice. They are Osama bin Laden, al Qaeda and their sponsors – the Taliban. They were in Afghanistan. And yet George Bush and John McCain decided in 2002 that we should take our eye off of Afghanistan so that we could invade and occupy a country that had absolutely nothing to do with 9/11. The case for war in Iraq was so thin that George Bush and John McCain had to hype the threat of Saddam Hussein, and make false promises that we'd be greeted as liberators. They misled the American people, and took us into a misguided war. Here are the results of their policy. Osama bin Laden and his top leadership – the people who murdered 3000 Americans – have a safe-haven in northwest Pakistan, where they operate with such freedom of action that they can still put out hate-filled audiotapes to the outside world. That's the result of the Bush-McCain approach to the war on terrorism." BARACK OBAMA, speech, Jun. 18, 2008

34. THE OBAMA "DOCTRINE"
By

Dr. Fred Monderson

Most Presidents leave office establishing a precedent that characterizes their administration as its "doctrine" and this position serves as a point of departure for a succeeding President who follows that path in defense of American lives, property and "interests." But, since there were different "problems" facing any administration, it stands to reason there would be more than one "doctrine." Notwithstanding, the preconditions for issuance of a "doctrine," whether from the birth of the new Republic, seems for the most part, response to a foreign threat that forces America to respond and signal the aggressor, the United States will use military, diplomatic and economic suasion to contest or combat whatever situation. While most presidents had situations that required this type of response, only some of their "doctrines" have become significant and have retained their viability down through the years. However, today President Obama, for his part, has not issued the "Obama Doctrine" per se, though the domestic and global downturn, Guantanamo Bay symbolism, threat of nuclear proliferation by nations pursuing military use of this capability, wars in Iraq and Afghanistan, environmental factors and global warming, energy dependence and new initiatives, and the Middle East

BARACK OBAMA
MASTER OF WASHINGTON DC

Palestinian-Israeli problem, nations struggling with poverty, relations with Muslims globally and now Somali pirates threatening shipping off the East African coast have not, as yet, elicited any clearly defined single or multiple "doctrine." What these current conditions do tell is that the "Obama doctrine" is a work in progress!

Historically speaking, perhaps the first American "doctrine" was issued by President George Washington in his "Farewell Address," wherein he suggested America should remain neutral in its dealings with European nations who have a propensity for conflict. In essence, be friendly to all nations, pursue alignments with none! Washington's "Neutrality Proclamation," his "doctrine" guided American foreign policy for more than a century until the nation entered World War I in 1917.

Barack Obama's Washington, DC Photo 248. Peace and prosperity.

While Thomas Jefferson did not issue a specific "doctrine" he was confronted by the actions of the Barbary Pirates who attacked American maritime shipping and held Americans captive in their dungeons in what is now Algeria. The President dispatched a naval and marine detachment that, by sea and land, overtook the pirates' stronghold and put an end to the Barbary Pirates.

FREDERICK MONDERSON

However, the most famous, long lasting and significant "doctrine" was that issued by James Monroe and entitled the "Monroe Doctrine." James Monroe followed that tumultuous age of the American, French and Haitian Revolutions, and the "War of 1812," America's "Second War for Independence," against the British Empire. After the French Revolution, Napoleon's imperial designs in Europe disrupted the Spanish Empire in Latin America and upon his final defeat, European Powers sought to recapture their holdings in the "New World." In the ensuing upheaval the Latin American holdings declared independence and became sovereign nations. James Monroe issued his "doctrine" in 1822, prohibiting European Powers from re-establishing claims to land in the "New World." Though a significant declaration, the United States was not equipped to enforce this "doctrine," but a belief holds there was a secret agreement with Britain to supply the ships in any show of force to uphold the "Monroe Doctrine."

For much of the 19th Century, the "Monroe Doctrine" created an enormous security and economic "American preserve" in the Americas. In 1903, exploiting this precedent, President Teddy Roosevelt issued the "Roosevelt Corollary to the Monroe Doctrine" which held the United States, will "invade any country which borrows its money and cannot repay." This way, Americans will help to regulate the nation's finances to insure the loan gets paid off. In this, he promised to "walk softly and carry a big stick," or as some has labeled it, "Gunboat Diplomacy."

In 1931, Japan invaded China and the United States sent it's then Secretary of State Henry L. Stimson to issue what became known as the "Stimson Doctrine."

This position held, "the United States will not recognize any country or venture that seizes land by force." Interesting how, once on the books, these pronouncements retain their viability. Roosevelt's Corollary was issued 81 years after **Monroe's Doctrine** and the U.S. response to Saddam Hussein's invasion of Kuwait came 60 years after Stimson!

In 1947, following World War II, President Harry Truman issued the "Truman Doctrine" which said in essence, "the United States will go anywhere to fight and aid anyone who resists the spread of Communism." This policy of "containing communism" or "containment" involved the U.S. in the Korean and Vietnam Wars, much cloak and dagger stuff and a proxy "Cold War" against the Soviet Union and China and their allies.

One of Richard Nixon's "doctrines" was "Detente" or "Let's talk" with the Soviet Union and China, the principal communist nations and in process he turned these adversaries into dialoging partners.

BARACK OBAMA
MASTER OF WASHINGTON DC

> WHAT SPECTACLE
> CAN BE MORE EDIFYING
> OR MORE SEASONABLE
> THAN THAT OF
> LIBERTY & LEARNING
> EACH LEANING ON THE OTHER
> FOR THEIR MUTUAL
> & SUREST SUPPORT?
>
> James Madison

Barack Obama's Washington, DC Photo 249. Words of Wisdom from James Madison.

FREDERICK MONDERSON

> KNOWLEDGE WILL FOREVER
> GOVERN IGNORANCE
> AND A PEOPLE WHO MEAN
> TO BE THEIR OWN GOVERNOURS
> MUST ARM THEMSELVES
> WITH THE POWER
> WHICH KNOWLEDGE GIVES
>
> James Madison

Barack Obama's Washington, DC Photo 250. More words of Wisdom from James Madison.

BARACK OBAMA
MASTER OF WASHINGTON DC

Barack Obama's Washington, DC Photo 251. Seated statue of James Madison with a young visitor in his shadow.

FREDERICK MONDERSON

Barack Obama's Washington, DC Photo 252. A taste of what's inside the Library.

Barack Obama's Washington, DC Photo 253. Looking back at the wonderful experience just encountered.

The Jimmy "Carter Doctrine" held "the United States will not negotiate with anyone holding American hostages." This was the argument or policy enunciated

BARACK OBAMA
MASTER OF WASHINGTON DC

in response to Iran's seizure of the American Embassy in 1979, and holding them for more than 1 year. This policy has been followed by all presidents since. However, Carter did have a policy that aimed at communism, as did his predecessors.

The "Reagan Doctrine" was aimed specifically at communism and the major communist nations and their allies. In regards confronting America's adversaries, his position was simply "we must build up to build down," and this involved an enormous build-up of American military might. In the process, the Soviet Union tried to match the American military outlay and as a result, the economic strain was too much so that the Soviet Union collapsed from within. However, there seems more than one description or multiple doctrines by individual Presidents. For example, Kenneth Franklin Kurz's *The Reagan Years A to Z*, Chicago: Contemporary Books (1996: 214-5) tells: "The Reagan Doctrine went beyond the traditional policy of containment, which sought to contain communism where it already existed by opposing its spread .... More often, containment was effectuated through diplomacy and foreign aid and the mere threat of military action. The nuclear sword of Damocles always hung over the proceeds."

Barack Obama's Washington, DC Photo 253a. Plaque of the Thomas Jefferson Building of the LIBRARY OF CONGRESS.

FREDERICK MONDERSON

Barack Obama's Washington, DC Photo 253b. Egypt as foundation on the "Knowledge Wheel," a profound concept emanating from the Library of Congress.

In a further explanation, he wrote: "Containment began in the Truman administration, and the principle produced a series of 'doctrines' meant to add each president's individual stamp on the Cold War. The Truman Doctrine held that the United States would aid any nation threatened by communist insurgency; the Eisenhower Doctrine vowed to keep communism out of the Middle East; the Nixon Doctrine pledged to honor all treaty commitments, uphold the Truman Doctrine (but with the caveat that the 'threatened' nation must supply the bulk of the manpower), and added the pledge to provide a 'Shield' if a nuclear power threatened one of America's allies or any other nation that the United States considered vital to American security."

Even more, the "Carter Doctrine, prompted by the Soviet invasion of Afghanistan, was in some ways a reprise of Eisenhower's, in that it concerned the threat of Soviet adventurism in the Persian Gulf. Carter announced that any Soviet action in the gulf region would be repelled by any means necessary, including military force. Kennedy, Johnson, and Ford seem to have refrained from adding their names to the doctrine pool."

Clearly there was more than one "doctrine" issued by the Presidents. Seems there was a doctrine for each type of threat the nation farced. One thing seems certain; when it came to communism the modern presidents were all in-tuned with the notion of "containment."

BARACK OBAMA
MASTER OF WASHINGTON DC

Barack Obama's Washington, DC Photo 253c. King Neptune and other mythological figures of the sea, devoid of their water in the fountain, outside the Library of Congress.

While the above presidents upheld the "containment principle," Kurz (1996: 215) wrote: "The Reagan Doctrine went beyond that principle in a push to try to win the Cold War outright, rather than maintain a balance of power according to the status quo. By the Reagan years, the fear of nuclear war subsided enough to permit such thinking in high government circles – either that or the Reagan administration was willing to count nuclear war as a calculated risk. In any case, the administration's foreign policies reflected the Reagan Doctrine in that the United States carried out both overt and covert operations aimed at combating Communist influence all over the Third World, particularly in Central America and the Middle East."

Following the World Trade Center attack on September 11, 2001, President George Walker Bush issued what became the "Bush Doctrine" which stated essentially "The United States will go anywhere and do anything to fight terrorism." In response to the enormous and deadly terrorist action, the grieving nation generated tremendous emotional capital that allowed President Bush to take us into Afghanistan and ultimately Iraq with its devastating results for the American image, and loss of military lives in an action that generated great global enmity towards America. Paul Gigot's "George Walker Bush" in James Taranto's

FREDERICK MONDERSON

Edited *Presidential Leadership*, New York: Wall Street Journal (2004: 212) put it best in the statement: "Bush has put his own stamp on foreign policy in two risk-taking ways. The first was to define a policy of prevention, sometimes called 'preemption,' that shattered the conventions of the inviolate nation-state that had held since Westphalia in the nineteenth century. Related to this was his decision to target not just the terrorists, but also their state sponsors. This Bush Doctrine was so outside the Washington consensus that the speech in which he first announced preemption was all but ignored. Soon enough, however, his critics figured out what was going on, especially as Bush moved relentlessly toward toppling Saddam Hussein in Iraq."

Barack Obama's Washington, DC Photo 253d. Clive Monderson of Guyana, on a visit to Washington, DC stands outside the Madison Building of the Library of Congress. That wonderful sentiment in the background reads: "What spectacle can be more edifying or more reasonable that that of liberty and learning each leaning on the other for the mutual and surest support." Elsewhere wisdom such speaks" "Knowledge will forever govern ignorance: And a people who mean to be their own governors, must arm themselves with the power of knowledge gives."

Into this mess, Bush's successor President Obama and his administration confronted many challenges from its inception and each response, tailored to the problem, could easily qualify as a doctrine. However, since none have been clearly enunciated, to posit a few "Obama Doctrines" would not be out of place. After all, the challenges are being met and being defined by the President's approach, demeanor and the quality input his excellent team of wise men have proffered.

BARACK OBAMA
MASTER OF WASHINGTON DC

Barack Obama's Washington, DC Photo 254. Young visitor stands before the Supreme Court building.

For example, in response to the negative publicity generated by the existence of Guantanamo Bay holding terrorist prisoners and the claim of some inmates that they were tortured, President Obama has decided to close the facility. The news of this development was heralded by the President who announced "The United States does not torture!" In addition, Mr. Obama insisted, in his response to the war against the terrorists pointedly stated, "We will capture Osama Bin Laden and defeat Al Qaeda." To the nations that not only challenge but offer threats to the United States, President Obama has insisted these nations "unclench your fist and we will extend a hand."

FREDERICK MONDERSON

Barack Obama's Washington, DC Photo 254a. Youngster stands in the Plaza of the Capital Building.

BARACK OBAMA
MASTER OF WASHINGTON DC

Barack Obama's Washington, DC Photo 255. The sign says it all!

Barack Obama's Washington, DC Photo 256. Washington's buildings are generally long but never too high.

FREDERICK MONDERSON

Mr. Obama made crystal clear, in his visit to Turkey when he addressed the Turkish Parliament, "The United States is not at war with Islam!" This unequivocal position, designed to clarify any misconceptions particularly in view of the previous administration's hard line attitude against terrorists masquerading behind the color of Islam, clarifies the new administration's position going forward. After all, most of the Muslims in the world today are not in the Middle East where many of the terrorists who wage war against the United States are located. Hence, to reiterate, there is "no war against Islam!"

Very early in his young administration, the President appointed a Middle Eastern Envoy with the intent of seeking to create peace in the Middle East. The "Obama Doctrine" in this issue, though not yet stated within the framework of such, is that the United States favors a "two-state peaceful solution with secured borders for Israel." The details will be worked out later where he insisted "Israel should return to its 1967 borders." Equally, the President drew a line in the sand when it came to Iran and North Korea who exhibited behaviors indicating these nations were intent on harnessing nuclear power, not for peaceful purposes, but with a military design. Iran's President indicated clearly they wanted to "nuke Israel" and the assumption is that his nation's nuclear program had a principal goal in mind, military use, despite the terrible cost they would have to pay if this cataclysmic action is carried out. Many people believe this is a very foolish act if followed through and the consequences are too horrible to imagine. That is why the President drew the line in the sand and declared essentially, "We will not permit Iran to have a nuclear weapon, and we will pursue all avenues to deny this nation such a capability because such would unleash unspeakable horror." In this, the "Obama Doctrine" then should be "No Nukes for Iran."

Walking a thin line in following North Korea's desire to possess nuclear capability, the Obama administration had faced a difficult time in slowing this effort. Much has been said about the questionable behavior of the leadership in North Korea, and President Obama has expressed alarm about the recent rocket launch by that nation. The President called this behavior very "provocative" and he resolves to do whatever he can to pressure North Korea into stopping it. His position is that the Korean Peninsula should not be made into a nuclear zone. In addition, the great fear is that a North Korea possessing nuclear weapons may lead to these devices finding themselves on the black market for sale to states who want to acquire the capability through surreptitious means. Even further, an even greater fear is that once North Korea acquires nuclear capability, then South Korea, Japan and neighboring states may seek same to counterbalance this threat, thereby destabilizing this region.

The President has again traveled abroad stopping in Mexico and will visit Trinidad and Tobago for a summit of Latin American nations. In Mexico he declared war on the drug cartels by going after their finances, beefing up Mexican-American border security, more stringently enforcing regulations regarding trade and travel

BARACK OBAMA
MASTER OF WASHINGTON DC

and intercepting money and guns going from America to Mexico. The doctrine could easily be "They shall not pass" as it relates to drugs going north and money and armaments going south, and taking a firm stance to stop the violence generated in the turf wars. He has, however, recognized the violence now manifesting in that region is fueled by the enormous American desire for drugs. Therefore, a more effective domestic strategy would be more education and drug treatment, with stiffer sentences for drug dealers.

As he heads to Trinidad for the "Latin American Economic Summit," or "Economic Summit of the Americas," the President has offered the 34 or so nations attending, "It's time for a change, a new direction, a new start." He insisted the meeting is to "jump-start job creation, promote free and fair trade and develop a coordinated response to the economic crisis." Of course, security and the flow of drugs to the United States will be important issues in the discussion, so too will be the embargo against Cuba. There is therefore, so many problem solving responses the Barack Obama administration has unfolded to address the many issues he inherited, for sure, history will be replete with Obama's "Doctrine." Hopefully, he will be remembered by those "doctrines" that advanced the cause of America's economic and security well-being.

Barack Obama's Washington, DC Photo 257. Souvenir of the important memorials in the DC area.

FREDERICK MONDERSON

Barack Obama's Washington, DC Photo 258. The trees in bloom.

BARACK OBAMA
MASTER OF WASHINGTON DC

"Racial equality is good for America as a whole –

Q: Is race still the most intractable issue in America?

A: [Those who worked on civil rights in the past realized that] to achieve racial equality was not simply good for African-Americans, but it was good for America as a whole; that we could not be what we might be as a nation unless we healed the brutal wounds of slavery and Jim Crow. Now, we have made enormous progress, but the progress we have made is not good enough. As many have already mentioned, we live in a society that remains separated in terms of life opportunities for African-Americans, for Latinos, and the rest of the nation. And it is absolutely critical for us to recognize that there are going to be responsibilities on the part of African-Americans and other groups to take personal responsibility to rise up out of the problems that we face. But there has also got to be a social responsibility, there has to be a sense of mutual responsibility, and there's got to be political will in the White House to make that happen." BARACK OBAMA 2007 Democratic Primary Debate at Howard University Jun 28, 2007

35. OBAMA: PROUD TO BE PRESIDENT
By

Dr. Fred Monderson

In an address at Central Intelligence Agency headquarters, President Barack Obama told it like it is to the employees of the nation's spy agency faced with confronting the aftermath of September 11, 2001 attack on the World Trade Center. The President boosted employee morale and praised the CIA for the work they do in keeping America and Americans safe, in the cloak and dagger world in which they physically operate or the analysis they do with the intelligence they gather.

This was a bold move on Mr. Obama's part as members of the Agency grew concerned about the implications of the release of the "Memo" depicting the CIA as involved in water-boarding and other forms of torture tactics of high value terror suspects. Some were becoming afraid, if captured in the field, how would this play out. Nevertheless, Mr. Obama received a boisterous welcome with raucous applause before and after he spoke, then he followed his customary act of reaching out to the people, shaking hands and appearing to be one of them. What is even more important is what the President said to those in attendance, such as "What's good for the agency is good for the country." Pointing out, "These are dangerous times but Americans must operate within the rule of law." Emphasizing the importance of the American way of life, Mr. Obama said, "We should uphold our ideals when it's hard not when it's easy." The President confessed, "We face a wide range of unconventional challenges," which makes the CIA "more important than ever." Expressing "exceptional pride" in the Agency's actions, he underscored the view; under times of "exceptional circumstances" they must work smarter, work more effectively than ever. This way, the best days of the Agency is yet to come! Further he told the audience, "Don't be discouraged that potentially we made some mistakes, we recognize them. We should be stronger and more secure when we deploy the power of our strength and our values." Trying to underscore his forward looking domestic and international agenda, Mr. Obama told his audience, "When you're a strong country, you can show grace."

Clearly then, in view of the rousing applause he received from the employees at end of his speech, the President, in defending the actions and praising the expected performance of the CIA, reassured the confidence of those there. In this he said they should be proud of their service and even more important, that he was just as "proud to be President."

Barack Obama's Washington, DC Photo 259. More Washington trees in bloom.

That Mr. Obama is "Proud to be President" is grounded in any number of realities relating to his rise to the Presidency and the significance of the office and the influence it exerts. This confidence building state of mind came about since the

BARACK OBAMA
MASTER OF WASHINGTON DC

whole world is familiar with President Barack Obama's rise from humble beginnings to acquiring a world class education at Columbia and Harvard, even becoming President of the prestigious Harvard Law Review. While race may, in the perception of many, have been an impediment to his social mobility; his genius, intellectual fortitude and calm demeanor coupled with a tenacity to work under any and all conditions, have helped Mr. Obama persevere.

He succeeded in his first job as a Community Organizer, learning in the trenches of social discontent, how to improve lives despite the many impediments such people face. Perhaps realizing change in the street is more easily come by when people have political and legislative clout, Barack Obama chose to run and was successful as a State Senator in Illinois. As his talent seemed to become apparent, given a chance to address the 2004 Democratic National Convention, Mr. Obama "brought the house down" gaining instant recognition of his stature as a rising star in the Democratic Party. This recognition was soon parlayed into a run for the position of Federal Senator from Illinois. As the nation began to cry out from the strains created by the Bush economic policies, regarding jobs, housing, and international scorn created by the wars in Iraq and Afghanistan, and the negative fallout from Guantanamo Bay terrorist prison, Senator Obama perceived a vacuum of leadership in the White House and had the brilliant idea "I should be President."

Barack Obama's Washington, DC Photo 260. Demonstrator at the "Rally on the Mall" shows off her banner.

FREDERICK MONDERSON

Barack Obama's Washington, DC Photo 261. This demonstrator is on his way to make a statement.

Barack Obama's Washington, DC Photo 262. This person also has a message.

As a respected family man with a loving wife, Senator Obama probably told Michelle of his intention to run for the Presidency. Yet, it's not inconceivable as brilliant a woman as Michele Obama is, she may have come up with the idea. Notwithstanding, perhaps only Michelle, besides Barack, believed he could win a race for such a prestigious post that required enormous sums of money, tremendous networking and consensus building strategies, coupled with physical

BARACK OBAMA
MASTER OF WASHINGTON DC

stamina and the mental wherewithal to persevere when the going really got tough. Well, we all know he blew away his opponent to win the Presidency.

Mr. Obama probably believed throughout that he would win and this says much for his confidence. As such, he probably studied the activities of previous great presidents in their preparation and transition strategies, and by November 5th, 2008, he could unfold a plan that encompassed the transition, his potential cabinet, the make-up of the White House staff and his series of plans and policies to tackle the mountain of problems and challenges facing the new President. He wanted to hit the ground running!

Perhaps the challenge of the job, the glare of the lights and attention, and the honor of representing America, motivated Mr. Obama tremendously, encouraging him to so splendidly be an ambassador of America. No matter what the critics, Republicans and their allies, have said about President Obama, being glad to lead the nation at home and abroad, he represented this nation exceptionally well. This is what makes him proud to be President and anyone with that outlook, very well liked by large segments of the nation, historic in his position, no one could believe Mr. Obama would fail to give his best in concern for and representing this nation. That is why the "fifth columns" and their non-cooperation strategies and the challenges every step of the way raise the question, why in these troubled times of the nation, would people such as the Tea Party Republicans so vehemently pull against the grain?

Still, all that notwithstanding, Mr. Obama seems to thrive on the challenges posed by the opposition, because he has the vision of where he wants to take the nation, possesses the tools and team, possesses broad support of the American people and that is what matters. Gradually as "Glimmers of hope" begin to emerge in the strategies his administration has deployed, such as profitable returns by banking giants Wells Fargo, J.P. Morgan Chase, Bank America and Citigroup, stabilizing of unemployment figures, tackling the foreclosure problem, beginning infrastructure projects, elevating immigration and health care to front burner issues, etc., the President can now "dust off his shoulder" and be congratulated for a wonderfully done work in progress. These, then, are some of the factors that make Mr. Obama "Proud to be President!"

FREDERICK MONDERSON

Barack Obama's Washington, DC Photo 263.

Barack Obama's Washington, DC Photo 264.

BARACK OBAMA
MASTER OF WASHINGTON DC

"People want to move beyond our divisions - I am absolutely convinced that white, black, Latino, Asian, people want to move beyond our divisions, and they want to join together in order to create a movement for change in this country. I'm not entirely faulting the media because, look, race is a factor in our society. There's no doubt that in a race where you've got an African-American, and a woman, and there's no doubt that that has piqued interest. They are desperate to move beyond the same, old arguments that we've been having and start actually getting something done in this country. The Republicans may have a different attitude, because they haven't been appearing before forums that are diverse. The policies that they have promoted have not been good at providing ladders for upward mobility and opportunity for all people. That is a fight that all of us will fight. But I don't want us to get drawn into this notion that somehow this is going to be a race that splits along racial lines." BARACK OBAMA 2008 Congressional Black Caucus Democratic debate Jan 21, 2008.

36. WITHER THE REPUBLICANS!
By

Dr. Fred Monderson

The Republicans in Congress are a peculiar group! Today they seem a far cry from caring for the "small man" as did Thomas Jefferson and about "healing the nation" as did Abraham Lincoln. Their behavior is manifested in the "dog-eat-dog" attitude Republicans have displayed towards Barack Obama, especially during the campaign and certainly after his triumphant victory in winning the Presidency of the United States. Concomitant and in the interest of being fair or should I say leveling the playing field in constructive criticism of the Republicans, let us remove the fact President Obama is the first African-American President. This way we can, for sake of argument, dismiss any claims that Republicans are attacking the President based on his race. Therefore, as some believe, destiny is immutable and that right and truth will triumph against untruth and injustice, no matter how long it takes. Dr. Martin Luther King Jr., believed "Truth crushed to earth shall rise" and "rough paths will be made smooth and crooked paths made straight."

Even a cursory look, if that was possible, at the Presidential contest, and even a "blind man could see" the Republicans waged a questionable contest, not on the prevailing issues, but more generally on the principle of *ad hominem*. A friend named Glen Davis always held to the view, "If the game is not played right it must be played over." If we apply this "grassroots logic" to the 2008 Presidential Campaign, Barack Obama and the Democrats won because their truths were immutable and they took the high road along that treacherous path. The Republicans, on the other hand, lost because history showed their policies and practices were poor at best, questionable perhaps, bordering on criminal, certainly unethical at worst.

Barack Obama's Washington, DC Photo 265.

Once the Presidential Campaign ended, the President-elect instantly unfolded his transition strategy and with good cooperation from the outgoing Bush Administration, the Obama approach planned to attack the problems – economic, infrastructure, foreign policy, the two wars, etc., in a meaningful manner designed to be effective. In view of problems faced, as framed by the experts, the nation was beset by probably the most serious domestic, economic and global challenge since the Great Depression. In such a crisis one would expect both sides of the aisle would be united to combat the threat to the nation's future viability.

As an example of this point, on December 7, 1941, after the Japanese attacked Pearl Harbor, President Roosevelt addressed Congress and received a universal and "united front" against Japan. Next, on September 11, 2001, after the attack on the World Trade Center, President Bush again got the same response from Congress. However, despite the grim picture painted of the current, particularly, economic situation, most Republicans seem unalterably opposed to the President's efforts, and this questions their "patriotism" at this time, despite what position they

BARACK OBAMA
MASTER OF WASHINGTON DC

are trying to project. Recently when I raised this issue with a colleague he emphasized opposition is a principal strength of the American Democratic tradition. Specifically he referred back to the challenge posed to Thomas Jefferson by Alexander Hamilton in the early days of the Republic. He told of Jefferson's budget being only $6 million dollars and how Hamilton seemed to resist every move Jefferson made. Hence, he tended to believe the Republicans were fulfilling a wonderful and time tested tradition of being in opposition!

Nevertheless, the current reality needs closer examination for when President Obama presented his Stimulus Bill to Congress, it passed the Democratic controlled House of Representatives even though not a single Republican supported it. The same outcome nearly happened in the Senate with only 3 Republican Senators supporting the bill; all this despite the President reaching out meaningfully to the other party to create bipartisan consensus. Mr. Obama included Republicans in his Cabinet and consulted with Republican theorists and advocates and even heaped generous praise on Senator McCain, his Presidential rival, at a bipartisan dinner. He visited the "Citadel of Republicanism" for dinner with George Will and Rush Limbaugh, among others. Yet, Mr. Obama faced the same non-cooperation when he presented his budget to Congress, again passed with no Republican support. As such, as the President innovated in his approach to combating the nation's challenges, the vitriolic criticisms continued from the Republicans and their right wing allies.

For every proposal or plan President Obama put forward, the Republicans opposed the idea. Yet, Obama moved forward with his agenda, unveiling a new plan practically every day, seeming to pay no attention to the opposition. Notwithstanding, there appeared to be cracks in the Republican armor. Rush Limbaugh, having "eaten at the King's table" emerged with a new salvo, "I want the President to fail in his endeavors." John McCain, on the other hand, distanced himself by remarking "I know there are a lot of people who are praying for the President to fail. I am not one of them." Equally, his daughter Megan McCain proudly boasted "I want the President to succeed!" This is because she and her generation represent the future, not only for the Republicans but for the younger set in general. In contradiction, there is a political ad making the rounds showing the "new face of the Republican Party." They are not showing Chairman Michael Steele but Newt Gingrich. Imagine! Newt, new? Gingrich recently emerged and began offering critical commentary of the President, gradually reinserting himself in the hierarchy of the Republican Party for a possible run for the Presidency in 2012. Newt as new, Gimme a break! Such forcefulness and clearly opportunistic maneuverings begs the question whether members of the Republican Party are following the lead of the new Chairman, who probably wants to take the party in another direction so as to be attractive to younger members and in particular whether it can attract African Americans, young and old!

FREDERICK MONDERSON

Barack Obama's Washington, DC Photo 266.

Barack Obama's Washington, DC Photo 267.

BARACK OBAMA
MASTER OF WASHINGTON DC

Barack Obama's Washington, DC Photo 268.

Upon close scrutiny, it seems some of the "presidential losers" gladly offer commentary on the office they once aspired to occupy. However, Governor Romney, for example, seeming to break ranks with Republicans, uttered "President Obama may not be wrong on everything." Perhaps after chastisement, he fell back in line after the Obama-Chavez debacle, saying the President was wrong for such a meeting with its psychological and propaganda potential ramifications. Such negativity, is in keeping with the contemporary Republican "slash and burn," tactics and their "scorched earth" forward thrust; and this is probably why their public approval ratings keep falling while that of the president keeps rising and is today higher than all modern presidents except perhaps John Kennedy, Dwight Eisenhower and Ronald Reagan in office about the same amount of time. If we look at Richard Nixon who scored the most far reaching foreign policy accomplishments than most modern presidents, he was not afraid to talk to America's enemies, who were much more powerful and ideologically more opposed to America than the "Chavez types" are today. Nixon made significant foreign policy inroads with the Soviet Union, China and North Vietnam in the "grand design" of his "structure for peace" wherein he unrolled "new approaches to friend and foe." In some ways the problems Barack Obama face today are not dissimilar to those of Nixon's age and Fredrik Logevall and Andrew Preston's *Nixon in the World: American Foreign Relations, 1967-1977* (Oxford, 2000: 31) gives a glimpse in summary of the age: "We live in a new world .... In a world of

FREDERICK MONDERSON

new leaders ... new people ... new ideas. Communism, Marxism, Socialism, anti-colonialism – the great ideas which stirred men to revolution after World War II have lost their pulling power ... Because we live in a new world, many of the old institutions are obsolete and inadequate. The UN, NATO, foreign aid, USIA were set up to deal with the world of twenty years ago. A quick trip around the world will show how different the problems are today." In a different mold, but the times and issues are probably similar and that is why Barack Obama has to innovate in his approach to dealing with world leaders and problems posed. This new thinking does not make him weak or in any way anti-American and ready to give away the store. After all, he has advisers and though he acts independently as President, he is still watched and analyzed by others near and far, particularly those who must choose whether to follow him or resign. And, to-date few have resigned from his cabinet-due to poor leadership. We must remember, Mr. Obama, unlike most presidents is more people friendly as he has demonstrated during the campaign and in many of the press conferences and other gatherings he has held. He is affectionate and comfortable in his person. He embraces people, not just shakes their hands. Some have even argued, the social scene at the White House has changed; he invites more people into that important "peoples' palace." That people friendly demeanor, his concern for the nation, hard working nature and grand outlook is what has kept his approval rating as high as it is.

During the last 8 years of Republican control of the government more Americans believed the nation was heading in the wrong direction. Then the Democrats may have criticized but not sabotaged the administration. Equally too, America's image abroad was tremendously tarnished, and as the global economic downturn manifested, that negative view helped in people blaming America for the world's economic woes. Obamas' campaign promises of change buttressed by his fast and decisive actions on economic and other issues on the domestic front, coupled with his outgoing nature, cool demeanor, wonderful smile and honest pronouncements have thawed the world's negativity. Naturally his critics, the Republicans principally, were quick to label him "soft," though he has only chosen to walk softly rather than wield his big stick. In this respect, President Obama was quick to point out; America's military might is only one aspect of its power. Its democracy, values, respect for law and order, ideals, ingenuity, freedoms and creative genius, its "basics," are collectively even more powerful. In fact, these attributes are what attracts so many immigrants to these shores and this is the carrot Barack waves much to the consternation of Republicans. Inherent here is the contradiction that a new president could parlay many of America's virtues, ideals and his opponents, many predisposed to be critical of his administration would challenge him for championing traits that they themselves believe in.

As Barack Obama progresses and the "glimmers of hope" become "points of light" and America could begin boasting of being "back in the saddle," the Republican fossils will have to yield to the real new faces of their party or become so embroiled in a "Civil War" in which their very existence would be at stake.

BARACK OBAMA
MASTER OF WASHINGTON DC

Meanwhile, President Barack Obama, a work in progress, would have turned around the American ship of state and begun sailing it into the calm waters under clear and sunny skies towards a future fueled by new and clean energy sources, competitive educational skills, scientific breakthroughs and these would signal the reality that better days are yet to come.

Barack Obama's Washington, DC Photo 269. Bikes and cars in the vicinity.

Barack Obama's Washington, DC Photo 270.

FREDERICK MONDERSON

Put billions of dollars into early childhood education - Latinos have such a high dropout rate. What you see consistently are children at a very early age are starting school already behind. That's why I've said that I'm going to put billions of dollars into early childhood education that makes sure that our African-American youth, Latino youth, poor youth of every race, are getting the kind of help that they need so that they know their numbers, their colors, their letters. Every dollar that we spend in early childhood education, we get $10 back in reduced dropout rates, improved reading scores. That's the kind of commitment we have to make early on. We've got to improve K through 12. That means not just talking about how great teachers are but rewarding them for their greatness by giving them higher salaries and giving them more support and professional development; and making sure that No Child Left Behind is not a tool to punish people, and we're not just basing how we fund our schools on a standardized test. BARACK OBAMA – 2008 Democratic debate in Las Vegas January 15, 2008

37. THE PRESIDENT ABROAD
By
Dr. Fred Monderson

Without a doubt the American people can be proud of how their President Barack Obama has performed abroad as he visited Canada and attended the G-20 Economic Summit in London, then his visits to France, Germany, Czechoslovakia and Turkey. Later he visited Latin America for an economic summit. When we consider the European disdain for America in wake of the invasion of Iraq and their actions, vis-a-vis, Donald Rumsfeld's arrogance – "The old Europe and there's the New Europe," and President George Bush's "go it alone" attitude and blaming those nations of Europe, particularly France that did not see it his way, the new fresh wind of change Barack Obama brings is welcome relief. Equally, closer to home, pressing problems in Latin America, need serious consideration for any future constructive relations.

He listened well in Canada, stated his views with this traditional ally and received a wonderful reception. Some consider this too soft a serious challenge that came when he "went abroad," Europe that is! In this assessment, from the moment Barack Obama stepped off Air Force One at Heathrow Airport, he has been acting Presidential, no matter what venue or country. In London, he met with the Prime Minister, had an audience and tea with Queen Elizabeth, attended the G-20 Economic Summit and then headed to Strasbourg, France, for a NATO meeting, and then he headed to Germany to celebrate the 60th anniversary of the founding of

BARACK OBAMA
MASTER OF WASHINGTON DC

NATO. After that it was on to Turkey for a meeting with Islamic students in a round-table.

Barack Obama's Washington, DC Photo 271.

After he got off Air Force One, traveling with Marine One and "the Beast," his armored Presidential mobile, the President moved about London with enormous security personnel deployed in wake of protesters and demonstrations taking place at strategic locations. Staying at the US Ambassador's residence, President Obama had a busy schedule ahead of him. Helene Cooper of the *New York Times*, Friday April 3, 2009, p. 1, "On Big Stage, An Overture" says: "It was a performance that ranged from mediating behind closed doors – Mr. Obama personally intervened in a spat between the French and Chinese leaders – to a carefully calculated news conference in which he reached deep into history, showed contrition for the failings of Wall Street, and forecast a road the world could no longer travel. Gone are the days, from *Pax Britannica to Pax Americana*, when Britain and the United States made the rules that others followed."

Many critics chose to wade into Mr. Obama seeking to down play his achievements on that first significant trip abroad. Nevertheless, he seems to have done very well. For that matter, the *New York Times* of Friday, April 3, 2009, reported the "Results of the G-20 Summit Meeting as the nations in attendance determined to combat the global economic downturn. These measures are as follows:

FREDERICK MONDERSON

- Increased resources for the International Monetary Fund 500 billion
- New Special Drawing Rights allocation shared among the 185 I.M.F. Members - 50 billion
- Increased lending by multilateral development banks 100 billion
- Increased support for trade finance 250 billion
- Additional lending to poorest countries financed by I.M.F. Gold sales 6 billion

Total   1.1 trillion

Other commitments they agreed to, include:

- To establish a Financial Stability Board, whose purpose will be to assess weaknesses in the global financial system and oversee action to correct them.
- To ensure regulators have necessary access to financial information.
- To require that hedge funds be registered and regulatory disclosure of their financial information, including leverage, to regulators.
- To develop means to control the use of illegal tax havens, in part by increasing disclosure requirements for taxpayers.
- To support greater transparency in the reporting of financial executives' compensation, and ensure that boards of directors play a greater role in the setting of executives' pay.
- To increase oversight of credit ratings agencies.

President Obama arrived in Iraq to pay tribute to the troops as their new Commander-in-Chief, but also to dish out medals, pound flesh with those in attendance, pose for photographs with them, and offer reassuring words of withdrawal. He received thunderous applause when he said, "It is time for us to transition to the Iraqis. They need to take responsibility for their country."

While not a planned or advertised Iraqi trip, it was logical after his two day stop in Turkey. In addressing some 600 of the nearly 140,000 troops in country, 10 of whom received the Medal of Valor, President Obama reassured the fighting men: "The main point I want to make is we have not forgotten what you have already done, we are grateful for what you will do, and as long as I am in the White House, you are going to get the support that you need and the thanks that you deserve from a grateful nation."

In his meeting with the Iraqi Prime Minister Nouri al-Maliki, President Obama told him: "The United States pursues no claims on Iraqi's territory and resources.

BARACK OBAMA
MASTER OF WASHINGTON DC

We respect Iraqi sovereignty and the sacrifices that you have made for your country."

Upon his return home, many of the "talking heads" in commentary on his overall trip abroad chose a "glass half empty" outlook to describe what it was he accomplished. Many others saw the glass as half full. After all, beside the G-20 Economic Summit, Obama attended social gatherings, held half-a-dozen news conferences and two campaign-style town hall meetings where people had a chance to hear him directly. Extolling his audience, he reinforced the view, "You will find a partner and supporter and a friend in the United States of America" if we can work together cooperatively. Explaining how sometimes it is difficult to get swift movement on issues, he pointed out, "Moving the ship of state is slow progress. States are like big tankers, they're not like speedboats. You just can't whip them around and go in a new direction."

Barack Obama's Washington, DC Photo 272.

FREDERICK MONDERSON

Barack Obama's Washington, DC Photo 273.

Barack Obama's Washington, DC Photo 274.

While he only got a promise of 5000 additional NATO troops for Afghanistan, a promise to pump billions into the International Monetary Fund and Russia's pledge on nuclear arms reduction, Mr. Obama was able to get invitations to visit Russia and China later this year. Some viewed the positive nature of the trip is

BARACK OBAMA
MASTER OF WASHINGTON DC

him "setting up his ducks" for later. Even more, his "ace in the hole" Michelle Obama helped win over many people, including the wives of leaders in attendance and in this respect, the first couple scored big.

One of the positives of Mr. Obama and a problem of his opponents, particularly the Republicans, he tries to remain upbeat, optimistic, with an attitude that sees more than the "half full glass;" while the opposition sees more than the "half empty glass." Or, as previously stated, Mr. Obama "sees the donut" while Republicans "see the hole!" In a press conference, while some reporters downplayed NATO's commitments, the President declared: "I am pleased that our NATO allies pledged their strong and unanimous support for our new strategy. We'll need more resources and a sustained effort to achieve our ultimate goals, but these commitments of troops, trainers and civilians represents a strong down payment on the future of our mission in Afghanistan and on the future of NATO." Adding further, that he felt "We already received the kinds of commitments that historically you don't see at a conference like this. Mr. Obama came away very pleased with his success and saw the gains as being even more significant later on." He then returned to the United States, address his domestic agenda and then set out again.

President Obama arrived in Mexico to support it's President Felipe Calderon, whose nation is experiencing unprecedented violence as drug cartels fight each other in competition for lucrative drug-transshipment turf to supply American demands. Obama affirmed, "We are absolutely committed to working in partnership with Mexico to make sure that we are dealing with this scourge."

Recognizing that Mexico is the main hub of Latin American drugs reaching the United States and guns and dollars flowing back through this corridor, the two men vowed to work together to stem the problem. But there are other matters under consideration, such as trade issues, climate change and new environmental energy initiatives, that the President will also raise when he goes on to the Latin American Economic Summit in Trinidad and Tobago, after his two day visit in Mexico. The question of immigration reform also loomed high in his plans for the future.

The nature of the problem of drug related killings of innocent civilians, drug dealing gang members, and law enforcement officials, as Secretary of State Hillary Clinton has explained, is the tremendous demand for drugs in the United States. Equally, gun sales have increased tremendously, masked under American right-wing extremists who are falsely fanning claims the president wants to curtail their 2nd Amendment rights to bear arms. Under this cloak, gun dealers are selling their merchandise indiscriminately domestically and the Mexican drug cartels are buying with their drug money. These weapons of mayhem are either being

FREDERICK MONDERSON

stockpiled at home by the right wingers or being shipped across the border to fuel the war among the drug cartels. This is what the two presidents, Mexican and American, hoped to combat.

After Mexico, the next stop was Trinidad and Tobago to attend the 5th Latin American Summit, where Mr. Obama hoped to set a new tone and to discuss trade, security and drugs flowing to North America. In addition, even though that nation was not represented at the Conference, the embargo against Cuba was a hot topic facing the President. He handled it well saying in essence, "Look, I made an overture to Cuba. The ball is now in their court to make some tangible changes before we go further."

Throughout the President took the attitude, "I did not come here to debate the past but to look to the future." He was concerned with the common prosperity of the entire region and hoped to help reform its failed regulatory economic system. He wanted a greater effort to combat inequality, create a broader foundation and strengthen that foundation. He insisted, "We must come together on behalf of the common good. This is a critical moment for the region. We seek an equal partnership with our neighbors. There is no senior or junior partner. We are just partners. You can't blame the US for every problem in the hemisphere."

Seeking liberty and justice in the region, and a concerted effort against poverty, corruption and racism, Mr. Obama equally insisted "illegal guns must not flow into criminal hands. We must seek to advance our common security." Jobs will go a long way to combat this trend. In all this, he insisted "We can't be prisoners of past policies. We must be concerned with making the lives of our citizens better." He recognized, the future of America is "inextricably bound to the people of this hemisphere."

Naturally, at home Mr. Obama's opposition foes have criticized him every step of his several journeys. Nevertheless, his public display this early in a new administration seems to indicate Mr. Obama is doing a terrific job on the international front as he is trying to do domestically.

BARACK OBAMA
MASTER OF WASHINGTON DC

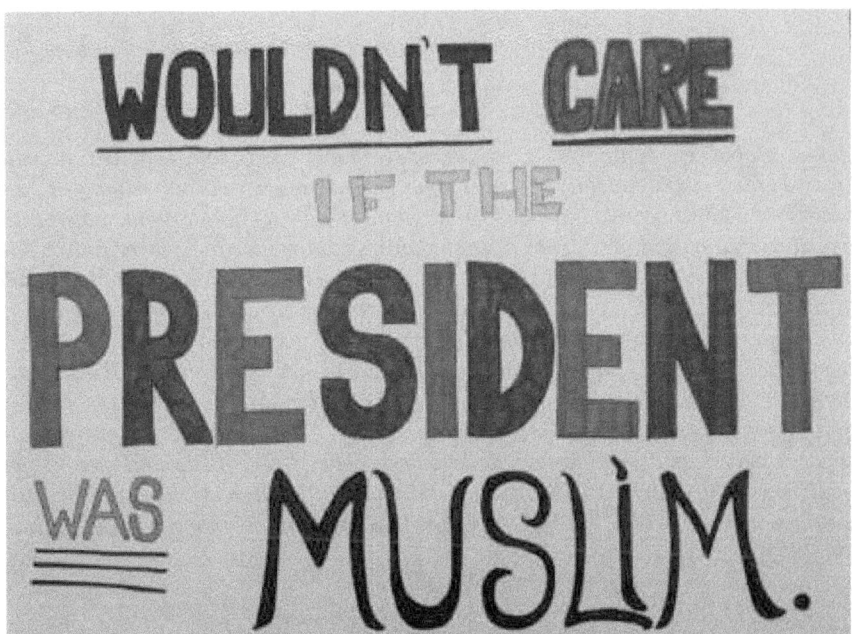
Barack Obama's Washington, DC Photo 275.

Barack Obama's Washington, DC Photo 276.

FREDERICK MONDERSON

"In a global economy where the most valuable skill you can sell is your knowledge, a good education is no longer just a pathway to opportunity--it is a prerequisite. And yet, we have one of the highest high school dropout rates of any industrialized nation. And half of the students who begin college never finish. This is a prescription for economic decline. So tonight, I ask every American to commit to at least one year or more of higher education or career training. This can be community college or a four-year school; vocational training or an apprenticeship. But every American will need to get more than a high school diploma. And dropping out of high school is no longer an option. It's not just quitting on yourself, it's quitting on your country. That's why we will provide the support necessary for all young Americans to complete college and meet a new goal: By 2020, America will once again have the highest proportion of college graduates in the world." BARACK OBAMA State of the Union Address February 24, 2009

38. THE BUCK STOPS WITH BARACK!
By

Dr. Fred Monderson

Every once in a great while along comes an especially great individual who not only levels the playing field but also moves the ball towards the goal line to score. History will show Barack Obama as a leader genuinely concerned with the future of his nation and has done everything possible in his first term to remedy the situation he inherited; despite the odds of succeeding, particularly and in spite of the tremendous efforts of the "stone throwers." Sure the buck stops with the top guy and even Barack Obama is sufficient of a pragmatist to recognize, to be in the left lane you must speed but also look out for "Smoky!"

BARACK OBAMA
MASTER OF WASHINGTON DC

Barack Obama's Washington, DC Photo 277.

Barack Obama's Washington, DC Photo 278.

FREDERICK MONDERSON

Barack Obama's Washington, DC Photo 279.

Not only has Mr. Obama recognized his "shovel ready" projects were not always "shovel ready," but he has made significant efforts to address those crucial sectors of the economic and social sectors of the America landscape that would aid progress in moving the nation forward. It's interesting no matter how much he employs the tremendous brain power of the American intellectual genius, he comes up short in affecting meaningful change in those critical areas of economics that it forces right thinking commentators to re-examine the starting point of the journey which should reveal unrevealed data that will show the pile to be shoveled was greater than thought because at the inception it was very well-camouflaged. Still, Obama stands ready to take responsibility for the condition of the ship of state he was elected to sail. That is because 'The buck stops with Obama!'

BARACK OBAMA
MASTER OF WASHINGTON DC

Still, the opposition never gives credit for the good things done, they only focus on what is negative and so because President Obama has not dramatically reduced unemployment, a significant barometer of the nation's lifeblood, people want his head, in some respects, literally. Though he has initiated the most comprehensive approach to health care reform that economically is a significant player in the nation's lifeblood, the opposition complains about this positive development.

Coming to power with two wars being waged in Iraq and Afghanistan, though he campaigned to end the nation's involvement significantly, once in the seat of responsibility and decision making, it becomes difficult to easily "cut and run." The President is Commander-in-Chief, but he is no battlefield commander strategist and must rely on his field officers who understand ground conditions. As such, he has to make mid-course corrections along the way so as save some credibility for the men and women who waged the struggle, died on the field of battle or were significantly impaired. Now critics challenge the President on every aspect of his actions in these theaters. Still, instead of these "tail try to wag the dog" they should stop being defective "fifth wheels" and instead put their shoulders to the wheel so as to insure we still have some credibility as the time goes by. Notwithstanding, while "uneasy lies the head" that wears the crown, the "Buck stops with Obama!"

Barack Obama's Washington, DC Photo 280.

FREDERICK MONDERSON

"I was drawn to the power of the African American religious tradition to spur social change. Out of necessity, the black church rarely had the luxury of separating individual salvation from collective salvation. It had to serve as the center of the community's political, economic, and social as well as spiritual life; it understood in an intimate way the biblical call to feed the hungry and clothe the naked and challenge powers and principalities. In the history of these struggles, I was able to see faith as more than just a comfort to the weary or a hedge against death; rather, it was an active, palpable agent in the world." BARACK OBAMA, Audacity of Hope.

"Volunteer in your neighborhood & we help pay for college - I know that the price of tuition is higher than ever, which is why if you are willing to volunteer in your neighborhood or give back to your community or serve your country, we will make sure that you can afford a higher education. And to encourage a renewed spirit of national service for this and future generations, I ask Congress to send me the bipartisan legislation that bears the name of Senator Orrin Hatch & Senator Edward Kennedy." Source: 2009 State of the Union address Feb 24, 2009

39. BARAK OBAMA:
A Majority of One.
By

Dr. Fred Monderson

"One man can become a majority if his truths are righteous and he firmly believes in the efficacy and forcefulness of his ideas." Fred Monderson.

When Senator Barak Obama conceived the idea to run for the Presidency of the United States of America, it's reasonable to believe not too many people expressed confidence in his ability to persevere for success. Perhaps his immediate family did! Nevertheless, when the brother decided to set out on that long and difficult journey, he may have said: "From Chicago, I travel to Maine then on to California." Metaphorically speaking, therefore, he took out and loaded his "Jeep," checked his tire pressure, oil, transmission, anti-freeze, spare tire, mechanical tools, money for gas and tolls, and considered motel and hotel accommodations along the way. Then he set out, believing "I can achieve this. I'm the one I'm waiting on."

BARACK OBAMA
MASTER OF WASHINGTON DC

Barack Obama's Washington, DC Photo 281.

Barack Obama's Washington, DC Photo 282.

FREDERICK MONDERSON

Barack Obama's Washington, DC Photo 283

As a community Organizer, Barak Obama formed a grassroots network that helped win him the Illinois State Senate seat. Pulled out, oiled and put back to work, his network again helped him win the United States Federal Senatorial seat. From the experience gained in the two Senate campaigns his staff people were now mobilized for Senator Obama's Primary and Presidential campaigns. So much so, with his knowledge as well as technical assistance he moved his movement up a notch and effectively utilized the Internet as a campaign tool. In this he achieved tremendous success in terms of fundraising and developed the ability to communicate with vast numbers of grassroots people and also to give instructions in terms of their assignments. His method of operationalizing his movement for effective and efficient operation was a significant contributor to his success.

BARACK OBAMA
MASTER OF WASHINGTON DC

Barack Obama's Washington, DC Photo 284.

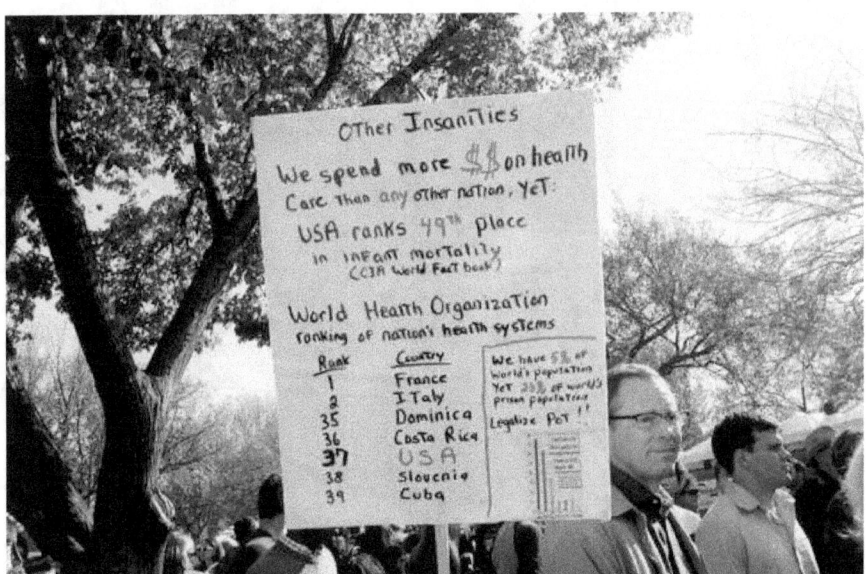

Barack Obama's Washington, DC Photo 285.

FREDERICK MONDERSON

Barack Obama's Washington, DC Photo 286.

BARACK OBAMA
MASTER OF WASHINGTON DC

Barack Obama's Washington, DC Photo 287.

Barack Obama's Washington, DC Photo 288.

There is "no force greater than an idea whose time has come!" Because of the confidence of his faith in himself, perhaps when others still doubted, Obama probably knew he could and would win the Presidency. Without a doubt he passed today's version of his critics standing by the roadside as he moved along his journey.

Barack Obama's Washington, DC Photo 289.

As such, it's not surprising, being wiser; he sees them as "little people trying to tie up Gulliver." However, Gulliver's skills in an age of technical sophistication, his tremendous work ethic and the extraordinary confidence he has always demonstrated in his many endeavors, keeps telling this man "you can do it;" because of his honest and sincere approach to the problem and honesty in stating his case before the nation.

BARACK OBAMA
MASTER OF WASHINGTON DC

Barack Obama's Washington, DC Photo 289a.

Despite the nefarious yet essential work of critics, America is sufficiently perceptive to realize, in Obama, we have a sincere and genuine leader, working at full throttle to rescue his nation, making courageous decisions, for he is also a student of history and must recognize, as a historical figure, his legacy will perpetually be scrutinized because of the time of his emergence on the American and world stage. That is why he may very well be saying, "Damn the torpedoes, I mean, critics, full speed ahead" because despite what they think they know, "I know different." This notwithstanding, in addition to being, Commander-in-Chief, Obama can still boast, "I'm a majority of one!" Or, as "possum playing" Mitch McConnell admitted: "President Obama is the only person who can sign the bill into national law."

FREDERICK MONDERSON

"I was drawn to the power of the African American religious tradition to spur social change. Out of necessity, the black church had to minister to the whole person. Out of necessity, the black church rarely had the luxury of separating individual salvation from collective salvation. It had to serve as the center of the community's political, economic, and social as well as spiritual life; it understood in an intimate way the biblical call to feed the hungry and clothe the naked and challenge powers and principalities. In the history of these struggles, I was able to see faith as more than just a comfort to the weary or a hedge against death; rather, it was an active, palpable agent in the world." BARACK OBAMA, Audacity of Hope

40. BARACK OBAMA: MAN FOR ALL SEASONS BY

DR. FRED MONDERSON

When the next election rolls around, despite the negativity spewed on Barack Obama, right thinking Americans will re-elect him President, a second time in office, because most realize, extra-ordinary times call for extra-ordinary leaders and Mr. Obama is an exceptional individual and leader with a genuine desire to rescue his nation from the perdition it did not deserve! After all, this is the principal reason he sought the Presidency in the first place. That is why this writer is confident America will not do a "Churchill" on Obama!

BARACK OBAMA
MASTER OF WASHINGTON, DC

Barack Obama's Washington, DC Photo 290.

Barack Obama's Washington, DC Photo 291.

FREDERICK MONDERSON

Barack Obama's Washington, DC Photo 292.

Let's face it, as a leader; Obama is the best thing America can muster right now! He is honest, thoughtful, and thorough; conscientious and hard-working; caring and concerned; a transformational leader; working for results.

Again facing it!

1.   Sure it's the economy stupid!

2.   At the start of his administration President Obama was praised for the great and efficient transition team he had put together and the great economic and scientific think tank comprising his team of experts.

3.   Timothy Geithner, his Secretary of the Treasury, was hailed as an economic wizard with a thorough and firm grasp of the American and global economic landscape who has worked unceasingly with the economic monster he inherited.

4.   Obama's Council of Economic Advisers was thought to comprise some of the best minds of the American pool with Ex-Fed Chief Paul Volker among equally awesome financial wizards.

5.   From day-one, these individuals have been "shoveling" away at the "economic heap" the Republican leadership had bequeathed Obama. Now, after all the reform measures put in place and the long days and nights of incessant work, it

BARACK OBAMA
MASTER OF WASHINGTON, DC

turned out there were "two back rooms" of the "stuff" they shoveled making the mountain "double" and "triple peaked."

Barack Obama's Washington, DC Photo 293.

Barack Obama's Washington, DC Photo 294.

Then, there's really the question of why, seriously, should we support Barack Obama? So, along comes the "Judas smiling" Republican horde pointing out all

FREDERICK MONDERSON

the supposed flaws in Barack Obama's armor and filtering this to the American viewing public in the most shameful and hood-winked confusing manner. They never admit to their culpability in manufacturing the "shovelable mountain," nor their sabotage of all the tools Obama has utilized despite their littering the landscape with their seeds of "No!" As the President has pointed out, "like Gordon" they "slid the American car into the ditch" and now want the keys to repeat their bad driving habits!

All the above, notwithstanding, honest questions for Republicans are, "Let us suppose we give you the keys to the American vehicle"

1. What would you do different than Obama has done in wrestling with the fracture of the American economy?

2. How long would it take you guys to repair the problem and set things right?

Now, since Republicans are incapable of giving a straight answer, "A La Ron Paul," we know "the Devil we have" as opposed to "the Devil we don't know;" the best bet is the Quintessential Obama, "Our Man For All Seasons."

Barack Obama's Washington, DC Photo 295.

BARACK OBAMA
MASTER OF WASHINGTON, DC

Barack Obama's Washington, DC Photo 296.

Barack Obama's Washington, DC Photo 297.

FREDERICK MONDERSON

Barack Obama's Washington, DC Photo 298.

Barack Obama's Washington, DC Photo 298a.

BARACK OBAMA
MASTER OF WASHINGTON, DC

Barack Obama's Washington, DC Photo 299.

Barack Obama's Washington, DC Photo 300.

FREDERICK MONDERSON

Barack Obama's Washington, DC Photo 301.

"My wife has been my closest friend, my closest advisor. And ... she's not somebody who looks to the limelight, or even is wild about me being in politics. And that's a good reality check on me. When I go home, she wants me to be a good father and a good husband. And everything else is secondary to that." BARACK OBAMA, Tavis Smiley Show, Oct. 23, 2006

41. MICHELLE OBAMA: MOTHER OF THE YEAR
By

Dr. Fred Monderson

In the selection of Michelle Obama for "Mother of the Year," "Why," becomes a legitimate question. In response, the answer is crystal clear that the face, persona, grace and beauty of the choice, and her warm, sensitive and intellectual abilities, coupled with the multitude of situations and activities in which Michelle has remarkably supported and represented her husband, accompanied him and as First Lady, the official face of the American nation, a role she pursues with distinction, unquestionably, the choice is therefore good and correct! Naturally, this is the opinion of one individual writer but many people, upon examination of the merits,

BARACK OBAMA
MASTER OF WASHINGTON, DC

will tend to agree. Also, Michele Obama is a legal eagle, highly intellectual, poised with suave, a confident woman, a fashion icon, and a well loved daughter, mother, wife, and domestic and foreign ambassador of the nation. She adores her husband, children, and is a professional who feels confident about her issues and programs of interest. She is also a terrific "White House Mother," well liked, displays a down-home personality that allows people easy access and she has also emerged as a symbolic figure who has motivated many people, young and old. She is thus "true to herself," "cool to hang out with," and strong, capable, cultured, sheikh, *ipso facto*, the contemporary quintessential mother!

Barack Obama's Washington, DC Photo 302.

FREDERICK MONDERSON

Barack Obama's Washington, DC Photo 303.

The title of "Mother of the Year" is an illustrious one with a lengthy history and only significant individuals are chosen for this distinctive award. In that vein, as a dutiful and loving son, I'm apt to say my mother, Mitta, and grandmother Cherise Preville have been the "Best Mother." However, now as we celebrate this time of recognition for the wonderful work, particularly African American, mothers have accomplished in the task of motherhood, in rural, urban and suburban America, we need to give special praise for their unselfish efforts. Their love, concern, caring and commitment deserve our unending adulation and support. Such a greeting comes from their sons and daughters, husbands and brothers and all well-wishers. This becomes even more real with the cards, perfume, gifts, candy, flowers, dinner, bubbly, entertainment, theater, etc., that they so rightly deserve. Such then, are affectionate sentiments extended to those loving, compassionate, uncritical, understanding, pleasant and forgiving mothers, stalwarts of the African-American family and that of the wider community.

For this Mothers' Day in the land of Red, White and Blue, an interesting connection can be established, when viewing the historical landscape of Africa for evidence of creative accomplishments of African motherhood.

In the beginning, Lucy or actually *Denk Nesh*, at 3.2 million years from the Hadar region of Ethiopia is an early ancestor of the African experience, and probably the first mother. Later, the "scientific Eve" has been identified as an African female who roamed the East African plains 150,000 years ago. Through DNA reconstruction she was been credited with being the "mother of all existing humans" on earth.

BARACK OBAMA
MASTER OF WASHINGTON, DC

The "Great Mother" of Kemetic/Egyptian cosmogony and mythology, Nut was married to Geb and they produced Osiris, Isis, Seth, Nephthys, and Horus. From this age of divine consciousness, down through the last prehistoric times, males being interred in shallow graves, besides other artifacts, had included carved figurines of these earliest African "mothers." Hathor, the "Cow goddess," makes her entrance on the divine stage from her Upper Egypt/Sudani origin. Now Bauval and Brophy in *Black Genesis: The Prehistoric Origins of Ancient Egypt* places this cow-goddess among the black people, true originators of pharaonic Egypt.

The first great dynastic mother was Aahotep, wife of Narmer and mother of Aha, his successor. The Narmer Macehead depicts this African queen seated besides her husband atop a flight of stairs as part of some celebratory occasion, thought to be their wedding. Hetepheres, wife of Snefru, founder of the fourth dynasty was mother of Khufu, grandmother of Khafre and great grandmother of Menkaure, builders of the great pyramids at Giza. What an illustrious progeny to which she gave life, courage and ingenuity, all attested by the greatest form of architectural accomplishments, mountains of splendid stone, magnificently erected, having defied time, to this day. Peseschet, "Lady Director of Lady Doctors" was probably a 4th Dynasty mother working in the medical field.

Von Bissing, a German Egyptologist, in *American Journal of Archaeology*, recounts an incident in the war between Heracleopolis and Thebes. Intef of Heracleopolis began the consolidation of Upper Kemet/Egypt after the collapse of the Old Kingdom and the First Intermediate Period, which led to establishment of the Middle Kingdom. Having mobilized his forces, Intef took the battle to Mentuhotep, the Theban. Coming out of a pass unto the Plains at Thebes he encountered Mentuhotep's superior army, ready and waiting. Thereupon, Intef called upon his mother to mediate with Mentuhotep's mother, Queen Aam, to broker a peace between the two forces. These mothers then presided over the peace as preparatory to challenge the Memphite prominence, to unify the nation and usher in one of the greatest periods of intellectual, literary and imperial expansion, consolidation and reorganization in ancient Egypt. Such an honor indicates the high esteem of the well-respected African mother! Such a mother, whose son is pictured "with black flesh" and very instrumental in establishing the continuity of Old and Middle Kingdom cultural, religious and scientific development in ancient Egypt, has a special place in the iconography of African historical reconstruction and the contribution of the great mothers.

The Middle Kingdom came to an end and gave way to the Second Intermediate Period that brought the Hyksos invaders who held the northern land of Kemet captive for over a century. Seqenenra I and his wife Tetisheri began a protracted war of liberation against northern domination that ultimately freed the land from the foreign invaders. Their offsprings Seqenenra II and Aahotep married and continued the struggle. Seqenenra II was felled by an axe blow to the head during

FREDERICK MONDERSON

the struggle at which time a palace coup broke out, led by "Tety the Handsome." Some have said Tetisheri but it's actually Aahotep who rallied the loyalists, put down the uprising, supported her son Kamose who expelled the Hyksos and saw his brother Ahmose establish the Eighteenth Dynasty ushering the New Kingdom. Then he married his sister, Ahmose Nefertari.

The sister-marriage now seems justified, for, having now won the country back, whom would Aahotep have chosen to support her son in the difficult tasks ahead. She would have chosen, none but the loyal Nefertari, his sister. Nefertari became a distinguished ancestress of the Eighteenth Dynasty, and together with her son Amenhotep I, they were later made gods with their own temple erected to worship them. Her grandson, Tuthmose I overran Palestine and provided strength, stability and wealth to Kemet. Much later in the Tuthmosid dispute between Tuthmose II, Tuthmose III and Hatshepsut, the woman who dared to seize power and rule for two decades, and who built the wonderful Deir el Bahari temple modeled after Mentuhotep's 500 year old masterpiece; she would later boast of her blood ties to the ancestress of the Eighteenth Dynasty, Ahmose Nefertari.

Another and even more important observation about Ahmose-Nefertari is her portrait in the British Museum. The bejeweled Nefertari, whose name is in a cartouche signaling royalty and is depicted as a regal fashionable lady "painted black" and wearing the fashion of the times, a long flowing robe of red, white and blue. Imagine! The first time the colors of our flag - red, white and blue are pictured in history we see then on a Black African Queen, 1500 years Before Christ!

Barack Obama's Washington, DC Photo 304.

BARACK OBAMA
MASTER OF WASHINGTON, DC

Barack Obama's Washington, DC Photo 305.

Barack Obama's Washington, DC Photo 306.

FREDERICK MONDERSON

Amenhotep III also of the Eighteenth Dynasty built a palace, Malcata, for his wife, the Nubian, Queen Tiy. Amenhotep IV (Ikhnaton, Akhenaten) launched the Amarna Revolution against the New Empire god Amon, destroying all images of him and establishing his god the Aten as supreme. Some have said if he had not used violence his profoundly religious ideas would have taken hold and things would have been better. Nevertheless, his mother, Queen Tiy in her pronouncements told his adversaries, "You have a right to disagree with my son, but if you harm him I will have you all put to the sword." That's a mother "watching her son's back."

The son Amenhotep IV married the Thadukhippa, daughter of Dushrata of Syria, whose name the Africans changed to Nefertiti the "fair one cometh." However, Aahmes-Nefertari meant "the most beautiful one!" However, he was overthrown and his god and their religion was rejected and Amon reinstated to reigned supreme as deity with his wife Mut, and their son Khonsu, forming the "Theban Triad."

Rameses II of the Nineteenth Dynasty built his magnificent worship temple at Abu Simbel and right next to it he carved another temple to his beloved Nubian wife, Nefertari, signaling the great respect he held for her. Some have reasoned Solomon pursued Sheba not particularly because of her extraordinary beauty but that her kingdom was greater than his and together they created Menelik I. Beauty coupled with power must have made her a great queen and mother.

During the Golden Age of West Africa, Ibn Battuta, Islamic traveler in that region, tells of the hospitality women, mothers, extended to the visitor who arrived at their village. Interestingly enough, Queen Nzinga may not have been a mother for she was too busy fighting the Portuguese slave traders who enslaved her people. Her resistance, nevertheless, symbolized an inclandestine abhorrence to degradation of the African mother and her offsprings during the horrendous middle passage, slave trade and slavery. Later, Yaa Asantewaa was the Ghanaian Queen Mother who fought and defeated a disciplined British army. Even still later, Harriet Tubman, as "mother of the Underground Railroad," was very busy heading north with brothers and sisters on the way to freedom. Sojourner Truth is another important mother we need to recognize. Both Mrs. Frederick Douglass and Mrs. Booker T. Washington supported their men in their much travail.

Into the twentieth century, the Educator Mary McLeod Bethune gave much that blacks would become educated to hurdle barriers in American scientific, industrial, educational, artistic, political, educational and economic enterprises. Amy Jacques Garvey resolutely supported her husband Marcus Garvey. Mitta Mary Monderson, who on March 6, 1957, dressed in the colors of the Ghanaian flag on the day of that nation's independence, "was laughed at" by brothers and sisters who were not yet nationalistically conscious, back then. Rosa Parks, mother of the Civil Rights Movement, Coretta Scott King and Betty Shabaaz, first nationalist mothers and

BARACK OBAMA
MASTER OF WASHINGTON, DC

now ancestors, have all been pillars of monumental resoluteness in defense of rights and human dignity for African Americans. In process they assisted America to move towards living out the true meaning of its creed.

Also, let us never forget the wives of W.E.B. DuBois and Paul Robeson, Dr. ben-Jochannan's Gertrude, Dr. John H. Clarke's Sister Cybil Williams-Clarke, Mrs. Angela Jitu Weusi, Dr. Leonard James' Marilyn, and Dr. Leonard Monroe' Nellie and Dr. Blakely, "Queen Mother of the Middle Passage."

So on this Mothers' day let us salute the many mothers, including Fannie Lou Hamer, Queen Mother Moore, Marcus Garvey's Black Cross Nurses, Winnie Mandela "Queen of the Black World" and those as Enid Forde, Marjorie Matthews, and Hazel Dukes who brought sunshine to board rooms; LaRay Brown of HHC, Patricia Hinds in ENDTC Health Care; and Mrs. Francis Hagler's concern about educating the young, also Lou Ann Dyer, Mrs. Taylor, the PTA mothers, Cherise Preville; Mother Carmel "Olga" Ward, Cherise Maloney, Megan Monderson, Sister Barbara and Claudia, Doreen John, and Fina, Gemma Grigsby, Ms. Maude Holloway, Elsie Richardson, Margaret Vinson, Connie Lesold and Ruth Goring in Crown Heights. Neville Norville's Claire, Violet Bennett, Myrtle Rogers, Doris Alexander, Angela Cooper, Queenie Huling, Gloria Brown, Edith Graham, Mavis Hill, Estelle Brown, Pat Richardson, Pamela Covington, "Miss Pearl" Weatherspoon, Enid Graham, Mavis Hill, and Aunty. To this we can add Renee Rowell of HHC, also Kashida Maloney, Suhail Pena, Carmen Rodriguez Monderson, Audrey Monderson, Keisha Monderson, Queen-Tiy Monderson, Jacqueline Monderson, Ethyl Foy, Melinda Melbourne, Rhonda Mormon, Charissa Wright, Winna Aulette, the Health Care Champions of Kings County Hospital Center Debra Tyndale, Mrs. Margaret Burke, Gloria Thomas, Jermaine Burge-Gaskin, as well as Ms. Rasheedah Nasir, Tammy Moore, Roshana Hinton, Alison Mulzac, Bernice Green and many more mothers.

This greeting also goes out to all the other mothers who vote, go to school, are in business and administration, cook, sew, teach, comfort, go to church, shop, wash, work, offer guidance to the young, doctor and support their black men!

Notwithstanding, Michelle Obama is celebrated as Mother of the Year because she has demonstrated unquestionably what a difference a woman can make in supporting her family during normal as well as challenging times. After all, she first declared to be "Mother-in-Chief" and still makes time to be with her kids, Malia and Sasha. Serving as a role model for her kids whom she raised to be enthusiastic and unselfish, she once boasted her mother was her role model! So let's give a big shout out to Michelle's mother, Mrs. Robinson! Equally, and without a doubt, Michelle has been tremendously inspirational in support of Barack Obama, but more importantly she held it down in that amazing year when

FREDERICK MONDERSON

Barack set out to "bring home the bacon." That role extended when she accompanied the President to the G-20 Economic Summit in London and mothered to the girls at Elizabeth Garrett Anderson School on April 2, and like a mother told the girls, "I am very touched. All of you are jewels .... You are precious and you touched my heart." She was certainly a hit in London earning the title "Mighty Michelle." When the "Mother of the British Nation" Queen Elizabeth reached for a hug, clearly this says much on Michelle's behalf! She was compared with Jacqueline Kennedy and Patty Reagan once said "Nancy Reagan likes Michelle."

An even more spellbinding statement of hers center on the unveiling of a bust of the abolitionist Sojourner Truth in Washington, D.C. recently. Michelle said: "I know Sojourner Truth would be proud to see me, a descendant of slaves, as the First Lady of the United States!"

We ought not to forget she works with military families trying to get them, particularly those returning from overseas duty, needed supplies and other forms of assistance in their transition from combat and other forms of service. She also inspires young men and women across the nation for them to get an education to be useful and live meaningful and contributing lives.

All in all, what kid would not like to boast, my mother is beautiful, "does her make-up most of the time," intelligent, very fashionable, a lawyer who helps with the homework, knows how to act on the world's stage, is sexy, warm, funny, likes to listen, a great mom, likes to welcome the kids in the neighborhood, inspires, gives good hugs, knows how to wield power and can say "No!" to the most powerful man in the world, as well as give him advice when it's needed. She is definitely my choice for "Mother of the Year!"

So therefore, we say have a Glorious and Happy Mothers' Day Michelle Obama and equally to all mothers!!! You have stood long and hard in struggle, trials and tribulation. Now stand tall and receive your richly deserved recognition and respect as the quintessential linchpin of your family and the nation, very much the essence of the human race!

BARACK OBAMA
MASTER OF WASHINGTON, DC

Barack Obama's Washington, DC Photo 307.

Barack Obama's Washington, DC Photo 308.

FREDERICK MONDERSON

"There is also no question that Guantanamo set back the moral authority that is America's strongest currency in the world. Instead of building a durable framework for the struggle against al Qaeda that drew upon our deeply held values and traditions, our government was defending positions that undermined the rule of law. Indeed, part of the rationale for establishing Guantanamo in the first place was the misplaced notion that a prison there would be beyond the law – a proposition that the Supreme Court soundly rejected. Meanwhile, instead of serving as a tool to counter-terrorism, Guantanamo became a symbol that helped al Qaeda recruit terrorists to its cause. Indeed, the existence of Guantanamo likely created more terrorists around the world than it ever detained." BARACK OBAMA, speech, May 21, 2009

42. Barack Obama and the Supreme Court

By

Dr. Fred Monderson

Even during the recent presidential campaign visionary commentators posited the view, if elected; President Barack Obama would have the chance to impact the Supreme Court by having to make appointments to that body. That was not unexpected since many of the sitting jurists were well beyond seventy years old. Of course, in an effort to keep their ideological positions alive, Supreme Court judges have a tendency to remain on the bench as long as their health and life lasts. One elder jurist, recently, practically died on the bench. Now, one of the youngest of the "black robes," Justice David Souter, a New Englander, appointed by the first President Bush, has decided to retire from the "best job in the world, in the worst city in the world." Justice Souter, therefore, gives President Obama the chance to make his first appointment to the bench.

As Justice Souter is a member of the "liberal" block on the bench, it's expected he will be replaced by an ideologically compatible person. However, it has been argued, since President Barack Obama is replacing a while male on the bench, his choice to fill the seat can be any number of possibilities. He could appoint another white male, or another black male, of course, ideologically opposed to Clarence Thomas; a white or black woman, a Hispanic, or Asian. In essence, the field of choice is wide open to the President. That is, there could be any other characteristics in his choice, but, most important is the knowledge, ideological orientation, writings, legal positions, and perhaps party affiliation of the individual who will make the grade. What is important, nevertheless, if it's a "young" appointee, the President will certainly leave his mark on the ideological orientation

BARACK OBAMA
MASTER OF WASHINGTON, DC

of the nation's legal lifeblood with its significant impact on the social realities, civil rights realities and political path of the nation for decades to come.

Barack Obama's Washington, DC Photo 309.

If President Obama is elected to a second term, given the ages of several other jurists, then he could be privileged to appoint additionally one or even two more "black robes." The chance to appoint one member is unusual, two is remarkable, and three is unprecedented. An experienced and respected constitutional scholar, Professor Ogletree, one of Barack Obama's teachers at Harvard University opined to change the orientation of the court his former student needs to appoint 4 justices. This, however, is doable if destiny dictates. Such a reality, therefore, requires President Obama to maintain his credibility, popularity and re-electability, requiring him to be around long enough to create this long lasting impact on the nation's legal system. Naturally, since the Senate will have to vote on the choice, the President will have to court Republicans even though the Democrats have a majority in that body. Even more, since all that is needed is a simple 51-vote majority in the 100-member chamber, an "up-and-down vote" is practically assured. Nevertheless, President Obama must consult across the board with Democrats and Republicans so as to encourage cooperation on issues beyond this particular case. Notwithstanding, as all presidents wish for the chance to make some appointment to the Supreme Court, this replacement for Justice Souter will define the Obama's presidency. Therefore, that person must be an intellectual and must also have diversity of experience, perhaps coming from another field other than a sitting judge.

In reflection, presidential power to appoint a Chief Justice of the United States Supreme Court allows him sometimes to impact the opposition, particularly if his numbers are up or down, as in the case of President George W. Bush. Importantly, some Presidents have had no impact on the Court, others get to appoint an Associate Justice and the lucky ones get to appoint the Chief Justice. Of course, the "not fortunate ones" do get to appoint judges to "inferior courts." Interestingly, in the Post World War II era, Republicans Eisenhower, Nixon, Ford, Reagan and both father and son Bush Presidents have impacted on the Court.

With President George W. Bush's leadership questioned on Iraq and Afghanistan and even his slow response to the catastrophe of Hurricane Katrina, many people began writing the final chapter of the sun setting on his presidency! His nominee Samuel Alito, to replace Justice Sandra Day O'Connor was in for a fight. Lo and behold, and sadly, Chief Justice William Rehnquist died suddenly and the President turned around and re-nominated John Roberts for Supreme Court Chief Justice. These two appointments did not disappoint anyone since they are Conservatives. However, an outsider, straight up the ladder, to be Chief Justice is indeed rare; yet, it's just the way things can turn around sometimes. To explain these dynamics, an attempt to trace the essentials of this extraordinary institution and its leading men allows this writer's readers a condensed glimpse at a process that affects their lives in more ways than one. Thus, we get a better understanding of the legal body which will be so much in the news in the months ahead.

The Constitution of the United States divided the power of the federal government into 3 Branches, the Legislative, Executive and Judicial. The Legislative Branch creates the laws, the Executive Branch executes the laws and the Judicial Branch interprets the laws. Under the first President George Washington, *The Judiciary Act* of 1789 created the Supreme Court with a Chief Justice and 5 Associate Justices. Over the years the numbers have grown to 8 Associate Justices and there have been attempts to change this now set number of 9 justices on this Supreme legal body. The Constitution also empowered the government to create inferior or lower courts. This judicial power gave the Supreme Court and other federal courts the authority to hear certain kinds of cases, relative to their expertise. Thus, together these courts have the power to rule in cases involving the Constitution, national laws, treaties, and states' conflicts. As such then, Supreme Court rulings have the power to shape government public policies on issues of great national and international concern from the beginning of the republic to today.

BARACK OBAMA
MASTER OF WASHINGTON, DC

Barack Obama's Washington, DC Photo 310.

Barack Obama's Washington, DC Photo 311.

FREDERICK MONDERSON

Barack Obama's Washington, DC Photo 312.

According to the Constitution, Article 3, Section 2, Subsection 1, the Supreme Court has General Authority and this judicial power "shall extend to all cases, in law and equity, arising under this Constitution, the laws of the United States, and treaties made, or which shall be made, under this authority; to all cases affecting ambassadors, to public ministers and consuls; to all cases of admiralty and maritime jurisdiction; to controversies to which the United States shall be a party; to controversies between two or more states; between citizens of different states; between citizens of the same state claiming lands under grants of different states."

Subsection 2 of the Constitution states: "In all cases affecting ambassadors, the public ministers and consuls, and those in which a state shall be party, the Supreme Court shall have *original jurisdiction*. In all the other cases mentioned, the Supreme Court shall have *appellate jurisdiction*, both as to law and fact, with such exceptions, and under such regulations, as the Congress shall make."

Keep in mind, the Constitution actually created only one court, the Supreme Court. It gave Congress the ability to establish lower or "inferior courts." More than two centuries later, under constitutional and judicial changes, the Federal Courts system has evolved into an institution that consists of three tiers. "At the lowest level are 94 U.S. District Courts. These are the courts where federal trials take place. The second level in the courts system includes 12 U.S. Courts of Appeal. These courts hear cases 'on appeal.' At the third level is the highest court of appeal, the Supreme Court."

BARACK OBAMA
MASTER OF WASHINGTON, DC

The Supreme Court in its capacity has heard cases from aid to church supported schools, affirmative action, campaign financing, civil rights, the Constitution, Executive Orders, impeachment, internment of Japanese Americans, interstate commerce, jurisdiction of justices, legislative veto, military actions, Mohammed Ali's refusal to serve in the military, poll tax, racial discrimination, racial quotas, reapportionment, right to be informed on charges, search and seizure, taxes, treaties, voting, work place rules and a whole lot more.

Even more important, however, in the "Checks and Balances" dynamic created by the Constitution, the Supreme Court can exercise checks on both the President and Congress. Because Judges are appointed for life and are free from executive control, they can sometimes, through "judicial activism," become "wild cards" on the bench and as such can declare Executive Acts unconstitutional and rule in unpredictable manners in the interest of the well being of the state even though this is not always the case.

Regarding Congress, these judges can, through the process of *Judicial Review*, declare acts of Congress, unconstitutional. This power to declare acts of Congress unconstitutional comes from the famous case of *Marbury V. Madison* in 1803, when Chief Justice John Marshall asserted the power of the judiciary and declared an act of Congress unconstitutional. In establishing the Judicial Review process, that is, the power of the Supreme Court to review any act of Congress, Marshall determined, it is the "unmistaken power of the Supreme Court to state what the law really is." Of course, nowhere in the Constitution does it say the Supreme Court is granted the power of Judicial Review. This practice gained legitimacy and became standard because it first occurred in the early legal history of the nation.

Different types of powers are granted under the Constitution. There are delegated and implied powers, and even concurrent powers. A *delegated power* is clearly stated, as in the case when the Constitution says the Executive has the power to give the State of the Union Address, to "appoint judges" or to "execute the law" or Congress has the power to "regulate interstate commerce," or to "coin money." The *implied power* means that given certain circumstances, the respective party can use a discretionary power. However, in the case of the Supreme Court, the founding fathers implied Judicial Review so as to keep an eye on the Congress and President. As they say, this is where John Marshall asserted this discretionary power. *Concurrent power*, in addition, is when both federal and state governments have the power to act simultaneously as in the case of "taxation" or "military" preparedness.

FREDERICK MONDERSON

Barack Obama's Washington, DC Photo 313.

Barack Obama's Washington, DC Photo 314.

BARACK OBAMA
MASTER OF WASHINGTON, DC

Barack Obama's Washington, DC Photo 315.

Irving Gordon in *American Studies* (1975: 222) says of the *Marbury v. Madison* decision: "Marshall reasoned that (1) the Constitution is supreme law of the land; (2) The Supreme Court is the final interpreter of the Constitution, and therefore (3) The Supreme Court may declare unconstitutional and inoperative any law contrary to the Constitution. Acting boldly and confidently, Marshall thus established the precedent of *judicial review*."

Even further, in subsequent years: "During Marshall's tenure (1801-1835), the Supreme Court did not invalidate another federal law but did declare several state laws unconstitutional. To 1975, the Supreme Court has held some 80 federal laws (out of 40,000 laws passed) and some 1000 state and local laws unconstitutional. Among democratic nations this power of the Supreme Court remains unique."

John Marshall was the fourth Chief Justice of the Supreme Court. *Marbury v. Madison* (1803) caused him to make a most significant impact on American constitutional law. According to Carl Brent Swisher's *Historic Decisions of the Supreme Court*, federalists and Jeffersonian Republicans vied for power and this forced the courts to act. "Jeffersonians were opposed to interference by a Federalist Judiciary. Yet, here Marbury, whom President John Adams had appointed a justice of the peace, was asking the Supreme Court to issue a writ of mandamus to compel Secretary of State Madison to give Marbury the commission entitling him to hold that office. *The Judiciary Act* of 1789 authorized the Supreme

Court to issue writs of mandamus to remedy wrongs of this kind, but the Constitution did not clearly authorize Congress to pass such an act." He said it was not the right of the court to issue a mandamus but it was the right of the court to review all acts passed by Congress.

There have been a number of cases both at the federal and state level declaring federal and state laws and acts unconstitutional. The first such significant civil rights case was *Dred Scott v. Sandford* in 1857 with Chief Justice Roger Taney presiding. Scott, an enslaved African in Missouri, taken into the free territory of Minnesota, was returned to Missouri. He sued for his freedom having set foot on free soil created by the Missouri Compromise of 1820 that declared such territory free. Taney ruled, in a very biased manner, as the majority opinion, that Scott was not a citizen and could not bring suit in a US court. Gordon (1979: 222) says further: "Assuming an activist stance, Taney stated further conclusions that (a) slaves are property, (b) Congress may not deprive any person of the right to take property into federal territories, and consequently, (c) the Missouri Compromise, which prohibited slavery in part of the Louisiana Territory, was unconstitutional."

There were other cases regarding the issue of constitutionality as *Schecter Poultry Corporation v. United States* (1935); *United States v. Butler* (1936); *Youngstown Sheet and Tube Company v. Sawyer* (1952), each having an impact on the constitution and American history and public policy.

At the state level, the significant cases were *Dartmouth College v. Woodward* (1819); *McCulloch v. Maryland* (1819); *Gibbons v. Ogden* (1824); *Wabash, St. Louis and Pacific Railway Company v. Illinois* (1886); and *Lochner v. New York State* (1905). These too are historic and the first discussed in American history and government classes.

Each Chief Justice has imprinted his mark on the Supreme Court beginning with the Marshall Court (1801-1835); the Taney Court (1835-1864); the Salmon Chase Court during Reconstruction (1865-1878); Hughes Court (1930-1940); Warren Court (1953-1969); Burger Court (1969-1986); and Rehnquist Court (1986-2005). Currently we have the Roberts Court (2005); this latter Chief Justice was appointed by the second President Bush. Many people have praised the last departed Chief Justice Rehnquist for his intellect despite his "narrow interpretation" of the Constitution. Chief Justice Rehnquist's immediate predecessors Warren and Burger have applied the concept of a "broad interpretation" of the constitution. The current Chief Justice Roberts is a "strict constructionist," who offers a "narrow interpretation" of the Constitution. "Strict constructionists" on the court reasoned, if it's not in the Constitution it gets no hearing, while "loose constructionists" take a more liberal stance and say, "well, let's open the door a little."

Andrew Jackson appointed Roger Taney Chief Justice in 1835 and in the climate of antebellum slavery he represented the evil face of a system that degraded and

BARACK OBAMA
MASTER OF WASHINGTON, DC

destroyed black men, women and children, in a horrendous experience whose influence still pervades in the social fabric of this society. This reality of historic racism can possibly be perceived in response to the devastation of hurricane Katrina in the "Black belt" states of Louisiana, Mississippi, Alabama, Georgia, etc.

An interesting point is appended here for clarification on an important ruling in Supreme Court history. President Abraham Lincoln appointed Salmon P. Chase of Ohio to replace Roger Taney. Page Smith in *The Constitution: A Documentary and Narrative History* (1980: 440) says the following: "In the first session of the Court after the new chief justice took his seat, John S. Rock of Massachusetts was admitted to practice before the Court. The *New York Times* published an account of the event: "The black man was admitted. Jet black, with hair of an extra twist - let me have the pleasure of saying, by purpose and premeditation, of an aggravating 'kink' - unqualifiedly, obtrusively, defiantly 'Nigger' - with no palliation of complexion, no let-down in lip, no compromise in nose, no abatement whatever in any facial, cranial, osteological particular from the despised standard of humanity brutally set up in our politics and in our Judiciary by the Dred Scott decision-this inky-hued African stood, in the monarchial power of recognized American Manhood and American Citizenship, within the bar of the Court which had solemnly pronounced that black men have no rights which white men were bound to respect ... By Jupiter, the sight was grand! 'Twas dramatic too." [The Court, incidentally, had never said that "black men have no rights which white men were bound to respect."]

Barack Obama's Washington, DC Photo 316.

FREDERICK MONDERSON

Barack Obama's Washington, DC Photo 317.

Frederick Douglass, in response to this Dred Scott Decision, according to Norman Hodges (1974: 96) declared: "The Supreme Court is not the only power in the world .... Judge Taney cannot bail out the ocean, annihilate the firm old earth or pluck the silvery star of liberty from our Northern sky."

In the era of Reconstruction (1865-1877) the Court faced the South in most of its rulings and seems to have continued in the vein of the Taney Court. Hodges (1974: 138) says: "The Supreme Court, too, played a significant role in the oppression of Black citizens. The federal court system, in its decisions, tended to reflect the political mood and temper of the times. The Supreme Court handed down a series of decisions that gravely compromised the power of the federal government to protect Black rights in the South. As early as 1878, the Court struck down a Louisiana ban on segregation in interstate transport because it was a 'burden' on privately operated interstate commerce. In 1882, it ruled against sections of the Enforcement Act of 1871 which stipulated punishment for persons acting in violation of the Fourteenth and Fifteenth Amendments. The Court continued its attack on Black rights in 1883, when it declared the landmark Civil Right Act of 1875 unconstitutional. This Act had given Blacks access to the 'full and equal employment of privately operated public facilities, such as inns, theaters, railroads, etc. The Court held that the Fourteenth Amendment prohibited state discrimination, rather than individual discrimination. Thus it deprived millions of citizens of the needed protection of federal enforcement of their constitutional

BARACK OBAMA
MASTER OF WASHINGTON, DC

rights. This decision particularly was used as precedent by the South to justify 'Jim Crow' laws, that were later enacted.'"

In wake of this, a number of terrorist groups such as the Knights of the White Camellia, the Ku Klux Klan and the White League emerged to terrorize Blacks and re-establish white supremacy in the south. Hodges (1974: 127) says further: "Hooded night riders erected burning crosses in Black areas at night and terrorized the Black populace with beatings, tarring and feathering, mutilations, threats, torture, and lynchings. Members of the Klan rode in conspicuous caravans at election time to intimidate the Blacks, and the brazen White League members sat at the polling places, in full view, with loaded guns on their laps in order to prevent the freedmen from casting their ballots. The Klan and its companion organizations stirred up hatred against Blacks and fermented riots against them at the slightest provocation or pretext." Little was done by the courts to curtail this form of 19th Century terrorism. Now we understand why individuals as Stokely Carmichael (Kwame Ture) and SNCC, in the 1960s, were so serious when they went to the South to register Blacks to vote!

All developments after Reconstruction led to the famous *Plessey v. Ferguson* (1896) case challenging a Louisiana law that required "Separate but equal" accommodations on trains and this extended to other areas. Accordingly, Hodges (1974: 145) noted: "The Court upheld the state law and gave constitutional approval to the 'separate but equal' doctrine. The Court denied that 'the enforced separation of the two races stamps the colored race with a body of inferiority ... if this be so, it is not by reason of anything found in the act, but solely because the colored race chooses to put that construction upon it."

FREDERICK MONDERSON

Barack Obama's Washington, DC Photo 318.

The dissenting Justice John Marshall Harlan of Kentucky wrote the minority opinion sating: "We boast of the freedom enjoyed by our people above all other peoples. But is it difficult to reconcile that boast with a state of the law which, practically, puts the brand of servitude and degradation upon a large class of our fellow citizens, our equal before the law. The thin disguise of 'equal' accommodations ... will not mislead anyone, or atone for the wrong this day done .... Our Constitution is color blind, and neither knows nor tolerates classes among citizens."

The NAACP was founded in 1909 and within half a dozen years was able to win a significant legal victory against a legal practice that severely curtailed black voting rights. Hodges (1974: 172) informs: "The supreme Court, in 1915, struck down the notorious 'grandfather clause' as unconstitutional. In 1917, the Court nullified a Kentucky law that provided for 'Jim Crow' communities in Louisville. And on the question of justice for Blacks, the Supreme Court ordered a new trial for a Black man convicted of murder by a jury from which his Black peers had been excluded."

In this past century, Charles Evans Hughes was appointed Chief Justice by President Herbert Hoover in 1930 and served during the New Deal era, often clashing with President F.D. Roosevelt. When the President threatened to "pack the court" with more judges to facilitate his agenda in this critical time, Hughes became liberal and helped pass two important pieces of legislation by a narrow margin of 5 to 4. These New Deal laws were: the National Labor Relations Act to guarantee collective bargaining and the Social Security Act that have had such far

BARACK OBAMA
MASTER OF WASHINGTON, DC

reaching implications for American public policy. Some say Roosevelt lost the battle but won the war!

Barack Obama's Washington, DC Photo 319.

FREDERICK MONDERSON

Barack Obama's Washington, DC Photo 320.

Nevertheless, during Roosevelt's tenure the Court became more liberal. "In 1932, in the first of two celebrated Scottsboro decisions, the Court ruled (*Powell v. Alabama*) that the defendants had been denied their right to counsel, and that such denial was a violation of their Fourteenth Amendment rights. In a second Scottsboro opinion in 1935, the Court held that Blacks had been excluded from Alabama juries over an extended period of time, and that this fact proved the existence of discrimination in violation of the accused Fourteenth Amendment rights. In these historic decisions the Supreme Court seemed to advance away from the racist tendencies that had perverted the dispensation of justice by some of its members in the past."

President Dwight Eisenhower appointed Earl Warren Chief Justice in 1953 and later admitted it was "the worst damn thing" he did, because Warren presided over the famous *Brown v. Board of Education of Topeka Kansas* in 1954. In the 1960s he began, according to John J. Newman and John M. Schmalback's *United States History* (1998: 602) exerting influence "on the criminal justice system, the political system of the states, and the definition of individual rights." Gordon (1984: 231) offered commentary on the liberal and activist course of the Warren Court in three major areas: "(1) in the Brown Case, the Warren Court unanimously held racial segregation in schools unconstitutional, thereby contributing to the movement for black civil rights; (2) In the Baker Case, the Warren Court held legislative apportionment to be a judicial matter, thereby furthering democracy through more equitable election districts …. (3) In several cases affecting persons accused of crime, the Warren Court insisted upon protection of their rights to a lawyer and against self-incrimination."

BARACK OBAMA
MASTER OF WASHINGTON, DC

Warren Burger was appointed Chief Justice by President Richard Nixon in 1969 to reflect his campaign pledge to appoint judges who would "interpret the law-not make the law" and "interpret the Constitution strictly and fairly and objectively." According to Gordon (1984: 233-34) while opposing judicial activism: "The Burger Court upheld busing to remedy *de jure* school segregation; however, in the absence of deliberate discrimination, it struck down inter-district school busing; it granted broad discretion to trial judges to close criminal pretrial hearing to the press and public but later reaffirmed the right of the press and public to attend criminal trials; it supported a voluntary affirmative action program in employment; it held that national defense took precedence over equal rights for women and approved draft registration only by males; it struck down a Texas law denying free public education to children of illegal aliens; it struck down the practice of Congress of overruling specific executive actions by the so-called legislative veto. The Court declared this practice a violation of separation of powers."

The last deceased, William Rehnquist, was an important modern Chief Justice whose conservatism turned back the liberal leaning of the Warren and Burger tenures. The *New York Times* Obituary of September 4, 2005, offered this commentary: "With a steady hand, a focus and commitment that never wavered, and the muscular use of the power of judicial review, he managed to translate many of his long held views into binding national precedent." The *Times* said further, praising his lengthy tenure: "But his ultimate success was also a testament to his own tenacity and skill. He combined an unfaltering sense of mission with high intelligence, patience, the strategic prowess of a serious poker player, which he was, and the attention to detail of an art-lover and serious amateur painter, which he also was. He had held many of his views since early adulthood, and he took the long view: with seeming nonchalance, he would plant a phrase in an opinion in the expectation that it would take root, blossom, and prove even more useful in some future case. Time proved him right, not always, but often enough."

FREDERICK MONDERSON

Barack Obama's Washington, DC Photo 321.

Major decisions of the Rehnquist Court, according to the *Daily News* of September 4, 2005 included: "*Texas v. Johnson* (1989) – The court ruled that flag-burning was protected speech under the First Amendment; *Planned Parenthood v. Casey* (1992) – The court, widely expected to overturn *Roe v. Wade* decision, reaffirmed the right to an abortion instead, but opened the door to new restrictions; *Lee v. Weisman* (1992) – The court ruled that sanctioned prayer at public school graduations violates the Constitution; *United States v. Lopez* (1995) – The court, led by Rehnquist, struck down laws that prohibited bringing a gun near a school; *Bush v. Gore* (2000) – In its most controversial opinion, the court decided 5-4 along political lines to end a recount of presidential election votes in the state of Florida, ending Al Gore's challenge to George W. Bush; *Stenberg v. Carhart* (2000) – The court struck down a Nebraska ban on 'partial birth' abortion and said all abortion restrictions must contain an exception for the health of the mother; *Dickerson v. U.S.* (2000) – The Court, led by Rehnquist ruled that taxpayer-funded school vouchers could be used for religious schools; *Gonzalez v. Gaich* (2005) – The court ruled that federal laws against medical marijuana trumped state laws allowing its use; *Roper v. Simmons* (2005) – The court outlawed the death penalty for prisoners who committed their crimes while under 18."

Those of us who remembered the Congressional hearings when Clarence Thomas was appointed as an Associate Justice were both proud and disappointed. He was replacing the venerable and venerated Thurgood Marshall as a black man on the court. However, for a black man, Clarence Thomas represented a surprisingly conservative wing of the court and he proved true to expectations on both sides of the divide. Nonetheless, he was at the time touted as being the youngest justice, will outlive many of the older ones and he will one day become Chief Justice.

BARACK OBAMA
MASTER OF WASHINGTON, DC

Years later he would confess at the Black Bar Association meeting of never realizing blacks would dislike his interpretation of the true meaning of the Constitution, against affirmative action, etc. Some thought he wanted to come home and be accepted by Black America. Nevertheless, "well played" and he "played well" according conservative standards, but was denied the elusive prize of becoming Chief Justice when President George Bush (Number 43) chose Mr. Roberts.

Barack Obama's Washington, DC Photo 322.

Now, with Justice David Souter's decision to leave the bench it places President Obama in a somewhat precarious position, because once appointed to the bench, the jurist has the security of service for life. In this, he is not sure how his appointee turns out; no President ever is! Presidents Franklin Roosevelt and Reagan were both disappointed with their appointments, while the second President Bush was not disappointed with his conservative pick. This then is one of the concerns facing President Obama. Nevertheless, "damn the torpedoes," let's proceed "full speed ahead," make this appointment and wait for the next one just around the corner.

FREDERICK MONDERSON

Barack Obama's Washington, DC Photo 323. Those three Washington, DC personalities, Michelle Obama, Abe Lincoln, Barack Obama, as souvenirs.

"I will never forget that the only reason I'm standing here today is because somebody, somewhere stood up for me when it was risky. Stood up when it was hard. Stood up when it wasn't popular. And because that somebody stood up, a few more stood up. And then a few thousand stood up. And then a few million stood up. And standing up, with courage and clear purpose, they somehow managed to change the world." BARACK OBAMA, speech, Jan. 8, 2008

43. BARACK OBAMA AND THE VOTING RIGHTS ACT
By

Dr. Fred Monderson

The **Voting Rights Act of 1965** and subsequent related Acts with the benefits and responsibilities they guarantee are dependent also on Civil Rights and the laws that flow from the conceptual intent of both statuettes; and only strict adherence to the letter of the law will ensure these laws serve the purpose for which they were intended. In *The American Political Dictionary*, Jack C. Plano and Milton Greenberg (New York: Holt, Rinehart and Winston, (1962, 1989: 108) have indicated, "The Voting Rights Acts were passed in response to demonstrations by black Americans protesting voting discrimination. Existing legislation that relied on slow-moving judicial procedures to control discriminatory

BARACK OBAMA
MASTER OF WASHINGTON, DC

practices had proved ineffective. Under the Acts federal registration procedures, thousands of minority voters were added to the voting rolls. The Acts have had a major impact upon southern and national elections, and numerous black officeholders have been elected. Federal intervention to expand the electorate was sustained by the Supreme Court through a broad interpretation of the Fifteenth Amendment."

Importantly, despite President Obama's election and claims of "post racial America" much needs to be done in terms of leveling the social, educational, economic and psychological playing field in America to truly advance this nation; for a culture, where as Dr. King advocated, Black Americans be judged, "not by the color of their skins, but by the content of their character."

Black voting rights have always been a problematic issue since the African-American constituency has had to struggle for the privilege of voting in elections from colonial days to today. In the former, a very miniscule percentage of this ethnic group has had the privilege to vote because in those days, wealth determined who was able to exercise the franchise and blacks qualifying were very few. Today, after a long history of laws regulating voting, for the general American voting pool and black voters in particular, the **Voting Rights Act** provides protection for black voting rights for a period of 25 years. That being so, there is always the concerns that the act may not be renewed and as such, blacks would lose the fundamental protections the act guarantees. Strangely, this concern only applies to black voters. However, while the likelihood of worst case scenario regarding loss of this right in these modern times would hardly ever materialize, the psychological and emotional strain associated with it raises fears that are not easily allayed.

Notwithstanding, the peculiarity at play this time around, interesting that because he is African American, potentially if the law expires, the President of the United States may have a problem with his vote and *ipso facto* he would not be able to stand or run again for a position he once held. Naturally, that scenario will perhaps never play out, but it focuses on how laws can contradict themselves in future developments. However, in order to analyze this conundrum one has to examine the evolution of the rights of blacks to vote and what were some impediments placed in their paths. Some of the president's aides, his wife Michele and daughters Malia and Sasha, and others of their generation can be victimized if the above scenario, though highly improbable, were to materialize.

FREDERICK MONDERSON

Barack Obama's Washington, DC Photo 324.

Barack Obama's Washington, DC Photo 325.

The Civil War Amendments 13th – freed the slaves; 14th gave citizenship to persons born in the United States; 15th gave black males the right to vote. At this time, women did not have the right to vote until 1921, and this right was granted because of their contribution to the World War I effort at home. With the rights and responsibilities came opportunities and challenges and the pressures to enjoy these promises. Nevertheless, the opportunities to exercise these rights were indeed struggles, for the opponents of black progress engaged in the most unimaginable full court press to deny such expressions and despite national law,

BARACK OBAMA
MASTER OF WASHINGTON, DC

private individual, groups and even local and state governments engaged in systematic efforts to deny black voting at all costs.

Barack Obama's Washington, DC Photo 326.

For example, Andrew Gumbel's *Steal This Vote* (New York: Nation Books, 2005: 135) recounts incidents perpetuated by Republicans in an 1898 election in Mississippi and elsewhere. He mentions efforts by states, in addition to gerrymandering and "state control of the electoral process to strangle voting rights of their black populations." He offers efforts to "pack black voters into the smallest possible number of legislative districts." Such things as restricting the "number of polling places of black-majority areas, put them twenty or even forty miles away from the densest population centers, change their locations without warning, disrupt transportation services such as river ferries on election day, and then run out the clock on those who make the long and uncertain journey by having Democratic Party poll watchers endlessly challenge their eligibility." There were also threats that Blacks with criminal records and outstanding warrants would be arrested if they showed up to vote. We could also add stuffing ballot boxes, threats and intimidation, etc., as well as changing the date of the election that acted as a ruse to get them to vote the next day. Some examples show such practices don't seem to go away and were attempted by Republicans in the recent 2008 presidential election. If a hundred years later we find these same practices, how could we argue for a "post-racial America?"

FREDERICK MONDERSON

Perhaps it was Voltaire who said, regarding Friday the 13th "Lets crush the accursed thing!" This is certainly the attitude we should take in viewing the ramifications surrounding the need to renew the **Voting Rights Act** every 25 years that pertains to blacks or African-Americans in this great nation. As such, the **Voting Rights Act**, renewed in 2007, further stigmatizes blacks in this great democracy and the "accursed thing" should be "crushed" because a segment is presently under challenge in the Supreme Court. A contrasting and disturbing reality is that a Russian immigrant whose country has nuclear weapons pointed at us; whether they will fire or not; can come to this country, work hard, maintain integrity and qualifies to become a citizen and win the franchise or right to vote. Equally too, we went to war against Germany, the French, Japan and these countries' immigrants can also become citizens and win the right to vote. The **Voting Rights Act** does not apply to these people once they acquire citizenship (natural or naturalized); residency (at least one month in an area); age (18 or older); registration (sign up to vote and choose a party or remain independent); and can thus participate in the General Election, Special Election or Primary Election.

Case in point! For the present California Governor Arnold Schwarzenegger, some wanted to change the Constitution to make him eligible to run for the Presidency. Yet, many wanted to deny Barack Obama's right to be President. Now, America would have been a global laughing stock having a married President, unfaithful to his wife and with a bastard child. Where is that woman who felt Obama was inadequate? Even more, black Americans whose ancestors slaved to build this country, defended this country against the warlike machinations of these same mentioned belligerents, despite Barack Obama's triumph, are still the victims of discrimination, bigotry, institutional racism, racial profiling, under-employment, police brutality and more, and have had a long struggle to pull the lever in elections. It must stay fresh in our minds that the former President of the United States George W. Bush, in his Second Inaugural Address, in 2005, called for an end to racism in America! After hundreds of years of this practice, despite Barack Obama's election as President, these ideas will remain, perhaps disguised. All of this helps to explain the road African-Americans have traveled, what were their experiences, where they are and the distance ahead. Let us not forget the obstacles along the way and those yet to be encountered.

There have been property ownership and religious requirements, poll taxes, sex discrimination, the effects of the "Three Fifths Clause" (1787) and the *Dred Scott Decision* (1857), which was challenged by the Civil War Amendments. Yet still, *Plessey V. Ferguson* (1896) (with its *separate but equal* philosophy) and the *Grandfather Clause*, outlawed in (1915)) ruling had to wait for the *Brown V. Board of Education* (1954) and the **Civil Rights Act of 1957** and **1960**. Nevertheless, the role of the court has been instrumental in Voting and Civil Rights litigation, seemingly ruling one way and then another. For example, Plano and Greenberg informs, "In 1980, the Supreme Court upheld provisions of the Voting Rights Act that prohibit changes in voting practices that have a

BARACK OBAMA
MASTER OF WASHINGTON, DC

discriminatory effect, even if not so intended (*City of Rome v. United States*, 446 U.S. 156). In another 1980 case, the Court refused to declare an at-large election system discriminatory because no black had ever been elected to a city commission even though blacks comprise about 35 percent of the city's population (*City of Mobile v. Bolden*, 446 U.S. 55).

This much said, some reflection needs to focus on Voting Rights in the United States of America, particularly as it pertains to African-Americans.

1.   Prior to the **Civil War in 1860** only the privileged could exercise the right of franchise and this excluded mostly all blacks, those enslaved, freed as well as poor whites. Women, black or white, were naturally excluded.

2.   The end of the war brought what came to be called the **Civil War Amendments**. The **Thirteenth Amendment** freed the slaves (1865); the **Fourteenth Amendment** gave citizenship to persons born in America and this meant black men and women were thus covered; the **Fifteenth Amendment** gave the right to vote to all males and hence black men were allowed to vote. That is, providing they were able to meet certain voting qualifications. However, the Southern states, just emancipated from the albatross of slavery, and within just over a decade, were yet able to reassert their odious political behaviors. That in spite of the role blacks played politically in **Southern Reconstruction** advocating universal male suffrage and free public education for the Freedmen. Blacks were elected to the national government. However, in the climate of Reconstruction, the **Radical Republicans** fought President Andrew Johnson's veto of the **Freedman Bureau Act** and the first **Civil Rights Act of 1866** that pronounced all Americans citizens. This was reinforced by the **Fourteenth Amendment** that repudiated the **Dred Scott Decision** and provided a shield against Southern states' **Black Codes** and in this a significant struggle ensued to insist on "equal protection of the laws" and "due process of law." There were others as the **Civil Rights Acts of 1870 and 1871** that make it "a federal crime for any person acting under authority of a state law to deprive another of any rights protected by the Constitution or by laws of the United States. Another authorizes suits for civil damages against state or local officials by persons whose rights are abridged. Others permit action against persons who conspire to deprive people of their rights."

FREDERICK MONDERSON

The Civil Rights Act of 1875 guaranteed equal accommodations in public places (hotels, railroads and theaters). Poor enforcement of this law led to the backlash of Jim Crow laws. Harold C. Syrett in *American Historical Documents* (1965) tells, the Supreme Court in 1883 declared this act of Congress unconstitutional "on the grounds that the Fourteenth Amendment did not forbid discriminatory actions of private individuals but only of states."

Irving Gordon in *American Studies* (1980) pointed out, politically: (1) Southern states required payment of a poll tax which discouraged blacks mostly poor, as well as impoverished whites, from voting. (2) Southern states established difficult and unfair literacy requirements, which effectively barred blacks, mostly little educated, from voting. (3) To preserve the vote for illiterate whites, some states enacted a grandfather clause, exempting from literacy requirements persons whose grandfathers had been eligible to vote before the Civil War. (4) The Democratic Party in the South denied membership to blacks and thus kept them from voting in party primaries. This had the effect of disenfranchising blacks, since Democratic nomination in the South, until well into the 20th century, was equivalent to election. By 1900 most Southern blacks did not vote and had negligible political influence. "

Barack Obama's Washington, DC Photo 327.

BARACK OBAMA
MASTER OF WASHINGTON, DC

Barack Obama's Washington, DC Photo 328.

Barack Obama's Washington, DC Photo 329.

FREDERICK MONDERSON

The Civil Rights Movement spearheaded the effort to not only desegregate but also to win the right to vote. **The Civil Rights Act of 1957** forced the Federal government to respect the voting rights of Blacks across the nation in that this act of Congress "created a bipartisan commission to investigate infringement of civil rights because of race, religion, or national origin. A civil rights division was established in the Department of Justice and authorized to seek injunctions against violations to voting rights." However, enforcement of such acts required extensive legal action that was cumbersome and time consuming. Yet still, the door began to be pushed ajar slowly. The non-violent protests of "sit-ins," "freedom rides," and "economic boycotts" all culminated in the **1963 March on Washington**. Dick Gregory reminded, Dr. King's speech was not about a "Dream" but about poverty, economic deprivation, employment, poor people, discrimination, etc., but the media and others co-opted it and emphasized naming it the "I have a Dream" speech.

The Civil Rights Act of 1960 "authorized federal courts to appoint referees if, in suits brought under the Civil Rights Act of 1957, the courts decided that Negroes had been deprived of voting rights because of race. In such cases, the referees were empowered to issue voting certificates, legally binding on state officials. The act required state officials to permit Justice Department officials to examine voting records and imposed federal penalties for obstructing federal court orders and crossing state lines to escape prosecution for bombing or arson."

The Civil Rights Act of 1964 noted "(1) Voting – The law prohibited election officials from applying different standards to black and white voting applicants and declared, as evidence of literacy, a sixth grade education. (2) Public Accommodations – The law forbade discrimination in most place of public accommodation: hotels, motels, restaurants, lunch counters, retail stores, gas stations, theaters and sports arenas. (3) Public Facilities – The law prohibited discrimination in government-owned or operated facilities such as parks, swimming pools, and libraries. (4) Federally Assisted Programs – The law authorized the federal government to withhold financial aid from the state and local programs involving discrimination. (4) Employment – The law prohibited discriminatory practices by most employers, employment agencies, and labor unions. To promote voluntary compliance, the law created an Equal Employment Opportunity Commission. The Twenty-fourth Amendment of 1964, aimed at five Southern states particularly, outlawed the use of poll taxes as a requirement for electing federal officials."

3. **The Voting Rights Act of 1965** was President Johnson's response to violence on the part of the Ku Klux Klan to deny voting rights to Alabama blacks. Out of 15,000 eligible black voters only 335 were registered because of intimidation and illegal practices. This spawned the Selma to Montgomery march to focus attention on the problem. The **Voting Rights Act of 1965** declared:

BARACK OBAMA
MASTER OF WASHINGTON, DC

"(a) In any state or county where less than half of the voting-age population was registered or had voted in 1964, all literacy and other qualification tests were suspended. This provision applied immediately to the five southern states and parts of two others. (b) The Attorney General was empowered to send federal examiners to any county practicing voting discrimination. These registrars were authorized to register all would-be voters who met the state's age and residency requirements. This provision replaced the time-consuming court processes required by previous laws. (c) The Attorney General was empowered to file suits challenging the constitutionality of state poll taxes." This provision affected four Southern states.

As a result, the **Voting Rights Act of 1965** and the other **Civil Rights Acts** helped increased the number of eligible southern blacks from 25 percent in 1957 to 65 percent in 1972. This voting strength enabled blacks to be elected to state and local offices and forced white candidates to appeal for black votes.

Barack Obama's Washington, DC Photo 330.

FREDERICK MONDERSON

Barack Obama's Washington, DC Photo 331.

Hence, the **1964 Civil Rights Act** "prohibited election officials from applying different standards to black and white voting applicants and declared a sixth grade education was evidence of literacy. The Voting Rights Act of 1965 suspended all literacy and other qualification tests in any state of county where less than half of the voting age population was registered or had voted in 1964. The Voting Rights Act of 1970 forbade all states from requiring literacy as a requirement for voting."

What is interesting is that all gains blacks made by amendment, legal statue or court proceedings aided minorities, women, children, disabled, and even persons accused of crimes. This brings us to the rights of prisoners. All across this nation black men and women are being incarcerated and losing the right to vote, and this is a situation President Obama has to address. He has to address this travesty because it could have an impact on national and state elections as well as on his own re-election campaign.

All this notwithstanding, in 1982, President Ronald Reagan signed the renewal of the **Voting Rights Act** for 25 years that expired and was renewed again in 2007. Jack Plano and Milton Greenberg (1962, 1989: 108-09) have explained: "The success of the Voting Rights Act results from the application of federal power to correct abuses at the state and local levels. Several million blacks and other minority voters have been registered since the law went into effect. In an important case in 1983, the Supreme Court upheld changes in city government that continued but did not worsen the racially discriminatory effect of the election system, against the position that the Voting Rights Act was intended to prevent perpetuation of past discrimination (*City of Lockhart v. United States*, 406 U.S. 125 [1983]). In 1986, in *Thornburg v. Gingles*, 478 U.S. 30, the Supreme Court

BARACK OBAMA
MASTER OF WASHINGTON, DC

ruled for the first time on the 1982 amendments to the Voting Rights Act of 1965 that require courts to look at the results of electoral practices and not merely the intent as expressed in regulations. In that case, which involved a redistricting plan using multimember districts, the Court ruled that the fact that some minority candidates were successful does not foreclose investigation into the extent to which minority voting is diluted."

Barack Obama's Washington, DC Photo 332.

When all is said and done, if blacks marshal their political strengths and advocate appropriately in alliances with liberals and people of like persuasion in legislatures across the nation, perhaps we can finally lay the Voting Rights Act in the Smithsonian Institution as a historic relic of a people's long struggle for equality, respect and right of self-determination. Then again, there must still be a means to keep the racists in check. That is, in addition to vigilance, unless America, in this most modern age still wants to be perceived as still wearing the shackles of a racist past.

FREDERICK MONDERSON

"The Declaration of Independence, the Constitution, the Bill of Rights—are not simply words written into aging parchment. They are the foundation of liberty and justice in this country, and a light that shines for all who seek freedom, fairness, equality and dignity in the world." BARACK OBAMA, speech, May 21, 2009

44. BARACK OBAMA AND THE POWER OF SYMBOLISM
By

Dr. Fred Monderson

Imagine a Black student standing among graduates, for example at Notre Dame University's Commencement, watching President Barack Obama receive a resounding applause as he walked to stand on the platform, then to the podium to give his Address. The significance of the President's visit, that of being a black President of the United States, the audacity of accepting the invitation despite all the controversy surrounding the choice of speaker, to be present at that historic moment in time, witnessing a prestigious academic institution giving an honorary degree to a constitutional scholar and the prospect of a Commencement Address that praises young graduates to engage the world and constructively build the future in the interest of humanity is phenomenal. However, the symbolism of being a part of all this is a powerful stimulus and motivator to a young mind setting out on a constructive path of who knows where into the future, and as such, this is an experience that comes once in a lifetime.

From the vantage point of being among the graduates, that young black student would experience any number of emotional, philosophical and spiritual reverberating highs to last a lifetime. As to the true meaning of a day as this; when a black person would be awarded a college degree as an alumnus of the President and also be privileged to witness the President of the United States give the address that begins the new journey of the rest of his life, is truly an unforgettable experience. The significance of the day is even more meaningful for the student because of the historic nature of the 2009 Commencement. For here is a Catholic University, celebrating 163 years dating back to 1846, a time when it was illegal for enslaved Africans in America to learn to read, much more be able to attend such an institution, to graduate and to see the President of the United States, an African-American, receive an honorary degree and have the honor of addressing its 2900 graduates, of which that student is a member.

BARACK OBAMA
MASTER OF WASHINGTON, DC

There was much press coverage and controversy in the days leading up to Sunday, May 17, 2010 and numerous questions as to why a Catholic University, guided by strict religious principles, particularly strongly anti-abortion, would not only invite to speak but also bestow an honorary Doctor of *Noris Causa* degree on someone, the President of the United States, who strongly believed in a woman's right to choose, as upheld by *Roe v. Wade*. Yet, in the aftermath of the pre-graduation publicity, protests, and arrests and even heckling drowned out by a rousing "Yes we can," President Obama had chose to speak, and delivered his message, because in his view, many of those who would be in attendance welcomed his appearance.

Father John Jenkins, President of Notre Dame University, in introducing President Obama, recounted a litany of accomplishments; while not spanning a great number of years, contradicted Arizona State University's contention that Obama had not achieved sufficient; which reflected the human side and simplicity of the man despite the powerful nature of the office he now held.

In his Introduction, Father Jenkins identified a sign on the East Bay of Notre Dame's Basilica that reads *God, Country and Notre Dame*. In his message, he recognized the President's trait of appealing to reason and his efforts to dialogue based on ethical principles, healing not being hateful, and engaging in responsible and respectful dialogue. He is endowed with tremendous human reason and emboldened to serve mankind, seek god and serve humanity, which is consistent with the mission of Notre Dame. His is a human reason, tempered by faith seeking common good in life. Notre dame is a primary and privileged place for dialogue between gospel and culture. The President listens carefully and speaks honestly. For that, a great deal of attention surrounded his visit to Notre Dame. He is one who does not stop talking with those who differ with him, and this is a quality the American people admired when they elected him. For that, his appeals transcends race and he is a healer, Father Jenkins concluded.

FREDERICK MONDERSON

Barack Obama's Washington, DC Photo 333.

Barack Obama's Washington, DC Photo 334.

BARACK OBAMA
MASTER OF WASHINGTON, DC

Barack Obama's Washington, DC Photo 335.

Before issuing the first among the eight honorary degrees on Sunday, Father Jenkins praised President Obama for his "enormous potential to impact the world for others." This ability culminated in his rise from being the child of a single mother whose family was on food stamps, yet, he engaged in a struggle for a quality education. He chose to serve the people of Chicago as a Community Organizer and worked alongside a diverse group of people. Significantly, from "relative obscurity" Obama triumphed in a political world; demonstrated a tremendous ability to build consensus and bring world leaders and opposing side together, which demonstrates his desire to ease hateful divisions among mankind. Even more important, Father Jenkins pointed out, President Obama, while realizing all the controversy awaiting him at Notre Dame, did not decline the invitation but chose to come and give his address. For this, it was not so much that the University in South Bend, Indiana was honoring President Obama but that Dr. Obama, a constitutional scholar in his own right, was honoring the University by coming to speak at that glorious occasion of its commencement.

For his part, President Obama, like so many great orators, punctuated his presentation with anecdotes of humor; began by being "honored to be here," "grateful to be part of your graduation" and reminded the audience, "Honorary Degrees are hard to come by;" in that he is "one for two," referring to his denial by Arizona State University. Recognizing his motivation to speak has "not been

FREDERICK MONDERSON

without controversy," he insisted no one should "shy away from things that are uncomfortable." He informed the graduates, they have "come of age at a time of great challenge in the world," but they were "privileged and have a responsibility to be constructively meaningful." He faulted the "global economic crisis caused by greed and short term thinking that was rewarded over hard work." Yet he admonished his audience, "We must find a way to live as one human family." This way, we must strive for "greater cooperation and great understanding among many people."

Quoting Dr. Martin Luther King, the President reminded those in attendance, "our fate is tied up in a single garment of destiny" and that "no one person or religion can meet world challenges alone." Therefore, "we must work together for humanity," even though "finding common ground is not easy." Continuing, he pointed out, "We too often seek advantage over others" and "bringing together people of goodwill can be difficult." Yet, he asked, "How do we work through these conflicts?" He insisted, we "remain firm in our principles without demonizing others on the other size" or making "caricatures" of them.

When he ventured into the abortion debate, he spoke of a doctor who wrote him insisting he use, "fair minded words" to find the "possibility of common ground." Rightly pointing out, "Abortion is a heart-wrenching decision for a woman." Therefore, he offered alternatives of reducing abortion, and the need to help that mother carry her child to full term. He suggested that adoption be made easier; that there be "support for women who give birth and honor the conscience of those who disagree with our views."

Recognizing that everyone is entitled to passion and conviction in their beliefs, President Obama insisted opposing views on abortion may be "irreconcilable" but we ought not to mock people to "caricature." He praised Notre Dame as a "lighthouse" that stands at the "crossroads" of religion, culture and love. Then he praised the graduates for the "maturity and commendable responsibility" they demonstrated in their approach to the issue of abortion and the controversy surrounding his coming to the university. Showing his respect for Catholic beliefs, he confessed how Cardinal Bernadine of Chicago and the Catholic Church helped him learn cooperation and understanding, and the importance of "finding common ground." He quoted Cardinal Bernadine who taught "you can't get on teaching the gospel until you touch hearts and minds." Then he told the graduates "you will be drawn to public service or to be an active citizen. You will be called to restore a free market that is also fair. You must stand as a light-house. Remember, you can also be a cross-road." He insisted the graduates "have confidence in the values with which you've been raised;" and that they "hold firm to your faith and allow it to guide you on your journey."

President Obama called on everyone in attendance to live by the "Golden Rule," to "Love One Another as you have others love you." He then issued a "call to love; call to serve. Call to share this law of love on your brief sojourn here on this

BARACK OBAMA
MASTER OF WASHINGTON, DC

planet." Praising Father Hessberg who President Eisenhower appointed to the Civil Rights Commission in 1957 to work on behalf of humanity and who also walked with Dr. Martin Luther King, Barack Obama believed those in attendance should "make the tradition of love a part of life." He reminded them "community service breaks down walls, fosters cooperation." Ending his speech, he reminded all, "life is never easy" and that "somehow we are all fishermen," expressing the view of Jesus when he admonished St. Peter to propagate the faith and be the rock on which the Church was built.

Father Jenkins, who described the President as someone who never stops talking with anyone who disagrees with him, also informed Mr. Obama, "you bring honor to this University by being our commencement speaker. You also felt honored at the crossroad and lighthouse. We thank you."

To be part of that tremendous experience, to bear witness to such history is an extraordinary motivator for that young black graduate and many students across the nation who can gain inspiration from the symbolism that President Obama represents.

Barack Obama's Washington, DC Photo 336.

FREDERICK MONDERSON

Barack Obama's Washington, DC Photo 337.

Barack Obama's Washington, DC Photo 338.

BARACK OBAMA
MASTER OF WASHINGTON, DC

"So long as our relationship is defined by our differences, we will empower those who sow hatred rather than peace, those who promote conflict rather than the cooperation that can help all of our people achieve justice and prosperity. This cycle of suspicion and discord must end." BARACK OBAMA, speech, Jun. 4, 2009

45.   OBAMA VERSUS THE MAN OF STEELE!
By
Dr. Fred Monderson

To create a good example of the concept being developed in this piece, I must take "Oldsters" to earlier showings of the classic movie, "In the Heat of the Night" starring Sidney Poitier. It was again shown within the last week. As the star actor pursued his killer suspect and "making waves" in Sparta, Mississippi; he was followed, chased and cornered by a band of racists bent on "teaching him a lesson." In the "nick of time" Lieutenant Virgil Tibbs was rescued by Chief Gillespie. The villains told the Chief, "Get rid of the Nigger or we will!" The TV station did not "bleep" the word "Nigger" after untold numbers of showings to "this age of political correctness." Again, when Endicott, the rich planter, slapped Officer Tibbs and Tibbs slapped him back, the black butler standing there was alarmed. Later, this "horrifying incident" was recounted when the butler met with all the hired help, much to their amusement and surprise that a fellow black could slap boss man Mr. Endicott and Chief Gillespie "did not shoot him in self defense." This part of the "Negroes gleefully enjoying the moment" was deleted from being shown as in the past for a number of years and is still missing today.

An even more interesting scene in the movie is when in a meeting between the Mayor, Chief Gillespie and the deceased businessman's grieving widow; who, emphatically insisted the "Negro officer remain on the case" to find her husband's murderer. After, in their discussion, the businessman Mayor said to Chief "Gillespie, Let the Negro officer remain on the case. If he catches the killer, we get the credit. If he fails, the widow requested him. It's a win-win situation for us, all around." Movies sometimes carry a powerful message!

FREDERICK MONDERSON

This brings us to Michael Steele, the new Chairman of the Republican Party, who only yesterday attached President Obama with a vehemence inclandestine, as he inaugurated a "comeback" program to redeem and revamp the Republican Party that has found great disfavor with the American people over the last two national elections, losing their majority in Congress and the White House to the Democratic Party headed by President Barack Obama. Of course, the 2010 election reversed much.

Many watchers believe Chairman Steele was only elected to head the Republican Party ten days after President Obama's inauguration. Analysts voiced the opinion, realizing their lost cause and the popularity of the first African American President, by electing Steele, he would split Obama's support among all voters and even more important, he would be a "great attack dog!" It would be a win-win situation all around, if he could succeed. However, the tremendously analytic and savvy Obama foresaw this approach and has stayed ahead of the "Republican pack" led by Michael Steele. This is an interesting deduction and needs more clarity.

The two individuals, President Barack Obama and Mr. Michael Steele, as leaders of the Democratic and Republican Parties, not only play important roles in fundraising for national, state and local branches of their respective party but set the tone and also help to get out the vote and campaigns for various candidates running for office. Just as important, however, is the leader's role in recruiting and training new and young members of the party and in helping to cultivate leadership qualities among them. That leadership is recruited and cultivated, whether Democratic or Republican, based on each party's core principles the individual then subscribes to. In fact, David Avella, executive director of GOPAC, formerly chaired by Steele is quoted as saying: "We have to, as a party, do a good job of training our candidates on how to connect with voters, how to make sure their message is getting to voters across their districts or across their states. We've got to do a good job of training them how to run winning campaigns, how to do the fundamentals, how to raise the money, how to put together door to door campaigns. We don't have to just do that with Black Republicans. We have to do that with all Republicans." Mr. Steele particularly thinks he must "engage the Black community" and cannot cede this group to the Democrats without a fight. He says, "I think that we failed when we stopped engaging, when we took an attitude that, 'Well they won't vote for us so why bother?' I think Black people have been largely dissed by both parties. Not just over the last eight years, but over the last 40 years." To remedy this, we must, "Talk to them, talk to them, engage them, be challenged by them, have them express their frustration and anger directly to us; have us to express why our solutions affect the Black community: Poverty, poor education, joblessness, incarceration, drug addiction, HIV AIDS Infection."

BARACK OBAMA
MASTER OF WASHINGTON, DC

Barack Obama's Washington, DC Photo 339.

Barack Obama's Washington, DC Photo 340.

FREDERICK MONDERSON

Barack Obama's Washington, DC Photo 341.

However, while Chairman Steele seeks to "engage" he is facing attacks from Democrats, understandable, but also from members within his own party, and has to contend with the likes of Rush Limbaugh, the talk-show host, former speaker Newt Gingrich and Vice-President Dick Chaney who are becoming more visible in the news. Even more important is the emergence of a resolution aimed at limiting Steele's control over party spending. According to Sean Yoes of NNPA, "The resolution would also install a comptroller or chief financial officer at the RNC who would report to the executive committee and not Steele. 'The Chairman shall appoint, with the advice and consent of the Executive Committee, a Comptroller or Chief Financial Officer who shall report to the Executive Committee.'" This reading does indicate, whether Mr. Steele knows it or not, his election as Chairman is not without restrictions. As they say, "Everybody is on a leash." Remember those days when you walked the dog on a three foot leash! Now, the leashes are 15 feet so the dog could be around the corner, but still tied to you. Again, everybody is on a leash!

Then there is also the occasional case in which an individual may switch party as in the recent case of Republican Arlen Specter Senator of Pennsylvania who switched to the Democrats, having switched from Democrat to Republican decades ago.

A little background information on the parties may be helpful. What we do know about President Obama's Democratic Party is stated, according to Jack C. Plano and Milton Greenberg in *The American Political Dictionary* (New York: Holt, Rinehart and Winston, Inc., (1962) 1989: 65-666) and that it is: "A major

BARACK OBAMA
MASTER OF WASHINGTON, DC

American party that evolved from the Democratic-Republican group supporting Thomas Jefferson. Andrew Jackson, regarded by democrats as co-founder with Jefferson, changed the name to Democratic Party in keeping with his ultra-democratic philosophy. Further development of party principles occurred under the more recent leadership of Woodrow Wilson and Franklin D. Roosevelt. Since 1932, the Democratic Party has dominated the American political scene, holding the presidency for all but the eight Eisenhower years (1953-1961), the eight Nixon-Ford years (1969-1977), and the Reagan years (1981-1989); it also has held a majority in Congress except for the four years 1947-1949 and 1953-1955, and in the Senate for the period from 1981-1987." Of course the Democrats held the Presidency in the Carter Years (1977-1981) and the Clinton Years (1993-2001).

As to its philosophy, Plano and Greenberg (1989: 66) continued, regarding the significance of the Democratic Party as a political entity: "Many studies show strong Democratic party preference by low-income groups, organized labor, young people, and religious and racial minority groups. In recent years, the Democratic Party has generally stood for freer trade, more extensive international commitments, a reduction in governmental regulation of the economy, and expanded civil rights guarantees. On the issue of states' rights, the party has reversed its early position and, in modern times, has consistently favored expanded national responsibilities. Its policies have generally been more liberal than Republican Party policies, although both parties include a coalition of liberals, moderates, and conservatives. Polls indicate that there are considerably more Democrats than Republicans registered to vote in the United States. Ideologically based groups that function in Congress within the Democratic Party include the liberal Democratic Study Group and the conservative Democratic Forum, often called the Boll Weevils."

On the other hand, the Republican Party, according to Plano and Greenberg (1989: 94) is: "A major American party, often called the GOP or Grand Old Party, that emerged in the 1850s as an antislavery party. The Republican Party is the successor to two earlier parties – the Federalist and the Whig. It became firmly established in American politics when its candidate, Abraham Lincoln, won the presidency in 1860 and successfully prosecuted the Civil War. The period from 1860 to 1932 was characterized largely by Republican dominance of the American political scene, but in the years since 1932 the Democrats have dominated the presidency except for the election of Dwight D. Eisenhower, Richard M. Nixon, and Ronald Reagan." Of course, we can add George Bush Number 41 (1988-1992) and George Bush Number 43 (2000-2008).

Regarding the significance of the Republican Party, Plano and Greenberg (1989: 94-95) continued: "Studies have shown that Republican support among voters tends to increase as their income, property-owning and educational levels rise.

FREDERICK MONDERSON

Traditionally, manufacturing, business, financial, and farming interests have been influential in the party except in the Deep South. The Republican Party has historically advocated individual initiative, free enterprise, fiscal responsibility, and sound-money policies. Its policies have generally been more conservative than Democratic Party policies, although both include a coalition of conservatives, moderates, and liberals. Ideologically based groups that function in Congress within the Republican Party include the relatively conservative Wednesday Group, and the relatively liberal Gypsy Moths. Historically, Republicans have favored a high protective tariff and isolationism, although in recent years the party has supported lower tariffs and various American international commitments. It has generally opposed the ideas of the welfare state and big government although it has given support to social welfare programs in recent years. Republicans generally have favored military interventions to cope with the threat of communism in the Third World, as, for example, in the 1983 invasion of the island of Grenada."

Barack Obama's Washington, DC Photo 342.

BARACK OBAMA
MASTER OF WASHINGTON, DC

Barack Obama's Washington, DC Photo 343.

Barack Obama's Washington, DC Photo 343a.

FREDERICK MONDERSON

Therefore, with Steele's election, the Republicans realized they had to make a significant turn-around otherwise the party would dwindle to practically nothing. After all, they have lost a significant number of their numbers, even the "Reagan Democrats" to the Democrats and also those voters now identifying with Independents. The new chairman insisted he would expand the party, compete among every group in the country and to quote him: "There is not one inch of ground that we're going to cede to anybody. This is the dawn of a new party moving in a new direction with strength and conviction." Lest we forget, that "new direction" did not come about until the "Sixth round of Republican balloting." He is further quoted as saying, "I've got to be the leader that will call the party to its great sense of self and its greater responsibility to all communities."

All this notwithstanding, as he contends with a very popular president, Mr. Steele should realize he has limitations, because he does not have all the keys to all the doors. Yet and importantly, he realizes the President is no "easy mark!" Still, Steele recently addressed state party chairmen, saying of Mr. Obama, "He's young. He's cool. He's hip ... he's got all the qualities America likes in a celebrity, so of course he's going to be popular" [but] "this is not American Idol. This is serious ... and we are going to take them on."

Steele said the GOP has owned up to the mistakes that caused its fall from power and is embarking on a renaissance. In the new salvo, Mr. Steele says to Mr. Obama, "The honeymoon is over. We are going to challenge those policies we think are wrong, and we are going to do so without apology and without a second thought." As if Mr. Obama is not listening and planning and going ahead with his agenda that the American people seem pleased with. Yet Mr. Steele continued even further, "We have turned the corner on regret, recrimination, self-pity and self-doubt. The era of apologizing for Republican mistakes of the past is now officially over. We have turned the corner. No more looking in the rearview mirror. From this point forward, we will focus all of our energies on winning the future."

At a recent Republican luncheon, Mr. Steele is quoted as saying "Mr. Obama's policies would lead to the most massive expansion of the old industrial age model of government that our country has ever seen. This popular politician is spending America into debt of such mammoth proportions that none of us can ever begin to calculate it or really understand it. The numbers are so big that they seem impossible." What he fails to acknowledge is that Reagan and Bush spending is largely responsible for the economic and social chasm that Obama inherited and only thinking big and big numbers can rectify this problem.

BARACK OBAMA
MASTER OF WASHINGTON, DC

Barack Obama's Washington, DC Photo 344.

Barack Obama's Washington, DC Photo 345.

Nonetheless, as Chairman Steele attacks, Obama continues to parry and carry forth his plans that seem to be working; and in his rescuing of the nation, the American people seems pleased as his numbers are still very high. This is because they believe in the sincerity, seriousness and integrity he brings to the job as President of the United States as he seeks results moving the nation forward, in the interest of all the people.

FREDERICK MONDERSON

"I reject the view that says our problems will simply take care of themselves; that says government has no role in laying the foundation for our common prosperity. For history tells a different story. History reminds us that at every moment of economic upheaval and transformation, this nation has responded with bold action and big ideas. In the midst of civil war, we laid railroad tracks from one coast to another that spurred commerce and industry. From the turmoil of the Industrial Revolution came a system of public high schools that prepared our citizens for a new age. In the wake of war and depression, the GI Bill sent a generation to college and created the largest middle-class in history. And a twilight struggle for freedom led to a nation of highways, an American on the moon, and an explosion of technology that still shapes our world. In each case, government didn't supplant private enterprise; it catalyzed private enterprise. It created the conditions for thousands of entrepreneurs and new businesses to adapt and to thrive." BARACK OBAMA, Address to Joint Session of Congress, Feb. 24, 2009

46. OBAMA'S MANY HATS AS PRESIDENT

By

Dr. Fred Monderson

From our earliest days we began wearing "hats," not the traditional hat or cap, but a particular responsibility where sometimes people are depending on us. The child is a student, son or daughter, brother or sister, grandchild, member of a choir, sport team, or marching band. The parent is a bread-winner, the first teacher, and homework helper, member of a group, church or some other type of leader. These functions and responsibilities are important and carry a lot of weight, sometimes. However, none carry a greater responsibility than that of the President of the United States. Sure, he has the unofficial responsibility of being parent, husband, group member, and so on; but he has the official responsibility of representing a whole nation domestically and internationally and the attendant dynamics that grow exponentially.

Article II, Section 2.1, 2.2, 2.3 of the Constitution spells out the powers and responsibilities of the President, but, as the nation has grown tremendously since its inception, so has his responsibilities. Thus, the many "hats" the President now wears are as **Head of State, Chief Executive, Chief Administrator, Chief Diplomat, Commander-In-Chief,** and **Chief Citizen.** However, while most are spelled out under Article II, Section 2, that of **Chief of Party** was not among the original responsibilities because

BARACK OBAMA
MASTER OF WASHINGTON, DC

when the Constitution was promulgated, as there were no political parties only concerned Americans who wanted to establish a free and strong government but also to provide safeguards against the President having too much power.

As **Chief** or **Head of State**, the President acts and speaks for the American nation and plays a number of roles in this respect. No matter what the peril faced by the nation; at the time, the President as the personification of the American people, must accept and entertain visiting heads of state and other dignitaries at the White House. The story is told that during the Cuban Missile Crisis, President Kennedy felt it necessary to hold a state dinner for the visiting Crown Prince of Libya. One could well imagine President Bush continuing this tradition after September 11, 2001.

The President is "Poster Boy" for any number of charitable and public service efforts. In fact, Robert C. Bone in *American Government* (New York: Barnes and Noble, 1970: 80) states: "As Chief of State the President must take time to give a boost to national highway safety campaign by receiving at the White House the safe truck driver of the year. He may be expected to pose with the child chosen for this year's March of Dimes Poster. Dedicating a new center for the performing arts or pressing a button to light the official Christmas tree, complete with holiday message, is another example of the President's role as Chief of State." Let's not forget his pardoning of a turkey as symbol of Thanksgiving. It's likely, if there's some national tragedy, whether flood, hurricane, tornado, bridge collapse, etc., the President may show up in solidarity with the victims. With nearly 200 independent nations in the world today, and that the United States maintains diplomatic relations with most, he must receive their ambassadors.

As **Chief Executive**, Article II, Section 2, Sub-section 2 and 3 grants the President power "to take care that the laws be faithfully executed." This means, once he has appointed public officials he can remove them for incompetence and violation of the public trust, that is, any of the millions employed by the federal government. This may very well be spelled out in conflict of interest regulations and thus he is responsible for the conduct of government officials.

FREDERICK MONDERSON

Barack Obama's Washington, DC Photo 346.

As **Commander-In-Chief**, President Obama oversees an enormous military machine, a far cry from just the Army and Navy in George Washington's day. Now, in addition to these two we have the Air Force, Marines, Coast Guard and he can call upon the National Guard militia of the various states. Importantly, President Truman in post-World War II days clearly pointed out: "If there is one unmistaken fact, its civilian control of the military in this country."

Oftentimes the nation finds itself embroiled in legitimate and illegitimate and justifiable and unjustifiable and popular and unpopular wars. World War II and the Korean Conflict were justifiable or popular wars. Viet Nam was unpopular. In many respects, Afghanistan was legitimate but Iraq II, when the facts became known, was not popular. As Senator from Illinois, now President, Barack Obama, opposed Iraq II, but he inherited it and after consulting with his top brass and field commanders, has announced an exit strategy, but he must still deal with the intricacies of having American combat troops in that country. Unmistakably, the view from outside is always different from the view from inside.

BARACK OBAMA
MASTER OF WASHINGTON, DC

Barack Obama's Washington, DC Photo 347.

Barack Obama's Washington, DC Photo 348.

FREDERICK MONDERSON

Barack Obama's Washington, DC Photo 349.

However, after the Viet Nam war debacle, in 1973 Congress passed the War Powers Act greatly curtailing the Presidents' powers to deploy military forces abroad. Bone (1970: 81) has explained: "The War Powers Act provides that within 48 hours of committing U.S. armed forces to foreign combat, the President must give Congress a full explanation in writing. If Congress does not declare war, the armed forces must be withdrawn within 60 days unless the President certifies that another 30 days are needed for safe withdrawal. After this period Congress can order an immediate withdrawal of American forces by passing a concurrent resolution, which is not subject to Presidential veto."

As the nation's **Chief Diplomat**, the President is solely responsible for foreign relations. As early as 1799, Chief Justice John Marshall declared the President the "Sole organ of the nation in its external relations and its sole representative with foreign nations." In 1936, during the "New Deal" tenure of Franklin D. Roosevelt, in *United States v. Curtiss Wright Export Corporation*, the Court in a 7-1 decision ruled, "The very delicate plenary and exclusive power of the President as the sole organ of the government in the field of international relations." Equally, the Secretary of State, Hillary Clinton, acting on President Obama's behalf, puts the credibility of the United States at stake in her dealings with other nations.

While the Constitution, Article I, Section I clearly states: "All legislative powers herein granted shall be vested in a Congress of the United states, which shall consist of a Senate and House of Representatives;" yet, as the leader of the nation, the President is the **Chief Legislator**. It's been said, nearly 90 percent of Congress' power to legislate is contained in Article I, Section 8, Subsection 1-17, while Subsection 18 contains the "necessary and proper clause." Also called the "elastic clause," it gives Congress more wiggle room to legislate for anything not

BARACK OBAMA
MASTER OF WASHINGTON, DC

covered in Subsection 1-17. Nevertheless, the President is the Chief Legislator, and as such the "buck stops" with him, for after all, he has to approve or disapprove any bill, approved by both houses of Congress, that reaches his desk! President Eisenhower has been quoted as saying "After all, the Constitution puts the President square into the legislative business." Therefore, as a significant player the President has to push his agenda by which he will be judged, check Congress and also try to reach a consensus with them.

One of the constitutionally mandated responsibilities of the President is that he gives the *State of the Union Address* to both houses of Congress. Other than the January following the November presidential election, this is given around January 20. Here he outlines a Comprehensive Plan he thinks Congress will follow. Once given, his Presidential Assistants who liaison with the Congress push this agenda to get it through the legislative body. When he is making nice with Congress, Bone (1970: 83) tells, he uses: "Personal phone calls to legislator's home states, appointment of a legislator's supporter to high office, and other inducements (or threats to withhold them). All these options play a part in the President's influence on Congress."

Even more important, the President has the **Power of the Veto**! Here he tells Congress "I don't want this bill, take it back and rework it!" In rare occasions both houses can muster 2/3 support for the bill in its original form and override his Veto. He can also use the **Pocket Veto**. Generally most bills are submitted just before Congress adjourns. Once they adjourn and he does not sign it within ten days, the bill is dead. **Moral Disapproval** means he lets the bill become law after 10 days without signing it. Then he can threaten to impound funds for a legislator's state. He can also call Congress back into session once it has adjourned; these legislators don't like to return.

From the time he accepts the nomination at the convention to be their candidate, whether he wins or not, he becomes **Head of his Party**. Oftentimes in elections for Congress or Governor, the "popular president" makes appearances for members of his party. In national elections, the **Coattail effect**, that is, people who win their contest being on the President's line, is a factor in support of the President's plans.

The President is the **Voice of the People**; he has to preserve the peace; and he has to manage the nation's prosperity, paying attention to rates of unemployment. Even more, the President, this particular President is involved in social activities and functions. He hosted a Seder that is a Jewish dinner around Passover, at the White House, for members of his team. He also invited gay parents and their kids to attend the White House Easter Egg Roll and he was

FREDERICK MONDERSON

actively rolling! He gives a weekly Saturday Radio Program outlining his plans and brings the nation up to speed on what to expect of his policies. The President is also *Chief Fundraiser* for his party, making stops or stumps across the country to raise funds for individuals running for national or local office.

Barack Obama was the first president to begin "blogging" on the White House Web site. He chose a nearby church for spiritual meditation and support and attends services regularly. The family got a dog named Bo, which is a tradition that has generated much media interest. With two young daughters and their young friends, he installed a swing set at the White House and often enjoys the cultural rounds such as seeing the Alvin Ailey Dance Troupe perform at the Kennedy Center. Sometimes he visits wounded veterans or even a children's hospital. At a Primary or Kindergarten school he reads to the class and takes questions from the little ones.

Oftentimes the winning, baseball, football or basketball, or even hockey, team is invited to the White House. The President is an avid basketball player and fan, and would invite his friends for a game regularly. He recently invited players of the Chicago Bulls and White Sox to the White House. He proved astute enough to pick University of North Carolina to win the NCAA basketball championship. Then he invited them to the White House. Many of these social activities not only continue a tradition but also show the social and human side of the man described as the most powerful in the world. Only this time he is African American!

Barack Obama's Washington, DC Photo 350.

BARACK OBAMA
MASTER OF WASHINGTON, DC

Finally, *World Book*, Volume 15, article "President of the United States," in a section entitled "A day in the life of the president" had this to say: "The president might begin a typical day by reading a few newspapers. A breakfast conference might follow with such top aides as the press secretary and the White House Chief of Staff. In the Oval Office, the president signs documents and reads letters, reports, and proposed legislation. Later in the morning, the president might discuss plans with congressional leaders or meet with the Vice-President. In the afternoon, the president might see people from various organizations. The president also might take part in a bill-signing ceremony, officially signing into law an act passed by Congress."

"In the evening, the president might sometimes attend a social function. The White House might host a formal dinner for a foreign official. While dining, the leaders might discuss trade problems, environmental protection, or other issues. The president might spend the late evening reading, perhaps a speech scheduled for the next day or a report on a foreign aid program."

Naturally his wife, Michelle, as First Lady, is a powerful asset, for she has an agenda that also keeps her busy. Highly intelligent, beautiful, tremendously fashion conscious, they make a wonderful working and social couple, and her support seems invaluable. At the Inaugural Balls they danced the night away. This past weekend they were in New York City, as the news reported, on a date, having dinner and taking in a play. Some weeks ago, the President and Vice President Biden dined at a hamburger joint as regular patrons would do and many were surprised to see these two powerful men, standing in line waiting their turn and even tipping the servers. The President and wife Michelle were known to slip out from the White House unannounced and without much fanfare to dine in the DC area.

Therefore, the many hats the President wears indicate how much of a challenge his job really is. All this notwithstanding, the position he holds is very influential, powerful and challenging, but somebody has to do it; and this time Barack Obama is the man!

FREDERICK MONDERSON

"I believe it is not in our character, the American character, to follow. It's our character to lead. And it is time for us to lead once again. So I'm here today to set this goal: We will devote more than 3 percent of our GDP to research and development. We will not just meet, but we will exceed the level achieved at the height of the space race, through policies that invest in basic and applied research, create new incentives for private innovation, promote breakthroughs in energy and medicine, and improve education in math and science. This represents the largest commitment to scientific research and innovation in American history. Just think what this will allow us to accomplish: solar cells as cheap as paint; green buildings that produce all the energy they consume; learning software as effective as a personal tutor; prosthetics so advanced that you could play the piano again; an expansion of the frontiers of human knowledge about ourselves and world the around us. We can do this." BARACK OBAMA, speech, Apr. 27, 2009

47. THE EXCITEMENT OF BARACK OBAMA
By
Dr. Fred Monderson

Barack Obama has generated an excitement perhaps unheard of in the political history of this nation and in turn he has become a media phenomenon, some say rivaling a rock star's turn out to see or hear his history making pronouncements and the ideas he plans to implement. From his ascendency on the national political scene at the Democratic Convention in 2004, Mr. Obama has remained a media darling as they followed him on his journeys at home and abroad and the excitement has never abated. For example, the *New York Times* Week in Review of Sunday, June 7, 2009, p. 1, depicts a spread of 12 photographs of a Simulcast showing people gathered in Cairo, Bahrain, Beirut, Calcutta, Baghdad, East Jerusalem, Damascus, Gaza, Los Angeles, Casablanca, Riyadh and Dakar to listen to Mr. Obama's deliver a speech in Cairo, Egypt, as he addressed Muslims regarding "the way forward" in their relationship with America. Naturally there were others listening elsewhere and like all his addresses, whether in town hall meetings, in board rooms, governmental bodies or even in outdoor arenas, the excitement was ear-shattering and this became standard expectation from Barack Obama, the icon!

Going back, clearly Mr. Obama injected an excitement into the primary and presidential elections, unprecedented in the 20th and 21st centuries in his demonstrated appeal to young and old, black and brown, white, yellow, red and gay and straight, protestant and catholic, Muslims, agnostics, atheists and legal and

BARACK OBAMA
MASTER OF WASHINGTON, DC

illegal immigrants. Even more, that interest and excitement generated by the man, his message, style, persona, consensus building ability, ability to listen and learn, and then for him to stand and deliver, have been remarkable experiences. Not since Billy Graham, who would take a single verse from the Bible and off he went, did anyone match Obama in verbal eloquence, motivating influences as well as focus on message and this did not end at the border of the United States. Interesting, everywhere he traveled abroad, as a Senator or as President, with or without his wife Michelle, the crowds turned out in tumultuous numbers, to show their love for him, savor his every word, hang on to his message and in the excitement, all this proved a challenge for his security detail determined to provide the best protection for their charge.

Barack Obama's Washington, DC Photo 351.

Whether it was a campaign stop in which Barack Obama attracted nearly 100,000 onlookers, as a US Senator in his first trip to Europe, Germany where quarter of a million Germans gathered to see the man with the motivating persona; and the tremendous turnout on November 4, 2008 when he was declared the winner of the Presidential Election and later that night people gathered and awaited for hours for his acceptance speech, the tumultuous gathering on the Great Lawn to witness his Inauguration; his trip as President to Canada, Mexico, Britain, France, Germany, Turkey, then Iraq, his return home; then on to Trinidad for the Summit of the Americas and finally his trip to Egypt to address global Muslims, etc., President Obama has generated an excitement that is unimaginable for one newsmaker.

FREDERICK MONDERSON

People seem turned on to the charisma, intellect, vision, honesty, and sincerity the President demonstrates as he tackles every issue, communicates his plans and intents and seems to reassure his audience, wherever. The sum total of these traits is what has endeared Barack Obama to the largest audience an American President has been able to muster in attempting to convey his message. This cool and courageous attitude is what sets him apart from most politicians and wins sympathy and the confidence of people everywhere. He demonstrates strength, thoughtfulness, decisive decision making and possesses a unique ability to convince people to agree with him.

President Barack Obama is not the ordinary politician because he tells the truth and this is what causes people to respect him and his enemies to fear or hate him. He easily disarms his opponents. Because he is a hard worker and his ideas, given time, seems to work or show promise, people are thus confident in his surroundings and his results and they trust him. Therefore, the man Barack Obama is a rare breed and his talents, temperament and thoughtfulness are just what this nation needed to help rescue it from the economic quagmire and international shamefacedness it became mired in over the last decades. Barack Obama is indeed a man of vision, tenacity and perspicacity who generates a great deal of excitement in every walk of his life. Consider the potentialities if we were able to clone him! Perhaps his devotion to family is the fuel that ignites his passion and fuels the excitement we have come to associate with the superman we call President Barack Hussein Obama!

Barack Obama's Washington, DC Photo 352.

BARACK OBAMA
MASTER OF WASHINGTON, DC

"I think the big challenge that we've got on education is making sure that from kindergarten or prekindergarten through your 14th or 15th year of school, or 16th year of school, or 20th year of school, that you are actually learning the kinds of skills that make you competitive and productive in a modern, technological economy." BARACK OBAMA, New York Times, Apr. 28, 2

48. So Obamasque
By

Dr. Fred Monderson

Shakespeare wrote "uneasy lies the head that wears the crown" and Robert Di Nero in the movie *Men of Honor* also starring Cuba Gooding, during Chief Beshir's trial for re-instatement after losing his leg, forcefully affirmed "I don't know why anyone would want this job" as a Navy Diver. At this critical time, with the financial strains of two wars in Iraq and Afghanistan; the challenges of international terrorism; a global financial system still reeling from the most significant economic downturn; domestic problems as Guantanamo, joblessness, Wall Street and banking mismanagement, local terrorism, the housing and health industries' painful realities, Republican injection and pursuing more partisanship in governing, both sentiments now apply to President Barack Obama towards the end of his first year in office. Naturally, the job as President of the United States of America with its many "hats," as well as being leader of the "Western Alliance," is a tough and challenging one, to say the least. However, his approach to the responsibilities has exemplified a unique flair in tackling these problems and simultaneously focusing on changing the face of America abroad, which can all be described as "Obamasque," characterized by deep contemplation then swift action. In a panel on Fareed Zakaria's *Global Public Square*, the commentator Peggy Noonan at least praised Mr. Obama by saying she was glad to see a "thinking American President." The friendly approach the President has utilized, caused Kishore Mahbubani, Dean Lee Juan Yew *School of Public Policy* at the National Singapore University to comment that, "Reflexive anti-Americanism around the world has subsided." Importantly, despite challenges from enemies abroad, Mr. Obama has gained the respect of high and low abroad because of the new direction he is taking the country.

FREDERICK MONDERSON

Barack Obama's Washington, DC Photo 353.

Early in the Presidential campaign when odds makers considered him a long shot, opponents emphasized his inexperience in a number of fields as foreign affairs, in three significant arenas, viz., Europe, the Middle East and Asia; and in global terrorism; the environment; threat of nuclear proliferation; the depth of the nation's economic plight and the global economic downturn; and the seriousness of the Wall Street malaise, the housing mess, lack of bank credit, joblessness, the rising health care concerns, his responsibilities to the military, and the list goes on.

On the one hand, as a freshman U.S. Senator whose fortunes were as a result of a meteoric rise to national prominence, on the other, as a highly intelligent, bright and thoughtful individual, he unquestionably brought tremendous talent to the job description as President. One of these strengths was the deep contemplation of a thoughtful and schooled mind. After all, contrary to John F. Kennedy's confession "I did not learn anything at Harvard," Barack Obama scaled the heights of that institution's legal domains coming, as he did, from Columbia University. The invaluable experience gained from his groundings as a community organizer in the trenches of Chicago's social inequities and with an unquenchable desire to succeed certainly fueled his ambitions to launch, sustain and win the campaign to be President of the United States. All along, obstacles of claims of inexperience; challenges of fund-raising; mass organizing; coupled with claims of being unpatriotic; socialist; being a Muslim; not a citizen; not to mention the audacity of a black man aspiring to the "secrets of the Presidency;" in these many trials Mr. Obama stood tall. It does says something of Mr. Obama that he met these many dragons' challenges and successfully slew them all to assume the mantle of leadership at this most troubling time of America's existence. Though there is division between church and state in American *de jure* and *de facto* thinking, only time will tell whether his "coming" was divinely inspired.

BARACK OBAMA
MASTER OF WASHINGTON, DC

Barack Obama's Washington, DC Photo 354.

Possessing a work ethic of unbelievable proportions, aided by the best legal, economic, military, foreign and domestic policy minds money can't buy, Barack Obama turned back the avalanche of America's descent into the abyss of failed economic statehood. As Walter Isaacson of the Aspen Institute has commented, "Saving the financial system was huge" and Obama gets the credit as this was accomplished despite unrelenting Republican rank and file obstructionism, while their allies simultaneously flanked him and falsely raised the banner of a questionable patriotism. The question should actually be who is the real patriot? In addition, Mr. Obama's financial brain thrust of infusing significant sums of cash in bank bailout, the auto industry hands on approach, as well as issuing Wall Street support was significant. His outreach to Asian nations as China, India, Indonesia and Japan is a result of his perhaps realization, according to Mahbubani, "The economic crisis has wreaked psychological damage on the world through deregulation, privatizing of financial resources and institutions." As a result of this, people in the know realize the "economic crisis has accelerated the shift of power to Asia." This is what Mr. Obama has realized and in his long view, he is trying to make sure "the US does not get it wrong with China for this will be very dangerous for the world." If he gets it right he may stave off the West's descent from economic prominence. This is what the Republicans could not see, still cannot see and perhaps will not be able to see since they did not see it looming on the horizon during their tenure.

FREDERICK MONDERSON

Barack Obama's Washington, DC Photo 354a.

That is to say, all things being equal, the afore-mentioned state of affairs only attests to the gravity of the situation created after 8 years of Republican *status quo ante* at the help of the nation's calamity. This is not to discount threats internal and external, and the manner which responses were effective or ineffective. It is reasonable to expect people's answer to "How am I doing?" by showing decreasing numbers in joblessness, a phenomenon not easily rectified, despite claims war footing is good for the economy. Just as in the campaign when he would "Study" areas of concern highlighted by his critics and emerge "Schooled" on these issues, Mr. Obama faced the reality of governing, for as Nell Irvin Pointer had pointed out, "You campaign in poetry and govern in prose," to describe Mr. Obama's taking the long view in his visionary approach. Significantly in this respect, Robert Caro praised the President for the magnitude of what he is trying to do since his "scope of ambition is great."

As he contemplated his intentions on Afghanistan critics charged this was so Obamasque! However, often not an Obama supporter, Peggy Noonan still confessed "I'm glad to see Obama is taking his time on Afghanistan."

Now, after much deliberation and the soundest judgment, President Obama decided to deploy 30,000 more U.S. troops to Afghanistan with the expectation there would be another 5,000-7,000 coalition forces added in what is emerging as a critical war of necessity owing to Taliban and Al Qaeda coalescing to threaten not just Afghanistan but also Pakistan. Clearly even his critics have had to applaud his "hard line" on terrorism. I suppose these adversaries "made him do it!" Even more, perhaps showing the multi-dimensionality of the thinking, Obama, despite critics as Jim DeMint's contention "he is doing too much too soon" Walter

BARACK OBAMA
MASTER OF WASHINGTON, DC

Isaacson pointed out, "A recession is the right time to tackle health care issues." Robert Caro, additionally affirmed, Mr. Obama wants to transform America and compared him to President Lynden Baines Johnson who wanted to create "social change in the midst of war." However, Mr. Obama must be mindful of Mr. Johnson's one term status.

Historically speaking, let us not forget, A. Philip Randolph told of how on eve of World War II blacks were hurting economically because of discrimination and not being hired in the war industries. Together with prominent blacks invited to dinner at the White House, he told President Roosevelt in a moving Presentation of the need for effective Presidential leadership to address the plight of black labor. Mr. Roosevelt listened intently, moved around the room sharing out cigars, sat down, lit his and said, "Very well, now go and make me do it!"

Sure, President Obama is busy in matters of state "raising all boats" and sees no need to selectively address this important aspect of "black issues" because he is "President of all the people." Well read as he is, he may have read or heard Malcolm X say, "The nation is so evenly divided between Democrats and Republicans, thus the black vote can be the deciding factor on who goes or stays in the White House and who goes to the dog house." This pearl of wisdom is rather appropriate in this upcoming 2010 mid-term election as the Republican war machine is coming full throttle, having gained some traction despite more partisanship in debating all issues particularly as experienced in the health care and jobless issues. Walter Isaacson, however, blames President Obama for not reducing the "poison of partisanship."

Again, as Malcolm commented on the photograph of the Irish smiling at the signing of a Presidential address of an Irish issue. Correct me if I am wrong, but no blacks are appointed Ambassador to Ireland. For that matter, there is a disproportionate or lack of sufficient black representation in the nation's State Department in the significant areas of policy execution, despite both Condoleezza Rice and Colin Powell's tenure as head of that department. Party affiliation aside, this is not an unusual phenomenon. Consider, as Joint Chief Colin Powell was accused of not promoting sufficient or hardly any black generals; Parsons was also accused of not promoting blacks in management positions; and Manning Marable was equally accused of not helping create more black PHDs at Columbia University. Since perception can weigh more heavily on reality, the President must seriously address black concerns of his base.

Actually, in the matter of disproportionality, percentage wise, check this out:

1. More blacks serve in the military to defend this nation and there are not sufficient general officers in all branches of the service.

FREDERICK MONDERSON

2.   Black unemployment rate is generally double the single digit rate for whites and in some urban areas black youth unemployment rate has been quoted as ridiculously high as 50 percent.

3.   The leading cause of death from AIDS, diabetes, heart attack, stroke, hypertension, cancer, is higher among blacks.

4.   Black elementary and high school dropout rates are highest of all groups.

5.   Black incarceration rates and those in the prison pipeline through the courts are highest.

6.   Blacks are more frequently victims of redlining and shady lending practices resulting in home foreclosures and schemes depriving them of their property. When we add the Hispanic element to these factors the numbers are staggering. This is what President Obama should be apprised of by Mr. Axelrod and other policy advisers and he should never forget Malcolm's "doghouse dictum."

Now, what we should do is "make him do it!"

1.   Gentlemen, we need a spring offensive in early April and a 15-year old Million Man March anniversary on Washington, DC, as a call to action on eve of the November National Elections. This is why Carlos Russell and the other elders established Black Solidarity Day on eve of the election to call attention to black voting strength and the need to address their issues.

2.   Gays and Lesbians, Labor and Immigrants have "called the President to the Mat." Now it's time for blacks to do the same.

3.   The President is too busy guarding the portals. We must scale the mountains at his rear and attack him from his blindside. Remember in 1980 when Senator Kennedy challenged Jimmy Carter for the Presidency and accused him of "tip toeing in the Rose Garden." Therefore, every black religious, civic and social organization across the nation must invite First Lady Michelle Obama to speak. Get her out of the Rose Garden and show her the disproportionality of the numbers! So much so, when the President flops down in bed after a busy day at the office, the First Lady can remind him, "Honey, my people are SUFFERING! If you do not address this issue PRONTO, I'm not bringing lunch to the office tomorrow!

4.   The President must realize, just as blacks are not getting jobs, black small businesses are not getting loans. They are also hurting nationwide.

5.   The President doesn't want, on his return to the NAACP to be reminded of his reminding them of their role in advancing the cause of equality through

BARACK OBAMA
MASTER OF WASHINGTON, DC

addressing the plight of blacks. From their mantle, that organization may more forcefully be able to implement a "make him do it" strategy.

Perhaps then, that studied "Obamasque" *modus operandi* may be reminded the chain is as strong as its weakest link. So be careful of the black ripple effect from down under, since the Republicans are waiting in the wings, mobilizing!

Now is an appropriate time, Mr. President, for swift action to address the plight of blacks!

Barack Obama's Washington, DC Photo 354b.

FREDERICK MONDERSON

"Whatever we think of the past, we must not be prisoners to it." BARACK OBAMA, speech, Jun. 4, 2009

49. FROM DRED SCOTT TO BARACK OBAMA
By

Dr. Fred Monderson

It's been a mighty long road from the humiliation of the enslaved African-American Dred Scott in 1857 to the triumphs of Barack Obama in 2008, and while there were many people toiling in the horrendous vineyards of the American social landscape, many dreamt of but still could not conceive of the "glory of the coming of the Lord;" certainly not this early election of the African-American Barack Obama as President of the United States of America. Fate is a peculiar phenomenon and though some people try to "hold back the dawn" of social progress, the spirit of humanity is sufficiently powerful it generates winds that eradicate obstacles and shines a tremendous light that illuminates the path to that greater glory, all people and states aspire to. However, and nevertheless, as "father time" takes his time in rectifying social injustices in a nation state, much suffering is experienced in the social dynamic of human interaction; and while persons may look to social institutions as the Supreme Court, the interpreter of the law and keeper of the people's conscience, their hopes are sometimes dashed if such bodies shy away from impartiality in the face of inequality of treatment of its citizens. Therefore, this impartiality and inequality or equality of and before the Supreme Court has been at issue throughout its history and is even more so today with President Barack Obama selection and nomination of Justice Sonia Sotomayor to the high court.

To imagine the changing nature of the United States Supreme Court, the conscience of the people, from the historic Dred Scott decision on eve of the devastating Civil War with the institution of slavery at its core, to the election of Barack Obama as enlightened President of the United States, in a move whereby he could now appoint one or more members to that body, is an unimaginable journey that's almost fairy-tale like. For an African American man to have risen from the stigma of the bowels of the American social order to see another ascend the zenith of its power structure and have the nation await his influence on a historic institution as the Supreme Court; which a century and a half prior, had ruled into law a black man was not an American citizen, could not bring suit in an American court of law in any state, and had "no rights which a white man was

BARACK OBAMA
MASTER OF WASHINGTON, DC

bound to respect" is a fantastic journey that "could only happen in America," is also a popular refrain. In retrospect, this is what the "Birthers," Bachmann and Trump, et al., were trying to uphold. Poor Keyes, imagine the multi-faceted ways he was "played!"

Barack Obama's Washington, DC Photo 355.

In its decision process regarding the black man, whose changing status from slave to negro with a small "n" to now African-American, the Supreme Court has had to rule countless times on issues regarding the status, rights and privileges of this significant segment of the American demographic community. In this the Court has ruled on *Dred Scott v. Sandford* (1857); *Civil Rights Acts* (1875) (1883); *Plessey v. Ferguson* (1896); *Grandfather Clause* (1915); *Regarding Negro Education* (1899-1927); *Abolishing White Primaries* (1944); *Segregated Graduate Education* (1946-1949); *Outlawing Segregation in State Owned Public Facilities* (1954-1964); *School Desegregation Decision* (1954); Rules *Segregation of Public Buses Unconstitutional* (1955); Upholds the 1964 *Civil Rights Act*; and many more particularly concerning the Negro, Black, African American. In these many decisions, the Supreme Court ruled in the interest of "positive law," though several times it reversed its own decisions or invalidated a lower court's ruling, whether positive or negative.

FREDERICK MONDERSON

The earliest and perhaps most significant ruling regarding Blacks in this country is the Dred Scott Decision. Scholars differ on Chief Justice Roger Taney's famous ruling in the suit *Dred Scott V. Sandford* in 1857; that he Scott, by American law was a slave, residing in a slave state, had been taken by his master into free territory and returned to a slave state to his prior condition; *Ipso Facto*, having set foot on free soil, should be permitted his freedom, but the Supreme Court ruled against him.

Constance Baker Motley's "The Legal Status of the Negro in the United States" in the *American Negro Reference Book* (Inglewood Cliffs, New Jersey: Prentice Hall, Inc., (1966: 484-485) recounts the case of *Dred Scott v. Sandford*, 19, Howard 393, 15L. Ed. 691. Contending that two questions required resolution: "First, whether Scott was a citizen of Missouri, and second whether Scott had been forced by being taken into free territory. The latter question involved a determination whether Congress had the power under the Constitution to prohibit slavery in the territories, thus making Scott a free man in Minnesota. Chief Justice Taney's adverse conclusions on these questions were concurred in by the majority. He held Congress did not have power to prohibit slavery and consequently the Missouri Compromise was unconstitutional. He held Scott was still a slave because the highest court of the state of Missouri had held in Scott's case when it was before it that under the law of that state a master did not lose his property right in his slave by taking him to a free state like Illinois. Taney ruled the Supreme Court was bound by this decision of the highest court of a state involving a matter of state law."

In the above situation, two operative ideas are identified. The first is that Scott, a man, a Black man, was regarded as property as is a horse, pig, shoe, any such thing.

The second idea is that of States' Rights; which means that, for example, just as Chapter 7 of the United Nations Charter prohibits any nation from interfering in the internal affairs of another state, so States' Rights allows states to determine in the best interest of its citizens even when this conflicts with the Constitution which is the supreme law of the land.

In regards the second question, the Chief Justice made the following determination, Motley (1966: 485) instructs: "Can a negro [sic] whose ancestors were imported into this country, and sold as slaves, become a member of the political community formed and brought into existence by the Constitution of the United States, and as such become entitled to the rights, privileges, and immunities, guaranteed by that instrument to the citizens? One of which rights is the privilege of suing in a court of the United States in the cases specified in the Constitution .... The only matter in issue before the Court therefore, is, whether the descendants of such slaves, when they shall be emancipated, or who are born to

BARACK OBAMA
MASTER OF WASHINGTON, DC

parents who had become free before their birth, are citizens of a State, in the same sense in which the word 'citizen' is used in the Constitution of the United States."

Motley continued even further, "Taney ruled that Negroes were not citizens within the contemplation of the Constitution. He based this on what he claimed to be the Negro's legal status throughout the civilized world at the time of the adoption of the Constitution. This statue was a non-citizenship status and, he said, 'so far inferior, that they [the Negroes] had no rights which the white man was bound to respect" One dissenting jurist, in contradicting this ruling wrote: "At the time of the ratification of the Articles of Confederation [which preceded the Constitution], all free native born inhabitants of the States of New Hampshire, Massachusetts, New York, New Jersey, and North Carolina, though descended from African slaves, were not only citizens of these States, but such of them as had the other necessary qualification possessed the franchise of electors on equal terms with other citizens."

Barack Obama's Washington, DC Photo 356. The Washington Monument seems to be part of this building's roof.

Scholars differ on Chief Justice Roger Taney's famous ruling regarding Scott's contention that he should be free having set foot in a free state, and should be permitted his freedom. As a student of *American History and Government* I have dealt with this issue for some time. Reading *The Constitution: A Documentary History and Narrative History* (New York: Morrow, Quill, 1980: 440) by the

FREDERICK MONDERSON

respected Page Smith, the author discusses a situation following Roger Taney's death and Salmon P. Chase's appointment by Lincoln to succeed the controversial Justice. "John S. Rock of Massachusetts was admitted to practice before the Court. *The New York Tribune's* account of the event is as follows: 'The black man was admitted, jet black, with hair of an extra twist – let me have the pleasure of saying by purpose and premeditation of an aggravating 'kink' – unqualifiedly, obtrusively, defiantly, 'Nigger' – with not palliation of complexion, no let-down in lip, no compromise in nose, no abatement whatsoever in facial, cranial, osteological, particular from the despised standard of humanity brutally set up in our politics and in our Judiciary by the Dred Scott decision – this inky-lined African stood, in the monarchial power of American manhood and American Citizenship, within the bar of the Court which had solemnly pronounced that black men, have no right which white men were bound to respect.... By Jupiter, the sight was grand! 'T was dramatic too.' [The Court, incidentally, had never said "Black men have no rights which white men were bound to respect."]"

While I accorded "respectable" to Page Smith, so too Constance Baker Motley was a respectable writer and she quoted the Court's document as saying the correct pronouncement. After all, Taney used "negro" not Black! Even more, this is an interesting caveat for many black scholars have held this is exactly what the Chief Justice determined and in many respects has been *de jure* and *de facto* state of relations. Recently, on ABC TV-7's **This Week**, the respectable conservative commentator George Will, in commentary reiterated that the Court had ruled, "The black man had no rights which a white man is bound to respect" and his facts are generally accurate. Therefore, in view of Barack Obama's recent nomination to the Court, I have chosen to sketch the path of legal challenge and the issues that brought us to the point where a Black man, the President, does have the right to replace a white male Jurist and his choice is to be respected.

Motley (1966: 506) discusses Charles Sumner, a lawyer of Massachusetts, who challenged that state's exclusion of Black children from attending public schools and sought to remedy this in Congress. His bill which became part of the 1875 Civil Rights Act sought equal treatment "on common carriers, in inns, theaters, other places of public amusement and in cemeteries" for Blacks. "However, before its passage, schools and cemeteries were stricken from the bill. The law was declared unconstitutional in 1883 by the Supreme Court in the *Civil Rights Cases*, 109 U.S. 1 (1883)."

BARACK OBAMA
MASTER OF WASHINGTON, DC

Barack Obama's Washington, DC Photo 357. Two interesting tourists on the lawn with the Washington Monument at their rear.

Plessey v. Ferguson (1896) is dealt with by C. Erik Lincoln's "The American Protest Movement for Negro Rights" in *The American Negro Reference Book*

FREDERICK MONDERSON

(1966: 464) where that author writes: "In 1896 a Supreme Court decision in the case of Plessey vs. Ferguson established the separate-but-equal doctrine upon which was built the legal institution of racial segregation, which was to circumscribe the activities and opportunities of Negroes in America for more than half a century."

Grandfather Clause (1915) - Constance Baker Motley in "The Legal Status of the Negro in the United States" (1966: 491) explains how efforts were made to deprive Blacks of the right to vote, particularly in the South. "The best known among these were the so-called grandfather clause, the white primary, the poll tax and the literacy test."

"The grandfather clause typically provided for continued registration of old voters and their lineal descendants. Registration pursuant to more stringent criteria was required of new voters. The white primary was a whites-only primary election to select candidates for the general elections. The poll tax made annual payments of a capitation tax a prerequisite to voting. The literacy test imposed a high standard of literacy to be judged by the registrar of voters. The registrar's judgment was largely uncontrolled. Generally, a voter applicant who could read, write, understand and/or interpret the Constitution to the satisfaction of the registrar qualified."

Regarding Negro Education (1899-1927) - "In 1899, the Supreme Court heard an appeal by a group of Negroes from Augusta, Georgia, who demanded an end to public support for two white high schools after the sole Negro high school had been discontinued. The majority opinion in *Cummings vs. Richmond County* held that the relief requested was improper. In 1908, the Court heard the case of Berea College vs. Kentucky, which involved the right of a privately chartered college to teach both races in defiance of the Kentucky law making segregation mandatory. The Court ruled against Berea on technical grounds. The case was generally accepted as a reflection of the Court's feeling that segregation was a matter better left to the states. The case of *Gong Lum vs. Rice* came before the Court from Mississippi in 1927. The issue was whether Mississippi could properly classify a Chinese child as "colored" and therefore require her to attend a Negro school. The Court upheld the Mississippi law and Chief Justice Taft took the occasion to offer a reminder that the "separate but equal" doctrine was still in effect; "had the petition alleged specifically that there was no colored school in Martha Lum's neighborhood to which she could conveniently go, a different question would have been presented ...."

Abolish White Primaries (1944) – The Supreme Court acted to abolish white primaries relating to cases in Texas and South Carolina because the former passed a law that read: "in no event shall a negro [sic] be eligible to participate in a

BARACK OBAMA
MASTER OF WASHINGTON, DC

Democratic Party primary election held in the state of Texas." The Court ruled against them and again, "The Democratic Party Executive Committee immediately adopted a resolution that only white Democrats could vote in its primary." The Supreme Court again ruled: "'The 14th Amendment, adopted as it was with special solicitude for the equal protection of members of the Negro race, lays a duty upon the court to level by its judgment these barriers of color."

In *United States v. Classic*, 313 U.S. 299 (1941), the Supreme Court ruled that "Congress had the power to regulate primaries where the primary is made by law an integral part of the machinery of Federal elections. The *Classic* case provided a new legal basis for attacking the white primary in Texas. In *Smith v. Allwright*, 321 U.S. 649 (1944) the Court seems to have reversed itself by siding with the Texas Democratic Party State Convention that "determined the qualification for voters." The Court again moved against South Carolina and was able to outlaw the white primary in that state.

The *poll tax* was eliminated in January 1964 and later the literacy test was also outlawed.

Segregated Graduate Education (1946-1949) – "In cases against the University of Oklahoma and the University of Texas, Negro plaintiffs carried to the United States Supreme Court between 1946 and 1949 issues sharply testing the right of the states to alter in any substantial particular the opportunities for graduate and professional study offered Negroes from that offered whites. Indeed in the Texas case (*Sweatt vs. the University of Texas*) the plaintiff's attorneys argued that no segregated Negro school actually could provide equal educational opportunities. They not only were materially inferior, but also offered the testimony by anthropologists, psychologists and educators to show that Negroes were as capable of learning as whites, that classification of students by race was arbitrary and unjust and that segregation was harmful to personality adjustment. The Court obviously gave weight to these contentions by ruling out segregation in specific instances and largely invalidating it in the field of graduate and professional training."

School Desegregation Decision (1954) - Motley (1966: 504-505) In *Brown v. Board of Education of Topeka, Kansas*, 347 U.S. 483 (1954) the "Supreme Court held that states cannot educate Negroes in separate educational institutions. This principle applies even where facilities afforded Negroes equal those afforded whites. Unanimously the Court ruled state enforced racial segregation is psychologically harmful to Negro children. Such harm, inflicted by the state, deprives Negro children of equal educational opportunities." The Court in this respect was upholding a decision of the Kansas Court which had ruled "'Segregation of white and colored children in public schools has a detrimental effect upon the colored children. The impact is greater when it has the sanction of the law; for the policy of separating the races is usually interpreted as denoting the inferiority of the negro [sic] group.' The Court also found that: 'A sense of inferiority affects the motivation of a child to learn. Segregation with the sanction of the law, therefore, has a tendency to [retard] the educational and mental development of Negro children and to deprive them of some of the benefits they would receive in a racial[ly] integrated school system.'"

In *Bolling v. Sharpe*, 347 U.S. 497 (1954) the Court recognized the Fifth Amendment prohibits any individuals being deprived of "life, liberty or property without due process of law." In this the Court ruled: "'Liberty under law extends to the full range of conduct which the individual is free to pursue, and it cannot be restricted except for a proper governmental objective. Segregation in public education is not reasonably related to any proper governmental objective, and this imposes on Negro children of the District of Columbia a burden that constitutes an arbitrary deprivation of their liberty in violation of the Due Process Clause."

Rules segregation of public buses was unconstitutional (1955) is discussed in C. Erik Lincoln's "The American Protest Movement for Negro Rights" in *The American Negro Reference Book* (1966- 471) that informs, "On December 13, 1956, in consequence of a suit brought by the NAACP, the United States Supreme Court ruled that 'state law requiring racial segregation on public buses was unconstitutional.' A year had passed, and the Negroes of Montgomery through direct action combined with litigation had won an important victory."

Barack Obama's Washington, DC Photo 358.

BARACK OBAMA
MASTER OF WASHINGTON, DC

Barack Obama's Washington, DC Photo 359.

Barack Obama's Washington, DC Photo 360.

FREDERICK MONDERSON

Outlawing segregation in state owned public facilities (1954-1964) - Virgil Cliff's "Educating the American Negro" (1966: 373) writes in regard to "Access to Public Facilities" that the Supreme Court has "divested 'Jim Crow' of all legal status in the public domain by construing the equal protection clause of the Fourteenth Amendment as a prohibition against state-enforced racial exclusion or segregation in every facility owned or operated by the state."

Upholds 1964 Civil Rights Act – John Hope Franklin in "A Brief History of the Negro in the United States" (1966: 94-95) has held: "The Civil Rights movement was greatly strengthened when, in an early test case, the Supreme Court upheld the Act of 1964 .... Negroes faced this their second century of emancipation not only with a new President whose stand on civil rights, housing, and poverty they generally supported, but also with a new civil rights law that many regarded as an indication that at long last the government of the United States was on their side. Perhaps the second century, some of them thought, would not be as difficult as the first."

Affirmative Action is a plan designed to remedy past discrimination against Blacks and by extension other minorities, physically challenged persons, women, etc. Over the years, as Black people have advanced, continued calls have been made to overturn this advantage. Jack Plano and Milton Greenberg in *The American Political Dictionary* (New York: Holt, Rinehart, Winston, Inc., (1962) (1989: 261) has noted: "Various federal and state statues require affirmative action to redress pass discrimination against or promote the employment of racial or religious minorities, women, handicapped workers, disabled veterans, veterans of the Vietnam era, and to some extent, the aged. Affirmative action usually involves a work-force utilization analysis, the establishment of goals and timetables to increase use of underrepresented classes of persons, explanation of methods to be used to eliminate discrimination, and establishment of administrative responsibility to implement the program. Good faith and a positive effort to remedy past discrimination must be shown. Affirmative action is required by law or regulation for all governmental agencies and for recipients of public funds, such as contractors and universities. Affirmative action is to be distinguished from antidiscrimination or equal opportunity laws, which forbid unequal treatment rather than requiring positive corrective measures. In 1978, the supreme court held that affirmative action programs are valid, but that explicit racial quotas are prohibited."

Again, Jack C. Plano and Milton Greenberg in *The American Political Dictionary*, New York: Holt, Rinehart and Winston, Inc., (1962) (1989: 324-325) informs in *Regents of the University of California v. Bakke* 438 U.S. 25 (1978), that the ruling: "Held invalid a state medical school admissions program based on a specific racial quota but upheld the use of race as a factor in admissions decisions.

BARACK OBAMA
MASTER OF WASHINGTON, DC

In the Bakke case, the Court ruled: (1) that where no previous racial discrimination has been found, a special admissions program setting aside a specific number of places for disadvantaged minority students violated both the equal protection clause of the Fourteenth Amendment and the Civil Rights Act of 1964, which bars exclusion of persons because of race from participation in federally financed programs; and (2) that it is constitutionally permissible for admissions officers to consider race, among other factors, in order to promote affirmative action programs."

Plano and Greenberg (1966: 324-325) says further regarding the significance of the Bakke Case that it: "is considered to be the most politically sensitive decision involving race since the 1954 ruling in Brown v. Board of Education of Topeka, 347 U.S. 483, which struck down state-imposed segregation of races in public school."

Plano and Greenberg (1966: 273-274) continued and described Equal Rights as "The movement to equalize the rights of men and women. Traditionally in American law, women have not enjoyed the same rights as men, and this has manifested itself in many areas of American life, including property rights, education, and employment opportunities." Even further, Plano and Greenberg (1989: 274) added regarding the significance of Equal Rights in that: "The concept of equal rights has had a dramatic impact upon American life, equal to, if not greater than, the impact of changing race relations. Many constitutional authorities believe that changes already brought about in behalf of women's rights as well as liberal application of equal protection of the law concepts diminish the need for an equal rights amendments .... The equal rights movement achieved two major victories in the 1960s – the passage of the Equal Pay Act of 1963, which requires equal pay for men and women doing similar work, and the Civil Rights Act of 1964, which forbids discrimination against women in hiring and other personal policies. An end to sex discrimination in education was ordered by Congress in 1972 and the Equal Credit Opportunity Act was adopted in 1974."

FREDERICK MONDERSON

Barack Obama's Washington, DC Photo 361.

Barack Obama's Washington, DC Photo 362.

BARACK OBAMA
MASTER OF WASHINGTON, DC

Barack Obama's Washington, DC Photo 363.

Barack Obama's Washington, DC Photo 363a. More of the Washington, DC trees in bloom.

FREDERICK MONDERSON

Plano and Greenberg (1989: 275) discuss *Fair Employment Practices Laws* that "Forbid private and/or public employers, labor unions, or employment agencies to discriminate in hiring or in other personal policies on the grounds of race, color, creed, or national origin."

We now come to President Obama's ability to impact the Supreme Court which is one of the most significant realizations in American socio-judicial orders within the last century. Considering the **Dred Scott Decision**, we have arrived at a great moment in Supreme Court history with social, civil rights, racial and a multitude of other implications; and America electing an African-American President with potential to impact that body has become a hot bed issue. Even during the presidential campaign, visionaries emphasized the importance of his election and that it would empower him to make appointments to the Supreme Court. Among the many meanings of Obama's election, an appointment to the Supreme Court was very possible given the ages of sitting jurists. However, his re-election to a second term increases the chances of possibly two or three more such opportunities and, as Professor Ogletree has predicted, if Obama wishes to really change the ideological make up of the Court, he has to make four appointments.

Makers of history have a tendency to also make predictions that do come true. In the case of Dred Scott, as he received the negative news regarding his petition to the Court, he may have silently in exasperation predicted the journey of empowerment that ultimately brought President Obama to the historic position he now enjoys. We know the pendulum of justice swings both ways, but it ultimately comes back to the middle!

BARACK OBAMA
MASTER OF WASHINGTON, DC

Barack Obama's Washington, DC Photo 363b. More trees in bloom.

Barack Obama's Washington, DC Photo 364.

FREDERICK MONDERSON

"No system of government can or should be imposed by one nation by any other. That does not lessen my commitment, however, to governments that reflect the will of the people. Each nation gives life to this principle in its own way, grounded in the traditions of its own people. America does not presume to know what is best for everyone, just as we would not presume to pick the outcome of a peaceful election. But I do have an unyielding belief that all people yearn for certain things: the ability to speak your mind and have a say in how you are governed, confidence in the rule of law and the equal administration of justice, government that is transparent and doesn't steal from the people, the freedom to live as you choose. These are not just American ideas. They are human rights. And that is why we will support them everywhere." BARACK OBAMA, speech, Jun. 4, 2009

50.   BARACK OBAMA: MAN WITH THE PLAN
By

Dr. Fred Monderson

Much has been said about plan and planning but not enough on a man with a plan or one who plans. After all, we know of the belief, "If you fail to plan, you're planning to fail" and you should "Plan your work and work your plan," and so on. However, Barack Obama, the new President of the United States obviously came to the quest with the idea of plan and also he must have realized "for me to be successful in this position, I must get "Plan down to science." As a result, if we trace his meteoric rise to the highest office in the land, clearly the notion of planning must have been an essential element in his arsenal of strategies to successfully accomplish his task. Within a relatively short time upon assuming the Presidency, in view of the enormous economic quagmire facing the nation and globally, President Obama was able to get Congress to pass a huge $785 Billion Stimulus Bill designed to provide jobs, infrastructure repairs, create initiatives in energy creation and revamp schools to encourage greater education reform and scientific and intellectual developments among other efforts to help secure America's future.

BARACK OBAMA
MASTER OF WASHINGTON, DC

Barack Obama's Washington, DC Photo 365.

As he unfolded his plans to rescue the nation from its dire position, President Obama announced his $75-billion Homeowner Affordability and Stability plan destined to help homeowners refinance their mortgages with the government sharing the cost with lenders low interest loans. In addition, he asked Congress to empower bankruptcy judges to be able to modify or rewrite primary residence

FREDERICK MONDERSON

mortgages. In addition, the Treasury Department infused an enormous sum of $200-billion, in addition to the $75-billion to assist the mortgage giants Fannie Mae and Freddie Mac to begin making loans to help millions of homeowners, many of whom stand to lose their homes. Treasury Secretary Geithner said regarding this effort: "The increased funding will provide forward-looking confidence in the mortgage market and enable Fannie Mae and Freddie Mac to carry out ambitious efforts to ensure mortgage affordability for responsible homeowners."

Barack Obama's Washington, DC Photo 366.

The president then launched a new plan to create a super train system in the United States by comparing our lack of this form of advanced transportation network with nations that have such and their intentions to improve even further. Saying this transportation initiative represents the "most sweeping investment in our infrastructure since President Dwight Eisenhower began the interstate highway system in the 1950s," he commented on China's advances in this area, France's and Japan's plans to improve to a 300-mile per hour super system. Planning to spend billions of dollars, more than 10 billion over a five year period, 10 areas throughout the country have been identified as hubs that will benefit. President Obama remarked: "Building a new system of high-speed rail in America will be faster, cheaper and easier than building more freeways or adding to an already over-burdened aviation system, and everybody stands to benefit." Further he added, "Money will be distributed based on merit, not on politics, not on favors, not for any other consideration, purely on merit."

BARACK OBAMA
MASTER OF WASHINGTON, DC

The Federal Plan to combat drug violence on the border with Mexico is designed to prevent spill-over into the United States. An article entitled: "Obama to Beef up Mexico Border Policy" *Daily Challenge* Wednesday, March 25, 2009, p. 3, notes: "The new federal plan, developed by the departments of Justice and Homeland Security, calls for doubling the number of border security task force teams as well as moving a significant number of other federal agents, equipment and resources to the border. It also involves greater intelligence sharing aimed at cracking down on the flow of money and weapons into Mexico that helps fuel the drug trade, senior officials said."

This plan will provide $700 million as well as five helicopters and new surveillance aircraft to help bolster Mexican efforts at crime fighting. They will also gain from new communications technology.

"On the U.S. side of the border, the goal is to use 'prosecutor-led, intelligence-based task forces that bring together all Department of Justice and Department of Homeland Security and other relevant law enforcement agencies' to disrupt and dismantle the drug cartels through investigation, prosecution, extradition of their leaders, and the seizure and forfeit of their assets" In this effort, Secretary of State Hillary Clinton and Attorney General Eric Holder visited Mexico and met with their counterparts who will be leading the fight to curtail and ultimately put the cartel apparatus out of business.

To help strengthen the U.S. side of the border further, the administration also plans to triple the number of Department of Homeland Security intelligence analysts dedicated to stopping Mexican-related violence. It also will "increase the number of immigration officials working in Mexico, double the number of 'violent criminal alien' teams on the border, strengthen the presence of border crime units and quadruple the number of border liaison officers working with Mexican law enforcement."

Agents from FBI, DEA, and BATFE will be stationed at the border with improved surveillance equipment. Secretary of State Clinton mentioned its US citizens desire for drugs that fuels the industry and associated violence.

The Geithner Economic Plan to assume toxic assets in banks is designed to remove these impediments and allow movement by these institutions to help stimulate the economy. Essentially, it requires pension funds, private equity and hedge funds, and mutual funds to invest in these negative assets that they could sell later for a profit. With government assurance or backing, the eventual viability of these loan and securities instruments, private investors would initiate competition among themselves and this would have a positive effect overall on the economy. He also

FREDERICK MONDERSON

challenged two of the three auto giants, General Motors and Chrysler Corporation to create plans to restructure themselves.

Barack Obama's Washington, DC Photo 367.

Barack Obama's Washington, DC Photo 368.

BARACK OBAMA
MASTER OF WASHINGTON, DC

Barack Obama's Washington, DC Photo 369.

President Obama asked his cabinet to find cuts totaling $100 million dollars while consensus is that this is too small given the multi-trillion dollar budget he submitted. Within this he signed a $410 billion spending bill that was designed to help restore confidence in and shore up the nation's financial condition.

It's generally agreed a President is most successful if his agenda is relentlessly pursued in the first and second years of his administration and President Obama is certainly holding to this belief. He has unleashed bills and plans sent to Congress designed to make his mark on the American historical landscape and in process create a better future for the young. For this he must be commended. However, when we consider the many obstacles placed in his path by Republicans whose non-cooperation approach proves the President is trying even harder to be successful. This says even more about the man and the efforts he expends to fulfill his promise to the American people when they elected him to the office.

While we cannot enumerate the many plans he has unfolded he has to get credit for working "27-hours per day" and much of his efforts seem to be working.

FREDERICK MONDERSON

Barack Obama's Washington, DC Photo 370.

Barack Obama's Washington, DC Photo 371.

His efforts to reform health care which has eluded presidents for decades since the Harry Truman era was delivered to the American Medical Association in Chicago, his home town. This venue did not aid his reception of the plan for it required great sacrifices from the Medical profession. Nevertheless, the President did say: "If we

BARACK OBAMA
MASTER OF WASHINGTON, DC

do not fix our health care system, Americans may go the way of GM; paying more, getting less and going broke." Trying to diffuse what he perceives as media and other efforts to derail his plan he again explained: "When you hear the naysayers claim that I'm trying to bring about government-run health care, know this – they are not telling the truth." Suggesting many changes in administrative and medical practices he seems to be pinpointing the problems and making a good faith effort to fix this escalating problem.

Another of the plans the President has unfolded designed to reshape financial regulation was commented on by Stephen Labaton in *The New York Times* Wednesday, June 17, 2009, page A 1 in which he explained: "The plan the president will formally announce on Wednesday would give the Federal Reserve greater supervisory authority over large financial institutions whose problems pose potential risks to the economic system. It would separately expand the reach of the Federal Deposit Insurance Corporation to seize and break up troubled financial institutions. And it would create a council of regulators, led by the Treasury secretary, to fill in regulatory gaps."

Therefore, what President Obama has been able to innovate in his method of planning attempts to address problems that have built up over many years and previous leaders have not really and seriously sought to correct.

FREDERICK MONDERSON

Barack Obama's Washington, DC Photo 372.

BARACK OBAMA
MASTER OF WASHINGTON, DC

Barack Obama's Washington, DC Photo 372a.

Barack Obama's Washington, DC Photo 372b.

FREDERICK MONDERSON

"Change will not come if we wait for some other person or some other time. We are the ones we've been waiting for. We are the change that we seek."
ARACK OBAMA, speech, Feb. 5, 2008

51. MICHELLE OBAMA AND THE GORILLAS
By

Dr. Fred Monderson

What the hell is going on? One day the racists attack Michelle and the next they attack Barack Obama, disregarding the fact he is the President of the United States!

During the recent Presidential Elections, Michelle Obama was attacked more often and more scurrilously than any candidate for the office and more important, more so than any First Lady. For one thing, she was caricatured in the *New Yorker* Magazine but this backfired because it mistakenly represented her as a loyal spouse who would fight to protect and defend her husband, now President Barack Obama. Equally too, in the early days of the attacks on Michelle during the campaign, then Senator Obama issued a warning which I reiterate, "If you're listening, lay off my wife!" However, now that he is President, a much sterner warning is very much in order.

The recent flap of the South African Republican activist Rusty De Passe who scurrilously referred to Michele Obama's "Gorilla Ancestors" is not only distasteful, out of order, but a disrespectful attack on the First Lady that seems very racist in its intent. Not only is it demeaning the First Lady, but it is well within the parameters similar such dangerous and racist attacks on Blacks comparing them to monkeys, gorillas, apes, and such odious comparisons. Afterall, he is of the age of the apartheid racists Winnie Mandela has long been fighting.

One could well imagine the ramifications of the responses if Gerald Ford's wife Betty Ford was attacked in a disrespectful and demeaning manner; the Response of Ronald Reagan if Nancy Reagan was so attacked; George Bush (No. 41) if Barbara Bush was so disparaged; George Bush (No. 43) if Laura Bush was similarly victimized. Therefore, a stern rebuke by President Barack Obama is very

BARACK OBAMA
MASTER OF WASHINGTON DC

much in order for the beautiful Michelle who means so much to him. Then again, if being Presidential means "he should grin and bear it" there are countless others who will not allow this to go unchallenged!

Barack Obama's Washington, DC Photo 373. Youngster stands in the fenced off area that shows the front entrance to the White House.

Recently, the *New York Post* caricatured President Obama with racial overtones linking him to an ape shot by two New York City policemen. In recent years we are reminded of a school teacher who likened one of her young pupils to a monkey and now this insult to the First Lady, despite what is said, is not accidental. Fact is the reality of racist white supremacy ideology is very apparent. The Internet Site Black Planet is reporting that after President Obama's spoke in Cairo, Jewish settlers began calling him "Nigger." It's as if the racists are expected to say things like that! While behaviors are long standing, the recent attacks on Michelle and Barack during the election and now this blatant attack on the First Lady and the hateful racist E-mails from Tennessee calling the President "Nigger" seems to be putting all of us on notice, and designed to cause tension and distress among the African-American community. We will have none of it!

It seems, all this stems from the resentment of having a wonderful and intelligent Black family in the White House. Even further, these developments seem to indicate the euphoria of President Obama's election has begun to wear off as he begins to tackle the arduous task of leading this nation during these trying times.

FREDERICK MONDERSON

This writer is reminded of an incident involving a colleague while a Doctoral student at Columbia University, some 25 years ago. As he presented a report on a researched topic in one of his classrooms in the "well," a white supremacy proponent heckled him, referring to his jawbone resembling that of an ape. Calmly he responded by saying one of the characteristics of the apes is a hairy chest. With that he opened his shirt to expose his hairless chest and dared the heckler to do the same. Instantly, the hairy chest individuals attending began holding their chests, refusing to unbutton their shirts and thereafter silence reigned.

Barack Obama's Washington, DC Photo 374. View of the Washington Monument from the area before the White House.

Name calling of African Americans in a pejorative and racist nature is replete in American history and is also an indication of the contempt held for these people in this country. Malcolm X liked to say all manner of people left their "Old World" homeland, viz., English or British, German, Italian, Turkish, Chinese, Japanese, Jew, Dutch, Dane, etc., and when they arrived here they retained their ethnic or national designation and cultural attachments, even though they integrated into the American body politic and cultural milieu. Not so with the African, captured in his homeland, transported to America, sold into slavery, brutalized, then called slave, 3/5 of a person, Nigger, Negro, colored, Black and many more nomenclatures between, before finally becoming African-American.

For Blacks, from the very inception, coming to America has been a struggle to survive, perennially a challenge to adapt and overcome and only with god's help have we been able to understand the terrorism and racial prejudice, unleashed in the perennial victimization against the humanity of people who are an integral part of American society. For it was the "crime against humanity" of the slave trade; the cruelty and viciousness of the slave experience; the physical and psychological

BARACK OBAMA
MASTER OF WASHINGTON DC

emasculation of being 3/5 of a person which indicated the depths to which the African persona had been degraded to be elevated to a fraction of a person; the emotional distress of constantly being trampled upon and the detachment and dislocation suffered in the unfettered terrorism of malcontent groups as the Ku Klux Klan, Knights of the White Camellia and the White Citizen's Council whose violence in the form of rape, tar and feather, arson, assassination, kidnapping, beatings, bombings, lynchings, murder and torture and all forms of hatred that knew no bounds, being fueled by racist white supremacy ideology and the literary and oral onslaught such as Dr. Hunt insisting the "Negro is a beast." Samuel Cartwright in 1857 declared the "Nilotic monuments indicate the Negro was a slave in Egypt from time immemorial." Little did this doctored and racist ignoramus know, blacks were the originators of Egyptian civilization! More important, are we to believe just as the descendants of the slaves are still with us, the descendants of the Ku Klux Klan, Knights of the White Camelia, White Citizens Council, and their terror cohorts have disappeared? No! Many may have replaced their hoods with business suits, but they are still functioning!

We know of Chief Justice Roger Taney's decision in the Dred Scott case; Jim Crow laws that were more draconian than the Black Slave Codes; the inequality of Share Cropping; the *Grandfather Clause* and voting rights; and *Plessey v. Ferguson*. Our people have weathered the targeting, black-listing, black-balling and assassination of our leaders; lynchings, tar and feathers, denial of meaningful jobs and quality education; refusal to recognize and respect the Black family; and confronting the brutality of the KKK and the likes of Bull Connor, we ought not forget racial discrimination and denial of civil rights; red lining and shady banking and real estate dealers; activities targeting Blacks including police brutality, black on black crime, vicissitudes of the Prison Industrial Complex, high Black unemployment, drugs and environmentally induced illnesses as diabetes, stroke, heart attacks, cancer, hypertension, AIDS and a whole lot more. So what's new?

All this notwithstanding, the African-American experience has not been all negative. These Americans can look back with pride on their African ancestors who evolved mankind; built the earliest and longest lasting civilization along the banks of the River Nile, providing ethical, philosophical, moral, scientific, mathematical and artistic creations and thought processes that influenced the pageantry of history. The Medieval Sudanic empires of Ghana, Mali and Songhay and the material and human wealth of Africa tremendously and constructively impacted America and the Western World. The free labor of Blacks transformed America and the first patriot to die in the American Revolution was a Black, Crispus Attucks. The first President of the new nation under the **Articles of Confederation** Mr. John Hanson, was a Black; the figure atop the Capital Building Dome is Black; technological patents by Blacks that abound especially in the 1870-1930 period enabled the early industrialization of the nation; Dr. Charles Drew invented blood plasma; the cell phone revolution; in sports, literature,

FREDERICK MONDERSON

medicine and Noble prize awards Blacks have contributed richly to American culture. Blacks have served honorably in every war America has fought not just to defend this great nation but also to acquire the skills to challenge and thwart the intent of those fueled by hatred of racial white supremacy ideology. Therefore, it is only when the constructive role Blacks have played in their heritage to humanity and in America is taught in the public schools and included in every curriculum will young people be armed with the knowledge to combat the destructiveness of racial supremacy.

Barack Obama's Washington, DC Photo 375. This is the "Starting Point of First Transcontinental Motor Convoy over the Lincoln Highway, July 7, 1919."

BARACK OBAMA
MASTER OF WASHINGTON DC

"In reaffirming the greatness of our nation we understand that greatness is never a given. It must be earned. Our journey has never been one of short-cuts or settling for less. It has not been the path for the faint-hearted, for those that prefer leisure over work, or seek only the pleasures of riches and fame. Rather, it has been the risk-takers, the doers, the makers of things -- some celebrated, but more often men and women obscure in their labor -- who have carried us up the long rugged path towards prosperity and freedom." BARACK OBAMA, *Inaugural Address, Jan. 20. 2009*

52. PRESIDENT OBAMA AND THE POWER OF APPOINTMENT
By

Dr. Fred Monderson

During the primary campaign candidates begin putting together various teams and this intensifies as the party's nominee is chosen at their National Convention. There could be teams of political campaign strategists, economic theorists and advisers, fundraisers, and teams that would search out the best qualified candidates for the numerous appointment positions to be filled if the candidate is successfully elected President of the United States. Other than the Vice-President who is chosen at the Convention to be running-mate to the party leader and equally brings some significant experience and capability to the ticket; the untold numbers who will constitute the administration must all be considered, screened, chosen, nominated, then most confirmed by the Senate which undertakes its own examination process before a final vote of confirmation can take place allowing the individual to serve in the Executive or even Judicial branch. Now, while the President can appoint to these two branches of the government, his appointive power does not extend to any congressional positions. The closest he comes to Congress is appointment of the liaison that will interact with both houses to help his legislative and other agendas that fall within the purview of these houses of Congress.

Edward Conrad Smith and Arnold John Zurcher (Editors) *Dictionary of American Politics*, New York: Barnes and Noble, Inc., (1944) (1966: 21) defies Appointment as: "The process, which may include both nomination and confirmation, by which a superior authority uses discretion in naming a person to hold an office. In some

FREDERICK MONDERSON

jurisdictions the issuance of a commission is necessary to complete an appointment. Ambassadors, other public ministers, consuls, and judges of the Supreme Court, together with several thousand others who have been designated by law as 'officers,' must be confirmed by the Senate. When it is not in session the President may fill vacancies by temporary appointments which expire at the end of the next session of the Senate. Appointments of inferior officers may be made under the laws of Congress by the President alone, by the courts, or by the heads of departments, independent agencies, and government-owned corporations. Most of those are chosen under civil service rules. In the States gubernatorial appointments generally require confirmation, and those made by heads of departments do not."

Louis Fisher in *The politics of Shared Power: Congress and the Executive*, Texas: Texas A and M University (1998: 118) writes: "The power to appoint agency officials is an essential tool used by both President and Congress to control the bureaucracy. In his report to President John F. Kennedy in 1960, James M. Landis counseled: 'The prime key to the improvement of the administrative process is the selection of qualified personnel. Good men can make poor laws workable; poor men will wreak havoc with good laws.' The potential of the appointment power has been narrowed by civil service regulations and other restrictions imposed by Congress."

Notwithstanding, Robert C. Bone in *American Government*, New York: Barnes and Noble, (1977: 73) in commenting on the President's Executive Powers states: "There are six powers that can be classified in the executive category. But it is worth noting that even in these the President shares authority with Congress on several important points. The President's executive powers are those of appointment, removal, administrative supervision, law enforcement, formulation of military policy, and conduct of foreign relations."

Even further Bone (1977: 73-74) writes: "The President's appointive powers are limited in two ways. First, Presidential appointments have to 'be made by and with the Advise and Consent of the Senate,' which is by no means automatic. (As of 1976, for example, 26 percent of all Supreme Court nominations had been rejected by the Senate.) Second, as a result of the continued expansion of the merit system of appointments since the Pendleton Act was passed in 1883, over 85 percent of all government positions are now outside the area of political influence. However, it continues to be accepted practice that the top decision-making positions in the government are at the disposal of the President. This list ... which was drawn up during President Eisenhower's first term (1953-1957), includes about 1000 top-level positions. Unless a Presidential nominee for one of these jobs in an unusually controversial figure, the Senate usually confirms the appointment routinely."

BARACK OBAMA
MASTER OF WASHINGTON DC

Nevertheless, there is always a cry to cut back on government size and spending and this has been a Republican Party mantra. Roger Hilsman in *The Politics of Governing America*, Englewood Cliffs, New Jersey: Prentice Hall, Inc., (1985: 136) provides some quotes regarding administrative attempts to scale back on the size of government such as: "'Reagan's administration is determined to cut down on the role of the federal government.'" "'The Carter Administration was determined to balance the budget.'" "'Nixon administration was conservative in domestic affairs but accomplish much in easing tensions in international affairs.'" Still, for example, the two decades since Reagan's tenure, the government has increased even more, adding departments that require more people to administer.

It is also interesting that young people pay particular attention to the things they say, for such utterances have a tendency to come back to haunt their authors. For example, President Obama recently nominated Judge Sonia Sotomayor to be a Supreme Court justice; and though she has been a jurist for nearly 17 years and has had a good record, the critical forces in the Senate have been paying more attention to a couple of statements she made that have nothing to do with her judicial record.

Therefore, in refocusing and tracing the evolution of the President's path to the point of nomination; from the moment he is declared winner of the national elections, and becomes President-elect, he sets in position his transition team, generally campaign loyalists who were the brains and brawn behind his success and whose responsibility it is to oversee a seamless transfer of power from the outgoing to the new incoming administration. This transition team including and comprising the search committee begin the process of replacing the old administration. They examine the thousands of resumes to fill the 2500-3000 White House staff members, secretaries and upper and middle management of the various departments, commissions, foreign service, judiciary as needed and promotions in the branches of the armed forces, agencies, and all areas the federal government has influence in employing personnel, including the ambassadorial team that represents the United States at the United Nations.

Hilsman (1985: 136) sheds some light on the appointment process in comparing that of the Nixon administration in the following statement: "At the time that President Nixon was putting together his administration, the *New York Times* defined administration as being 'one President, one Vice President, 12 Cabinet appointees, 300 sub-Cabinet officials and agency heads, 124 ambassadors, and 1700 aides, assistants and confidential secretaries. Another guide to the definition of an administration is a document published each election year as a public service by one of the committees of the Senate. It lists not only the jobs that make up an administration but all of the patronage and Schedule C jobs available to a new administration (a Schedule C job is one that the occupant has no tenure and is expected to change with each new administration.) Variously called the green book and the shopping list, it has also been called the plum book because it describes the available political 'plums.' The *Times* article and the plum book are only rough guides."

Indicating during the mid-eighties there were some 2000 appointments new presidents would make and that some 500 are policy making jobs, at that time there were only 12 Cabinet posts. This number has increased to 15 positions by the time of the Obama administration and thus, clearly the number of appointments is closer to more than 3000. Nevertheless, Hilsman (1985: 136) continued: "Most of these top jobs require confirmation by the Senate. Cabinet members, deputy secretaries, undersecretaries, and members of regulatory boards and commissions all require such confirmation. So do certain members of the Executive Office of the President, such as the director of Office of Management and Budget, members of the Council of Economic Advisers, and the director of the Office of Science and Technology. White House aides do not require confirmation, presumably on the theory that they are personal aides to the president. Commissioned Officers of the Army, Navy, Air Force, Marine Corps, Coast Guard, Foreign Service, and certain other officials require Senate confirmation, but they are not usually thought of as being members of the administration."

The White House team generally comprises the National Security Adviser, the Chairman and members of the Joint Chiefs of the Military, a Council of Economic Advisers, and security advisers and analysts as well. Then are appointed the Secretary of State for foreign relations; the Secretary of Defense to coordinate military activity at home and abroad; Secretary of the Treasury for economic policy and practice; and the Attorney General to ensure the law is effectively administered. While a general or admiral heads the various branches of the armed forces, viz., Army, Navy, Marine Corps, Air Force, Coast Guard, a civilian Secretary is also appointed for each branch, inasmuch as the Constitution provides for civilian control of the military. In his attempts to be bi-partisan, President Obama recently appointed a Republican, John McHugh as Secretary of the Army.

For much of his first year in office, while he must tend to the pressing demands of the various hats he wears, President Barack Obama is also preoccupied with making appointments of party loyalists, searching for the most qualified individuals to fill respective positions and also to demonstrate a spirit of bi-partisanship by selecting members of the opposition party who could "live with his policies." After all, if the President calls or offers a position in the government, who would turn him down? But this belief does not always hold true. Senator Greg Judd turned down President Obama's offer to be Commerce Secretary. On the other hand, his cabinet appointments were withdrawn by former Secretary Tom Daschle as Secretary of Health and Human Services and Governor Bill Richardson as Commerce Secretary, because these individuals had problems with their taxes and as such, became embarrassments for the President.

BARACK OBAMA
MASTER OF WASHINGTON DC

John J. Patrick, Richard M. Pious and Donald A. Ritchie in *The Oxford Guide to the United States Government* Oxford at the University Press (2001: 25) under "Appointment Power," informs: "The Constitution (Article 2, Section 2) gives the President the power to nominate and, with the advice and consent of the Senate, appoint officers of the United States. The Constitution also provides that Congress by law may vest the appointment of 'inferior Officers' in the President alone, in the courts of law, or in the heads of departments. Presidents also appoint and promote all military officers subject to Senate consent." They continue (2001: 25) even further: "The President appoints 1,000 top officials, who bear titles such as secretary, under secretary, deputy secretary, and assistant secretary to the departments."

In these appointments, the President's team researches each candidate's background thoroughly so the President can "choose wisely." However, as the above appointment were withdrawn because these individuals had problems with their taxes, once Congress did put them through the rigors of examination they would have been rejected, bringing a sort of shame to the administration. Even though nominations were being made since the beginning of the Republic, that development is interesting for as Patrick, Pious and Ritchie (2001: 25-26) have pointed out: "Prior to the 1950s only seven cabinet nominations were turned down. More recently, Dwight Eisenhower's nomination of Lewis Strauss for secretary of commerce in 1959 and George Bush's nomination of John Tower for secretary of defense in 1989 were defeated. Some nominees will withdraw before a Senate vote if the President senses they will be defeated; President Jimmy Carter withdrew the nomination of Theodore Sorensen for the position of Director of Central Intelligence in 1977, and President Bill Clinton withdrew his first two nominees for attorney general, Zo Baird and Kimba Wood, because of Senate opposition in 1993. In 1962 Congress refused to create the Department of Urban Affairs because President Kennedy made it known that he intended to appoint Robert Weaver to head it – and he would have been the first African American in the cabinet. By 1967 President Lyndon B. Johnson won congressional approval for the department and then for Weaver's appointment."

In the case of Governor Bill Richardson and Senator Tom Daschle they realized their candidacy would bring dishonor to the President at a time when he was in the throes of getting settled in his Administration. This, however, is not unique. Louis Fisher in *The Politics of Shared Power: Congress and the Executive* (Texas: Texas A and M University, 1998: 119) explained: "The appointment process is taken seriously because it is assumed that 'who you get *in* government directly affects what you get out of government.' The number of senate rejections cannot be measured by floor votes. Of forty major nominations rejected from 1961 to 1977, only four were rejected on the floor. Nine were rejected by committee vote, while twenty-seven nominees were forced to withdraw. Ernest Lefebvre, nominated by President Reagan in 1981 for a top post in the State Department, was a casualty of this process. After the Senate Foreign Relations Committee voted 13-4 to disapprove his nomination, Lefebvre asked Reagan to withdraw his name. A number of recent nominees have experienced the same fate. Victor Stello, Jr., picked by President Bush [father] for a position in the Energy Department, withdrew his name in 1990 after it became clear that the Senate would not confirm him. Other Bush nominees fell by the wayside without a formal Senate vote. Hundreds of potential nominees are never even submitted by the White House because of Congressional opposition."

This type of rejection is not confined to Republicans for the Democrats also have their lumps. As an example, Fisher (1998: 119) mentions: "Several Clinton nominees chose to withdraw their names after encountering resistance in the Senate: Zoe E. Baird, nominated for Attorney General; Lani Guinier, selected to head the Justice Department's civil rights division; Stanley Tate, scheduled to head the Resolution Trust Corporation; and Anthony Lake, who abruptly withdrew as nominee for CIA director; Henry W. Foster, Clinton's choice to be Surgeon General, withdrew his name in 1995 after running into a Senate filibuster."

Much was said in the Primary and Presidential Elections about Barack Obama's ethnicity as African American. He was accused by black and white. Some blacks accused him of "not being black enough" and others accused him of "being too black." Yet, we are informed by Kevin Chappell's "Power Behind the Power" in *Ebony Magazine* (May 2009: 64-77) which features a photograph of top blacks in the Obama Administration, naming "Lisa Jackson, administrator of the Environment Protection Agency; Eric Holder, Attorney General; Valerie Jarrett, senior adviser to the President; Susan Rice, U.S. Ambassador to the United Nations; Melody Barnes, Director of the White House Domestic Policy Council; Joshua DuBois, Director of the White House Council for Faith-Based and Neighborhood Partnerships; Ron Kirk, U.S. Trade Representative; Desiree Rogers, White House Social Secretary; Mike Strautmanis, Chief of Staff to the Assistant to the President for Intergovernmental Relations and Public Liaison; and Rob Nabors, Deputy Director of the Office of Management and Budget." These represent the President's "Black Inner Cabinet" reflecting his appointment capability, though some go through the Congressional approval process.

But it's not always about politics, sometimes the arts also figure in the equation. The *New York Times* newspaper of Thursday June 4, 2009, p. C 1 featured an article by Robin Pogrebin entitled "Obama Names a Republican to Lead the Humanities Endowment" which states: "President Obama intends to nominate Jim Leach, a former Republican congressman from Iowa who is now a professor at Princeton University's Woodrow Wilson School of Public and International Affairs, as the next chairman of the National Endowment for the Humanities, the White House said on Wednesday." The article quoted Mr. Obama as saying: "I am

BARACK OBAMA
MASTER OF WASHINGTON DC

confident that with Jim as its head, the National Endowment for the Humanities will continue on its vital mission of supporting the American public access to the rich resources of our culture." Accordingly, "The endowment is a federal agency with a budget of $155 million that gives grants to support research, education, preservation and programs in the humanities." Mr. Leach is quoted as saying: "America somehow thinks that leadership relates to governance, and it certainly does. But society is much bigger than governance, and some of the truly great leadership of our society is outside the governance arena. Our culture is more shaped by the arts and humanities than it often is by politics. And in difficult times the arts, sciences and humanities vastly increase in significance. And this is one of those times."

President Obama is therefore empowered to appoint qualified people to fill positions in the government, yet constrained by Congress' role and the potential problems of nominees who have slipped through the screening net bring with their resumes. Nevertheless, the job has to be done and he chooses, appoints and trusts they will be confirmed. He also hopes they will faithfully and successfully carry out the policies he has outlined in keeping his promise to the American people that he would faithfully carry out the laws and manage the nation's economy in a constructive, coordinated and conducive manner that promotes the welfare and prosperity and defend America and Americans at home and abroad.

Barack Obama's Washington, DC Photo 375a. Youngster in front of the Postal Museum.

FREDERICK MONDERSON

"I don't want to pit Red America against Blue America. I want to be President of the United States of America." BARACK OBAMA, speech, Nov. 10, 2007

53. THE QUINTESSENTIAL OBAMA
By

Dr. Fred Monderson

The "Quintessential Barack Obama" is one who brings thoughtful contemplation to assessing an issue that ultimately has national or even global significance. While this attribute may have characterized his personality in private life, it came to the fore during the Democratic Campaign and the Presidential race as well. During these contests, when Barack Obama was confounded and confronted with an issue not considered one of his strong suits, he would "go to school," and later the public would learn he consulted his "team of wise men" versed in the important issues such as foreign policy, domestic policy, economics, national security, all that were directly related to his duties and responsibilities. Naturally, this "ace in the hole" concept was baffling to his opponents and the media, yet he pulled it off. This became apparent when an important issue surfaced requiring immediate action or concrete solutions, and Barack Obama did not respond as was supposedly expected. Finally, when queried, he gave what came to be later characterized as the "Quintessential Obama" answer. So as not to "conjure up a negative connotation," Barack Obama's contemplation reflects his wrestle with the serious problems and then he gives his "come up with constructive answers" that address the issue, positively.

As an example of the thinking of the man, the recent pirate standoff off the Somali coast raised the question, "What is President Obama doing about it?" and the answer in response was the "President is keeping abreast of the situation." Well, that response caused a local commentator to remark, "This is the quintessential Obama." Whether or not this defines the "Quintessential Obama," because he chose to study an important issue is debatable, since so many other traits can truly define the man. After all, unlike so many others, President Barack Obama has demonstrated rather than "shoot from the lip" to delay and study an action and seek a broad based consensus to be more schooled and educated in his response. Listening to what you say and contemplating an action before the fact is an extraordinary trait most decision makers lack. World figures are not excluded from this *modus operandi* and the potential successes of such a strategy.

BARACK OBAMA
MASTER OF WASHINGTON DC

Ancient Egypt is one of the earliest of civilizations that has had a tremendous impact on its age and subsequently. It was replete with pharaohs, kings, leaders with tremendous abilities, who produced successful outcomes. These, however, were primarily fighting pharaohs, warrior kings, whose challenges were a far cry from those of a leader and times such as a Barack Obama and his challenges.

Barack Obama's Washington, DC Photo 376. "Zero Milestone."

There was one particular pharaoh, Rameses III, a warrior king of the 20th Dynasty. In his time of leadership, during the late New Kingdom, the Egyptian state stood on the precipice of its relative decline and he had to contend with mobilized and newly energized enemies of his nation. In *The Splendor that was Egypt* (New York: Philosophical Library, 1957: 61) Margaret Murray has written: "Rameses III was the last of the fighting pharaohs. He deliberately delayed any attack until he

FREDERICK MONDERSON

was ready. Then he made his assault with complete success: 'The foreign lands and countries are stripped and brought to Egypt as slaves; gifts are gathered to satisfy the gods; provisions and supplies are like a flood in Egypt. As for those who invade his boundary, his Majesty goes forth against them like a flame in dry herbage. They flutter like birds in the net, their legs struggling in the basket. The land of Egypt lives with untroubled heart; a woman can go about at her will, with her veil upon her head, she can go as far as she pleases.'"

Times may be different but that classic art of contemplation in making decisions of the state is a trait only the very best leaders possess and effectively demonstrate. This is what Barack Obama seems to so sincerely and effectively manifest.

The whole notion of the "Quintessential Obama" seems to have publicly surfaced during the Presidential Campaign when, as a freshman, Senator Obama was accused by many things, including being inexperienced in such matters as foreign policy. Between campaign stints, Barack would "go to school" on his opponents and emerge knowledgeable about any topic, whether domestic or the global economy, foreign policy, national security, etc., and he would unexpectedly best his opponent. Here lay the foundation of the notion of what was later described as the "Quintessential Obama." This pattern of deep contemplation on any issue, undergirded by the expertise provided by Obama's team of "wise men," proved the wherewithal for the new President to study the issues as they appeared. It also helped as he prepared for the many matters of state. Studying the issue is not all Obama has done, but the manner in which he articulated his position after such contemplation has always been clear, sequential and convincing.

In *The Politics of Expertise* (1977) Guy Benvenise used three "takes" or analytic approaches to examine the American response in the Cuban Missile Crisis during the Kennedy Administration. Perhaps we could use three cases for study to assess (in one man's view) how President Obama responded to these situations, in light of the tremendous criticism directed towards him and how he has handled some foreign policy developments.

In his acceptance speech on the evening of November 4, 2008, President Obama said among other things, to those nations who have a problem with the United States, "If you unclench your fist, we will extend a hand." Therefore, the three "case studies" we can use include the "pirates debacle;" "Chavez contact;" and "outreach to Iran."

BARACK OBAMA
MASTER OF WASHINGTON DC

Barack Obama's Washington, DC Photo 377. The National Christmas Tree, lit by the President during the Christmas season.

The details of Somali pirates seizure of the Mares-Alabama and subsequent developments are well known. As the situation unfolded and the captured Captain Phillips appeared in danger, President Barack Obama decisively determined on a course of attack and gave the Navy Seals the go ahead to "take out the pirates." The success of this venture proved the President decisive and quick acting that saved the life of an American hostage. For this success he was applauded by both supporters and critics.

Everyone knows the Venezuelan President Hugo Chavez has demonstrated an anti-American tirade for the longest, even calling former President Bush the devil at the United Nations and then calling President Obama stupid. Nevertheless, following his trip to Mexico, Barack Obama then traveled to Trinidad and Tobago for the Fifth Summit of the Americas to discuss trade, security, guns, drugs, jobs in a new "approach to relations" with Latin America. Among other things, Hugo Chavez approached President Obama for what seemed a well-choreographed handshake and later presented him a book written about Western and American economic "rape" of Latin America. Later, Obama explained he thought it was a book Chavez had written and would have given him one of his. However, it was the handshake and friendly chit-chat that caused the uproar at home where Republicans had a field-day criticizing the President for being "civil." This is basically a part of his nature and Barack Obama rightly argued, a handshake does not threaten American interests! After all, he did say "if they unclenched their fists we would offer a hand."

The third case in point is the President's decision to outreach to Iran in an effort to diffuse tensions between the two countries, but also to neutralize Iran's nuclear military option while acknowledging that country's right to pursue nuclear power for peaceful purposes. This new approach, as was laid out in his Presidential Primary and National Election campaigns he promised to undertake "negotiations without preconditions."

To explain the President's foreign policy approach as a strategy, we point out, during the "Cold War" the concept of "who lost what" emerged as a point of assessment and departure for many Presidents in their foreign relations policies. We know Nixon "won China and Russia;" Reagan won the "cold war;" and Jimmy Carter "lost Iran." From the time of Iran's seizure of American hostages in 1979-1980, the emergence of the show "Nightline, America Held Hostage," all subsequent Iranian elections emphasized hatred towards America with slogans such as "Death to America" and "Death to Imperialism." With these realities in mind after nearly thirty years of strained relations between the two nations, as vigorous dialogue unfolded in the 2009 Iranian Election, and for a change the themes did not involve America in any way. The candidates and their debating points focused on the nation's economy and the country's continuing global isolation due to sponsorship of terrorism, pursuit of nuclear power for military purposes and threats to Israel as well as denial of the holocaust. All along President Obama watched and thought of the best way to approach these developments.

Former Secretary of State Henry Kissinger and National Security Adviser Brzezinski believed the President was doing the right thing. Mr. Obama does not want to allow the Iranian regime to use the US as a "political football" or "political foil" or substitute the protesters and reformers with the United States as their punching bag.

In retrospect, Obama set the bar high in his run for the Presidency as the world watched the phenomenal dynamics of American electoral politics, where only the most hardy and tested prevail. The world watched in fascination as America elected its first African American President and commentators, pro and con, predicted Barack Obama would be tested by international developments. Now, as the Iranian election ended, the results declared and untold numbers gathered in the streets to protest what they determined was election fraud, many looked to President Obama for leadership on this issue. Many looked to him to make a

BARACK OBAMA
MASTER OF WASHINGTON DC

statement in condemnation of the results, but in his quintessential manner, he studied the developments before he finally said the protesters should be heard. He said he was "deeply troubled by the violence he saw on Television." He reaffirmed, the "democratic process of free speech and the right of people to peacefully dissent are universal values" and that the Iranian people should be free to express such. It is indeed sweet irony that after the Iranian revolution in 1980 and decades of sour relations with the United States, an American President could be called to speak out for the rights of Iranians. This certainly says much for the credibility of President Obama as a respected world leader.

Barack Obama's Washington, DC Photo 378. Photographic imagery showing the Christmas tree lit and image of President Franklin D. Roosevelt.

Now, if the election results were questionable such developments pose any number of challenges to President Obama. Having won a hotly contested American election with the world focused on its legitimacy, any negotiations with an "illegal regime" may cast doubts on any agreements worked out therewith. Such negotiations will also lend legitimacy to a questionable act by a government whose intentions on the world stage are questionable. Nevertheless, in a mature spirit President Obama has treaded lightly and began to deploy some of his quintessential strengths. As leader of the western world especially and a global icon, President Obama has tried not to inflame tensions in his approach to Iran. While he has employed his consensus building strengths among many nations who can all influence events in Tehran, he has steadfastly sought to avoid American "meddling" in Iran's internal affairs, while striving for the right balance. While he has taken the position of not wanting to insert America into the process of what is unfolding there, he has insisted as the *New York Times* article by Helene Cooper on Sunday, June 21 has reported "Obama Says 'Justice' is needed for Iranians," wherein "The Iranian life that is lost. We call on the Iranian government to stop all violent and unjust actions against its own people." However, while he has a public posture and takes a great deal of heat especially from Republican critics, who knows precisely what he may be doing in private.

However, confronted with the changing realities of the situation on the ground, some strategists have argued the President has struck the right tone and Senator Barbara Boxer of California has said, "We don't want our fingerprint on this issue." Senator John McCain wants a more forceful condemnation of events in Iran. Equally, Republicans in both houses, on the other hand, disagree, arguing for a more focused strongly worded and unequivocal response in support of the people in the streets. As such, and subsequently, in view of continuing Iranian government repression and fatalities in the streets, the US Congress passed a non-binding resolution condemning the atrocities. This has forced President Obama to express more forceful comments about the rights of the demonstrators. He quoted Dr. Martin Luther King, as reported by Helene Cooper, "The arc of the moral universe is long, but it bends toward justice. I believe that. As I said in Cairo, suppressing ideas never succeeds in making them go away. The Iranian people will ultimately judge the actions of their own government. If the Iranian government seeks the respect of the international community, it must respect the dignity of its own people and govern through consent, not coercion." He has, as President, to focus for the long haul on how he will deal with Iran after this issue becomes settled, because his primary interest is negotiations to halt Iran's sprint to possess nuclear weapons and destabilize the Middle East. Now, in any future negotiations with the Iranian Administration, the President can approach with more respect, confidence and wink "I know what you did last summer!"

While the President's behavior in this issue has been exemplary in regards Iran, that quintessential behavior was clearly demonstrated in his address to the American Medical Association regarding the need for Health Care reform. Inasmuch as he hated to quote former House Speaker Newt Gingrich, the President reiterated its "easier to track a Federal Express package that it is to keep track of a patient's health care records." Indicating that American Health Care is in critical condition, it is creating escalating costs, it's like a ticking time bomb and such costs are unsustainable, he presented a formidable argument to the medical body beginning with eliminating paper records and replacing this with computer generated record keeping. Naturally, there were views expressed on both sides of this issue.

BARACK OBAMA
MASTER OF WASHINGTON DC

An even further example of "Quintessential Obama" can be gleaned from a *New York Times* article on Wednesday, June 17, 2009, p. 1, entitled "Obama Enlisted Broad Consensus on Finance Rules" which states: "President Obama's plan to reshape financial regulation, which he will unveil Wednesday, is the product of weeks of meetings among government officials, financial experts, lawmakers, industry executives and lobbyists, many of whom were invited to help the White House draft the proposal." An even further example of Obama's "schooling" is explained in Stephen Labaton's article which states: "But executives from an array of industries caught up in the financial crises came to Washington over the last several weeks to make their case for how the new regulatory landscape should look. They came from big banks and small ones, insurance companies and stock exchanges, hedge funds and mutual funds, and were joined by officials from consumer groups and big labor – often with conflicting views." This is clearly a wonderful example of some aspects of the contemplative Barack Obama who consults then comes up with a position he so eloquently articulates, which for the most part proves to be innovative and ultimately successful.

Therefore, it's evident President Barack Obama is certainly unlike most American Presidents, certainly different from most world leaders and unquestioned a leader who is thoughtful, articulate, oratorical, compassionate, concerned with a tremendous ability to listen; and is extremely sincere as he seeks to provide moral and effective leadership to steer the ship of state of his nation into the calm and constructive waters of a secure and bright future that will benefit subsequent generations.

FREDERICK MONDERSON

Barack Obama's Washington, DC Photo 379. Another view of the Washington Monument.

Barack Obama's Washington, DC Photo 380. Street scene.

BARACK OBAMA
MASTER OF WASHINGTON DC

"The strongest democracies flourish from frequent and lively debate, but they endure when people of every background and belief find a way to set aside smaller differences in service of a greater purpose." BARACK OBAMA, press conference, Feb. 9, 2009

54. BARACK OBAMA AND THE POWERS OF THE PRESIDENCY
By

Dr. Fred Monderson

Barack Obama is arguably the most powerful man in the world today, because as President of the United States, he is Commander-in-Chief of a formidable military organization and as Chief Executive he also oversees the federal bureaucracy partnering with the largest and most powerful economy in the world. As Head of State he represents one of the most scientific, intellectual, industrial and creative nations on the planet. However, he is constrained by a constitutional system, by the distribution of powers, and a system of freedom of expression that checks and keeps his power in balance and paradoxically can remove him from office. In the recently concluded national elections, then Senator Joe Biden (now Vice-President) told of his visit to Libya in "times of old" where he met Col. Khadafy, the Libyan leader. Then the Libyan head of state tried to convince Senator Biden how potent his country's form of democracy was in comparison to that of the United States. Caught somewhat unprepared and with his back seemingly against the wall, Biden asked Col. Khadafy, "Can your people remove you from office?" To which the response was a resounding no! Biden then had history on his side in the impeachment cases of President Johnson who succeeded Abraham Lincoln; Richard Nixon who was succeeded by Gerald Ford; and the 42nd President Bill Clinton who, while impeached or charged, was found not guilty. This then represents a check on the President's power as defined by Article II, Section 4 which reads: "The President, Vice President, and all civil officers of the United States, shall be removed from office on impeachment for, and conviction of, treason, bribery, or other high crimes and misdemeanors."

This caveat underscores the true nature of the two systems of government and equally measures the powers of their leaders. The power, therefore, that Barack Obama commands as President is enshrined in the U.S. Constitution, written laws and even in social practice. That is, while he wears "many hats" his many "powers" are stated or implied and derived and are also referential. This drives home the point Senator Biden wanted to make to Colonel Khadafy, that though our leader is powerful, he is also constrained by balances in the American system of federal, state and local government. This we call power, checked and balanced! Robert C. Bone in *American Government* (New York: Barnes and Noble (1977: 72) best summarizes this relationship as envisioned by the founding fathers. "In broad outline, the president was to be virtually an elected king. Prestige was to be his lot. By the nature of the electoral system, he was intended to be removed from partisan politics or popular pressure. As the [constitutional] convention conceived the office, the President was not to lack power, but his power was to be subject of checks, and it was to be shared."

The power an American President is able to wield can be described as direct and indirect. Those direct powers are four in number. For example, Article II, Section 2.1 states: "The President shall be commander in chief of the [military] ...; he may require the opinion in writing of the principal officer in each of the executive departments upon any subject relating to the duties of their respective offices and he shall have power to grant reprieves and pardons for offenses against the United States, except in cases of impeachment." Article II, Section 2.3 indicates further, "The president shall have power to fill up all vacancies that may happen during the recess of the Senate, by granting commissions which shall expire at the end of their [the Senate's] next session."

The President also has the power to make treaties with other nations, providing he seeks "advice and consent" of the Senate and two-thirds of the Senators vote in favor of any treaty. Equally, he can appoint ambassadors, consuls and junior officers, judges of the Supreme Court providing Congress has the opportunity to vest or examine their fitness for the position as representatives of the United States.

Article II, Section 3, spells out 5 duties of the President. It's generally agreed, around January 20th or so, he has to report to Congress and give the **State of the Union Address**. He has to make sure the **laws of the United States are faithfully executed** as he affirmed in the Oath of the Office. On extraordinary occasions, for example, the day after Pearl Harbor, right after 9/11 or any such developments, he may **convene both Houses**. His recent Address to Congress after the Inauguration is one such example. If Congress is not generally "In Session," he can still convene them; and if they cannot agree on an adjournment date, he can adjourn Congress. He can **receive ambassadors** or heads of states as in case of the recent visit of the British Prime Minister Brown, the Palestinian President Abbas, or the Israeli Prime Minister Netanyahu, and he must **commission all officers of the United States**.

BARACK OBAMA
MASTER OF WASHINGTON DC

Beyond these, governmental power is classified in three areas as Executive, Legislative and Judicial. Bone in *American Government* (1977: 73) says: "There are six powers that can be classified in the Executive category. But it is worth noting that even in these the President shares authority with Congress on several important points. The President's Executive powers are those of appointment, removal, administrative supervision, law enforcement, formulation of military policy, and conduct of foreign relations."

Barack Obama's Washington, DC Photo 381. Plaque in honor of John Saul, Horticulturist.

FREDERICK MONDERSON

The appointment power of the President allows him to nominate judges to the nine-member Supreme Court, appoint untold numbers to the lower federal courts, Secretaries of the various departments, members of the White House Corps, and the various federal offices. With the power to appoint comes the power to remove and whenever, in the President's opinion, an individual has not performed at the best of his or her ability or is guilty of some infraction of the law, conflict of interest, or not on board with his agenda, that person can be removed from office. The President has the power of administrative supervision in that he requires reports from the various branches of his administration and the expectation is that their performance is optimal in keeping with his agenda. Federal law enforcement takes precedence over state and local police, even though the latter have a tendency to cooperate with federal authorities. Law enforcement comes under the office of the Attorney General, a position appointed by the President. As Commander-in-Chief the President is assisted by his generals in planning military preparedness and strategy, as well as waging war. While the Secretary of State heads the diplomatic corps and speaks for the President when conducting foreign relations, the President is ultimately responsible for conducting any relations with other nations.

Beyond the expressly stated powers granted the President, in the American political system there are many forms of powers that can be invoked as necessary. Some are stated and some are not. For example, Article I, Section 8, Sub-section 1-17 lists the powers granted Congress but the document also lists delegated, enumerated or listed, implied, reserved and much more. What is most significant, however, is the **Distribution of Powers**. In this regard, Plano and Greenberg in *The American Political Dictionary* (1989: 35) discusses: "An underlying principle of the American constitutional system designed to prevent tyranny by assigning powers to different governments and agencies and by checking the exercise of power. The distribution takes the following forms: (1) dividing power between national and state governments under a federal system; (2) separating power among the three major branches of the government – legislative, executive, and judicial – giving each branch a check upon the operations of the others; (3) selecting the personnel of the three branches by different procedures and electorates, assigning them different terms of office, and making them responsible to different pressures; (4) limiting all governments by specific constitutional restrictions."

The significance of this distribution of powers is further commented on: "Through a complex distribution of authority, the framers sought to prevent all governmental power from falling into the hands of any individual group. They feared majority tyranny as much as minority or individual tyranny. Hence, they provided for a wide distribution of authority, limited in scope, and designed to effect a balancing of interests. The distribution of powers has been modified by the expanding role

BARACK OBAMA
MASTER OF WASHINGTON DC

of the national government, the increasing influence of the President over legislation and foreign affairs, and the development of independent regulatory agencies that exercise some legislative and judicial power in their supervision of the economy."

Thus, the distribution of power gives rise to separation of powers, giving each branch of government specific powers, limiting their terms in office and allowing them to be part of the checks and balance system that, in a way, fragments power so that the same individuals do not make the law, enforce the law and interpret the law at the same time. Plano (189: 47) informs further: "The separation of lawmaking, law enforcement, and law interpretation is designed to prevent tyranny. It also serves to make the three branches responsible to different pressures. At the same time, the system frequently results in lack of unity between the legislative and executive branches, particularly when they are controlled by different parties. This fragmentation of power is a major factor in the operation of the American governmental system. The judiciary plays the critical role in maintaining the branches within their assigned powers."

To provide a more complete understanding of "powers" as defined in the American political system, the following terms and appropriate definitions are provided so the general readership may be appraised of some insights into governmental terminology.

Concurrent Powers as stated in the constitution are applied to the same powers being exercised by the federal and state governments. The power to tax, the power to borrow money, and the power to police, to maintain courts and to charter banks and local governments are examples of concurrent powers.

Delegated Powers or sometimes listed as enumerated powers, and it has been said, constitute nearly 90 percent of the powers granted to Congress. Article I, Section 8, Sub-section 1-17 are the "Delegated" or "Enumerated Powers" granted to Congress. These are as follows:

To lay and collect taxes, duties, imposts, and exercises, to pay the debts and provide for the common defense and general welfare of the United States; but all duties, imposts, and exercises shall be uniform throughout the United States;

To borrow money on the credit of the United States;

To regulate commerce with foreign nations, among the several states, and with the Indian tribes;

FREDERICK MONDERSON

To establish a uniform rule of naturalization, and uniform laws on the subject of bankruptcies throughout the United States;

To coin money, regulate the value thereof, and of foreign coin, and fix the standard of weights and measures;

To provide for the punishment of counterfeiting the securities and current coin of the United States;

To establish post offices and post roads;

To promote the progress of science and useful arts by securing for limited times to authors and inventors the exclusive right to their respective writings and discoveries;

To constitute tribunals inferior to the Supreme Court;

To define and punish piracies and felonies committed on the high seas and offenses against the laws of nations;

To declare war, [grant letters of marquee and reprisal] and make rules concerning captures on land and water;

To raise and support armies, but no appropriation of money to that use shall be for a longer term than two years;

To provide and maintain a navy;

To make rules for the government and regulation of the land and naval forces;

To provide for calling forth the militia to execute the laws of the Union, suppress insurrections, and repel invasions;

To provide for organizing, arming, and disciplining the militia, and for governing such part of them as may be employed in the service of the United States, reserving to the states, respectively, the appointment of the officers, and the authority of training the militia according to the discipline prescribed by Congress;

To exercise exclusive legislation in all cases whatsoever, over such district (not exceeding ten miles square) as may, by cession of particular states, and the acceptance of Congress, become the seat of government of the United States, and to exercise like authority over all places purchased by the consent of the legislature of the state in which the same shall be, for the erection of forts, magazines, arsenals, dock-yards, and other needful buildings; - and

BARACK OBAMA
MASTER OF WASHINGTON DC

Implied Powers: "The Elastic Clause." To make all laws which shall be necessary and proper for carrying into execution the foregoing powers, and all other powers vested by this Constitution in the government of the United States, or in any department of officer thereof.

Section 9 lists Powers Denied to the Federal Government. It:

May not interfere with the slave trade prior to 1808;

May not suspend the Writ of Habeas Corpus except in Emergency

May not enact a Bill of Attainder or an Ex Post Facto Law;

May not levy a direct tax except in proportion to population;

May not levy an export tax;

May not favor the ports of one state over those of another;

May not spend federal funds without Congressional approval and public accounting;

May not grant titles of nobility.

There are also powers denied the states as the unconditional denial of various powers; Conditional denial: May not levy import and export taxes without the consent of Congress and as a Conditional denial: the states may not prepare for and wage war (Except in emergency) without the consent of Congress.

Reserved Powers are reserved to the states or people and mentioned in the Tenth Amendment of 1791. It states: "The powers not delegated to the United States by the Constitution, nor prohibited by it to the states, are reserved to the states respectively, or to the people."

FREDERICK MONDERSON

Barack Obama's Washington, DC Photo 382. Soldiers' Memorial off from the White House area.

Exclusive Powers are powers specifically delineated to the national or state government. An example of an exclusive power is to conduct foreign affairs granted to the President as part of the national government. An exclusive power granted the state is the power to charter local governments, such as New York City. Keep in mind, the Constitution only provides for the national and state governments. Local governments such as the City of New York operate under a charter and can be terminated. However, since New York City is such a cultural, economic and demographic powerhouse, its termination is hardly likely.

War Powers – The Constitution grants the President War Powers to wage war in defense of the nation. Plano and Greenberg (1989: 521) describes War Powers as, those powers "granted to Congress to tax and spend for the common defense, to declare war and make rules concerning capture, to raise and support armies and provide a navy, to enact military law, and to oversee the state militias. Moreover, the elastic clause permits Congress to do whatever is necessary and proper in executing these powers. The President, as Commander in Chief, has the inherent power to do whatever is necessary to protect the nation, subject to judicial scrutiny. In times of crisis, Congress delegates legislative powers to the President as 'emergency powers.'" These authors commentary on the significance of War Powers notes: "Although defense and war powers are subject to constitutional limitations in the same way as other powers, they have been stretched to the limits during serious crises. Presidents Abraham Lincoln, Franklin Roosevelt and Harry

BARACK OBAMA
MASTER OF WASHINGTON DC

Truman regarded the war powers as a special and undefined category of powers that can be exercised whenever the security of the nation is threatened. Congress, the public, and the courts have generally accepted the primacy of the President's role and his exercise of vast powers during time of war. Under conditions of modern warfare, the war powers include control over the domestic economy as well as the military phases of the conflict."

Resulting Powers are powers derived from a number of powers and hence, they are "powers that result from a number of powers, rather than inferred from one of the delegated powers." Plano and Greenberg (1989: 46) says resulting powers are "an extension of the implied powers doctrine. They make possible an exercise of power that logically follows from a series of granted powers. For example, the United States Criminal Code provides that the violation of any national law is subject to punishment. The Constitution does not explicitly delegate this power, nor is it implied by any single grant of power. Rather it 'results' from the aggregate of power delegated to the national government."

Police Powers are described as the "authority to promote and safeguard the health, morals, safety, and welfare of the people." Plano and Greenberg (1989: 43) stated further: "The national government, exercising only delegating powers, does not possess a general police power. Many national laws enacted under the commerce and postal powers, such as those that prohibit shipment of impure drugs in interstate commerce or mailing of obscene literature, are, however, examples of what may be termed 'federal police power.' State laws enacted under the police power may legally invade national jurisdiction if such laws are pertinent to the health, safety, or welfare of the people of the state, such as a state law regulating grade crossings for interstate trains."

FREDERICK MONDERSON

Barack Obama's Washington, DC Photo 383. The United States Treasury.

Inherent Powers are also known as 'prerogative powers,' and "derives from the fact that the United States is a sovereign power among nations. The Supreme Court has pointed out that even if the Constitution made no mention of it, the national government could still, for example, make international agreements or acquire territory. Whether or not the President has inherent powers to meet emergencies in international affairs by virtue of his position as chief executive is a matter of dispute." Even further, the significance of inherent powers is given that: "Since the national government is one of delegated powers, justification for its actions must be found either directly or by implication from a specific grant of power. In the field of international affairs, however, the United States must be presumed to have the same power as any other nation in the world. Many presidents have taken unauthorized action to meet emergency situations, notably Abraham Lincoln during the Civil War. However, in 1952, during the Korean conflict, the Supreme Court ruled that the President could not seize private property (steel mills) without authorization from Congress."

Implied Powers refer to the authority, according to Plano and Greenberg (1989: 38) whereby it is "possessed by the national government by inference from those powers delegated to it in the Constitution. For example, the power to draft men into the armed forces may be deduced from the power delegated to raise armies and navies. The implied-power concept derives from the 'necessary and proper' clause in Article I, section 8, which empowers the national government to do all things necessary and proper to carry out its delegated powers."

BARACK OBAMA
MASTER OF WASHINGTON DC

When President Barack Obama assumed the Presidency on January 20, 2009, he set about to confront the many challenges he inherited and as such, began exercising the many powers granted or implied, by his position. At that time the nation was in one of its most serious economic downturns in history and only the powers available to the national government allowed the president, within less than six months in office, to be able to turn back the tide in all the significant areas of distress. President Obama has certainly demonstrated a unique ability to utilize the many powers granted by the American governmental system.

Barack Obama's Washington, DC Photo 383a. How picturesque that barriers become art.

FREDERICK MONDERSON

"What Washington needs is adult supervision." BARACK OBAMA, *fundraising letter, Oct. 2006*

55. THE IDIOCY OF ALAN KEYES
By

Dr. Fred Monderson

The world is principally peopled by two types of people of significance, winners and losers, for the most part. Not to discount the great multitude between who choose not to be bothered with the vicissitudes of either aspirations. They chose to remain outside the realms of either reality for many good reasons. While the laws of average dictates, all factors being considered, you win some and you lose some. Nonetheless, Alan Keyes, a Republican, seems to be perpetually enshrined in the loser's column but whether or not he relishes this designation he seems bent on perpetuating that record.

Let me take you back to the time of the Three Stooges! One episode featured a boxer, Gunboat Johnson, who had an impressive record of 50 fights with 49 losses and 1 drawn decision. After the draw, he spent six months in hospital recuperating. In so many ways, he mirrors the record of Alan Keyes, who when the Republicans seem to be saddled with a losing proposition, extricate this guy from the shelf and run him. I remember my deceased friend Sylvester Leaks in another context, had called this "running losers."

Now, according to CNN, July 17, Lou Dobbs, 7:00-8:00 pm, Mr. Keyes has joined forces with Orly Taitz to file a lawsuit to invalidate the Obama presidency because they believe the President is not a native born U.S citizen. These two are in association with a US Army Major who refuses Afghanistan deployment because in theirs and his mind, the President is not legitimately Commander-in-Chief and therefore cannot order him into a war zone. I think this group won the "Wing Nut Award" and whether they have chosen to accept is another matter!

Recently, my relative, a soldier in the US Army, was deployed to Iraq and he, in his infinite wisdom, could not envision such an addled egg idea. It also begs the question as to what the hundred-thousand-plus soldiers on the front lines in Iraq and Afghanistan are thinking about. Let us not forget the million plus members of the US Armed Forces including the Joint Chiefs who follow the command of President Obama. We could include all the security agencies, the cabinet, the

BARACK OBAMA
MASTER OF WASHINGTON DC

Supreme Court and you name it, all these entities that recognize Mr. Obama's legitimacy. Alan Keyes and his cohorts' actions are happening in an age when we are told of "post-racial America" and the need to end affirmative action. The sad part is, this tragedy has a black face on it.

Barack Obama's Washington, DC Photo 384. Street scene after the "Rally on the Mall."

I am reminded of an approach made to me back in the 1980s. In predominantly Democratic Brooklyn, an individual wanted to recruit me, a Democrat, to run as a Republican candidate in the 43rd AD or any adjoining Assembly Districts. I was told, "all you have to do is submit your name. There's lots o money to be made." My answer was, "I'm a Democrat and cannot be bought."

As I listened to the program that featured Alan Keyes, Orly Taitz, Errol Lewis and another, hosted by Kitty Pilgrim in place of Lou Dobbs, I was amazed how this issue of President Obama's birth has been examined *ad nausea* and Kitty, before she allowed any commentary quoted from four investigations made into President Obama's birthright. The interesting one was made by Hawaii's Republican Governor who pointed out she supported John McCain in the Presidential election, yet, authenticated Obama's birthright legitimacy!

The barraged unleashed by Kitty's guests included such terms as "Obama Deranged Syndrome" and that "World Net Daily" is running a "Scam" in their efforts to keep a false idea alive and raising money in the process. Another individual associated with this group "daily prays for the death of President Obama!" Alan Keyes should remember, "Birds of a feather flock together" and

FREDERICK MONDERSON

"show me your company and I'll tell who you are." Another term expressed for that group was "nuts." However, this is even more serious and Alan Keyes should be ashamed to be associated with this.

Everyone should be familiar with the stances Republicans have taken in opposition to every program the President has proposed, whether they are the objections to the Stimulus Plan; requests for money in support and deployment of forces to Iraq and Afghanistan; his Health Care Overhaul; and so many others. Yet, none of these Republican powerhouse politicians could contemplate and follow up such an elaborately far-out-of-this-world idea. I think, in Mr. Keyes' mind's eye, this idea would become truly legitimate when the Iranian President raises it as President Obama sits across him from at the negotiation table. While Mr. Obama may say, "Mr. Fox, I know how you got there," the Iranian would reply, "Mr. Keyes has questioned your birthright." Amen!

Nevertheless, imagine the thoughts of Speaker Nancy Pelosi and Senate leader Harry Reid, Democratic leaders in the House and Senate respectively, as they faced down Republican full-court presses with the possibility that their leader's credibility was questionable. They could not be as inordinately entrenched in their beliefs about the authenticity of the President's credibility and agenda and equally as obstinately opposed to idiocy of the likes of Alan Keyes' newest flavor.

Keyes is the perennial candidate, perennial loser and perennially cannot get elected dog catcher. Being consigned to political obscurity, like the living dead, he refuses to remain buried. One has to remember and ask, "What's the going price to embark on such a ridiculously futile venture to gain publicity for an individual and a cause more suited for the trash heap of history than the time, cost and effort as an asinine quest?"

BARACK OBAMA
MASTER OF WASHINGTON DC

"This notion that's peddled by the religious right - that they are oppressed is not true. Sometimes it's a cynical ploy to move their agenda ahead. The classic example being that somehow secularists are trying to eliminate Christmas, which strikes me as some kind of manufactured controversy." BARACK OBAMA, Street Prophets interview, Jul. 11, 2006

56. OBAMA'S STIMULUS AND DANCE OF LEGISLATION
By

Dr. Fred Monderson

Hypothetically speaking, as Senator Barack Obama winds-down his election campaign, his wonderfully organized and creative mindset not only focused on the dramatic requirements of the final full-court press to the tape recognizing the calamitous state of the economy, he began looking ahead with a stimulus strategy. Much of this was imbedded in his platform pledges and probably on election night perhaps after a two hour rest and self-congratulatory accolades, he began tinkering with the grand plan he envisioned for rescuing the economy based on the parameters he had already outlined.

With his major objective accomplished, President-Elect Obama next began more frequent consultation with the economic team he had been meeting with, along the campaign planning his economic strategy, framing the parameters of his rescue plan. Now, the "Shadow economic advisers" emerged into full-public recognition to support and give credence to Mr. Obama's strategy to deal with the full-blown and daily realization of the rapidly deteriorating American economy with rising unemployment, collapsing housing market, the Wall Street mess, world economic down turn, etc. Therefore, his economic agenda, spelled out in the stimulus package was now being flushed out by a team headed by Paul Volker, former head of the Federal Reserve System. Meanwhile, as Obama countdown to Inauguration and assuming the mantle of the Presidency, the economic quagmire worsened and elements of the critical public began clamoring for President-Elect Obama to step in and stem the bleeding economy suffering from higher job loss, more people filing for unemployment benefits, more foreclosures, turmoil on Wall Street, bank closures, suicides as the easiest way out, etc. In addition, trouble began to brew overseas and all Mr. Obama would utter: "There's only one president at a time."

FREDERICK MONDERSON

President Bush, on the other hand, now fully grasping the reality of his place in history, could only nod in appreciation that, at least Mr. Obama still afforded him the opportunity of gracefully exiting the stage he occupied over the last eight years. Therefore, and recognizing Obama was a class act, resolved to give unqualified support to the transition team of his successor to make it as smooth as possible, so number 44 would get a head start to clean-up the mess number 43 made as steward of the nation. Meanwhile, the sour grapes Republican Congressional delegation began closing ranks, planning to lower the boom on Obama when he comes around seeking bipartisanship "pushing his economic stimulus bill."

Barack Obama's Washington, DC Photo 385. Ionic column colonnade at the Department of the Treasury.

There are several types of Bills or laws presented to the House of Representatives or Senate for consideration and debate before it reaches the President's desk to sign it into law. There are public and private bills and these require the president's signature. Then again there are Joint Resolutions, Concurrent Resolutions and Resolutions that do not require the President's signature.

William A. McClenaghan's *American Government* describes a **Bill** as: "A proposed law; a public bill applies to the entire nation; a private bill applies only to certain people or places." A **Joint Resolution** is "A proposal for some action that has the force of law when passed; usually deals with special circumstances or temporary matter." A **Concurrent Resolution** is "A statement of position on an issue, adopted by the House and Senate acting jointly; does not have the force of law; does not require the President's signature." A **Resolution** is a

BARACK OBAMA
MASTER OF WASHINGTON DC

"measure dealing with some matter in one house; does not have the force of law; does not require the President's signature."

A money bill, such as the stimulus bill is a different matter. Accordingly, Article 1, Section 7 of the Constitution "All Bills for raising Revenue shall originate in the House of Representatives; but the Senate may propose or concur with amendments as on the bills."

The Constitution clearly states money bills can originate from the Executive Branch or the Legislature through the House of Representatives. At the time, no one fully realized the depth of the financial crisis facing the nation. That being so, President Obama came into office with his plan as the conceptual framework was envisioned by the economic minds he was able to muster during the transition period.

"Federal Stimulus Plan Information

Our country faces its most serious economic crisis since the Great Depression.

With a new government in office, several economic reforms have been put into action to help revitalize the economy. This Federal Stimulus Plan aims to:

Create new good jobs in America
Provide relief for struggling families
Increase assistance available to homeowners
Provide assistance for business owners
Increase funding for programs like **Government Grants** to help US citizens.

"Barack Obama upped the ante on his economic recovery package"

January 10, 2009

Next Steps For US Citizens

The Federal Stimulus Plan will provide relief for US citizens through a variety of programs. If you are a US citizen in financial distress or simply want to improve your financial situation, it is recommended you take the following three steps to help improve your financial situation:

Obtain a free credit report to better understand your financial situation

FREDERICK MONDERSON

Lower your interest payments and consolidate your debt

Refinance your mortgage to lower your payments and prevent foreclosure

Programs That Provide Immediate Help

As an alternative to tax cuts, the government is providing economic relief to US citizens as part of the Federal Stimulus plan. Government grants, debt consolidation, and housing assistance will all play a key role in the Stimulus Plan as a way to provide assistance to those in need. In addition, there are several other programs and services available to individuals that can help you.

Additional Programs: Government Grants

Demand will be high for these programs and many people have already applied. Although billions of dollars have been set aside for the Federal Stimulus Plan, the funds will only last for a limited period of time. If you are interested in applying for one of these programs, you should do so immediately before the funds are depleted.

Application kits have been assembled and contain additional information about how to apply. View the available programs to determine what funding is available to US citizens and to find out more about how to request assistance. Learn more about which programs are available to you and what types of funding you may qualify for."

BARACK OBAMA
MASTER OF WASHINGTON DC

Barack Obama's Washington, DC Photo 386. Regular building made of red stone.

"If the people cannot trust their government to do the job for which it exists - to protect them and to promote their common welfare - all else is lost." BARACK OBAMA, speech, Aug. 28, 2006

57. OBAMA, 'DOIN' TOO MUCH'
By

Dr. Fred Monderson

There is an old cliché, "Damn if you do, and Damn if you don't" and the attitude of this 'wide brush' painting has emerged as a consistent strategy critics of President Obama have employed to seedling his path with negativity as he wrestles with the myriad problems facing the nation. Claiming that Obama is 'Doin' too much,' his critics, principally Republicans, have tried to box him in by having to defend his good work, but this approach has not been effective because these adversaries have grossly underestimated their opponent. This is evident in the 'Thumpin' he administered his opponents in the recent Presidential election and

FREDERICK MONDERSON

the program he instituted to rescue the nation, from the quagmire 8 years of Republican Administration rule created.

Hitting the ground running, a number of President Bush Executive Orders were, with great speed, overturned. In his effort to reduce the nation's dependence on foreign sources of energy he encouraged the development of wind energy. He supported development of hybrid electric cars with advanced batteries, while insisting that carmakers reduce emissions and encouraged experimenting with clean coal energy. Staying busy, the President appointed a number of czars, such as urban, car and stimulus designed to keep track of how the region, industry or money is doing.

Underestimating the intellectual brilliance of Barack Obama and the quintessence of "team Obama," caused the Republicans the election. Even more important, as the President ignores his critics, he goes about pursuing his program underscoring his success and the failure of his opponents' strategy; as reflected in the changing realities and the American people's positive assessment of Obama and negative assessment of the Republican opposition.

The wonderful thing about President Barack Obama is that while he recognized his adversaries and their criticisms, he ignores them and goes about his business pulling new plans and ideas out of his symbolic "hat." Important that, ignoring the opposition is a very potent exhilir in dealing with all types, particularly problem people. There is an interesting story of "ignoring" told about His Excellency Haile Selassie, Emperor of Ethiopia, who came to America to attend some important state function in the 1950s, with the British Queen Elizabeth in attendance. In as much as he had been on the throne longer than the Queen, protocol dictated during the preliminary introduction into the social setting, Haile Selassie preceded the Queen. Naturally, within the social racial constraints of pre-civil rights movement American society, this protocol arrangement played well in the black community.

BARACK OBAMA
MASTER OF WASHINGTON DC

Barack Obama's Washington, DC Photo 387. Two Ionic columns adorn the PNC Bank, part of Bank of America.

In follow up to the Emperor's visit, a black newspaper sent an African-American reporter to Ethiopia to interview the king. Upon arrival at the Audience Hall, he thought he saw a regal figure sitting on an elevated throne at the rear of a very large room. On entering he was informed of protocol for proceeding he was to stop, kneel at each of three cushions placed one before the other, as he got closer to the throne area. In his eagerness and perhaps American arrogance, he simply kicked these aside and approached the king. There was still some distance between him and the throne, but there was a figure seated there. Yet, as the reporter tried to speak to the person, he got no response. Puzzled, he was not sure if it was a statue or a real person because he could see no movement of the seemingly cold figure. The next day there was a reception at the palace and the reporter, bent on getting his story, was there, so he snaked his way towards the monarch and forcefully reached to touch Selassie, only to realize he was entangled with a real person who seemed as cold as a statue. Meanwhile, the king seemed to be looking for help from his assistants, as if to say, "Get this clown off of me." Moral, he got the Selassie stare, cold shoulder and silent treatment!

Who knows if Barack Obama ever heard of this incident but when it comes to ignoring his critics and opponents, he does a very good imitation of Emperor Selassie as he Obama goes about his work of thinking, proposing and following through on programs and plans to carry out his mission.

Recently I met an elder, Mr. McPherson and asked him, "Sir, what do you think of this Obama thing?" He replied, "The President is doing a very good job. He doesn't want to get in a direct confrontation. They are criticizing him at every turn but he is not talking, ignoring them, just going about his business." Such an attitude, demeanor, is indicative of a very confident man, but also one who

FREDERICK MONDERSON

understands the gravity of the task before him. I am reminded of something General George Patton said sometime in 1944, before the invasion of Normandy. When many officers at a meeting seemed too self assured and were underestimating the Germans, General Patton cautioned that despite what appeared an impending victory, "We could still lose the war!" This is the same way with President Obama, who feels he has no time for idle chatter and counter-productive speculation and negative vibes. He realizes "We're not out of the woods as yet." Despite the positive showing of the economy, Wall Street rebounding, housing starts despite the foreclosure situation, efforts to get stimulus shovel ready projects on the way, plans to assist the auto industry, get the financial system past the bank stress test and get credit flowing, and all the rapid infusions of capital into the financial system that may not give the expected returns; still, there is much more work that would need to be done. Therefore, Obama is keeping his pedal to the metal.

Perhaps the thing that sets the Obama Administration apart from that of the Republicans in Congress and their allies in the print and electronic media is the fact he is probably smarter than them and this may be the reason he defeated them in the last election. In addition, because he is serious and deeply concerned about the American condition and takes his job seriously, he is not about letting up. This attitude underscores the nature of the man, his brilliance and perhaps with a view to the future, that is, his re-election and how history will record his efforts at this critical time in American history. Good luck Barack, you're not doing too much, perhaps only you can see there needs to be more done. After all, many still do not see the gravity of the situation you inherited.

Barack Obama's Washington, DC 388. Twelve Ionic columns on an elevated ledge.

BARACK OBAMA
MASTER OF WASHINGTON DC

"If we want this country to succeed in the 21st century, we've got to lay a new foundation for lasting prosperity." BARACK OBAMA, town hall meeting, Aug. 15, 2009

58. OBAMA AND COMPROMISE
By

Dr. Fred Monderson

Throughout the election campaign, among Senator Obama's strong suits was the ability to build consensus and with this compromise could be considered a twin attribute. Upon assuming the Presidency, he set about proposing and pushing legislation in Congress and this involved compromise in all fights. For example, within a relatively short time after his inauguration President Obama submitted an 800 Billion plus spending bill to Congress. With the democratic majority in the House of Representatives the measure was generally passed without one Republican vote. In the Senate, on the other hand, with some compromise three Republicans crossed the aisle to join the Democrats and passed a bill of a lesser sum of 785 Billion. In many other situations in his relation with Congress, President Obama compromised to get his way. For instance, as the Chief Legislator, the President would submit the broad framework of a piece of legislation and ask Congress to flush it out with the necessary compromises to create a bill he could sign when it reaches his desk.

All this notwithstanding, the notion of compromise has had a tremendous history in American politics, stemming from the early days of the Republic; and it has remained a viable alternative to grid-lock on Capitol Hill. The **Great Compromise** of the Constitutional Convention allowed for the creation of the three branches of government with the small and big states feeling there was balance in the arrangement of division of power in both houses. Notwithstanding, technically, the year 1787 has had more significant historical compromises than any other year in American history and government, ever.

The first significant **Compromise in 1787** had to do with the slave trade. In England, focus on abolition of the trade became magnified in the Somerset Case pursued by Granville Sharpe in 1772 in which Chief Justice Mansfield finally ruled in the interest of "positive law" that "English soil is too sacred to permit slavery." This came in response to British plantation owners practice of taking their slaves from the West Indies back to England to live more socially elevated in their homeland. By 1778, thanks to the work of abolitionists Clarkson, Buxton, Sharpe and others Parliament was petitioned through resolutions to outlaw the slave trade. As the new American nation began wrestling with its political dynamics in formulating the United States Constitution, the foreign activism spread to America and the slave trade became a national issue.

Jack C. Plano and Milton Greenberg's *The American Political Dictionary* New York: Holt, Rinehart, and Winston, Inc., (1962) (1989: 29) offers commentary on the commerce and slave trade compromise generally considered: "An agreement reached at the Constitutional Convention of 1787, giving the national government power to regulate foreign commerce, requiring the consent of two-thirds of the Senate to treaties, and prohibiting the national government from taxing exports or interfering with the slave trade until 1808." The significance of this is stated as: "A substantial number of people opposed ratification, but strong opposition to the Constitution rapidly dwindled after its adoption. The Anti-Federalist group, however, became the supporters of Thomas Jefferson, whose views on the nature of the Union, as distinguished from those of Alexander Hamilton and other Federalists, continue to be influential and controversial in American politics today. The Anti-federalists were also known as "Democratic Republicans" and, in time, evolved into the Democratic Party."

The **Three-Fifths Compromise** gave the South the right to count their slaves in the population calibration to determine representation in congress. It meant in essence, five blacks would be counted for 3 whites. Davidson and Batchelor (1991: 204) explained how this compromise was worked out as the delegates debated: "They agreed that three fifths of the slaves in any state would be counted. In other words, if a state had 5,000 slaves, 3,000 of them would be included in the state's population count." Some critics have argued, after having reversed the process of evolution in the institution of slavery, Blacks were now elevated to becoming "three-fifths of men." Some have further argued, despite progress across the board made over the last two centuries, some whites still regard Blacks in the same manner. Some ideas never die.

The **Compromise of 1820** arose during the height of debates on admitting new states in territory west of the Mississippi River. The previous year, 1819, there were 11 free and 11 slave states. Thus, the question of maintaining balance between Slave States and Free States or north and south states, all having to do with representation in Congress, had taken on great significance. As Missouri applied for admission to the Union, the question that became important was whether it would "come in" as a Slave State. In that case, the south would have a majority in the Senate. James West Davidson and John E. Batchelor in *The American Nation* New Jersey: Prentice Hall, (1986) (1991: 373) explained events

BARACK OBAMA
MASTER OF WASHINGTON DC

as they unfolded: "Senator Henry Clay proposed a plan that both the North and South accepted. During the debate over Missouri, Maine applied to become a state. Clay called for admitting Missouri as a slave state and Maine as a free state. Clay's plan was known as the Missouri Compromise. It kept the number of slave and free states equal. As part of the Missouri compromise, Congress drew a line across the southern border of Missouri at latitude 36 degrees 30 inches North. Slavery was permitted in the Louisiana Purchase south of that line. But it was banned north of the line. Missouri was the only exception."

As **Manifest Destiny,** (The destiny of the white man to capture and hold North America) and industrialization fueled economic changes in the nation, drums of war began beating as slavery loomed even greater in America's history. As such, men of great talent wrestled with the nation's direction as a divided country. Names as Henry Clay, Daniel Webster, Stephen Douglas, and John C. Calhoun began to play even greater roles in unfolding events.

The Compromise of 1850 came to dominate events at mid-century. Davidson and Batchelor (1991: 377) described provisions of the new compromise. "The Compromise of 1850 had four main parts. First, California was admitted to the Union as a free state. Second, the rest of the Mexican Cession was divided into New Mexico and Utah territories. In each territory, voters would decide the slavery question according to the idea of popular sovereignty. Third, the slave trade was banned in Washington, D.C. However, congress declared that it had no right to ban the slave trade between slave states. Fourth, a strict fugitive slave law was passed." The Fugitive Slave law allowed slave catchers to kidnap and return runaways and this did not go well with Blacks! Many viewed this as "Open Season" on "Free" and Runaway enslaved Blacks."

The **Compromise of 1877** was a turning point in Reconstruction after the devastation of the Civil War. The election of 1876 was in dispute and a Compromise vote allowed Rutherford Hayes to become president because he had privately promised to end Reconstruction that was changing the South, giving Blacks a more prominent role in voting and electing representatives who had their interests in mind. As the South regained supremacy, terror became the order of the day. Nevertheless, in the Dance of Legislation, Compromise has come to play an important role to get any work done in the Congress. Given the cards he must play, President Obama is turning out to be a master of compromise. In the December 2010 extension of the Bush Tax Cuts he compromised and in the now infamous Debt Ceiling" issue he compromised. Yet, Speaker Boehner boasted "I got 98 percent of what I wanted." Days later Wall Street dropped 500 points and Standard and Poors downgraded American bond ratings as "Mr. Boehner and his group laughed all the way to the bank!"

FREDERICK MONDERSON

"Americans ... still believe in an America where anything's possible -- they just don't think their leaders do." BARACK OBAMA, *fundraising letter, Sep. 1, 2006*

59. PRESIDENT OBAMA AND AFFIRMATIVE ACTION
By

Dr. Fred Monderson

President Barack Obama faces the challenge posed by the need for Affirmative Action in an age when its critics argue 'America has elected an African American President and hence in a post-racial society there is no need for Affirmative Action. However, such a position is highly debatable, for many people use the spurious argument that African Americans are the sole beneficiaries of Affirmative Action and in their circular argument that brings us back to the election of President Obama so they believe there is no longer such a need. Yet, Affirmative Action benefits, besides African Americans, women, firefighters, physically challenged individuals, and even veterans. Therefore, aiming at the African American group in a pernicious assault, really affects a greater population. Even more important, the group singled out, despite what is said is in greater need of Affirmative Action today given Blacks are the last hired and first fired; their pay grades or scale is less than that of whites; their rates of unemployment, especially among the young, are higher than those of whites; their color is a prime element for suspicious actions of racial profiling, questionable character and abilities; bank 'red-lining;' housing discrimination; victims of police brutality and random violence; and prolific candidates for the Prison Industrial Complex; and these do not exhaust potential victimization methods African-Americans are subjects of. To fully understand the dynamics of the situation facing President Obama one should be acquainted with Affirmative Action's meaning, origins and relevance.

Jack C. Plano and Milton Greenberg in *The American Political Dictionary*, New York: Holt, Rinehart and Winston, Inc., (1989: 260-261) defines Affirmative Action as: "A plan or program to remedy the effects of past discrimination in

BARACK OBAMA
MASTER OF WASHINGTON DC

employment, education, or other activity and to prevent the recurrence. Various federal and state statutes require affirmative action to redress past discrimination against or promote the employment of racial or religious minorities, women, handicapped workers, disabled veterans, veterans of the Vietnam era, and to some extent, the aged. Affirmative action usually involves a work-force utilization analysis, the establishment of goals and timetables to increase use of underrepresented classes of persons, explanation of methods to be used to eliminate discrimination, and establishment of administrative responsibility to implement the program. Good faith and a positive effort to remedy past discrimination must also be shown. Affirmative action is to be distinguished from antidiscrimination or equal opportunity laws, which forbid unequal treatment rather than requiring positive corrective measures. In 1978, the Supreme Court held that affirmative action programs are valid, but that explicit racial quotas are prohibited."

Barack Obama's Washington, DC Photo 389. The US Treasury.

Plano and Greenberg (1989: 273-274) again equates **Equal Rights with Affirmative Action** in describing it as: "The movement to equalize the rights of men and women. Traditionally in American law, women have not enjoyed the same rights as men, and this has manifested itself in many areas of American life, including property rights, education, and employment opportunities. State laws vary widely, although many are protective of women rather than directly discriminatory. Women's suffrage led to a gradual narrowing of legal differences, but with increasing intensity since the 1960s, an extensive body of new laws and

FREDERICK MONDERSON

administrative regulations, as well as court decisions, has provided protection against sex discrimination. In March 1972, Congress proposed to the states a constitutional amendment that provided that 'equality of rights under the law shall not be denied or abridged by the United States or any state on account of sex.' The seven-year time limit for ratification expired in March 1979 and Congress, in an unprecedented move, extended the deadline to June 1982. Still, the proposal failed to receive the thirty-eight state legislative approvals necessary for ratification."

Affirmative Action is also equal to the notion of "Comparable Worth" and it certainly benefitted the Women's Liberation Movement. Plano and Greenberg sees the significance of Equal Rights in that: "The concept of equal rights has had a dramatic impact upon American life, equal to, if not greater than, the impact of changing race relations. Many constitutional authorities believe that changes already brought about in behalf of women's rights as well as liberal application of equal protection of the law concepts diminish the need for an equal rights amendment. Others note that an amendment will give rise to a host of constitutional problems relating to the traditional roles of men and women. The equal rights movement achieved two major victories in the 1960s – the passage of the Equal Pay Act of 1963, which requires equal pay for men and women doing similar work, and the Civil Rights Act of 1964, which forbids discrimination against women in hiring and other personnel policies. An end to sex discrimination in education was ordered by Congress in 1972 and the Equal Credit Opportunity Act was adopted in 1974. A 1978 enactment prohibits discrimination against pregnant women in any area of employment. Pension rights of widowed homemakers, and of working mothers who temporarily leave jobs to raise families, were put under protection in 1984. In 1986, the Supreme Court declared sexual harassment to be unlawful sexual discrimination under the Civil Rights Act of 1964."

To this day the nation is struggling with the merits and need for Affirmative Action in a "Post-Racial America." Evidence of how President Obama has been treated in and out of Congress certainly indicates we're not "out of the woods" in a "Post-Racial America" and further underscores the need for Affirmative Action and Equal Rights.

BARACK OBAMA
MASTER OF WASHINGTON DC

Barack Obama's Washington, DC Photo 390. Monument in the park.

Barack Obama's Washington, DC Photo 391. Plaque indicating the US Department of the Treasury has been designated a Registered National Historic Landmark.

FREDERICK MONDERSON

"America is a land of big dreamers and big hopes. It is this hope that has sustained us through revolution and civil war, depression and world war, a struggle for civil and social rights and the brink of nuclear crisis. And it is because our dreamers dreamed that we have emerged from each challenge more united, more prosperous, and more admired than before." BARACK OBAMA, speech, Jun. 4, 2005

60. PRESIDENT OBAMA AND WAR POWERS

By

Dr. Fred Monderson

Throughout its history America has fought many wars from the colonial conflict knows as the French and Indian, the Revolutionary War for Independence to the current wars in Iraq and Afghanistan that President Barack Obama has inherited. Only Iraq and Afghanistan and Viet Nam have lasted long enough (excepting World War II) to involve more than one President to be commander. Franklin D. Roosevelt's lengthy tenure covered World War II and he died in 1945 to be succeeded by Harry Truman at the war's end. Viet Nam, on the other hand following the French defeat at Dien Bien Phu in 1954, first involved President Dwight Eisenhower in the 1950s, then John F. Kennedy, his successor Lyndon B. Johnson, then Richard M. Nixon and his successor Gerald Ford who saw America's involvement in Viet Nam end in 1975. Afghanistan and Iraq were begun by President George Bush (No. 43) and inherited by Barack Obama (No. 44). In times of war the President's powers are tremendously expanded because the lives of Americans are placed in danger and as Commander-in-Chief, he holds some responsibility for the safety of all Americans, whether morally or otherwise.

Inasmuch as the Constitution last determined the President is solely responsible for foreign policy matters and the Supreme Court has reinforced this legality; up until Viet Nam, the Commander-in-Chief was the principal force behind deployment of troops abroad and waging war. The War Powers resolution has sought to curb this power of the President by establishing guidelines on how he could wage war.

However, the Constitution specifically gives Congress the powers to declare war and establish protocols though day-to-day waging of conflict is the President's. Article I, Section 8, Sub-sections 11-16 of the Constitution provides guidelines for

BARACK OBAMA
MASTER OF WASHINGTON DC

Congressional authority in this matter. Congress has the power: "To declare war, grant letters of marquee and reprisal, and make rules concerning capture on land and water; to raise and support armies, but no appropriation of money to that use shall be a longer term than two years; to provide and maintain a navy; to make rules for the government and regulation of the land and naval forces; to provide for calling forth the militia to execute the laws of the Union, suppress insurrections, and repel invasions; to provide for organizing, arming, and disciplining the militia, and for governing such part of them as may be employed in the service of the United States, reserving to the States respectively, the appointment of the officers, and the authority of training the militia according to the discipline prescribed by Congress."

Plano and Greenberg (1989: 521) define War Powers as: "Although defense and war powers are subject to constitutional limitations in the same way as other powers, they have been stretched to their limits during serious crises. Presidents Abraham Lincoln, Franklin Roosevelt, and Harry Truman regarded the war powers as a special and undefined category of powers that can be exercised whenever the security of the nation is threatened. Congress, the public, and the courts have generally accepted the primacy of the President's role and his exercise of vast powers during time of war. Under conditions of modern warfare, the war powers include control over the domestic economy as well as the military phases of the conflict."

Congressional authorization was not applied to the first two conflicts, the French and Indian Wars (1756-1763) and the Revolutionary War (1776-1783). The French and Indian Wars were waged under colonial administration. Irving L. Gordon in *American Studies: A Conceptual Approach* New York: AMSCO School Publications, Inc., (1975) (1980: 67) explained the change from initial friendliness to subsequent hostilities between the white settlers and (Indians) Native Americans. He states: "In notable cases, the Indians showed friendship to the first white settlers. In Virginia, Massachusetts, and New York, the Indians provided the settlers with food and helped them survive the early difficult years. In Pennsylvania the Indians signed a treaty with William Penn who, although he held a land grant from the British Crown, insisted that the Indians be paid for their lands. With time, European settlers became more numerous; they began to cheat and mistreat the Indians and to pressure them for additional lands. In Massachusetts the preacher and social reformer Roger Williams condemned colonial seizures of land without paying the Indians and insisted that the Indians, not the British Crown, were the rightful owners. Along the North Atlantic Coast, settlers and Indians fought each other in numerous 'Indian Wars' in which both sides committed atrocities and brutalities. The settlers, sometimes aided by Friendly Indians, proved victorious. They decimated the hostile Indians and drove out the remnants, usually westward toward and beyond the Appalachian Mountains."

FREDERICK MONDERSON

Requirements made on the colonists by British authorities led to events that precipitated the Revolutionary War for Independence. Events such as the Proclamation of 1763 which reserved lands west of the Appalachians for Native Americans, prohibiting settlements there and insisting settlers in these lands remove and this began an activism that ultimately led to the Declaration of Independence (1776) and Revolutionary War (1776-1783), at the end of which the new nation was born. The governing council that prosecuted the war elected General George Washington, of **Fort Necessity** fame, who through trial and error and setback and success, was able to defeat the British and assure the new nation's republic beginnings. A body of wise men crafted the United States Constitution that gave Congress and the President Powers to protect the nation from threats of a military nature.

The next significant military engagement was the War of 1812 waged against the British whose navy harassed American maritime vessels at sea, boarding these vessels and "impressing" Americans into British naval service. President Sam Adams, it is thought, badly managed this engagement, that at conclusion of hostilities the British got the better hand. All except the "Battle of New Orleans" in 1815 where General Andrew Jackson administered a resounding defeat on British forces, unknowingly, days after the armistice had been signed. This was the only honorable outcome of the war reflecting favorably on the American psyche.

In an age when America was in the throes of internal improvements, African American struggles for freedom, reform movements, southern sectional rebellion under threats of Nullification and abolitionism, Manifest Destiny pronouncements pushed American expansion westward coming into conflict with Native Americans out west and Mexicans resulting in the Texas revolt in 1836. A decade later in 1845 Texas was admitted to the Union and this generally led to war with Mexico. These were events that the Constitution did not make provisions for but the philosophy of expansionism drew America into the conflict that ensued and as Irving L. Gordon (1980: 76-77) explained: "The admission of Texas was resented by Mexico and helped bring about the Mexican War. The United States was victorious and in 1848 acquired California and the American Southwest – together called the Mexican Cession. In 1853 the United States purchased from Mexico a small strip of land, now part of southern New Mexico and southern Arizona. This strip of land, containing a railroad pass through the mountains to California, was known as the Gadsen Purchase."

Following the Lincoln-Douglas Debates culminating in the Election of 1860 that Abraham Lincoln won, Southern states withdrew from the Union. The South considered Lincoln hostile to the institution of slavery and South Carolina having challenged the national government as early as 1832 in the Nullification movement, issued an Ordinance of Secession dissolving the bonds of the Union.

BARACK OBAMA
MASTER OF WASHINGTON DC

Six other nations joined this rebel state and upon outbreak of hostilities four other southern states joined in rebellion. Irving Gordon (1980: 298) commenting on **Causes of the Civil War** noted: "historians have long disputed regarding the causes – especially the primary cause – of the Civil War. Some have insisted that the primary cause was slavery as a moral issue. Others have focused attention elsewhere: (a) on the Constitutional issue – do states have the right to secede or are we one nation indivisible, (b) on political developments – the South's realization that eventually the North and Western support would secure control of the central government, (c) on fanaticism by extremists of both sides and on blundering leadership, (d) on differences in civilization between a static South dominated by a planter aristocracy and a dynamic North reflecting democratic values, and (e) on economic differences between the South and North."

With the fate of the nation hanging in the balance Abraham Lincoln emerged as the principal figure in the Civil War and his generals were fully behind him.

The further significant military engagement was the War with Spain called the Spanish American War of 1898. Historians generally seek causes to all wars and in an age when the Industrial Revolution was sweeping America; the close of the frontier with western land now fully populated; and American Nationalism, these developments pushed the nation to further expansion and creation of an empire beyond its borders. This outward interest led to war with Spain as reflected in a number of developments characterized as humanism, economic interests and yellow journalism as well as the skinning of the US Ship Maine.

While the **fundamental causes of World War I**, as a result in competition in the colonial areas by European powers, were listed as nationalism, imperialism, militarism and international anarchy as a result of the assassination of the archduke in Sarajevo, America did not enter the war until 1917 when these shores were actually threatened by German American intentions. In fact, Irving L. Gordon in *American Studies* gave as reasons why America entered World War I as follows: (1) Unrestricted Submarine warfare by Germany (sinking of the Lusitania in 1915; the Sussex pledge; further unrestricted submarine warfare); (2) Allied Propaganda; (3) Hostility towards Germany; (4) American Economic Interests; (5) American Idealism; and (6) American Security.

After World War I, in another two decades World War II exploded and again America was forced to enter in 1941 after Japan attacked the American base in the state of Hawaii at Pearl Harbor. However, by this time the war in Europe had been in effect from as early as 1939, though the climate of aggression could be traced even as far back as time of the Stimson Doctrine in 1931. Perhaps the same causes of World War I were responsible for World war II such as totalitarianism, militarism, nationalism, and imperialism as well as subsidiary causes as the failure of appeasement, lack of collective security and a stubborn American neutrality as it struggled with the problems of the Great Depression.

Ever since World War II communism has played a central position in American wartime strategy and the accumulated approaches have shaped modern tactics aided by development of American superiority in military technology that has given this nation in warfare.

Viet Nam certainly shaped Congress' role in holding the President responsible for waging war or simply deploying American forces into any theater of operation. Such "limitations" were bequeathed President Obama as he inherited wars in Iraq and Afghanistan, the war on terrorism as well as the challenges of Somali pirates and even deployment in Libya and the more sophisticated responses to events in Somalia and to Al Qaeda in the Arabian Peninsula. Nevertheless, as evidenced by his independent deployment of forces to Libya after successfully pursuing Osama bin Laden, President Obama has clearly demonstrated he has the right advisors and as Commander-in-Chief has a thorough grasp of military events and is waging war as a true commander.

Barack Obama's Washington, DC Photo 391a. Painting of the entrance to the Union Station with "Old Glory" flying proudly to the left.

BARACK OBAMA
MASTER OF WASHINGTON DC

"The success of our economy has always depended not just on the size of our gross domestic product, but on the reach of our prosperity, on the ability to extend opportunity to every willing heart -- not out of charity, but because it is the surest route to our common good." BARACK OBAMA, Inaugural Address, Jan. 20. 2009

61. MAN OF STEELE OR RUST?
By

Dr. Fred Monderson

Michael Steele came into leadership of the Republican Party owing to the unintentional "affirmative action" manifested as a result of Barack Obama's ascendency to the US Presidency. He was probably the only one who did not discern the circumstances of his *Fortuna*! Even political novices were aware his election, in later rounds to elect a leader of the Republican Party, was to place him as a "spook who sat by the Republican door." Equally, despite his new role, his influence was probably not intended to be very effective in the deepest echelons of the inner sanctum of Republicandom. His job, stated or unstated, known or unknown to him, was to lead the "pack attack" to derail the "Obama Express." What other conceived purpose such a timely elevation could be attributable to, seemingly, than to set one black man against the other! Unfortunately, trusting soul that he wanted to be, Mr. Steele probably never took the time to fully assess his new found fortune and what "selling one's soul to the devil" really entails, was a reality easily discernible to thinking individuals. The shades of one of Malcolm's dictums apply. You guess which one!

Let's face it, Barack Obama' election victory was a result of tremendous faith in his beliefs and capabilities, extraordinary coordination, exemplary old-fashioned politicking and unending hard work that appealed to a broad mass of people, particularly the young, who were yearning for change after Republicans had run the American economy and overall national well-being into a ditch. Or, should I say Bush!

Mr. Steel, not an overwhelming favorite of the caucus by any means, was chosen, seemingly, by default from a mediocre field after several rounds of voting. Some credit Mr. Steele's victory to that old-fashioned American panacea, the compromise! Nevertheless, his election as Chairman of the Republican Party was hailed as another significant step forward for Republicans and America. Many hailed racial and social progress in America having a black president and leader of the Democratic Party and another black, Michael Steele, Chairman of the Republican Party. Many heralded post-racial change in America. Then both men

FREDERICK MONDERSON

set out to work in their respective areas of responsibility. Barack Obama, as President of the United States set out to rescue, restructure and rebuilt his nation's financial and health care systems, its housing industry and infrastructure, stem the tide of unemployment and hopefully create new jobs, and even repair the world's perception of its image of America. Michael Steele, as the new kid on the block, set about riding two tigers. First, caught in the euphoria of seeing a black man now leading the Republican Party and recognizing Blacks were at the core of Obama's support, the new chairman set out to "Engage the Black Community," skepticism of some early observers notwithstanding. Second, Mr. Steel found himself in the forefront of a movement, who, under cloud of American patriotism, were subscribing to more sinister intents.

Honestly, no one fully realized the chasm of the ditch the Republicans had "slid" the country into; and naturally Obama suffered some setbacks in his desired goals of moving his nation forward. Meanwhile, those who created the problems, masquerading as patriots cheered at the "President's misfortunes" stemming from Republican "slash and burn" positions of "No" as he valiantly fought as a real patriot.

In his constitutional obligation as Chief Legislator, Mr. Obama encountered the most vitriolic obstructionist responses in tackling the tough issues now confronting the nation. Relationship responsibility is such that the captain is held accountable for everything that occurs on his ship, on his watch, and this is the standard so many held Mr. Obama to. Unfortunately, Mr. Steele's Republican Party had taken a non-cooperative not even critical support attitude towards the new President, earning the title "Party of No!" Every measure, every proposal, every law, practically every appointment the president proposed was met with a negative response. But, the nature of politics is such opposition is expected, even welcomed. However, this time, the movement's seeming intent had taken on a different tone. It was more caustic, sinister, albeit, some saw it as racist!

Tracing the opposition to Mr. Obama's candidacy for President, it was easily apparent; the audacity of a black man running for President of the United States of America was not well received by some elements, despite broad support across a wide spectrum. The racial, both under and over, tones were very apparent. To recall, as a candidate for president, Barack Obama was accused of being a socialist; inexperienced; a Muslim; unpatriotic; "not like us;" "too black" and "not black enough;" "palling around with terrorists;" a non-citizen and therefore ineligible to hold the office. Republicans have an uncanny way of playing the race card. Some may even recall the sign, when he ran for mayor, "Rudy G. fights Racism," but all that was to no effect as Rudy Giuliani turned out to be the most polarizing Chief Executive in New York City's history.

Alan Keyes, that perennial loser, led the charge even after the election, to challenge the President's birth certificate's authenticity. In keeping with one of

BARACK OBAMA
MASTER OF WASHINGTON DC

Malcolm X's assiduous insights, Alan Keyes probably said, "Bosses, I will bring that black man down from the high offices." Perhaps he was recruited. Then again, one can believe Republicans know how to pick winners! They certainly know how to pick losers! Of course, Mr. Keyes lost again when the courts ruled Mr. Obama was a citizen. Old tigers never lose their stripes and CNN's AC 360 recently interviewed a Texas state legislator, Leo Berman, who is "reinventing the Birthers' wheel," challenging Mr. Obama's citizenship. Together with a state legislator from Arizona, they are even proposing a new law to this effect designed to keep Barack Obama off their state's Presidential Primary in 2012. We know Texas knows how to choose winners but how did this fellow manage to "slip in." Arizona on the other hand, is home state of the minister who prayed for Obama's death and the black protester with guns!

This assault and all such on Black Lawmakers by Republicans and their allies similarly fall within the purview of Mr. Michael Steele as their leader. However, notwithstanding Mr. Steele being in charge, the "Republican coalition" seemed fueled by racial animosity as it attacked Mr. Obama and his policies under the guise of "tea party" shenanigans. Civil protest is in keeping with the American way but overboard caricature of Mr. Obama, many have argued, "crossed the line." Not unlike a Rorsarch blot, many saw racial animosity in the behavior of opposition to Mr. Obama; unfortunately in alliance with Mr. Steele's party's grand scheme to "Stop Obama" and create his "Waterloo." In the reaction to the French Revolution in the period 1791-1793, the Englishman Edmund Burke, in his *Reflections on the Revolution in France*, wrote, "The only thing necessary for evil to triumph, is for good men to say nothing." In the ensuing mayhem, Mr. Steele remained silent! So too did the higher echelon of Republican leadership. Are these good men?

Despite overwhelming evidence Mr. Obama was a lawful citizen and eligible to be President, the "Birthers," unintentional allies of the Republicans, kept up a steady drum roll that he held the office illegally. What is interesting, these nefarious individuals, who seems to have an extra-political agenda, are not only disrespecting Mr. Obama, the Presidency of the United States but also making the world wonder about American stupidity. Even more important, such behaviors intending to strike at Mr. Obama actually demeans the practitioners who in turn are demeaning the Office of the Presidency of the United States of America and the world watches and wonders about those ringmasters whose circus activities are laughable.

We know of DeMint's "Waterloo" and Sarah Palin's "Let's take back our America" and President Obama "is not like us." Even Mitch McConnell publicly stated his goal is to make Obama a "one term President." So much so, one English commentator on Fareed Zakaria's Global Public Square offered "Mr. Michael Steele and Sarah Palin should be careful of what they pray for." He seemed to imply the "Tea party" "cart had gotten ahead of Mr. Steele's horse;" its "tail was

FREDERICK MONDERSON

wagging his dog!" Nonetheless there has been no condemnation of "Birthers" actions, no call to publically denounce them as being "un-American!" One has to wonder, are they Republican operatives, paid or otherwise? Meanwhile, Obama continued working to change America's perception abroad, enacting health care reform, working to fix the financial system, taking on Wall Street, stopping the unemployment slide and creating new jobs, offering scientific incentives for clean energy innovations as well as developing methodologies and strategies designed to improve and advance the educational standards of the nation.

Just as Mr. Obama faced an uphill task to repair American state of affairs, Mr. Steele had somewhat similar task for the nation had grown dissatisfied with the Republicans. His party had lost significantly at the 2008 polls with Democrats coming into control of both houses and the presidency. About at his task of rebuilding the Republican Party, fund raising, encouraging and fielding new candidates while just saying "No," Mr. Steele very early encountered criticisms that he was more interested in self-aggrandizement, was accused of financial mismanagement and frequent verbal gaffes, as their "cart began running ahead of his horse." Still, be bore down and with chaotic conditions becoming favorable for Democrats, Republicans won the mid-term 2010 elections in a landslide.

Barack Obama's Washington, DC Photo 392. Greened walkway sporting US flags.

Fortuna like justice is blind. So, how come Mr. Obama is "doing so poorly" in the polls yet it's been predicted no one will challenge him for the Democratic Nomination in the 2012 Presidential Election. Yet, Mr. Steel's Republican Party has "Shellacked" the Democrats at the Mid-term election and still Mr. Steele, the Party leader, is being challenged from all angles, even by some of his best friends and backers such as Saul Anuzis, Jim DeMint, Morton Blackwell, Reince Priebus and even been criticized by Gentry Collins. Is it that Mr. Steele did not "attack and bite" Mr. Obama sufficiently or is it that the "Man of steel has begun to rust!"

BARACK OBAMA
MASTER OF WASHINGTON DC

"We live in a culture that discourages empathy. A culture that too often tells us our principle goal in life is to be rich, thin, young, famous, safe, and entertained."
BARACK OBAMA, speech, Jul. 12, 2006

62. FIASCO ON THE MALL BY

Dr. Fred Monderson

"They came to restore sanity and/or fear"

For the most part, the rally on the national Mall on Saturday October 30, 2010 was a mixture of masquerade, comedy, satire, and surprisingly a show of force, for, of all people, Barack Obama. Much of the intelligent crowd came for the comedy or to decry the ringmasters Jon Stewart and Stephen Colbert; but they came expressing their own views on placards, banners and in costumes that were colorful and to a point. One thing seemed clear, President Obama has a tremendous following across this nation and a great many of the estimated 200,000 people who showed up either demonstrated their support for the president or expressed disdain at the seeming popular "Tea Party" movement and other forms of extremisms, or comedy or otherwise of that hue.

If anything, we need to be careful in digesting the messages of the news media's writers, reporters and analysts' messages, for, after all, their "findings" are designed for ratings.

Naturally it was not all Obama, for there was some support for sanity, some concern about fear and some, sad to say support for the wackiest but also for meaningful expressions of credible issues that address bread and butter matters. Musical entertainment was supplied by performers Cheryl Crow, Kid Rock, John Legend and Tony Bennett and other celebrities including Kareem Abdul-Jabbar,

FREDERICK MONDERSON

were in attendance. Clearly, from this writer's limited view in a sea of that many, there was none of that vile condemnation of the President as shown in the racist venom that had characterized past "Tea Party" rallies. Let us not forget the original "Tea Party" was born of anger directed against the British. By British law they were criminals!

The sinister portrayal of the President that depicted a racist underbelly of the "Tea Party" movement seemed gone. One sign showing the "seated Witch Doctor" instead showed Stephen Colbert with a moustache instead but that is not to say those disgusting depictions of Mr. Obama were missing only this writer did not see any. As such, this whole gathering took on a Halloween/carnival atmosphere; yet still was more optimistic, heartening, while also conveying a political message. Some of the messages read as follows: "Tea Parties are for little girls;" "Obama-Biden;" "Tea Party puts the dumb in Freedom;" "Integrated Law-Abiding American Muslim;" "I will take Hope over your Bush/Dick any day;" "War, That's Insane;" "Stop Socialism: Boycott public roads, bridges, air traffic control, public sewers, fire fighters, police;" "End Afghan War;" "Don't tread on me any more than is absolutely necessary;" "Stop the Daily Show's Islamo Commie, Judeo-Nazi, Homo fascist, socialist femi-grizzly character dressed up as The Unemployed man attack on America." "Love Small-Government: Somalia is lovely in the Fall;" "War is usually not the answer;" "Dear News Media: Freedom of Speech Doesn't = DIAHHREA of the mouth!" "Immigrants have always been a problem: Ask any Native American;" "Keep your nuts to yourself;" "Vote lawyers out;" "Stephen Colbert is unfair to bears;" "Fear is the Mind Killer;" "Smile;" "Restore sanity!!! Glen Beck Not Playing with a Full Deck;" "I'm Here, Start Rally!"

"If you listen to Fox You got a head full of Rocks;" "I hate crowds;" "Change Doesn't Happen Overnight;" "Just Ask me;" "DC Voting Rights: Statehood for DC;" "Get High on Sanity, Not Tea;" "Just Say No to Republican Tea baggers;" "Sanity not Hannity;" "I may like political humor, but you should take my vote seriously;" "Don't Tea on my leg and tell me it's raining;" "I like Pie – Pie makes me Obese;" "Hyperbole is destroying America;" "You Can't have your country back – Mine Now;" "Yes We Can! DC Statehood Now;" "Can't we all just get along?" "Maybe No one asked nicely – End the War(s) now. Please?" "Sanity – It's a trap;" "Wouldn't care if the President was Muslim;" "Keep Fear Alive: I'm Afraid I'll miss my bus back to Toms River, New Jersey;" "Restore Sanity, Deplore Hannity."

When asked why they came to the Rally, the following responded: Katie Polak said she came: "To compare this Rally with Glen Beck's Rally."

John Morgan thought: "The Daily Show is so entertaining; I'm here to show the flag." Luz MacArthur from Orlando, Florida stated: "Most of us are moderate and need to be represented." "We must restore sanity because of the division in our

BARACK OBAMA
MASTER OF WASHINGTON DC

country. It is time for Dialogue. There is no monopoly on truth. We have to get along!"

Rachel Friedman said she brought her parents to the spectacle: "To get together to celebrate Sanity." Janet Brown, formerly of New York in 1968 believes "They can't take DC statehood back." With the exception of the original 13 states in the Union, each additional state was admitted through an Act of Congress. So, if Congress acts "They can't take the statehood back!"

Sheryl Holmes asked: "Can't we all get along? It is the only way to get America moving forward."

Meliss Robinson thought, "Sometimes fear is useful."

In a later lecture at the Thurgood Marshal Cultural Center that day on 12th Street, the noted Dr. Charles Finch III, added: "The Tea Partyers Are Dumb. They are setting themselves against the Destiny of Heaven." He believes, "There is a force at work that no human power can work against. It comprises Personification, Justice, Wisdom, Healing, Protection." Then he mentioned four archetypes in the will of heaven:

1. Ras Tafari, the Ethiopian Emperor Haile Selassie, the "Conquering Lion of Judah."
2. The Million Man March.
3. The Election of Barack Obama, which was not supposed to happen.

He was honest in saying he did not know what the fourth archetype was or whether it had arrived.

These people want Statehood for DC because it will guarantee 2 Black Senators and rights to vote on national Legislation.

As a final reflection, while the news media in print or electronic, reported on the "Rally" it downplayed any evidence of support for President Barack Obama, who appeared more favorable than any of the persons who had criticized him.

FREDERICK MONDERSON

Barack Obama's Washington, DC Photo 393. Backdoor of the White House, where deliveries are made.

Barack Obama's Washington, DC Photo 394. From one fountain to another.

BARACK OBAMA
MASTER OF WASHINGTON DC

"From the day I took office, I've been told that addressing our larger challenges is too ambitious; such an effort would be too contentious. I've been told that our political system is too gridlocked, and that we should just put things on hold for a while. For those who make these claims, I have one simple question: How long should we wait? How long should America put its future on hold?" BARACK OBAMA, State of the Union Address, Jan. 27, 2010

63. REFLECTIONS ON BARACK OBAMA
By
Dr. Fred Monderson

Barack Obama has been attacked from the right, not fully supported by the left and queried by the center in American politics; but notwithstanding, he has successfully brought America back from the perils of the economic brink, and changed the world's perception of American leadership. Recently, the president announced U.S. troop combat mission in Iraq is complete and having passed some of the most comprehensive legislation in recent American history, incentivized efforts to promote fuel and energy saving devices and effectuated strategies to improve and enhance education performance while setting this nation on a path of future prosperity and a brighter future; clearly, therefore, we see a Black Man Working (BMW). All this in an environment of vigorously challenged cooperation within some 18 months of assuming the Presidency and could have been even more with constructive cooperation from his Republican opponents. What a remarkable achievement in a performance that has demonstrated to the world that a black man can lead and raise a family reflective of the highest standards of this important social unit.

What are the lessons any clear sighted and objective observer can learn from, as Yogi Berra would say, regarding "observing" Mr. Obama?

First and foremost, Barack Obama is an exceptional visionary leader; cool, calm, collected with a passion to serve his country. However, when we consider the unrelenting attacks on the man, his character, style, personality, leadership ability, patriotism, memory, birth status, "wavering eye," threats of physical harm, no American leader has been subject to this form or level of inclandestine vituperativeness, while still charged with leading a major nation of the stature of the United States. Some critical observers have not discounted the fact Mr. Obama is a black man and have attributed his ethnicity as a major factor for the basis of these attacks and insidious characterization. Nonetheless, Mr. Obama is well-liked at home by broad segments as well as abroad because of his calculated and constructive leadership, his broad smile, athleticism, and overall father-figure as reflected in his beautiful family.

Barack Obama's Washington, DC Photo 395. Protest display just across the street from the back door of the White House.

Two significant milestones were reached on the American political landscape in the year 2008. The first occurred when Mr. Obama was selected at the Democratic Party's Nominating Convention to be its standard bearer in the November elections. The second milestone occurred when Mr. Obama was elected, in a landslide, President of the United States. As events unfolded, Americans and the world-at-large viewed these developments as significant. In fact, a great many hailed "post-racial America," as it marched confidently into the future. However, there was work to be done.

Fortunately Mr. Obama's transition team not only studied the bureaucratic structure shaping the American social landscape but also sought to understand the dynamics of the economic, political and social firestorm they were getting involved with. Significantly, the outgoing Bush Administration made every effort to facilitate a flawless transition to the incoming one, for principally two reasons.

BARACK OBAMA
MASTER OF WASHINGTON DC

Importantly, this was a historic win. The first African American to be elected President of the United States and so many eyes were and would be focused on his administration to see whether Mr. Obama could effectively captain the ship of state, while America confronted its many challenges. Second and even more significant, the Bush Administration had perhaps finally realized the gravity of the state of conditions under which the nation had succumbed in the many key financial and economic sectors, especially, during their tenure in office. For this latter, they wanted to "get out of town" quickly!

Nevertheless, with a clearly delineated set of goals and objectives contributed from input by recognized experts in their fields of expertise, the Obama administration set about tackling the formidable tasks that lay ahead. Securing the remaining TARP funds, passing a Stimulus Bill, tackling and securing Passage of Health Care Reform, bailing out Wall Street and passing Financial Reform, rescuing the auto industry, challenging and then seeking to stabilize the Housing Market, assisting State and Local Governments enabling them to continue providing essential services as police, fire, unemployment insurance and more were significant achievements. The task was formidable made more so by a seemingly virulent Republican Party opposition with allies in the likes of a supernova "Joe the Plumber," perennial loser Alan Keyes, viral and insidious masquerade elements within the "Tea Party movement," all while demonstrating stand-up leadership in waging two wars in Iraq and Afghanistan, confronting and targeting masterminds and practitioners in the "war on terror" as well as contending with incessant threats to his personal safety particularly driven by pernicious and ill-conceived propaganda that not only was Obama going to institute a socialist take-over of America but deny the right to bear arms, despite the many constitutional safeguards in place. In reaction, right wing militia groups, inclandestine Republican allies, stockpiled tremendous arsenals of weaponry supposedly to defend themselves from the supposed revolutionary changes the super black man would bring. These delusional individuals spent lots of money on arms and are still armed and dangerous!

FREDERICK MONDERSON

Barack Obama's Washington, DC Photo 396. This group could vocally be heard praying for President Obama.

Barack Obama's Washington DC Photo 397. Chef Jerome from "Old School Diner" all the way from Savannah, Georgia, with "JJ" and Keisha show support for the Obama family.

BARACK OBAMA
MASTER OF WASHINGTON DC

Envision a scenario where a leader must execute the functions and responsibilities of his office, in difficult and "new normal times," where only consistently creative policies and practices address the nuts and bolt issues of American realties such as the environment, climate change, infrastructure repairs, job creation, energy, student and teacher performance, and research and development in the fields of science and technology. Let us not forget, border security and the need for ever-present vigilance to combat foreign and domestic terrorism all while blocked by a political party whose only one word is "NO!" the likes of Alan Keyes's "Birthers Movement" of losers; right wing electronic and print media's animosity towards the President fueled by "wing nuts" the likes of Rush Limbaugh, Glen Beck, Hannity Combs, Fox News; and so many others and everything else that comes with the job, all! Of these latter we can add threats from Iran and North Korea, challenges to America's allies, need for hard, straight-forward and equitable negotiations with treaty states and the necessity of high level appointments that meet the criteria of excellence in their respective fields of experience. As Commander-In-Chief he must win the respect of those he commands. In addition, regarding the need to fundraise and provide leadership to his party, he must represent the country abroad in the most professional and respected manner.

Barack Obama's Washington DC Photo 397a. Chef Jerome from "Old School Diner" along with Carmen, all the way from Savannah, Georgia, show support for the Obama family.

FREDERICK MONDERSON

As a constitutional scholar, President Obama has certainly surveyed the history of the American Presidency and become familiar with historians' treatment of the occupants of that office. Coming as he has, after a "failed presidency," Mr. Obama could only provide effective leadership. He has certainly not been tainted by scandal, but has been concerned with the future of his party, concerned about the foreign policy issues that his predecessors either sustained or been troubled by. He must also focus an eye towards re-election and his place in history, not only as the first African-American President but also as the 44th President of the United States. In addition, in American culture, Number 44 has consistently provided a number of exceptional performances. On June 6, 1944, the Allies launched the final assault that resulted in victory that ended that conflict. In baseball, Hank Aaron, Willie Mays and Reggie Jackson have been incredible performers and sportsmen wearing the number 44. While only George Bush and Barack Obama know what was in the letter addressed to Number 44 from Number 43, the latter may have cautioned, "You have a number to live up to!"

Now, with an economy stubbornly flat despite enormous efforts, Mr. Obama and his democrats are constant targets of his Republican opponents who have convinced large segments of the landscape 'they don't know what they're doing;' and their alternative may very well be the maladies Obama inherited and is still confronting. Thankfully, many people now realize the full reality of Mr. Obama's inherited state of the nation was worse than at first thought. Imagine, all that's been done and here we are still in this deep chasm! Are we to believe the Obama Administration did not in good faith set up to clean up the mess of the Bush Administration? We now seem to understand not only was the basement full of horse manure at takeover, there was also a hidden sub and sub-sub basement with the stuff and that is what exudes the lingering stench! Despite this reality, Democrats have not put Republicans on trial for their past performance and intent to make the rich a priority through whatever means, outsource American jobs as they have done in the past and have silently stoked or given aid to anti-Obama sentiments that have aided their road-block strategy.

Nevertheless, excepting this unprofessional view of Republican actions and intentions and the outlined speculative possibility of character traits Mr. Obama brought to the national political stage and the presidency, knowing he represented a proud race of people; an intelligent, loving and no nonsense wife and two lovely daughters, in Barack Obama we have a leader cut from the finest cloth, studious, a consummate politician and man of impeccable character. As such he must be the leader of the American people, that despite their ideological persuasion or party affiliation they will still recognize and treat him as "Our Leader."

BARACK OBAMA
MASTER OF WASHINGTON DC

"I always believe that ultimately, if people are paying attention, then we get good government and good leadership. And when we get lazy, as a democracy and civically start taking shortcuts, then it results in bad government and politics."
BARACK OBAMA, MSNBC interview, Sep. 25, 2006

64. SHIRLEY SHERROD – SUPERSTAR
BY

DR. FRED MONDERSON

In another context, Dr. Yosef ben-Jochannan said, "After they had beaten and battered us, we sent in the women." While at this point the context is unimportant, the concept is truly significant. In the current situation, the superwoman at the center of the brewing racial story, Shirley Sherrod, is indeed a remarkable person, who, because of her religious beliefs and spiritual foundation has not only done good but also trumped evil and done so in a perpetuating manner. Therefore, out of this unfortunate circumstance can come enormous benefits to the cause she has valiantly served and perhaps she is one of those messianic figures the black struggle for civil rights and empowerment needs to move it significantly along its path of fulfillment.

Professor Leonard James of New York City Technical College of the City University of New York imparted to his students, as part of the methodological plan of historical evolution, how internal and external factors have a tendency to steer developments of any situation creating unexpected outcomes in any given phenomenon. A good example of this recent development, Mrs. Sherrod was in her lane, in her element, doing her good, unnoticed; when an "evil scientist" hatched a sinister plot in the vein of his nefarious intent often seen as a racially insensitive conservative blog. This then is a good example of an external event having an internal impact. Therefore, the unintentional significance of the current development is that it is or can be wrong for the right reasons. Hence, Ms. Sherrod's skills and visibility can be utilized as an activist.

"Old folks" have often spoken of a mythical situation where two pugilists, one black and one white, were going at it in a boxing match. A blind white man went to "see the fight," but he had a companion who gave him a "blow by blow account" of the action as he kept asking "What's happening now?" As the companion related the developments, he got to where he related, "The white man

FREDERICK MONDERSON

has the black man plummeted, and he has him down." The blind white man responded, "The black man is down! Keep him down, for when the black man raises, hell raises!"

One has to believe the right-wing web journalist Andrew Breitbart has indeed raised Mrs. Sherrod with his grossly back-fired misrepresentation of this angelic soul. Equally, another context saying, "Hell hath no fury like a woman scorned," can apply to the misogynous behavior of the sinister blogger "evil scientist" who has given birth or new force to an old star that can manifest in a multitude of situations. In that, Mrs. Sherrod has been working quietly under the radar doing rather constructive work in the field of agricultural assistance as head of the Agriculture Department's Rural Development Office in Georgia. Despite her temporary setback in being "put through hell;" she had been given a powerful new platform provided by an unrepentant Breitbart and his right-wing cohorts who used a doctored video of a speech she made at a branch meeting of the NAACP in March to make her look racist. This journalistic mishandling was then given extensive print and electronic media coverage without verifying the veracity of the claims made against one unjustly accused. Now the media is reporting Andrew Breitbart has been invited to Headline a Republican National Committee Fundraiser scheduled for August 12-13, 2010. This invite to the media provocateur and those allied with the "Tea Party Movement" not only calls into question Republican associations, but creates opportunities and underscores the work Mrs. Sherrod needs to be involved in.

Now, with a raised profile, the many years of her experience manifesting good in challenge to evil; as symbol, she can assist in generating a whole host of movements particularly a national dialogue on race that can work for good in the African-American experience and America in general. As the saying goes, "God works in mysterious ways, his wonders to perform." As such, what has happened to Mrs. Sherrod in the rush to judgment firing of this innocent woman, can serve as a motivating factor not simply to generate discussion on race in America but importantly to fire up a nascent movement of black consciousness and activism. The Sherrod star has risen and by all accounts, this fighter for good is ready to do "The Lord's Work!" Imagine the progress that would ensue in race relations if the President invited a face-off with Ms. Sherrod and Prof. Gates against Andrew Breitbart with Officer Crowley as referee or moderator!

BARACK OBAMA
MASTER OF WASHINGTON DC

"I'm happy to get good ideas from across the political spectrum, from Democrats and Republicans. What I won't do is return to the failed theories of the last eight years that got us into this fix in the first place, because those theories have been tested, and they have failed. And that's what part of the election in November was all about." BARACK OBAMA, press conference, Feb. 9, 2009

65. BARACK AGAINST THE REST
BY

DR. FRED MONDERSON

Having scaled the 30-day, 100-day and now 1-year milestones, President Barack Obama faces the triple dilemma of having accomplished so much thus far, having to contend with an unrelenting opposition entrenched in its archaic mentality, is fervently obstructionist, and whether he should continue his chosen path for the good of the country as he sees it. Of course, no one walks away from power, but Cincinnatus of ancient Rome did it and so too General Obasanjo of Nigeria, though he returned. President Obama, for his part cannot do this, though it would be unprecedented, foolish, laughable even more important, illegal because he took an oath to uphold and execute the laws of the Constitution which mandates he serve at least one term of four years. The great presidents are those elected to a second term, accomplish essentially the broad parameters of their agenda and end their term without scandal.

As the first African-American, those unalterably opposed to the man, whether ideologically or for racial reasons, would love to not only see him fail as a leader but to be hit by scandal that impugns his character. Therefore, beyond their "I told you so's" they would hope to derail any credible non-white male leader who in time would have the tenacity to seek the office especially if such leadership would benefit the nation at a critical period in its history.

FREDERICK MONDERSON

Barack Obama's Washington, DC Photo 398. Full-body colorful female figures lining a main street in Washington.

Plotters have a tendency to fail because no matter how they shape the parameters of their scheme, there are variables not considered, some underestimation of the "target" and the remarkably unpredictable nature of chance or Fortuna. Fortunately, Barack Obama is a strong candidate for at least two of the three criteria as sketched.

While not particularly a racial comment, there is folkloric reference where, "somewhere in the Islands" a young man went to see his dad at work in a bank decades ago, sort of the "good old days." What the lad saw, his black father in a sea of white clerks, like "a fly sticking out in buttermilk." In their later recounting, the father informed, "I did not get this job because I had the same education as my white counterparts, but because I have more." That makes us see; "fully equipped" Barack Obama came "fully equipped!"

Mr. Obama's successes in becoming President of the United States had nothing to do with an idea whose time had come, *Fortuna* or his gracious smile. He was victorious because he had a brilliant mind, a tremendous work ethic, possessed the tenacity to stand and be counted, the good sense to ally with equally intelligent individuals who would buttress his ideas, encourage his efforts, contribute in a team spirit mentality, and he having the love and support of a family who, when the going got tough amidst his 97 percent perspiration and 3 percent inspiration, encouraged by hard work that kept motivating his unquenched desire to pull it all together to make success a reality. The challenges Mr. Obama faced to confront

BARACK OBAMA
MASTER OF WASHINGTON DC

his challengers would make lesser men question whether the rigors of the journey were worth the price of victory or whether to persevere to persevere. Still he believed the journey was worth the sacrifice!

Barack Obama's Washington, DC Photo 398a.
An Ad for the National Museum of Women Exhibit on display in DC.

Everyone ought to be familiar with the rocky road to the White House he has traveled. What people are not quite familiar with is the totality of problems America faced, how close to a failed state this nation had come and whether, with wars on many fronts, he had not snatched victory from the jaws of defeat at the hands of erstwhile adversaries who kept circling the wagons.

A synopsis of what faced the new 44th President of the United States is compounded by the notion that some ideas die hard. We know on the campaign trail then Senator Obama was accused of being inexperienced, a socialist, not being a citizen, being unpatriotic, not wearing the flag on his lapel, being too black, not black enough, associating with terrorists and even more. A year after becoming President, a "woman of questionable character" called the Rick Sanchez show on CNN and referred to "that boy in the White House" because the President had the temerity to challenge Wall Street and the banks in recent statements. Thus, while some of the overall vitriol has swept itself under the rug, these are still there! So where we have this Congressman (R- Colorado) calling the President of the United States of America a "tar baby." In the House they refer to each member as

FREDERICK MONDERSON

the Distinguished Gentleman from this state of that state. In the Senate they refer to each other with the same level of respect. Yet, these people do not respect the office of the President nor the man, President Barack Hussein Obama. Even Reverend Al Sharpton has had to upbraid that perennial candidate for the presidency, Pat Buchanan, as the **Gwinnett Daily Pos**t, Friday August 5, 2011, p. A 8, reported, "after Buchanan referred to President Barack Obama as 'your boy' when saying Obama caved in past negotiations and was likely to do so in the future." Sharpton responded, "He's nobody's boy. He's your president, he's my president, and that's what you have to get through your head." He probably meant "thick skull." On that same page, the President is shown as a teacher before the blackboard that read: "Do not call Tea Partiers 'Terrorists' or use the word 'Jihad." Whereupon one of the six students in the picture raised his hand and asked: "Can we still refer to them as 'stupid, knuckle-dragging, frothing at the mouth anarchistic, right-wing nut jobs?"

With the failure of AIG and Bears Sterns and the crisis on Wall Street that acerbated a global economic tsunami, the incoming President faced the reality that the auto industry, essentially General Motors and Chrysler Corporation, were in serious trouble and had to be rescued. Failure of these auto giants would have had devastating consequences with a ripple effect across the economic landscape of the nation. Be reminded, when President Barack Obama took over, the nation was losing 800,000 jobs per month. Today, its adding some 100,000 plus jobs, but this is not enough, but he's working while appealing to Congress to come up with a plan. Will the Republican controlled House of Representatives come up with a plan to help, that is still to be seen.

Equally too, foreign auto makers would probably have wedged themselves beyond extraction in this industry and the backbone of American auto ingenuity would have been broken. Therefore, the auto industry had to be rescued! Moving quickly the President with his majority in Congress passed the Recovery Act that provided broad tax cuts, extended unemployment insurance, provided aid to states to fend off layoffs of teachers, firefighters and police officers and initiated the rebuilding of roads, bridges, tunnels, ports and things of this nature. In addition, he initiated a slew of new initiatives including the need for new and clean renewable energy sources, addressed global warming and the environment, the need for revamping of schools, the curriculum and compensation for good teachers and need to fire bad teachers. He offered incentives to generate creative ideas in education and industry. Yet, the nation hemorrhaged from the loss of jobs. This notwithstanding, what people seem to have lost sight of is over the years, corporate greed manifesting in downsizing and outsourcing had steadily stripped the American work force of potential jobs and as times got hard, the job pool got smaller and thus unemployment rates rose. However, in time the numbers have shown the escalating job loss have been reduced tremendously.

BARACK OBAMA
MASTER OF WASHINGTON DC

Barack Obama's Washington, DC Photo 398b. Kings County Hospital Center's Community Advisory Board members, Dr. Fred Monderson, Jermaine Burger-Gaskin, Gloria Thomas, Agnes Abraham, unknown, (in rear) Mr. Terrence La Pierre and Mr. Morgan Gabrielle, and Sarana Purcell aide to Assemblyman Karim Camara, making a Health Care statement on the steps of New York City Hall.

Like everything else, it pays to look down the road and in doing so; President Obama realized Health Care costs were on an express runaway track. Thus he devoted an inordinate amount of time to educating people to this reality to ease the burden of the nearly 50 million Americans who do not have health care coverage while informing those who have that theirs too will erode soon enough. Recently on the steps of New York City Hall there was an enormous rally and press conference called by the Health and Hospital Corporation that essentially provide the backbone of public medical care in the city. While for years the public hospitals, Kings County, Coney Island, Queens General, Harlem Hospital, etc., have borne the brunt of caring for those with and without health care insurance, the "fat cats" of private hospitals got fatter. Now with the health care crisis escalating, they began to feel the heat and chose to be part of the protest movement because it's only a matter of time before the tsunami of costs reaches their shores. This is essentially what President Obama has been preaching to those who have health care insurance. It's only a matter of time before rising health care costs erode your benefits, that is, if we do not have meaning health care reform.

FREDERICK MONDERSON

For people who will settle for failure as an option, their first and biggest mistake is underestimating the challenge or obstacle confronting them. Equally, like any path one travels, a record is created, footprints left that, in time, can be seen as "where you sit is where you stand" or "where you stand is where you sit." If President Obama had not had the wherewithal to confront and overcome the obstacles placed in his path perhaps the nation would have been worse off than it is today. However, considering from where he brought it back, on the brink of economic collapse, the home, auto and banking industries hemorrhaging, unrelenting terrorist challenges with two wars raging, challenges of the global economic downturn, the world's view of America and the need for regulation across the board at home in financial, legal and political realms; one has to wonder if his challengers could have done as well. Of course, there is still a long path to tred because of past mistakes by people who lead the nation.

Barack Obama's Washington, DC Photo 399. Souvenirs of the Washington Monument.

In a recent town hall meeting in Ohio, telling his audience how challenging and confining the White House is as an office and that he was glad to get out to meet the people, and recognizing the challenges and obstacles he faced, the President reminded those in attendance: "I did not run for this office to run away. I ran for President to confront challenges to rebuild our economy, create good jobs, and improve the quality of schools and, yes, make health care affordable." He sketched the scenario of opponents and "talking heads" who, in analyzing this and

BARACK OBAMA
MASTER OF WASHINGTON DC

that, strategized "Well, if we stop Obama, etc." Thus, he reminded his audience, "This is not about me. This is about you." That being so, all forms of behaviors call into question who is the real patriot and whether the actions of those who opposed the President so vehemently and maliciously can be considered patriots or rebels and whether their actions are in the best interest of America.

Mr. Obama has proved to be a realist and confessed at the town hall meeting, if he had taken the "path of least resistance" everyone would have been happy but nothing would have gotten done. He reminded, the first things he did was pass the **Lilly Ledbetter Act** for equal pay for men and women and addressed the credit card dilemma. He wanted to restore home values, provide quality education, open up the process of government, cut waste and inefficiency in Washington and create a tough Consumer Protection Agency. To the banks, rescued and now doing so good he insisted: "We bailed you out and now we want our money back." Then reflecting on developments in Massachusetts he again reminded, no matter what, he wanted "Real Health Insurance reform and intends to hold the insurance industry accountable." He will press for financial regulation reform, invest in higher education, encourage initiatives in clean energy and finally praised the "strong, resilient, perseverance of the American people." Then he reminded all, there were "better days ahead."

Barack Obama's Washington, DC Photo 400. Souvenir replica of the White House.

FREDERICK MONDERSON

Barack Obama's Washington, DC Photo 401.

"With the magnitude of the challenges we face right now, what we need in Washington are not more political tactics -- we need more good ideas. We don't need more point-scoring -- we need more problem-solving." BARACK OBAMA, press conference, Mar. 17, 2009

66. The President's Cabinet and the Order of Succession

By

Dr. Fred Monderson

The Cabinet is as old as the Presidency and in its present composition and functions it is evolving to this day. The Constitution created great responsibility for the President and even though it did not spell out the Cabinet as a specific entity, George Washington, the first president, created this entity to assist him in the many functions he then undertook. To do this, the Cabinet was born. However, while today there are some 15 cabinet positions, in the beginning of the young Republic, there were only 4 such departments or executive posts. These were state, treasury, war (today Defense) and Attorney General (then Justice).

BARACK OBAMA
MASTER OF WASHINGTON DC

Providing commentary on views on the early Cabinet, Bob Bernotas in *The Federal Government: How it Works*, New York: Chelsea House Publishers (1990: 56) writes: "The Constitution does not provide for a cabinet, and no law requires the president to form one. The idea of an advisory body to help a leader make decisions goes all the way back to the political theories of the Greek philosopher Aristotle (384-322 B.C). In the United States, however, its usefulness has been debated as far back as the earliest days of the new nation. Benjamin Franklin believed that a cabinet 'would not only be a check on a bad President but be a relief to a good one.' Alexander Hamilton argued that, on the contrary, the cabinet would prove to be either 'a clog upon his good intentions' or 'a cloak to conceal his faults.'"

However, Jack C. Plano and Milton Greenberg in *The American Political Dictionary* (eight Edition, New York: Holt, Rinehart and Winston (1962) (1989: 164) clarifies the composition of the Cabinet in that: "By custom, the heads of the major departments (State, Treasury, Defense, Justice, Interior, Agriculture, Commerce, Labor, Health and Human Services, Education, Housing and Urban

Development, Energy, Transportation, and Veterans Affairs, are members of the Cabinet, and the President may also invite the Vice-President and other officials to sit in on Cabinet meetings." Today, Homeland Security is added to this collection of departments due to the increase issues of terrorism and other challenges to the interior department.

The Order of Succession in the event the President is incapacitated begins with the Vice-President of the United States followed by the Secretaries of State, Treasury, Defense, Justice, Interior, Agriculture, Commerce, Labor, Health and Human Services, Housing and Urban Development, Transportation, Energy, Education, Veterans Affairs and Homeland Security.

In the Obama Administration, the respective heads of the following positions also have Cabinet-rank status. These include the White House Chief of Staff, Environmental Protection Agency, Office of Management and Budget, United States Trade Representative, United States Ambassador to the United Nations and members of the Council of Economic Advisers. Of course, the Press Secretary who represents the President in explaining his daily positions to the Press Corps can also be considered a member of his Cabinet. I suppose we could throw in the National Security Adviser, head of the Terrorist Task Force and the Head of the Joints Chiefs of Staff.

FREDERICK MONDERSON

Barack Obama's Washington, DC Photo 402. Standing before the flags of the nation, a final salute to those coming and going.

"America can do whatever we set our mind to. That is the story of our history, whether it's the pursuit of prosperity for our people, or the struggle for equality for all our citizens; our commitment to stand up for our values abroad, and our sacrifices to make the world a safer place. Let us remember that we can do these things not just because of wealth or power, but because of who we are: one nation, under God, indivisible, with liberty and justice for all." BARACK OBAMA, remarks on the death of Osama Bin Laden, May 1, 2011

67. STATE OF THE AMERICAN UNION
By
Dr. Fred Monderson

In this State of the Union Address, President Barack Obama delivered a powerful message regarding problems facing the nation but more particularly emphasizing his vision for the nation over the next year. Touting some of his successes, failures and future prospects, commentators have declared this is one of Barack Obama's characteristic speeches.

Article II, Section 3 of the Constitution states, the President "shall from time to time give the Congress information of the State of the Union and recommend to their consideration such measures as he shall judge necessary and expedient; he may, on extraordinary occasions, convene both Houses, or either of them, and in

BARACK OBAMA
MASTER OF WASHINGTON DC

case of disagreement between them with respect to the time of adjournment, he may adjust them to such time as he shall think proper; he shall receive ambassadors and other public ministers; he shall take care that the laws be faithfully executed, and shall commission all the officers of the United States."

Pointing out the President can change any time for the State of the Union Address but customarily at the beginning of the legislative session in January, Jack C. Plano and Milton Greenberg in *The American Political Dictionary* (New York: Holt, Rinehart and Winston, Inc., 1989: 180-181) comments on the significance of this important legislative mandate. "The importance of the State of the Union message lies primarily in its placing the initiative for developing a broad, comprehensive legislative program in the hands of the President. At the opening of a new legislative session, members of Congress busy themselves with routine organizational matters and minor legislative proposals until the President presents them with his legislative program. In his message, the President discusses the major problems facing the nation and recommends statutory solutions. His message is followed up in subsequent months by scores of bills drawn up in the executive departments and introduced in Congress by "administration" congressmen. Presidents usually deliver their State of the Union messages in person. Radio and television have greatly increased the importance of these messages, and the President now speaks not only to Congress but also the American people. The media offers the opportunity to dramatize policies and objectives and to gain support for them by arousing public opinion. Some presidents have delivered a second "State of the World" message to Congress focusing on foreign policy problems. "State of the State" and "State of the City" messages are typically delivered by governors and mayors to their state legislatures and city councils. Oftentimes, State Assemblymen and even State Senators deliver "State" of their "district" messages and even in Brooklyn, we now have a "State of the Borough" address.

Generally commentators use the previous address as a barometer to determine and speculate as to the nature of the President's direction in his talk and to examine whether he had accomplish the things delineated in his speech. His 2009 Introduction to the Congress, just brimming with the confidence of a successful run for the Presidency and having some understanding of the state of affairs, he sought to secure from Congress TARP funds from the previous Bush Administration and things being so bad, by 2010 he was able to convince the law-making body the Stimulus Bill would work wonders. In the 2010 Address the issue was how to stop the profuse hemorrhaging of the American economy, financial system, taxes, bank and industry bailouts, housing, jobs, education, the Middle East conundrum, terrorists, nuclear proliferation by Iran and North Korea, global warming, energy independence, American research and development of clear energy and a whole lot more.

FREDERICK MONDERSON

Barack Obama's Washington, DC Photo 403. Souvenir replica of the White House.

"We worship an awesome God in the blue states and we don't like federal agents poking around in our libraries in the red states. We are one people, all of us pledging allegiance to the Stars and Stripes, all of us defending the United States of America." BARACK OBAMA, Larry King Live, Oct. 19, 2006

68. RALLY AROUND BARACK!
By

Dr. Fred Monderson

"Time will tell" is full of merit and without a doubt; we must now "Rally around Barack" because he has proved he's well on way to becoming one of the great Presidents of the United States of America, certainly for the new century. Such a view is credible for a number of reasons including Mr. Obama's full-fledged grasping and grappling with the economic, domestic and international conditions facing the nation and, despite all the negativism, he seems to be prevailing in his vision. However, unlike the woman at his town hall meeting who publicly criticized the President and he took it smiling while the *New York Post* and such *ilks* gave her unprecedented coverage, front page and all, because as an African American she dared to call out the President; many supporters who understood the

BARACK OBAMA
MASTER OF WASHINGTON DC

big picture never wavered in their support and such loyalty now seems to be paying just deserved rewards, as the merits of Barack Obama's strategy and unrelenting hard work continues to unfold.

Perhaps the farmer with his conception of the agricultural season requiring the process of tilling the field, planting the seeds, watering the ground, weeding the shoots and allowing the plants to bud, grow, develop and mature for the harvest could identify with the genuine efforts of Mr. Obama. Opponents, competitors, critics and even "haters" on the other hand, have shown their true colors of contempt in the unrelenting attacks on Barack Obama from the time he demonstrated audacity to run for the Presidency of the United States. This bold move for a black man to run for the Presidency called into question a number of factors global observers used as a yardstick to evaluate the presumed state of America in the young century.

In wake of "opposition scorched earth" methods, the words of Edmund Burke in his *Reflections on the Revolution in France* (1792) that "The only thing necessary for evil to triumph is for good men to say nothing" rings true today, as it related to assaults on the integrity of the Senator and now President Barack Obama and for that matter the Office of the Presidency which he represents and uphold. When we reflect on the inhuman characterization of Barack Obama in the "birth of the Tea Party movement" and the unrelenting assaults on his human, civic and intellectual personality as represented by the "Birthers Movement" one has to wonder about the deafening silence of those leaders, men of conscience, who claim to speak to and for America. Not only the President, but such attacks are shameful affronts on the American people.

Principal among questions stated and unstated were whether America was ready for a black President? Could a black effectively run such a major entity as the United States? Was he sufficiently experienced to contend on the world stage as a major statesman? Could his new face and voice change the world's image of America, particularly in view of its perception over the last decade or so? And, even more important could Barack Obama run a credible campaign to be elected President of the United States? To all observers, the answer to the last question was the unleashing of a well orchestrated surprise machine that snowballed in organizational sophistication as he took his opponents down a "dusty road," and the rest is known history.

Pitfalls along the way included that nascent "Tea Party" movement in alliance with the Republican Party that vindictively characterized the intelligent gentleman candidate Barack Obama who, not only organizationally gifted but remained glued with his "eyes on the prize," looking "straight ahead" and ignoring "Cat calls" and insidious intent. Yet, as Barack took no action towards such behaviors, some

FREDERICK MONDERSON

clamored "we want our country back" because he is "not like us." Equally they though he was "inexperienced" and even if elected, would soon be "challenged" by nation states' "bad boys."

All the while the President set out tackling the problems he inherited. Even more sinister, given the domestic and global mess bequeathed this new Chief Executive and Commander-in-Chief, the "Birthers" kept up their attacks. Black Republicans including Alan Keyes and the much publicized "black protester with guns" in Arizona whose church leader was "praying for Obama's death" were the most sinister. Notwithstanding the latter state of affairs, in view of the task ahead of economic, financial and fiscal collapse desperately in need of monetary regulation, a hemorrhaging job market, foreclosures, etc., and with international ideological competition; to accuse the president of being unsuited for office was a blindsided attack that disrespected the institution of the Presidency and the man who held that office. Let us not forget, the older attacks during the campaign of Mr. Obama of not being a citizen," "unpatriotic," "too black," "not black enough," that he "forgot the name of a soldier whose bracelet he wore" and to boot opponents rolled out "Joe the Plumber" who parroted a false notion that "Obama was a socialist." Yet, in time, the *New York Post*, in a political cartoon, showed Obama flushing "Joe the Plumber" down the bowl!

Just as Obama's opponents could not honestly admit to the mess their Republican cohorts had created in the American economic, financial, international and political climate, even Mr. Obama did not, at first, comprehend the size of the mess he inherited. Nevertheless, he set about tackling the problems requiring banking and financial and economic reforms; paying attention to problems of housing starts and foreclosures; expressing concerns about jobs, health care, educational reforms; and touting the need for energy independence through innovative research and development of wind energy, energy from the sun, and new forms of battery power, all designed to reduce the nation's dependence on foreign oil. Couple this with the international situation, and the ramifications of two wars in Iraq and Afghanistan, as well as challenges posed by North Korea, Iran, the Middle East quagmire and the global threats of Al Qaeda and the potential of domestic terrorism, to not aid but tear down the President at this time was truly un-patriotic, un-American.

We cannot forget during and after the campaign, physical threats to Mr. Obama increased manifold as right wing groups stockpiled military hardware to combat a perceived threat Mr. Obama represented. Still, many American "leaders of repute" said nothing though law enforcement agents tightened their scrutiny so as to ensure the president's safety. Added to this, the *New York Post* printed a political cartoon showing two policemen shooting the President disguised as an ape. This action stirred the irony of particularly Obama's black supporters and many liberal whites across the nation who never let the *Post* forget. Nevertheless, the President

BARACK OBAMA
MASTER OF WASHINGTON DC

continued his tremendous efforts of fulfilling the functions of the many hats he wore.

Of course, the big assignments come to mind first: historic health insurance reform, even though he lost his biggest ally and champion of this bill, Edward Kennedy, and this passage is today reining in the insurance companies and helping control the cost of care for millions of Americans; Wall Street reform, which put in place the toughest consumer protections ever; passage of the bill to close Guantanamo Bay prison and the move to begin trials of those incarcerated there; and bringing an end to combat operations in Iraq with the intent of bringing more than 100,000 troops home.

And there is so much more the Obama-Biden team helped achieve that is right now improving lives across this country.

The first act Mr. Obama passed as President was the Lilly Ledbetter Act giving women equal pay status as men.

The team passed the Recovery Act, which saved and created more than 3 million jobs, provided the largest middle-class tax cut in a generation, and made landmark investments in clean energy, infrastructure, and education.

They made critical investments in General Motors and Chrysler, saving tens of thousands of jobs - and perhaps these companies - and spurring a rebirth of the American car industry which could have gone into oblivion.

The administration wrote into law student loan reform and credit card reform, which ended the worst abuses of the banking industries and are making lending fair for American families.

FREDERICK MONDERSON

Barack Obama's Washington, DC Photo 404. Souvenir replica of the Capitol Building.

The Barack Obama Administration put two new Supreme Court justices on the bench -- Sonia Sotomayor and Elena Kagan, who bring rich and diverse experiences to the Court and if re-elected he would have the potential to appoint even more justices perhaps changing American jurisprudence for decades. The potential of such an act irks many and has spurred much animosity towards the President. This possibility may have motivated the Republicans even more to "Stop Obama."

The Administration has begun to reset America's relationship with the international community, from the ratification of a new START nuclear arms treaty with Russia to tough new sanctions on Iran to strengthening America's long-term partnership with a unified Iraq and to engaging China to rein in its close ally, North Korea.

The very thorny "Don't Ask, Don't Tell" legislation which was the right thing to do -- not only because it makes the military stronger at a time when it needs to be the strongest, but because Americans are seeking that military might with an abiding sense of justice. This and more was accomplished in a two year period.
We do recognize the November mid-term election that saw Republicans regain the House of Representatives sent a strong message to the President and the Democrats that, despite what has been done to turn things around; the country wants to go in a new direction. Still, countering conventional wisdom by applying the great resources of his thinking economic and other forms of advisers particularly Paul Volker, as the economy began to improve, the President was able to wrangle a new tax-cut bill despite the lame-duck status of a democratic

BARACK OBAMA
MASTER OF WASHINGTON DC

congress, though some have argued Republicans, despite their rhetoric about deficits are more interested in MONEY through their mantra of tax cuts that benefits the wealthy.

Like everything else, "time does tell" and the nation, like the enormous battleship that it is, has slowly begun to turn and as things unfold, Mr. Obama's numbers are improving. This is because the recession is over, businesses are hiring, unemployment rates have dropped, housing starts have increased, Mr. Obama has insisted, having pulled the economy back from the brink, he wants to put it in overdrive. With such efforts, the prospects of Mr. Obama's re-election seem to get even better. While some have blamed the recent violent murders in Arizona on anti-Obama inspired rhetoric that seemed to motivate an unbalanced individual, the President went to Tucson to pay tribute to those victims and sent a powerful message of healing. Some have hailed his reconciliatory message designed to heal and unite the nation, so much so, one of his harshest critics and credible opponents Senator John McCain, came out and praised Mr. Obama's healing words, while Condoleezza Rice, former Secretary of State on Pierce Morgan's new show remarked "Mr. Obama is a decent man and doing his best for this country." Therefore, it is time to "Rally around Barack" to show his detractors, supporters and the world, Mr. Obama is indeed a good man doing the best he can to turn the nation around and help it recover from the quagmire of the last decade. And, with this we must rally and stand behind Barack Obama!

Barack Obama's Washington, DC Photo 405. Youngster in practice to become President one day as Michelle salutes and President Obama smiles approvingly.

FREDERICK MONDERSON

"Like no other illness, AIDS tests our ability to put ourselves in someone else's shoes -- to empathize with the plight of our fellow man. While most would agree that the AIDS orphan or the transfusion victim or the wronged wife contracted the disease through no fault of their own, it has too often been easy for some to point to the unfaithful husband or the promiscuous youth or the gay man and say 'This is your fault. You have sinned.' I don't think that's a satisfactory response. My faith reminds me that we all are sinners." BARACK OBAMA, speech, Dec. 1, 2006

69. PRESIDENT OBAMA AND CONGRESS
By

Dr. Fred Monderson

From the earliest days of the Republic, Presidents have struggled in their relationship with Congress, for after all, the Legislative body holds the purse strings to the economic road map the President sketches and tries to implement. This relationship is dictated by a number of factors depending on whether his party is in the majority of the 435 member body of the House of Representatives or the 100 members of the Senate. Whether he can persuade some members of the opposition to cross the proverbial aisle and support him or whether his "coat-tail effect" can help incumbents or new candidates get elected; and the extent to which he can endorse, campaign for or raise money for local candidates who can win their race for Congress and then support the president's agenda as its presented to the lawmaking body for passage, are all important probabilities the President can affect. Even more, the President's relationship with Congress is much more complex than simply economic matters for policy, appointments, security concerns, deployment of troops for military action overseas, protection of the environment, wild-life refuges, civil rights enforcement and protection and promotion of the general welfare and more are all affected by the President's relationship with Congress.

As a Congressional "insider" and having been a member of the Senate, President Obama had become acutely aware of these upper house workings. He probably built-up friendships and working relationships with colleagues and instantly began exploiting this knowledge in proposing and moving his agenda through this body, as the nation's Chief Legislator. In the House of Representatives he depends on his

BARACK OBAMA
MASTER OF WASHINGTON DC

majority leaders and in the experiences and abilities of Rahm Emanuel, his Chief of Staff.

The role of Congress, as an important entity in the American governmental structure was born in controversy and shaped to be a complimentary, counterweigh or force to help; yet, be a check on the President or Executive branch, becoming too powerful in the political equation.

In the period between realizations that the Article of Confederation was an inadequate document to forge a United States of America and promulgation of the U.S. Constitution, the issue of representation became a serious contention. Small states were fearful that large states would dominate the government and they would lose their individual identity. As the delegates to the Constitutional Convention wrestled with the issue, the Virginia Plan, the New Jersey Plan and finally the Connecticut Compromise emerged with the latter exerting more influence on the structure and function of American government and what role Congress would play as the new nation was launched.

The New Jersey Plan offered by William Patterson, proposed a unicameral or single legislative body or house was devised to revise rather than replace the Articles of Confederation. Robert C. Bone in *American Government* (New York: Barnes and Noble, 1977: 16) notes: "While it retained the Confederation's single vote for each state and supremacy of the legislative branch (which would elect a plural executive) the New Jersey Plan greatly strengthened the powers of Congress. Its acts were to become the 'supreme law' over all state laws; and its powers were to be expanded to impose taxes and regulate trade." The Virginia Plan by James Madison, on the other hand, proposed the "establishment of a national government 'consisting of a supreme Legislative, Judiciary, and Executive.' The lower house of the legislature, 'elected by the people of the several states,' was to choose the upper house. The Judiciary was to be chosen by the legislature as whole, as was a 'national executive,' with the question of whether the executive was to be single or plural left open. Roger Sherman proposed the 'Connecticut Compromise,' notes Bone (1977: 16) that "provided for a House of Representatives based on proportional representation with the slave population of any state counted as three-fifths of its actual number. In contrast, the Senate was to be composed of two members from each state, to be chosen by the state legislatures."

Sherman's contribution to the structure of American government went beyond this framework impacting in two significant ways more than two centuries later. Sherman framed the debate and status of the black man by "elevating' him to "2/3 of a man" and for two centuries his social relations in the society have been influenced by this philosophic and human relations inequity. Perhaps, even more meaningful, has been the notion of "compromise" in government for when

FREDERICK MONDERSON

opposing forces have been entrenched in their positions, the notion of compromise has helped to break the grid-lock to get legislation or the issue under consideration moving in the interest of all.

A recent and good example of compromise is seen with President Obama's Stimulus Bill presented to Congress within weeks after his inauguration. The issue seemed divided along party's ideological lines with the Republicans in both houses seemingly unalterably opposed to the President and the Democrats' position on the Bill. Yet, three "moderate" Republicans broke ranks and compromised their party's obdurate stance to vote with the President in this one. Thus, as happened countless times when "horns were locked" Sherman's notion of "Compromise" has helped to break the gridlock and move the issue forward. Still, we see the Republicans were against the President from day one.

"In a global economy where the most valuable skill you can sell is your knowledge, a good education is no longer just a pathway to opportunity – it is a pre-requisite." BARACK OBAMA, Address to Joint Session of Congress, Feb. 24, 2009 "The answers to our problems don't lie beyond our reach. They exist in our laboratories and universities; in our fields and our factories; in the imaginations of our entrepreneurs and the pride of the hardest-working people on Earth. Those qualities that have made America the greatest force of progress and prosperity in human history we still possess in ample measure." BARACK OBAMA, Address to Joint Session of Congress, Feb. 24, 2009

Barack Obama's Washington, DC Photo 406. Press Secretary in the making, "Giving them the business!"

BARACK OBAMA
MASTER OF WASHINGTON DC

Barack Obama's Washington, DC Photo 407. Souvenir of the US Capital Building with its majestic dome.

"It is time to put in place tough, new common-sense rules of the road so that our financial market rewards drive and innovation, and punishes short-cuts and abuse."
BARACK OBAMA, Address to Joint Session of Congress, Feb. 24, 2009

FREDERICK MONDERSON

Barack Obama's Washington, DC Photo 408. The author doubles as the top guy!

"The only way to fully restore America's economic strength is to make the long-term investments that will lead to new jobs, new industries, and a renewed ability to compete with the rest of the world. The only way this century will be another American century is if we confront at last the price of our dependence on oil and the high cost of health care; the schools that aren't preparing our children and the mountain of debt they stand to inherit." BARACK OBAMA, Address to Joint Session of Congress, Feb. 24, 2009

BARACK OBAMA
MASTER OF WASHINGTON DC

"We should never forget that God granted us the power to reason so that we would do His work here on Earth - so that we would use science to cure disease, and heal the sick, and save lives." BARACK OBAMA, speech, Dec. 1, 2006

70.   OBAMA AS EDUCATION REFORMER BY

DR. FRED MONDERSON

Like so many of his creative approaches to problems in the American social and economic body-politic, President Obama now turns to address the issue of education, an important issue upon which the future of America will depend heavily. Within education itself, a number of issues bear upon and will affect the grand design to not simply rescue America from the quagmire it has steadily slipped into over the last decades but to help brighten the chances of success and prosperity in future years. Throughout his campaign Mr. Obama assessed the state of education, viz., instruction, facilities, personnel, strategies, remuneration, creativity, vision and the role and responsibility of government to provide the funding and moral support to elevate American education to a pinnacle that serves as a beacon and pace setter to empower tomorrow's leaders. This way, in the partnership of educational empowerment America must remain a trendsetter in science, medicine, technology, social studies and behavioral mannerisms. However, while this ideal is attainable, it is far from current and in order that this becomes a reality there must be a concerted and meaningful partnership between government, educators, administrators, parents and students. Notwithstanding, in order to achieve the best results, the political drama surrounding education must play itself out in the best interest of American education in general and the students' well-being and progress in particular.

Yet, while these ideals are worthy aspirations, the reality is that American education is in crisis for a number of reasons, primarily owing to the notion of social equality and adequate access, the broad funding designed to encourage achievement and the nature of creativity from all who could better the lot of all. Because America is a great and expansive nation where the seedlings of great

FREDERICK MONDERSON

minds are first nurtured, then the requisite support ought to be given without emphasis on favoring one group or region over another. A very good example to underscore an analogy with regional financial disbursement can be drawn from the role and make-up of the military. Whether in peace or war, America draws its citizen soldiers equally from every city and state in the nation to serve in every branch of its services. This they do with distinction in performance of duty, sometimes giving life and limb. Therefore, similarly that dedicated service and recruitment for defense of the Republic, consideration for educational support ought to be equal regardless of person or region. This seems to be the ideal Senator, now President Barack Obama, preached and now seeks to achieve in order to correct the deficiencies and set the nation on a path that elevates and sustains America as a leader in the multiplicity of educationally oriented engines that drive the progress of modern civilization.

The fact of the matter, for some, American education is in the doldrums in segments of the inner cities, some rural areas and particularly among minorities. The path to this dismal state of affairs is long, studded with moments of brilliance and gloom; and for African Americans progress of the earliest educational initiatives, viz., head start, etc., the flow and ebb will hopefully be enhanced by more flow.

Barack Obama's Washington, DC Photo 409. After the "Rally on the Mall," Dr. Charles Finch gave an intellectually stimulating lecture on "Pathways from the Nile: Genesis of the Cultures of the Western Sudan."

Barack Obama's record as an education advocate has been extensive and the following is shown from "Beyond the Beltway" site.

- Volunteer in your neighborhood & we help pay for college. (Feb 2009)
- $2,500 tax credit for all four years of college. (Feb 2009)
- Quitting high school is quitting on your country. (Feb 2009)
- Invest in early childhood education and higher education. (Aug 2008)

BARACK OBAMA
MASTER OF WASHINGTON DC

- Fight for social & economic justice begins in the classroom. (Jul 2008)
- Make math & science policy a national priority. (Jul 2008)
- To compete, students need at least H.S. & college degree. (Jun 2008)
- Pay for college education for those who commit to teaching. (Jun 2008)
- We need real commitment to education; instead we got NCLB. (Jun 2008)
- $10 billion to guarantee early childhood education for all. (Jun 2008)
- Merit pay ok if based on career instead of a single test. (Apr 2008)
- Evolution & science aren't incompatible with Christian faith. (Apr 2008)
- Mother home-schooled Obama in English while in Indonesia. (Apr 2008)
- Children's First Agenda: zero to five early education. (Feb 2008)
- $4,000 college tuition for 100 hours' public service a year. (Feb 2008)
- Put billions of dollars into early childhood education. (Jan 2008)
- Need after-school and summer programs with good parenting. (Jan 2008)
- Get parents re-engaged in educating the children. (Dec 2007)
- Nationwide program to reconstruct crumbling school buildings. (Sep 2007)
- STEP UP: summer learning opportunities for disadvantaged. (Aug 2007)
- We left the money behind for No Child Left Behind. (Aug 2007)
- Pay "master teachers" extra, but with buy-in from teachers. (Aug 2007)
- Supreme Court was wrong on school anti-integration ruling. (Jul 2007)
- Incentives to hire a million teachers over next decade. (Jun 2007)
- Pay teachers more money & treat them like professionals. (Jun 2007)
- Cut banks out and add $4.5 Billion to college loans. (Mar 2007)
- More teacher pay in exchange for more teacher accountability. (Oct 2006)
- Guarantee affordable life-long, top-notch education. (Jun 2006)
- Sex education needed to help children discuss molestation. (Oct 2004)
- Provide decent funding and get rid of anti-intellectualism. (Jul 2004)
- Address the growing achievement gap between students. (May 2004)
- Will add 25,000 teachers in high-need areas. (May 2004)
- Free public college for any student with B-average. (Jul 1998)

School Choice

- I doubled charter schools in Illinois; but no vouchers. (Oct 2008)
- Vouchers don't solve the problems of our schools. (Oct 2008)
- Fact Check: McCain for national reforms & also DC vouchers. (Oct 2008)

FREDERICK MONDERSON

- Supports charter schools; it's important to experiment. (Feb 2008)
- We need a sense of urgency about improving education system. (Sep 2007)
- Sends kids to private school; but wants good schools for all. (Jul 2007)
- Public school system status quo is indefensible. (Oct 2006)
- Supports charter schools and private investment in schools. (Jul 1998)

Voting Record

First Senate bill: increase Pell Grant from $4,050 to $5,100. (Aug 2007)

- Sponsored legislations that recruit and reward good teachers. (Sep 2004)
- Voted YES on $52M for "21st century community learning centers." (Oct 2005)
- Voted YES on $5B for grants to local educational agencies. (Oct 2005)
- Voted YES on shifting $11B from corporate tax loopholes to education. (Mar 2005)

All this, notwithstanding, President Obama continues to emphasize, encourage and offer incentives so American education can constantly improve to retain the nation's cutting edge position among the best nations of the world as education will always remain the source of knowledge and power.

Barack Obama's Washington, DC Photo 410. Youngster stands before Union Station entranceway with flag poster that reads "God Bless America."

BARACK OBAMA
MASTER OF WASHINGTON DC

"The single biggest threat that we face is a nuclear weapon or some weapon of mass destruction. What that means is that we have to be extraordinarily aggressive and vigilant in controlling nuclear proliferation. We have a nuclear proliferation treaty and strategy that has failed. I think it failed in Iran. It also failed in North Korea. That has to be rewritten and renegotiated. And I think that we have to rapidly accelerate the manner in which we are locking down nuclear materials in the former Soviet Union. You know, the Lugar-Nunn bill has shown itself to work. Unfortunately, right now it's on a thirteen-year timetable, in which the United States puts in resources to make sure that those resources are secured. I think we can rapidly advance it to the point where we get it down to four years."
BARACK OBAMA, debate, Oct. 12, 2004

71. BARACK OBAMA: THE GREAT VISIONARY
By

Dr. Fred Monderson

Every once in a great while a visionary comes along whose passion, intellectual fortitude, a great work ethic and tremendous appeal to masses endears him or her to multitudes over great distances. Barack Hussein Obama is one such individual whose election was a day that changed everything and whose visionary capabilities has mesmerized the American people causing them to trust and ultimately elect him President of the United States of America, a position of tremendous influence at home and abroad. This likability has helped those who have felt victimized by American policies and practices his visionary nature has created the environment whereby he has blunted the enormous anti-Americanism developed over many years. Supporters may have been overlooking but certainly not forgetting the challenges posed to his personal safety and well-being.

Case in point, everyone, in and out of Iran seemed pleased that the upcoming election reflected the democratic process at work and that the people would get a chance to elect those who most represent their ideals. The debates and other election actions promised much for progress in Iran as the world watched. The thing conspicuously absent in the debates was the mention of America, the "great Satan." Within two days some 80 million votes were counted and the winner declared. The people took to the streets to protest what they seem to rightfully believe, the elections were stolen. In the United States, Republicans especially began criticizing President Obama for not speaking out about the Iranian government's responses to their people protesting about their election results.

Barack Obama's Washington DC 411. Folks getting ready to ride the train at Union Station to perhaps head out of town.

The visionary character of President Obama coupled with the input from his team of "wise men" determined he should not comment on developments on the street in Iran. In as much the name of America was not a part of the election nor was it being mentioned in the street, the United States should guardedly monitor developments on the ground but maintain a balanced approach. Republicans on the other hand, wanting a more forceful response began criticizing the President for not speaking out on the election results. Senator John McCain, as is customary, publicly labeled the election results a fraud. This "shoot from the lip" attitude of his is characteristic of the expressions he voiced at the last Russian invasion when he spoke out while Senator Obama consulted with "wise men" and other officials familiar with foreign security issues, before he spoke. Similarly, while the President took a cautious approach to the developments, in his first comments about the election results, the Ayatollah Khomeini blamed America and Britain and Israel for interfering even though the US had not done so. Therefore, it seems President Obama's cautiously neutral stance was really the best way to go so as to maintain America's non-involvement in Iranian developments.

BARACK OBAMA
MASTER OF WASHINGTON DC

Barack Obama's Washington, DC Photo 412. Souvenir replica of the White House.

Thomas Jefferson in his *First Inaugural Address* on March 4, 1801 stated: "But would the honest patriot, in the full tide of successful experiment, abandon a government which has so far kept us free and firm, on the theoretic and visionary fear that this government, the world's best hope, may possibility want energy to preserve itself?"

The visionary nature of President Barack Obama seems to have surfaced as early as his first graduation from Columbia University when perhaps he began believing some force may have been helping to shape his destiny. Graduating from Harvard University Law School, that same guardian spirit seemed bent on directing his path leading him to Chicago rather than Wall Street for visions of the future may have seen the ultimate mess that would surface later while Mr. Wonderful would also be there to come to their rescue.

FREDERICK MONDERSON

Barack Obama's Washington, DC Photo 413. Ringing the bell in front of Union Station.

BARACK OBAMA
MASTER OF WASHINGTON DC

"It's only when you hitch your wagon to something larger than yourself that you will realize your true potential." BARACK OBAMA, speech, Jun. 16, 2006

72. OBAMA: UNEASY LIES THE HEAD
BY
DR. FRED MONDERSON

President Barack Obama has been the subject of criticism from right, left and center and this proves anyone can be criticized by people all the time. From the inception of his assuming the mantle of leadership of this great nation, Barack Obama has been the victim of personality attacks, policy attacks and even attacks on principles; that is, from the perspective of those leading the attacks. Everyone is familiar with the pre-election attacks on his patriotism, experience, religious affiliation, social connections, elitism, even the perennial and nauseating attacks on his birth status designed to disqualify his right to hold the Presidency. Whatever happened to "Joe the Plumber" who coined the notion Obama was a socialist? He was last seen in a *New York Post* political cartoon being "flushed down the bowl" by Obama! Remember the claim Obama won't know what to do as President when the "3:00 AM phone call comes." That is not altogether correct as evidenced from his handling the Somali Pirates and from his relentless and ultimately successful pursuit of Osama ben-Laden!

President Obama was criticized on the economy as the job marked greatly hemorrhaged losing more than half a million jobs per month and he had not instantly rectified the situation in less than two years that had taken more than a decade to create. Now the economy is adding jobs in the low hundred thousands, even though this is still not enough to get the nation out of its state of national job stagnation. Some experts have argued some American jobs will never return since so much was lost to outsourcing. The President was criticized for aiding Wall Street, the Automobile Industry, Banks, and his use of TARP and Stimulus funds. Failure of those significant sectors of the economy would have had devastating and long lasting consequences for those industries and the nation as a whole. Meanwhile the "Birthers Movement" continued their "fools' errand" challenging Mr. Obama's citizenship while undermining the credibility of the Office of the Presidency and that of Hawaii State officials who "certified Mr. Obama was born in that state." Put all the weight on the good mule meant Mr. Obama was also criticized for the housing crisis that resulted in massive home foreclosures, greatly reduced new housing starts and a tremendous decline in home value as well as the fall of lending giants including FANNY MAE and FREDDIE MAC.

FREDERICK MONDERSON

Through all that turmoil, ignoring the misogynistic rhetoric, President Obama went about his duty of improving America's image abroad, putting America first, laying the foundation for America's resurgence as the world's technological leader, sponsoring a new generation of clean air and clean energy initiatives to reduce the nation's dependence on foreign oil. But even more, Mr. Obama emphasized education as a cornerstone of the future competitiveness of the nation. He offered incentives to spur more creativity in approaches to educational successes. He also unveiled plans for upgrading the nation's transportation system emphasizing the need for a high speed rail system to be competitive with other nation's who have active high speed means of transportation. Completing this sweeping new approach to American initiative, and utilizing stimulus funds the President began disbursing such dollars to move America forward on the economic front by repairing roads, bridges, airports, tunnels and ports. He extended unemployment insurance and helped states burdened by economic conditions as demands grew.

He took to the airwaves and expended much time encouraging people to be patient and creative to help themselves in these troubled times in which he never stopped working to make things better. He endeavored and supported all sorts of creative social projects that could give people a sense of usefulness. He kept insisting in these difficult times, Representatives of the people should support "the flag' rather than be intransigently committed to political party ideological talking points aimed at the 2012 election rather than compromise in the best interest of the nation. Republicans never stopped running for Congress after the 2008 and 2010 elections with an eye to 2012. What is interesting, in the 2010 elections many "Tea Party" Republicans made what would appear a "pact with the devil" by signing a "no tax agreement" to get support to be elected. Despite what they may say, this is not putting America first for the man who now controls "their mortgage" have them on a leash. So much so, even though America's credibility stood on the cliff's edge, breaking rank meant the "devil could call for their souls," despite the rationale of blaming the debt on the shoulders of future generations. Retired Senator Alan Cranston publicly decried their arrangement.

Through all this, Mr. Obama demonstrated outstanding leadership that turned the tide despite criticisms, threats, unduly caricature and Republican obstructionism. In addition, as Commander-in-Chief, he continues to prosecute two wars in Afghanistan and Iraq, while checking militants in Pakistan through drone attacks. In addition, he never let up on domestic terrorism, Mexican border violence, and sundries issues such as earthquakes, Somali pirates, tsunamis, radiation contamination in Japan and nuclear safety at home, NASA's space program and a whole lot more, even welcoming winning teams to the White House.

Some commentators have argued street protest to address social grievances pioneered by blacks in this country, was taken over by the "Tea Party" and this tactic was instrumental in their successes in the 2010 mid-term elections. Now "in

BARACK OBAMA
MASTER OF WASHINGTON DC

power" people begin to see the challenges the "Tea Party Movement" posed to genuine leadership and now their heads lie uneasily because of their proposed draconian methods not much dissimilar to their attitude towards the now President Obama in their initial coming together where he was characterized and caricatured in the most disrespectful and uncivil manner. So much so, the public's watch word to the "Tea Party" has become "wait till the next election," when, like the proverbial "tea" they will be "thrown overboard." This is primarily because the Republican horse is being controlled by its cart full of some 80 freshmen "Tea Party" Congressmen who will not budge on compromise, that quintessential American legislative equalizer, the "compromise."

When President Obama made his "Address in Cairo" he stressed the need for reforms by Middle Eastern governments that focus on needs and aspirations of their people such as jobs, education, freedom of speech and right to peacefully assemble and protest grievances. He was quick to point out these are among the pressing issues that lead to pessimism and attract young people to terrorism. Seemingly none of the leaders paid attention and some two years later Tunisia and Egypt erupted in peaceful revolution forcing their leaders from power. Now Libya is mired in a serious rebellion that raises questions about Gadhafi efforts to preserve his hold on power while the nation flagellates itself and his power has gradually declined. The same can be said for Syria whose unleashed military forces are decimating its own citizens in a desperate struggle to "hold back the dawn." Even Bahrain and Yemen are greatly challenged, all reflective of a new awakening as the "Arab Spring" has challenged repressive regimes that will do anything to retain power, and as such, protests remain viable promising a "long, hot summer" and an "early fall."

Perhaps his critics viewed President Obama from the ankle down and seemingly only see less than 10% of the man. Its known, Mr. Obama came to national public attention with his 2004 Democratic National Convention speech. There, applauded for a speech reflective of a brilliant mind;, he came with the highest American educational background which resulted in his being elected President with the revelation he had amassed a war chest of millions of dollars and millions of followers in his database. Even from the time he ran for President, as a thinking man, whenever faced with insufficient knowledge of any topic, Mr. Obama would "go to school" by consulting some of the most knowledgeable advisors on the particular issue. Hence he gained a reputation for studying every issue before making his considerable judgment and decision. It is arguable such an approach enabled the turnaround of national conditions. We see his imprint in reforms in the financial system through new federal regulations; albeit Wall Street and the banks are stronger, strengthened, they're making and disbursing money; unemployment has dipped through job creation from both public and private hiring, yet much more needs to be done; new housing starts are evident foreclosures are down, and houses are regaining some of their lost value; the domestic automobile industry,

FREDERICK MONDERSON

particularly General Motors, Chrysler and especially Ford Motors are more competitive and holding their own in market share.

Questions as to how far the Republicans and their "Tea Party" allies will go are tied to their repeat success at the next, general or Presidential Elections. In a hopeful boast new Gingrich had predicted the Health Care Reform will be repealed in 2013, the first year of the next Federal Administration presumably headed by him. Some now recognize this as wishful thinking on part of another of those aspirants to the office Mr. Obama now holds. It is surely wishful thinking as the wheels of Mr. Gingrich's wagon have begun to come off over the rough terrain he must travel at the start of a long, uphill road!

ON UNION STATION CORNICE, CENTER, Washington, DC

Fire – Greatest of discoveries enabling man to live in various climates, use many foods and compel the forces of nature to do his work

Electricity – Carrier of light and power – Discoverer of time and space – Bearer of human speech over land and sea – Greatest servant of man – Itself unknown.
Thou hast put all things under his feet.
Sweetener of hut and of hall – Bringer of life out of naught – Freedom o fairest of all – The Daughter of time and thought
Man's imagination has conceived all numbers and letters – All tools, vessels and trade – All philosophy and poetry and all politics - The truth shall make you free

The Farm – Best home of the family - Main home of national wealth – Foundation of civilized society - The natural providence.

The old mechanic arts controlling new forces – Build new highways for goods and men – Override the ocean and make the very ether carry human thought – The desert shall blossom as the rose.

RIGHT SIDE

Let all the ends thou aimst at be thy country's. Thy god's. And truths be noble and the nobleness that lie in other men sleeping but never dead – will rise in majesty to meet thine own.

LEFT SIDE

He that would bring home the wealth of the Indies must carry the wealth of the Indies with him. So it is in traveling – A man must carry knowledge with him, If he would bring home knowledge.

BARACK OBAMA
MASTER OF WASHINGTON DC

"Washington is a beautiful city. It's very nice living above the store; you can't beat the commute. It's just sometimes all you hear in Washington is the clamor of politics. And all that noise can drown out the voices of the people who sent you there. So when I took office, I decided that each night I would read 10 letters out of the tens of thousands that are sent to us by ordinary Americans every day -- this is my modest effort to remind myself of why I ran in the first place. Some of these letters tell stories of heartache and struggle. Some express gratitude, some express anger. I'd say a good solid third call me an idiot -- which is how I know that I'm getting a good, representative sample. Some of the letters make you think -- like the one that I received last month from a kindergarten class in Virginia. Now, the teacher of this class instructed the students to ask me any question they wanted. So one asked, "How do you do your job?" Another asked, "Do you work a lot?" Somebody wanted to know if I wear a black jacket or if I have a beard -- so clearly they were getting me mixed up with the other tall guy from Illinois. And one of my favorites was from a kid who wanted to know if I lived next to a volcano. I'm still trying to piece the thought process on this one. Loved this letter. But it was the last question from the last student in the letter that gave me pause. The student asked, 'Are people being nice?' Are people being nice?" BARACK OBAMA, remarks at University of Michigan, May 1, 2010

73. VOTE OR DIE! Well, By Dr. Fred Monderson

The next general election in November 2012 is tremendously important for a number of equally important reasons; particularly national and state, whether combating voter apathy or expressing concern about the "new normal," national trend or the President's performance, people must understand the importance of voting. As someone who has voted in every election since 1972, I was dismayed by a comment made around the time of the primary last September. Asked whether he was going to vote in New York this individual responded "No! I don't like the politics of Albany!" As such then, a critique of his behavior as well as voter apathy in general is very apropos, because only by voting can he change such behaviors.

Some people need to be reminded the struggle for the right to vote, particularly by blacks and women in America has been a long, difficult and challenging experience fraught with deception, bloodletting and disappointment. Still, while the disenfranchised won the right to vote, there has been and still continues a movement to disfranchise particularly black segments of the voting constituency.

FREDERICK MONDERSON

Hence, any form of "voluntary disfranchisement" should not be condoned since we already have the Prison Industrial System disenfranchising Blacks at a rapid rate!

The Civil War (1860-1865) resulted in the "Civil War Amendments." 13th, 14th, and 15th that conferred freedom, citizenship and the right to vote on the *freed* African American, but also on citizens, native born or naturalized. To exercise that first ballot experiment, African Americans travelled a rocky road to the voting booth. They were subjected to voting restrictions through literacy tests, fraught with problems; poll taxes that didn't always apply; property taxes even if persons didn't own property; intimidation and disqualification at the poll; deceptive signs that misdirected voters away from the polls; and the "grandfather clause" that trapped first time voters. Don't get me started with the Ku Klux Klan and Knights of the White Camelia; all terrorists by today's definition, who intimidated and killed blacks through lynching, tar and feathering and other forms of disfigurement. Finally, when black people persevered, at great personal risk and elected their representatives these officials had to battle prejudice and discrimination on the way to and from and at the legislative chamber.

This experiment collapsed with the end of Reconstruction and those the voting rights legislation were designed to help lost a great deal in the 100 years that ultimately gave birth anew to the Civil Right Movement. After tremendous struggle at great personal cost, the *1964 Civil Rights Act* gave Americans the *1965 Voting Rights Act* with the mandatory renewal clause every 25 years. The irony of this latter reality is that though African Americans are among the most loyal Americans, they are subject to this discriminating and dehumanizing experience. Let's face it. Germans, Italians, even the British, French as well as Japanese and Russian Americans, people who have killed and threatened America and Americans in wars, are not subject to this legal handicap. Nevertheless, despite all of this, the power of the ballot to elect African Americans and be influential in other races is a reality that cannot be wasted.

In South Africa, the great majority had been prevented from voting and when given the opportunity that historic vote pictured extra-long lines that vindicated Nelson Mandela's ordeal and the worldwide struggle to free him and South Africa.

In this country, the audacity of Barack Obama to run for and win the presidency was a tremendous opportunity for African Americans, young voters and other minorities and people in general to cast that historic vote.

On the national level, many people have criticized President Obama for not delivering on the change he promised, expecting a magic wand "fix it" for what ails America. Conceptually speaking, the belief was that he would have rapidly

BARACK OBAMA
MASTER OF WASHINGTON DC

built up a "skyscraper of change" that would have addressed unemployment, housing, financial and economic reform opportunities, energy, education, internal improvements, health care, while waging two wars in Iraq and Afghanistan and fending domestic terrorist threats at home and combating Somali pirates all at once. These many challenges and more the President faced against a recalcitrant scorched earth obstructionist policy driven Republican Party and their allies in and out of government and particularly after the 2010 elections with one goal in mind, Stop Obama at all costs! What was not evident up to now is that the Republicans had built a "sub-valley" size hole that the President had to fill before he could reach ground level. That is like "filling the substructure, constructing the structure to build the superstructure of clean energy;" a better and a more robust education and science endeavor, with economic, financial and capital reform coupled with improvements in housing, health care and all forms of job creation designed to improve the condition of all Americans, particularly by putting the economy on a stronger footing. Yet, there are those persons who believe in the vision of President Obama and understand the nature of the opposition and, as Maryland Democratic Senator Barbara Mikulski remarked in regards the impending debt ceiling crisis with catastrophic implications, America "cannot fall, cannot falter," cannot fail! This is essentially the position President Obama has worked unrelentingly to bring about.

As such, much of his base is committed to vote in unprecedented numbers to ensure his agenda gets the support it deserves. That is to say, "Vote or Die!"

FREDERICK MONDERSON

Barack Obama's Washington DC Photo 414. Front door to the White House.

74. REFLECTIONS ON THE NEW OBAMA AGE
By
Dr. Fred Monderson

President Obama has been villainized by many persons particularly those who lay claim to being "analysts;" and one has to wonder how such persons can be trusted, having shown their biased, some have called, bigoted, underbellies. The thing that can be said for Mr. Obama, he takes these insults in stride allowing others to see the ridiculous lengths people would go to insult the President of the United States! In aftermath of the raid on Osama bin Laden's compound, at the height of the "last hurrah" of the "Birther charade," a political cartoon in the *New York Post* showed President Obama instructing his forces "the next compound you will raid will be Trump Towers." Well, this never materialized for Donald Trump soon self-destructed and reclused himself as a Presidential contender, though claiming "victory" for having Obama surrender his birth certificate. Is he a "winning loser" or what? Nevertheless, the thoughtful brilliance of Obama is seen in his standing

BARACK OBAMA
MASTER OF WASHINGTON DC

still and allowing such critics to bake and finally eat their own "crow pie!" Does he know, "Quitters never win and winners never quit!"

Republicans, unable to tarnish Obama's brilliance in never ending critique of his social policies, constantly revert to *ad hominem*. One can wonder how Republican "big guns" as McCain, Palin, McConnell, Boehner, DeMint, etc., feel after a "busy day at the office," when get home, flop down on the sofa, unfold the newspaper or turn on the TV, to be greeted by fallout of "One of our guys," called President Obama a "dick" or as Rep. Wilson did in the Chamber of the House, telling the President "you lie" etc. Again, after his speech to the nation on the impending debt ceiling quagmire, Representative Joe Walsh (R. Illinois) even arguing against Speaker Boehner's new "Proposal" remarked President Obama should "stop lying!" The question is, do the likes of these guys "high-five" each other, get on the phone to offer congratulations for another notch of insult in their belt or squirm in their seats, having unlocked Pandora's, I mean, the Republican's "box" of the evils of non-cooperation with the president, perhaps because he is African American? Do these Republicans and their "Tea Party allies" realize they're actually insulting the Presidency and the American people, equally showing their "other or hidden side."

Equally, a new "shoot from the lip" attack on the character of the President was made by Mark Halperin, a commentator on MSNBC who thought he was on "delayed feed," and called Mr. Obama a "D" word that was not Democrat! The CNN ticker's newsflash read "MSNBC panelist suspended after Obama insult." While Republicans may, perhaps, be able to claim Mr. Halperin is probably not a "card carrying member" of their club, "independent critics" opposed to Mr. Obama are on their side of the line and therefore as such, perhaps, are unintentional, allies.

On CNN's "**In the Arena**" with Elliot Spitzer, former Governor of New York, a Mr. Abrams, seemed one of the first honest voices, in commenting on MSNBC's action in response to Mr. Halperin's remarks following the President's press conference. He expressed: "This is not something you say about the President of the United States!" However, such is indicative of behaviors towards the man. Equally, let's not forget the Colorado, in a "Post Racial America" calling the President a "tar baby!"

What this teachable moment indicates, even "nice looking" "normal" people can drop "bombs." So, what is it about President Obama, except his race, that really motivates people to speak so loosely and disrespectfully about this man of character, intellect, intent, humanity! Equally, we recently heard a Republican Senator, on the floor of the House of Representatives, say, "The President should be ashamed ...." For what should he be ashamed? He did not reach to grab under

FREDERICK MONDERSON

some person's ankle in a public restroom! He has never been "hiking the Appalachian Trail." He never sent salacious e-mails to Congressional Pages, President Obama has not fathered any illegitimate children and nor been unfaithful to his wife! What is it the world sees in Mr. Obama that disgusting elements at home do not?

To show their far out nature, in the smoke and mirrors euphoria that clouded "Arnold's" rise to become Governor of California, many Republicans began championing the notion of "changing the constitutional requirement" that a presidential candidate be native born, so that Arnold Schwarzenegger could run for and, hoping to win, become President. How beautiful that Pied Piper's tune sounded! Unfortunately he had pooped on the party but bottled it up in a closet that was finally opened. Meanwhile, other "allied wings" of the Republican Party incessantly, vehemently and inclandestinely with much vituperativeness denied Barack Obama's citizenship and right to be President! As betting men, these Republicans, in their "tunnel vision," chose the potential long shot as a safe bet, while ignoring the safe bet as a long shot. In other words, they were hoodwinked and willing to choose a fellow Republican for President who cheated on his wife, sleep with the help, fathered an illegitimate child and lied to cover it up over an intelligent and respectable married man with a beautiful wife and two lovely children who consistently manifest ideals even Republicans want in a family man and who works feverishly in a job he was elected to.

For argument sake, let us suppose the covered farce was successful and Arnold elected President of the United States, after having the constitution changed and deluding all Americans. So here we have him abroad attending, let's say, a G-8 meeting with all the bells and whistles euphoria; him "flying the flag" and there he is waving on the platform with leaders of the other great nations awaiting the photo op! Meanwhile, customary anarchists are arrayed outside, picketing. Now, here comes **Wikileaks**' leader Assange who releases the ethically damaging information about Arnold's illegitimate behavior. Try to think of Danny Kaye's "kid" blurting out, "Look at the King!" Can you imagine the embarrassment and mileage our enemies would get in criticizing America for this immoral chasm!

Here again, on that Spitzer program, another Republican Congressman boasted and took credit for saying the "President should be ashamed," for whatever. Now, here we have an intelligent, professionally and academically qualified Mr. Obama, whose intellect, stamina and strategies and tactics awarded him the US Presidency. Most people, whether in government or not, who have disparaged Mr. Obama constantly, do not have the intellectual fortitude or academic accreditation brought to the office as this man genuinely committed to seriously challenging problems facing the office he inherited. Word has it, in the academic age of the 1970s especially, when young Adjuncts and Professors applied for teaching positions, particularly in the Community Colleges, the people in control of "P and B" would demand the highest qualifications from these new people. These "educrats," on the

BARACK OBAMA
MASTER OF WASHINGTON DC

other hand, had "slipped in" with degrees in "Basket-making" and "Pottery" and now controlled those powerful committees. Did Mr. Obama's critics come in through the back door of "Basket-making" or "Gerry-Mandering?" and now in those positions of power, are they manifesting their true intentions?

Case in point! CBS recently aired a documentary about the 50-year old murder of Louis Allen, Civil Rights advocate, a proud veteran of World War II, who lived in a town called **Liberty**, Mississippi. His suspected murderer, according to the best estimates of the FBI operative Cynthia Diddle, still walks the streets. This is just one of more than 100 racially motivated murder cases that have remained unsolved, and though some of the active participants have died out, others are still alive. One thing pointed out in the documentary; in the age of southern racial terrorism from the Nineteenth Century onwards, anyone who wanted to be elected to any office in much of that post-bellum South, whether sheriff, deputy sheriff, town clerk, county post, dog catcher, etc., had to belong to some terror group such as the "Klan" and had to actively carry out their mandate of intimidation, even murder. It's reasonable, such persons' descendants never left their region, perhaps evolved new strategies and tactics and could very well be the chief architects of the anti-Obama assault in Congress and elsewhere. If such, family ties probably got these people into those positions of power in the government and elsewhere and now seems they have forgotten this is the age of "post racial America."

Again, perhaps if these people had the educational, intellectual and even moral qualifications Mr. Obama possesses they would not be so outlandish in their behaviors. With a sound educational background, one sees the world and people differently!

The Congressman also added the President launched his re-election campaign nearly two years before the next election date. What he did not include, President Obama has been under attack before he became President, while he is president, on his way to re-election, and will be attacked even after he is re-elected and perhaps after he leaves office in 2017. Republicans never stopped running particularly after their 2010 victory in Congress. Well, let the American people do the math about these people and their intentions to take this country back to the 17th Century "Stone Age!" Blacks certainly never forget the long and arduous road they traveled and still travel! This time, however, they've learned a few tricks along the way!

Now, as the nation faced it's most catastrophic and embarrassing debacle, Republicans fiddle obstinately obdurate in opposition to helping the President's efforts to move the country to a better state. The current obstacle of raising the debt ceiling to avoid an unthinkable and embarrassing default, pits Republicans particularly those of the 2010 wave who en-masse signed a "no-tax pledge" and were elected and now adamantly oppose the current economic measures. Why? Because they're on that "man's leash!" In a recent press conference President Obama said to his opponents "If you want to be a leader then you have to lead." In many people's views, the "Party of No" has not led and refused to say "What they will say yes to!" They seem to be single-mindedly focused on "Getting that Nigger out of the White House!"

The interesting thing is the debt ceiling has been raised nearly 100 times, some 78 times since 1968, 18 times under Ronald Reagan, under Bill Clinton and 7 times under George Bush; yet Republicans will not allow one passage under the Democrat Obama trying to preserve the full faith and credit of the United States. Congressional insiders as Mitch McConnell and John Boehner have certainly voted many times to raise the debt ceiling, so why not now! What these two leaders have finally realized, "What they prayed for" in "Stop Obama" may very well be "America's Titanic" in its economic default with its tremendous implications that Peter Siris in "Debt Game's a Big Loser" (New York *Daily News*, Tuesday July 12, 2011, p. 35) calls "irreparable harm to the economy and the financial markets."

Still, a contrast can be made of President Obama by two individuals whose assessment underscore his leadership and betray the "penny-ante" nature of the critic. Case in point, former governor and presidential contender Tim Pawlenty appeared on CNN's Candy Crowley's **State of the Union**, Sunday, July 24, 2010, 9:00 am.

Saying he long favored the House passed and Senate rejected "Cut, Cap and Balance" measure, along with a Constitutional Amendment, which in a way, showed why he's at the bottom of the Republican list and high among losers. Thus Mr. Pawlenty accused President Obama of not having a plan. He went further saying the President "does not have courage." That he is "hiding in the basement" and offers "fake rhetoric" and "sophistry." Even more, decrying "the country is sinking," "the country is drowning," Pawlenty accused Mr. Obama of not being able to "walk and chew gum;" a comment which underscores his inabilities and recent denying "not dropping out soon" from the presidential race due to poor ratings.

On the other hand, **Presidential Historian** David McCullough, author of *Truman, John Adams*, and now *The Greater Journey*, appearing on CNN's Fareed Zakaria's **Global Public Square**, Sunday, July 24, 2011, 10:00 am, began by saying "I admire President Obama tremendously." The President has had to face "problems few Presidents have had to contend with and he has handled himself very well" Continuing that "no one human being should be charged with handling such great responsibility" he emphasized "what really matters is what's written in the book of history." Being "optimistic," "distressed" and even "stunned" at current state of affairs, he emphasized that "exceptional presidents are the

BARACK OBAMA
MASTER OF WASHINGTON DC

exception" and that "George Washington was our greatest President" Mr. McCullough responded to the question "What makes a great President?"

Somehow he seemed to be including President Obama the following individuals who must have:

(1)   The capacity to move the country to do better;

(2)   The power of the written and spoken word;

(3)   An ability to stick to your principles;

(4)   To work with people who you disagree with or do not like.

Mr. McCulloch put great store in "We too will be judged by history."

Americans have begun to judge both parties, but seem overwhelmingly to blame President Bush (No. 43) and Republicans for the current economic mess.

Treasury Secretary Timothy Geithner is of the view, "It's unthinkable this country would not meet its obligations" and that "We cannot leave the threat of default hanging over the American economy."

In discussing cuts in the current negotiations, Senator Diane Feinstein on CNN's State of the Nation, expressed: "The wealthiest should help with this crisis and it should not be on the backs of people least able to afford it." That 39 Senators support the position of the "Gang of Six" (3 Democrats and 3 Republicans) she pointed out Republicans have said "No to Simpson-Bowles and No to the Gang of Six." Sad to say, "Something that can be done very simply is being held hostage in a high stakes game."

FREDERICK MONDERSON

75. Barack Obama
Master of Washington DC
Postscript
By
Dr. Fred Monderson

Again, in the movie "Men of Honor" starring Robert De Niro and Cuba Gooding, the Master Chief De Niro told the young recruit, "I don't know why anyone would want this job" as a Navy Diver because of the inherent difficulties in the responsibilities. These were indeed Men of Honor! The same could be said of Barack Obama, himself a Man of Honor, as he recognized the plight his nation faced and stepped up to the plate to provide indispensible leadership in service to rescue America from the economic freefall wrecking havoc on financial, housing, employment and environmental spectrums across the landscape whose greatness was sorely threatened. The image of this nation had suffered tremendously from dynamics relative to the invasion of Iraq and other foreign policy blunders that helped amplify the notion of the "ugly American" as reflective of this great land. To this we may add the two wars, a prescription drug plan not paid for and a tremendous tax cut for the wealthy by the Republican controlled government. We may equally add the current debacle, "America held Hostage," as the Republican controlled House of Representatives unflinchingly refused to compromise their signed "No Tax" pledge made to an individual for his support before the 2010 elections even though such a stance threatens not just the American economy but has worldwide economic implications for other nations as China, Japan, Saudi Arabia, who hold American debt of immense value. They will question the worth of their holdings and after this "squeeze play brinksmanship" they will certainly up the interest on future loans. On the domestic front any default threatens higher interest rates for mortgages, credit card debt and even automobile loans; among other things.

Nevertheless, taking stock, we see the struggle to combat the threat of terrorism, dropping the ball on Afghanistan and problems created from emerging centers of terrorist hotspots concurrent with the global economic crisis resulting in aftermath of September 11, 2001, despite the tremendous effort of Barack Obama to rescue the American economy from going over the cliff, playing political games Republicans, uninterested in compromise "as some may say," are about to "drive the car into the ditch again." On July 29, days before the Tuesday default deadline, Terry Young Tweeted on CNN "The Tea Party is ruining our country." Mildred Hawkins Tweeted "Play in the Park not with my Social Security." Even Ernie Powell pleaded, "Don't cut Social security. Do not make deals to cut Social Security." Thus, in a local New York tabloid newspaper a Voicer pointed out, by

BARACK OBAMA
MASTER OF WASHINGTON DC

November 2010, the economy was getting better, we were on the mend, adding jobs and seeing housing starts on the rise, and the "Tea Party Republicans" took over and reversed all this! In this time of heightened expectations, for many people the "fat lady's song" now seems more inevitable.

However, before that final curtain, we must reflect how along came this African American possessing the wherewithal of what "Dutch Schultz" in the movie **Hoodlum** characterized "Bumpy Johnson" as having, "watermelon for nuts;" confident in his capability to wage a credible campaign to become President of the United States as faith or Divine Province would have it. He persevered, and Arming himself with a formidable transition team and with full cooperation from the outgoing Bush Administration, Barack Hussein Obama successfully assumed the mantle of President of the United States and leader of the "Western" and "Free World," a position hardly conceivable for a man of color!

Not one to rest on his laurels, his team of the ablest administrators and advisers the American reservoir of thinkers could muster enabled his forthright challenge of the formidable situation. Obama confronted the complicated issues from financial and economic reform and housing and unemployment to clean air and environmental and education and infrastructure problems while weathering the storms of Republicans obstructionism and other allied criticisms. Racial and social pejorative characterization took center stage while the President still focused determinedly on terrorism at home and abroad amidst two wars, challenges of Somali pirates, tsunamis, earthquakes, tornados, hurricanes, environmental issues, global warming, rogue nations, competitors, etc., all the while keeping a smiling even "game face," in his message to all the world, America is not finished yet! Now without question, despite the current gloomy situation, Obama's confidence again, says to the world, America is still not finished yet! His exceptionalism was shown in the first round as he laid great store on health care reform! In all this, kudos should go to the brilliant Michelle Obama, who, after each challengingly brutal day when only she would see the "wounds on the President," would tend and bandage them, and send her man out the next day to fight in pursuit of the highest ideals of the American dream he stood for. Facing the wolves, while still looking like a "new penny" Obama characteristically smiled at the world to show the strength of character and resilience of American patriotic not partisan leadership and of its people's resilience even in difficult times.

Yet still, imagine the unmitigated gall of his detractors as Obama continued to steadfastly defend this nation and these same people's right to criticize him as he worked to fulfill the Divine Mandate, be enamored in the love and respect of a wonderful family and the continued loyalty of deep thinking visionaries who truly understood the nature of problems confronting America. Equally, how heroically and gallantly Mr. Obama pride-fully serves and fulfills expectations of an

FREDERICK MONDERSON

electorate, some of whom do understand the nature of things and determine this is the quintessential leader to steward the American ship of state at this critical time.

Being a critic is one of the easiest jobs there is, for all one has to do is say no! However, in this cherished expression is betrayed a selfish and massive realization of what is the calculated measured response to succeed. To take a page from Edmund Burke in his **Reflections on the Revolution in France 1791-1793** that "little minds and empire go ill together;" and though this new age is past the time of empires, the sentiment is, however, still valid, because President Obama's successes betray the "Lilliputian nature of his critics" particularly of the radical fringe and other opponents suffering from Obama Deranged Syndrome, as compared with his giant thinking and indispensible leadership capabilities in service to his beloved nation.

Questions for critics generally and particularly those blacks who specifically argue "Mr. Obama is not doing enough for black people," are simply this, "Have you written or called Senator Mitch McConnell asking what he meant by publicly stating his mission is to 'make Obama a one term president.'" "Has he given up this cherished quest?" Or, "Have you bothered to call or write Senator Jim DeMint asking him to explain what he meant by 'Stop Obama?' or 'His Waterloo?'" "Have you further queried these individuals to request a 'Report Card' on how they are doing with their public boast?" "Have these 'Little Caesars' expressed any condemnation of the significant Washington players who lay 'minefields' Mr. Obama has to tread while challenged to function effectively?" Have they grasped the gravity of the problem critics and opponents have created for Mr. Obama particularly today with this debt ceiling quagmire. In the House, Representative Jackson recently posed questions to Republicans, "Why this President? Is it because of his race?" Has anyone bothered to hold Republicans responsible for "tying Mr. Obama's hand" in dysfunctional not divided leadership in Washington? Have they bothered to question Republicans for pulling the rug from under the President? Why are people not incensed about Tea Party behavior?

With the debt crisis deadline looming, one could well imagine Mr. McConnell "playing possum" before his big "thumbs up." Even Speaker John Boehner has had to bark at his "leashed Tea Party Republican freshmen" "Get your ass in line!" Meanwhile President Obama is sailing his ship to port and dinner with his beautiful wife and lovely kids; until tomorrow when government business again calls or to be awaken to answer the "3:00 AM phone call!"

Recently former Federal Reserve Chief Alan Greenspan said, "Something basically bad is going on. It's not just the economy. It has affected the American spirit." The anti-Obama racism that characterized opposition to Mr. Obama's candidacy and Presidency remained unchecked and finally snowballed into a crash infecting the moral fiber of the nation. Edmund Burke prediction, "The only thing necessary for evil to triumph is for good men to say nothing." No one rebuked the

BARACK OBAMA
MASTER OF WASHINGTON DC

"Birthers," Pastor Anderson praying for the death of the President, the "black protester with guns," right wing groups arming themselves, birth and expansion of the "Tea Party Movement" and its insidious characterization of the President, their "selling their souls to the devil" in a signed entrapment that forces them to hold America and the economy hostage with resulting catastrophic consequences. These are all part of the malaise that has brought this country once more to the brink. But not to worry, for like before, "Captain Obama" will again save the day.

As such then, if I may echo Mr. David McCullough's sentiments, Mr. Obama must be tremendously admired, for he is doing a damn good job, all things considered. Though the opposition has not let up from day one, the President has maintained a cool hand and head while amassing a tremendous amount of legislation that benefits all Americans, particularly his insistence in investing in education, both secondary and higher to cultivate those "ideas, ingenuity, foresight, the most valuable resources" Mr. McCullough identified. The President's emphasis on research and development especially in clean energy sources and attention to infrastructure upgrade, etc., has been a focused interest on a better future for the nation. The American people are not stupid or ideologically cemented in stone to realize, in an age of little bipartisan cooperation, Obama is a hardworking leader, with the best intentions assisted by ablest advisors, tackling a difficult job he inherited while having to face down recalcitrant Republicans. Just as "Tea Party" Republican Members of Congress have refused to break their "No Tax" pledge, DeMint and McConnell may be playing possum, but they, more than likely, have not reneged on their publicly stated mission to sabotage Obama. But it is not Obama they are sabotaging but the American people and their children's future.

As pointed out elsewhere and more for effect, the brilliance of Mr. Obama is clearly evident in the manner in which he couches his legislative package in language that gets passage through the Congress yet still targets those most in need, particularly the same black people some black critics claim to be so concerned about. Unfortunately these people cannot seem to extricate themselves from the maze of their figmented imagination as they continue to circle in confused and repetitious patterns of criticism not in the nation's best interest. President Obama, certainly as a Community Organizer, understands the significance of the social "safety net."

In his latest display of unifying leadership, Mr. Obama had called his opposition; some of the same people who have fanned the flames against him; because he wanted to make a last ditch effort to raise the debt ceiling and equally address the nation's mounting economic woes in meaningful deficit reduction talks. However, hoping to rekindle a little Republican spirit of cooperation, he reminded these lawmakers, they are in Washington to face tough problems facing the American people. As such, they must come together to assist in placing the economy on a firm footing. However, to be successful, he insisted; on entering the White House for these talks, they must leave their political rhetoric at the door, find common ground and make tough decisions to eradicate the impending financial crisis facing the nation. Still, to the last minute, Republicans not willing to compromise have created uncertainty that promise big taxes on the American people, as Senator Mikulski has reported, will result in "high interests on car loans, houses, credit cards, cuts in discretionary spending, and more."

We would all be looking at solutions instead of problems today if the radical Republican fringe leading the charge in Congress and their allies against Mr. Obama, assumed a more cooperative attitude at the start of his tenure. As such, America would have been well-along to addressing the problems of jobs, housing, environment, energy, education, financial and fiscal reform, health care, even the debt ceiling, etc. Such is the work of true patriots, instead of laying minefields on the American social and political landscape. Again, as evidence of compromising leadership, as opposed to Republican obduracy, Mr. Obama said to avert the impending catastrophe he would take heat from his Democratic Party members and would put Social Security, Veterans' benefits, Medicare and Medicaid on the table but would only cut these entitlements under the right circumstances. However, he would acquiesce in cuts in discretionary spending, save monies in Iraqi and Afghanistan drawdown, cut tax subsidies for ethanol, and some other private subsidies. Insisting the wealthy should pay their share with some tax increases, closing tax and corporate loopholes, he still admonished Congressional leaders in Washington that he was hoping for a "changing of hearts and minds; that they act like Americans; act like adults; act for the good of the country."

Thus, to complete his Mandate to recharge, redirect and refocus this nation of tremendous intellectual and moral potential, Mr. Obama needs another 4 more years to get the economy back to working, generating faster growth, and bring the prosperity he initially envisioned. Thus, now is the time for all good people to remain committed and not be sidetracked by people with other agendas. We must vote in unprecedented numbers to re-elect Mr. Obama to show the first time was not a fluke; that we believe in him, his sincerity and work ethic in service to make America a better, more human and prosperous nation for all its citizens. This, as the ship of state sails towards a bright future's promise under the philosophic construct espousing the fatherhood of god and the brotherhood of man!

SOME FINAL OBSERVATIONS
1. CRITICAL SUMMARY

Given the tortuous history of Black people in this country and treatment of President Barack Obama, overwhelmingly we seem reminded "Black people are part of the American household but not part of the American family!"

BARACK OBAMA
MASTER OF WASHINGTON DC

1. INTERPRETATIVE SUMMARY

Predictable, self hate of blacks which unfortunately is reflected in large numbers of blacks due to the constant barrage of negative images/stereotypes to which they are subjected; psychic scarification of the black experience lasting some for 400 years; predictably induced a sense of inferiority and self-hate. Thus, when these wounded people see a black person in a position of the highest office in America, they attack that person because:

a) They feel that he ought not to be there
b) The hatred of themselves requires a hatred of him because he looks like them. This is not helped by the unending efforts of the racists and their cohorts.

2. CRITICAL SUMMARY

Elected Representatives speak for their constituencies so therefore, Representative Doug Lambourn (R-Colorado), calling the President a "tar baby" is based on a reasoned presumption if he did not feel his constituency agrees he would not have spoken such. The question is whether after he has demeaned the Presidency, will they re-elect him and if so, what will this say for his constituency?

2 INTERPRETATIVE SUMMARY

There is a deeply entrenched tendency to redicule, dehumanize, African peole and their descendants by using the concept of black as being indicative of genetic inferiority. The irony is, increasingly scientists agree that the human family has evolved from the early anthropoid apes and this includes the entire human family.

3. CRITICAL SUMMARY

Speaker John Boehner disrespectfully refused to return the President's phone call, yet he could boastfully proclaim after the deal, "We got 98 percent of what we wanted." Guess what? Days later Wall Street lost 500 points and Sand P downgraded America's credit rating. Well, they succeeded in showing this happened under the presidency of a black man! Talk about "Post-racial America!"

3. INTERPRETATIVE SUMMARY

FREDERICK MONDERSON

In the mind's eye of the Speaker, he was not dealing with the President of the United States but with a black male. Therefore, the highest office in the land is treated with contempt because of the color of the person holding the position. Little did he realize, he had not extorted or demeaned the President of the United States but held hostage the American people and seriously impaired the dignity of the United States as a leader of the democratic world. Still, President Obama had the compassion to hug Boehner, who did not respond, and this shows the Presidence's elegance of mind and nobility of spirit after the insult which is a fundamental criteria of class, his not responding to Boehner in kind.

4. CRITICAL SUMMARY

Senator Mitch McConnel in that *New York Times* August 1, 2011 photo giving the thumb's up and "rat that just ate the cat" smile in powerfully indicative of one who had set out to "make Mr. Obama a one-term President."

4. INTERPRETATIVE SUMMARY

Senator Mitch McConnel did not hold President Obama hostage but held the American people hostage. He extorted from the debate the wishes and desires of his party and their base. Is that the aspiration of a US Senator? Is that what a US Senator is all about? What then is the role of a US Senator?

Senator Mitch Mcconnel has therefore exposed himself as anti-democratic and racist. That thumbs up image says "I got that Nigger!" But he really got the people of the United States because as a Senator his intent and actions should be of a higher order and principled. That role is to deliberate and further the interests of the nation and principles of democracy not to demean the leader.

4. INTERPRETATIVE SUMMARY

The President was willing to make compromises that would benefit all the people of the United States. This is what a leader of a democracy is supposed to do for democracy means government by the people and President Obama was elected by the people.

5. CRITICAL SUMMARY

BARACK OBAMA
MASTER OF WASHINGTON DC

Representative Gabrielle Gifford was shot because she supported the imaginative possibilities, democratic initiatives and policies of President Obama's leadership. She left her rehabilitative center where she was recovering from the terrorist attack in Arizona to come to the House of Representatives in Washington, DC, to vote in support of the House measue of President Obama's initiative.

5. INTERPRETATIVE SUMMARY

The superb leadership of President Obama led Representative Gifford to leave her rehabilitation center where she was recovering from wounds inflicted by a native terrorist to come to Washington to support the initiative of President Obama. There is no question her courage and commitment as a Representative of the People played a decisive role in the positive results of the vote. Lochner's shooting of Representative Gifford is analogous to the thumb's up signal from McConnel and indicative of the terrorist meantality and the stop Obama syndrome so many have demonstrated.

Finally, Black Folks may be considered crazy but they are not dumb! They realize the real intent of all this is so the record would show the only time this nation has really defaulted is under the Presidency of a black man. Such actions are clearly evident racism is not dead. But the sagacity and eloquence of President Obama is seen when he placed the matter before the American people and asked them to decide for themselves within the context of fair and unfair; just and unjust. In the context of fairness and unfairness, for example, why should senior citizens, students and the poor bear the burden of cuts in order to balance the budget while millionaires, the rich, the powerful, such as the President are free from making any financial sacrifices to achieve the same end since their wealth increased tremendously over the period when the the debt ceiling was raised and the national debt escalated? Now the Tea Party Republicans "hold the have nots" hostage in this miscarriage of economic justice as their base laugh all the way to the bank!

In the final count, given the tremendous obstacles which have faced the transformational President Barack Obama including ridicule and defamation to racist characterization and threats of bodily harm amidst highly complex national and international issues, it ought to be evident to any reasonable person or persons that he has filled the Office of President with skill, compassion, personal integrity and intellectual autonomy. Present and future reasonable persons will conclude, that President Barack Obama ought to be numbered among the most effective masters of the political arena of the United States in general and Washington, DC in particular.

FREDERICK MONDERSON

WHERE OBAMA STANDS TODAY

Sounding upbeat yet frustrated by a Congress that keeps bickering among its members playing politics at the American people's expense, President Obama addressed an audience at a factory in Holland, Michigan, aided by Stimulus dollars that's making new forms of batteries for Hybrid cars with potential for suppliers jobs across the country that can benefit many from this new form of energy supply. Pointing out America has some of the most knowledgeable workers, with great ingenuity, drive and optimism with a powerful work ethic, he urged those in attendance and those viewing on television to complain to their Representatives, "Don't go back to Washington to bicker, but put country ahead of party and pass meaningful job creation bills." Then he listed the following proposals that Congress should act on:

1. Extend the Payroll Tax Cut that would allow customers with extra money to generate greater demand for domestically produced goods.

2. Pass the Road Construction Jobs Bill that would enable people looking for jobs to repair roads, bridges, seaports, etc.

3. Pass an Agreement on Trade Deals that would strengthen the opportunities for America to sell high priced items as cars, and other technology in foreign ports.

4. Reform the Patent System that would further encourage American ingenuity in technological areas as new and creative forms of energy.

5. Tailor a Jobs Bill that would target Veterans returning from overseas service especially those who are skilled in handling high priced technology and heavy equipment. I might add encourage school attendance through the GI Bill so these veterans can take advantage of educational opportunities as a way to improve their intellectual and technological skills.

6. He wants to end subsidies for oil and gas companies doing very well for as we know, these entities report significant profits from their businesses. Also cut subsidies for successful corporations. He also wants to tax corporations, close loopholes and raise taxes on the rich. That's why he wants Americans to pressure their representatives to also compromise on a sensible plan to address the deficit problem that is burdening America.

Pointing out the world is watching what's going on, he insisted "there is nothing wrong with our country, but there is something wrong with our politics." Himself a victim of "people playing political games," the President reminded listeners of the need to pressure their Representatives to especially enact his jobs measures. He

BARACK OBAMA
MASTER OF WASHINGTON DC

confessed people want him to recall Congress but he feels "The last things we need is Congress spending time arguing in Washington."

President Obama recognized and confessed these are challenging times as events around the world unfold, and that "some things are beyond our control, but we can control our responses to these challenges." Nevertheless, the President reminded all comers "Don't bet against America. Don't bet against our ingenuity."

www.ingramcontent.com/pod-product-compliance
Lightning Source LLC
Chambersburg PA
CBHW070003010526
44117CB00011B/1417